W9-CNQ-129

FINANCIAL FREEDOM THROUGH ELECTRONIC DAY TRADING

VAN K. THARP
BRIAN JUNE

McGraw-Hill

New York   San Francisco   Washington, D.C.   Auckland   Bogotá
Caracas   Lisbon   London   Madrid   Mexico City   Milan
Montreal   New Delhi   San Juan   Singapore
Sydney   Tokyo   Toronto

Library of Congress Cataloging-in-Publication Data

Tharp, Van K.
    Financial freedom through electronic day trading / by Van K. Tharp and
Brian June.
        p. cm.
    Includes bibliographical references.
    ISBN 0-07-136295-9
    1. Electronic trading of securities.   2. Investments.   I. June, Brian.
II. Title.
  HG4515.95 .T49   2000
  332.64'2'02854678—dc21

00-062448

McGraw-Hill

A Division of The McGraw·Hill Companies

Copyright © 2001 by The One Minute Trader Corporation. All rights reserved.
Printed in the United States of America. Except as permitted under the United
States Copyright Act of 1976, no part of this publication may be reproduced or
distributed in any form or by any means, or stored in a database or retrieval
system, without the prior written permission of the publisher.

1 2 3 4 5 6 7 8 9 0   AGM/AGM   0 9 8 7 6 5 4 3 2 1 0

ISBN 0-07-136295-9

This book was set in Palatino by North Market Street Graphics.
Printed and bound by Quebecor World/Martinsburg.

This publication is designed to provide accurate and authoritative
information in regard to the subject matter covered. It is sold with the
understanding that neither the author nor the publisher is engaged in
rendering legal, accounting, futures/securities trading, or other professional
service. If legal advice or other expert assistance is required, the services of a
competent professional person should be sought.

> —*From a Declaration of Principles jointly adopted by a Committee*
> *of the American Bar Association and a Committee of Publishers.*

McGraw-Hill books are available at special quantity discounts to use as
premiums and sales promotions, or for use in corporate training programs.
For more information, please write to the Director of Special Sales,
Professional Publishing, McGraw-Hill, Two Penn Plaza, New York, NY 10121-
2298. Or contact your local bookstore.

This book is printed on recycled, acid-free paper containing a
minimum of 50% recycled, de-inked fiber.

This book is dedicated to my son, Robert Tharp.
Robert is growing into a fine trader.
By keeping in mind the principles
that I want him to know as he grows as a trader,
Robert has provided me with an objective
for writing this book.

V. T.

Valerie, Meghan, and Olivia
You are my earthly treasure. My heart is with you!

B. J.

CONTENTS

PART THREE

LAUNCHING YOUR TRADING ROCKET   177

Chapter 8

FOREWORD

When I was first asked to write a foreword for this book, I was mystified. Although I've been a trader for 24 years professionally and traded for myself for even more years, throughout that time, I've never been a day trader. So why me?

The answer comes in two parts: First, I've always said that I was a businessman first and a trader second. Trading is a business for me. *Financial Freedom through Electronic Day Trading,* unlike most books that I've read on trading, takes the process of trading and shows how to treat it like a real business. Most electronic day traders have little chance of success, but those who apply the business approach that Van Tharp and Brian June present in this book will be way ahead of the crowd.

Second, trading is trading. Principles of good trading span the time horizon from long-term traders, like myself, to short-term traders like Brian June. No matter what the time period, a successful trader needs to do a lot of things right to produce profits. The markets are fairly brutal. They have a way of weeding out the amateur and making fools of those who believe they've figured it all out.

After reading a draft of the book, I realized that, just like longer-term trading, short-term trading is largely driven by the trader's mental abilities and condition. That's where Van comes into the picture and why he and Brian teamed up to write this book. Van's been coaching traders for a long time, and I have seen the positive effect that his coaching has had on traders striving to improve their performance. I have even used some of his techniques in other parts of my life, like my golf game—but that's another story.

In addition, there is interesting teamwork between Brian and Van in this book. Van is a coach for traders, while Brian has been a successful CEO. Brian has added a very businesslike approach to

Van's coaching principles of success. Both of them lay the steps out for the reader in a very clear and succinct manner.

I believe there is a direct correlation between the amount of preparation one does as a trader and the bottom-line results obtained. Thus, the first part of this book is all about preparation and laying out a business plan for your success. And the key to this preparation is knowing yourself. As you begin to understand yourself, you can look at your beliefs about trading and your beliefs about yourself. Next you can determine what your mission in life is. That's a big step, because as the authors point out, if your trading goals and objectives are not congruent with your mission and your own definition of yourself, you probably are doomed to failure from the beginning.

Chapter 3 of this book is one of the most interesting chapters I have ever read about trading. The authors show you in a logical, step-by-step fashion how to lay out a complete business plan for your trading. You learn how to develop your business mission, understand and bring all your resources to the task of trading, develop the right type of trading entity, and identify your trading edge and your trading style. The authors take you through all the steps and even give you a sample business plan at the end. That material alone is worth many times the price of the book.

Part Two of the book also addresses issues that are very seldom covered in trading books. You'll learn about hardware and software configurations that are important to getting the right start. In addition, core trading issues like expectancy and position sizing are covered in great detail. These are key areas for everyone to understand, and they are presented to the reader right up front.

Part Three of the book deals with specific hands-on aspects of trading. You'll learn specific techniques for dealing with what comes up during the day and specific trading strategies. This book is not going to give you some magic formula to follow where, lo and behold, day trading is easy. To be successful in trading, I'm convinced that each trader must find his or her own way. If that is not done, you cannot have the mental courage to stick with your strategy when it has a rough period. The book will give you the impression that there's a lot to think about when attacking a challenge like day trading. Knowing what you're up against is more than half the battle. Preparing yourself to overcome those obstacles will win the battle.

If the trader doesn't have the mental side of the game in good shape, the rest of it doesn't matter. The markets will find your weak spot and exploit it and you'll be one more *former* trader. Done well, trading should be about as exciting as breathing. Getting to that state is simple for some, almost impossible for others. Van and Brian are using this book to help others understand the important issues involved in day trading and provide some very helpful suggestions on how to avoid some of the pitfalls and develop your own day trading strategy.

Finally, the last part of the book deals with how to handle mistakes and refine the process. How do you know when you've made a mistake? How do you correct mistakes? What are common mistakes that most day traders make? The last section of the book deals with the whole process of refining your plan and continually evolving it. These are all essential aspects of success in trading.

The bottom line? There's a lot of interesting information on trading in this book for all sorts of traders, short term or long term, but for the day trader, it should definitely help build a strong foundation to overcome the challenges that lie ahead.

Best of success in your trading.

Thomas F. Basso
President, Trendstat

Imagine you work for a large company. Whether you're the janitor or the CEO or somewhere in between, you still feel as if your time isn't your own. You are a slave to the system. You constantly have to do tasks you don't believe in or enjoy—and you do them because you're told, "It's required." You're constantly faced with regulation and bureaucracy. You have a number of people in the company whose sole purpose seems to be to figure out why *you* can't do what you think is important for the company. Most of what you end up doing seems to have nothing to do with productivity, making money, or even making improvements in the way the company does business. Indeed, you might feel like a corporate slave.

Perhaps you're in a technical field where you've always called your own shots. Only now, you spend more time on bureaucratic red tape than actually doing your job. Your avocation isn't what it used to be; it's just not as much fun anymore.

Does one of these scenarios sound familiar? Does it sound like where you're working now? Would you like more freedom to get away from the constant bureaucracy and corporate infighting? Do you want to be freer while making as much or even more money? Then read this book!

You see, both of the authors of this book went through that kind of life. Both of us were very unhappy, and both of us found freedom through trading—Brian June as an electronic direct-access trader and Van Tharp as a swing trader and trader's coach. If we did it, then it is also *possible* for you to do it. This book is your road map to a new personal freedom—a financial freedom through electronic day trading.

While we believe that you can attain this kind of financial and personal freedom, it does require that you pay a price. The statistics suggest that 95 percent of all day traders lose money—most lose it all. And the reason most lose it all is because they approach everything from the wrong perspective. They have natural inclinations and biases to do all the wrong things. In fact, there is so much misinformation in the education system that most people don't stand a chance. It's not necessary to be an A student in order to be a successful trader. As a matter of fact, because of some of the biases required to achieve that academic standard, that may make it more difficult to become a successful day trader. Yet, believe it or not, most of the misinformation is not deliberate.

People tend to ask the questions that tell them what they want to hear. This has given rise to a whole host of information vendors (newspapers, television, stock tip hotlines, to name a few) that prey upon this tendency. Not to say that these industries are knowingly dispensing misinformation; they're merely answering the questions that people *think* are important, such as:

- What's the market going to do now?
- What stocks should I buy now?
- I own XYZ stock. Do you think it's going to go up? (If you say no, then they'll keep asking other people until they find a person who agrees with their opinion.)
- Tell me how I can get into the market and be right most of the time.

There is a large industry available to give you the answer to such questions. You hear ads for workshops and seminars that show you how easy day trading is and how you can make a small fortune. You then pay tuition to attend a seminar that will (1) show you how to get rich by using their software and (2) provide you with a few strategies for picking the right stocks. Unfortunately, what they are teaching you has nothing to do with the real secrets of successful trading. Instead, they are showing you why 95 percent of all day traders lose money and why most lose all their money and sometimes money from their friends and relatives as well.

Our goal in writing this book is to show you another way. The authors are both experts in success technology. Brian June was a corporate executive who transformed himself into a successful electronic day trader. Van Tharp is a top coach for traders and a modeler of trading excellence. So it should come as no surprise that Brian wrote the technical and strategic chapters, while Van wrote the theoretical and behavioral finance chapters.

Brian June was the CEO of a high-technology company. However, he was caught in the corporate rat race, just as much as anyone else that worked there, dealing with regulatory and management issues that had nothing to do with top-line growth production. The bigger his company got, the further it got from the entrepreneurial dream. As a result, he used his extensive business experience to design a plan to direct himself toward financial freedom as an electronic day trader. Brian was already an expert at business and technology, so he simply applied his knowledge and developed a series of steps to help himself become a successful day trader—which was all fine and dandy until he realized there were gaps in his knowledge, missing steps if you will.

Fortunately Brian found a personal coach, Van K. Tharp, to provide the missing steps. He thoroughly studied Van's *Peak Performance Course for Investors and Traders* until it was second nature to him. He attended a number of Van's workshops and then applied the material to fit his mission and trading goals. And soon he became one of the 5 percent—an electronic day trader who survived and prospered.

Van Tharp has a Ph.D. in psychology and has been helping traders as a coach since 1982. A coach is someone who attracts talented people (like Brian) and then teaches them the fundamentals of the craft and helps them attain peak performance. Van is also a modeler of success who uses NeuroLinguistic Programming as a tool to determine what successful traders do in common. In that regard, he's modeled the trading process, the trading research process, the wealth development process, and the ultimate key to market success—position sizing. Furthermore, Van is a successful short-term trader in the stock market. He's applied and adopted his own models.

We believe that we have formed a synergistic team in writing this book together—coach and successful business entrepreneur turned successful electronic day trader. As a result, this book brings you the latest techniques in business success and applied behavioral finance. In this book, we show you how to lay a foundation for success that those 95 percent just will not do. Our goal is to show you how to follow the path the 5 percent take.

We have combined both of our backgrounds to create a real humdinger of a section on the software and technology—the tools of the trade so to speak. And we did it in a way that won't make you run looking for a manual to explain it all.

Last, we have combined the skills of a top coach and a very successful pupil. What does it take to master the process of becoming a successful trader in a tough, tough arena? We've done it and developed a *step-by-step plan for you* to get through the process. We'll take you right inside of Brian June's mind and bring you his specific success strategies. Dr. Tharp presents broad-based strategic guidelines that can be personalized to your unique needs. These guidelines will be the framework of a greater understanding of the market and how you think about it.

We'll show you *global strategic plans* that will help any trader, and *specific trading tactics* that you can adapt to fit you. Furthermore, all this is presented to you within the framework of applied behavioral finance—helping you to adopt success techniques that really work. We've blazed a trail for you to follow to successful electronic direct-access trading, showing you the pitfalls and the gold mines but leaving your exact course strictly to you. It's an exciting journey toward financial and personal freedom, and we salute you for taking it.

Virtually all studies show that people learn more easily if they can have some fun while doing so. To that end, we have made a deliberate attempt to write in an easy, if not at times whimsical, style. We've also tried to make the tone conversational, so we use "I," "me," and "we" a lot.

We suggest that you read sequentially, from the beginning to the end, at least your first time through. For the most part, earlier material builds the foundation for later sections. If you then want to, you can go back to any specific material as a refresher. We hope you'll use this book as a handbook of direct-access trading, referring to it often as you build your trading career.

We have divided this book into four primary parts: Part One is about preparation and laying out the plans for success. This information and the exercises are so critical to your success that we can virtually guarantee that only those who complete Part One will achieve the highest success, the 5 percent!

Part Two addresses the more mechanical aspects of trading, such as hardware and software configurations. We also address specific trading mechanics such as expectancy and the ultimate key to trading success or failure—position sizing.

Part Three deals with the "hands-on" aspects of trading. How do you select stocks? How do you profitably get through the trading day? How do you deal with what comes up during the day? What are the keys to success? We go through several actual trades, walking you through each one step-by-step. The strategies and tactics we use here are timeless. Some are terrific in bull market conditions; others are great in bear markets. The examples chosen are taken from mid-1999 to mid-2000, specifically to show their flexibility. Of course, this is the material most people relish, and in the right context, it is important to trading success.

Part Four deals strongly with applied behavioral finance. For instance, in Chapter 13 we show you all the key elements behind peak performance trading. When you understand the material in this chapter, you'll know why only 5 percent trade successfully.

Finally, we'd be remiss if we failed to mention the distinction between knowledge and experience. For a moment, imagine reading a book entitled *How to Fly an Airplane*. Assuming for the moment that you have no prior aviation training, you read the material faithfully. You even take an examination on your knowledge and get a 100 percent correct score. Would you then attempt to actually go fly the plane without a flight instructor? Most of you would not—simply because doing so would, in all probability, result in catastrophe! Yet far too many newer traders kill their trading capital by reading a book and then trading without the benefits of an experienced trader by their side. If you have never done direct-access trading, we urge you to *be cautious, especially in the beginning*. If possible, find an experienced trader (one who's making money on a consistent basis) who will guide you through the process. We believe that by doing so, you have the best chance of becoming one of the 5 percent that does find financial freedom through electronic day trading! And we hope this book gives you a rich source of material that plays a truly significant role in helping you to reach your dreams.

Van K. Tharp, Ph.D.
Brian June

ACKNOWLEDGMENTS

This book is a product of a great collaboration between Brian June and myself. Brian has taken many of the principles I've developed for traders and transformed them into business principles for traders. I love the approach, and I'm deeply grateful to him. In addition, my first book took 3 years from start to finish. Brian, with his businesslike approach, was able to help us finish *Financial Freedom through Electronic Day Trading* in less than a year.

I especially want to acknowledge the love and tremendous support of my wife, Kalavathi Tharp. Without the kind of support you have provided me with, Kala, this book would probably not exist. You light up my life.

In addition, I'd like to thank my staff at IITM for their support in completing this book. They include Jo'Ann Donders, Cathy Hasty, Barbara Murray, and Tamika Williams. Thank you all for your support.

I've been working with traders and investors for 18 years now. During those 18 years, numerous people have helped shape the thinking that has gone into this book. All of you, who contributed in any way, have my deepest thanks and appreciation.

Van Tharp

* * * * *

The world is full of possibilities and opportunities. One of the greatest is the opportunity to learn from others. This book is a concrete example of the tremendous growth that occurs when we learn from our predecessors. My life has been transformed by the work of hundreds of authors and traders who have come before, blazed trails, won and lost, and then had the fortitude to tell the world of their trials and travails by writing about their experiences. I thank all of you.

To the students who have attended our Electronic Day Trading Seminars, I thank you. I've learned and grown exponentially as a result of our time together.

I'm also truly grateful to my friend Nelson Hansen, who has freely given me his time, resources, and talents for over 10 years. He gave me the time and freedom to become a full-time trader and to write this book. Thank you, Nelson!

Of course, many people were involved in the production of this book, especially the great team at McGraw-Hill, including Jeffrey Krames, our publisher; Ela Aktay, our editor; and Jane Palmieri, our editing supervisor. Their assistance and guidance was invaluable.

I'd also like to thank Lori Pharis, who faithfully and quickly transcribed many hours of dictation, and John Coleman, who took time from his very busy schedule as a magazine editor to produce the graphics in this book.

Fellow trader and friend R. A. Ishibashi gave freely of his time and talents as he helped with trading ideas and suggestions—this book is much better as a result. Thanks, R. A.!

I also owe a debt of gratitude to Kala Tharp, who has been a source of inspiration for me. Her determination and internal strength are phenomenal. Kala makes things happen and simply will not take no for an answer! Thanks for being there, Kala!

Some people give beyond measure. D. R. Barton is one of those people. D. R. put forth a Herculean effort to help produce this book. He helped me brainstorm ideas, created outlines, helped with graphics production, and spent countless hours in the editing process, to the point of being a cocreator of this book. He spent a week with me at my home, working late into the night and rising early to continue the creation. We spent hundreds of hours in phone conferences together. Very simply stated, this book would not exist without D. R. Along the way we have become very good friends. Although "thanks" somehow seems inadequate for what you have done, D. R., I give you my heartfelt thanks!

Of course, this book would not exist at all without Van Tharp. Van's influence on my trading is almost impossible to adequately describe. Prior to meeting and getting to know Van, my trading results were sporadic. After spending hundreds of hours in training and time with Van and his revolutionary teaching materials, my trading was transformed! I cannot thank you enough, Van!

Most of all I, want to thank my wife of 25 years, Valerie. She, probably more than anyone else, can attest to the challenges of writing this book. She supported me during the long hours, late evenings, and weekend writing marathons that were required to complete this work. This book would not exist without her support. I know no other person of her strength, integrity, and love.

Brian June

## PART ONE

How to Develop a "Laser-Guided Rocket" to Trading Success

Hint: *This Is the Material Most People Want to Skip!*

Master traders have long known that successful, profitable, long-term trading is the result of diligent work. Unfortunately we live in the "super lotto" age—an age of "get rich now!" This mindset is part of what draws so many into the world of trading. And advertising perpetuates the myth of instant riches. Unfortunately most of those drawn into this world quickly burn out, consuming untold sums of money in the process.

So this first section details what it *really* takes to be successful and profitable through direct-access trading. In fact, most of the material in this section is applicable to any type of trading or investing. What it really takes to be a successful trader has *everything to do with you* and *almost nothing* to do with the "right" broker or the "right" software or the "right" stock. Do you really want to hear this? You see, for many it's easier to believe that there is a "holy grail" or a "laser-guided rocket" that will suddenly lead them to trading mastery. And the good news is that there *is* such a holy grail. It's just that you've probably been looking for it in all the wrong places for far too long. So charge forth! Read and devour the three chapters in this section and you'll learn where to find it! If you have the "right stuff," you *will* find the laser-guided rocket to trading success.

## CHAPTER 1

The Journey to Trading Mastery

Deep within man dwell those slumbering powers . . . powers
that would astonish him, that he never dreamed of
possessing . . . forces that would revolutionize his life if aroused
and put into action.

Orison Swett Marden

THE MIND OF A MASTER TRADER

Steve leaned back in his Italian leather lounger. As he perused the
information on his monitor, a little grin appeared on his face. Bright
colors danced quickly across his market-maker screen. Earlier that
morning, Intel announced that it was going to add another $6 bil-
lion capital investment to its chip-producing capability. Intel had
been in a rather strong uptrend recently. In fact, over the past
month or so, it had made several new annual highs. In a recent
NASDAQ pullback, however, Intel, along with most every other
stock, had suffered from a mini-bear market.

This was of little concern to Steve—he loved to trade both
sides of the market. He regularly traded Intel; he knew it inside and
out. Steve had been trading Intel for better than 2 years and knew
as much about the stock as most market makers on the stock. That

mindset was very rare for a day trader, and Steve knew it. Most day traders just jump on anything that moves, but that wasn't Steve's style. He was a man of preparation.

You see, before Steve had become a full-time day trader, he'd been a dentist for more than 15 years and had run a very successful practice. Business planning was a normal part of his routine, as was science and preparation. No, Steve would not participate in any gunslinger "shoot-from-the-hip" style of trading, because he knew better. He knew he'd never be able to compete against the market makers if he did that. So he'd spent 2 years trading Intel, learning all about it.

He knew its average true range every day. He knew its high, low, open, and close every day. He knew that it tended to open on gaps and fill those gaps in the first 15 minutes or so after the opening. He knew who the "axes" were on Intel. He knew that Morgan Stanley and Goldman Sachs were normally two of the most active market makers in the stock, and he knew how good those market makers were.

On this Monday morning, he was almost ready to trade Intel, but not quite. At 8:04 a.m. Eastern Standard Time, CNBC's Joe Kernen mentioned the news story on Intel—Intel would invest $6 billion into new chip production facilities. Steve thought to himself, "Boy, Intel ought to be a great trade today." But he wasn't going to go on just any fly-by-the-seat-of-the-pants mission to trade Intel. Instead, as soon as Kernen mentioned the news, Steve pulled up his news feed and looked at the story from Reuters. He read the story over quickly to get a sense of how Intel would use the money it would pour into the chip production and when it would do so. He printed out the Reuters story, just to have a hard copy next to him.

He threw Intel up into his daily candlestick chart (see Figure 1–1), took a look at the trend, and mentally applied some trend lines. He then noted both support and resistance areas so that he knew where it had traded over the past 2 or so weeks. Last Friday, Intel had traded between $131⅜ and $137. It closed at $136¹³⁄₁₆, near its high. Based upon this recent price action and today's news, he fully expected that the market makers would try to gap Intel up on the open.

Steve's finely honed trading instincts started to kick in, and he began to watch the premarket activity on Intel. Trades were going

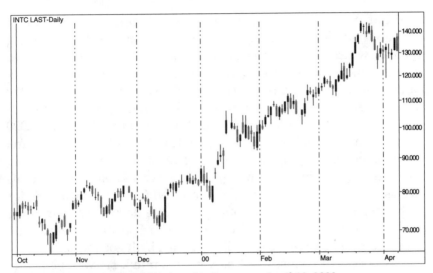

Figure 1–1 Intel daily candle chart leading up to April 10, 2000.

off at $144 and $144½, almost 8 points above where it had closed last Friday. Steve thought to himself, "Intel closes the gap quite often. Looks like we're going to get a good gap this morning." He watched Intel trade from approximately 8:15 to around 8:45 o'clock that morning. Premarket it had already traded over a million shares. Interestingly, it had held strongly onto the gap. This wasn't such a big surprise because, after all, Intel had just reached its annual high at slightly above $145 a few trading sessions earlier. This morning's news would bring out the greed in traders, who would want to score as Intel (they hoped) soared to new and even loftier heights.

Steve decided immediately to execute his plan. He would try to short a 1,000-share lot right before the opening, hold it for 10 or 15 minutes into the opening, and then cover his short as the gap began to close. And then, depending upon the overall market and the relative strength of Intel that day, he'd either reverse and go long on the pullbacks or continue to short the highs.

9:17 a.m. Steve had been carefully watching the time & sales window on Intel all morning long. He'd watched the stock trade as high as $144½ and as low as $137 (fairly typical of erratic premarket conditions). Currently it was $140 × $140½. It appeared to Steve that the pace had slowed down a little bit and that the strong buying interest, which was so prevalent just after the new release, had waned somewhat. Steve now watched the prints carefully. He prepared to short 1,000 shares. He put 1,000 shares into his order entry screen, checked the "Short" button, and got into "pounce" mode.

He noticed a trader on Island (ISLD) bidding $140 for 1,000 shares, so he hit the "Sell ISLD day" button on his trading software. Immediately he was short 1,000 shares at $140. "Trading on Island can sure get great fills," he thought. Steve had a satisfied look on his face as he glanced up at Joe Kernen on CNBC. He reached over for his hand-ground Colombian coffee and took a deep drink. Steve was totally relaxed and very satisfied with his short position. He thought, "I should be able to make my 10:30 tee time if all goes well."

All of Steve's senses had now been ignited. He watched carefully as Intel bounced up and down during this preopening activity. A few prints went off at $141, fully 1 point above his short, but they were small 100-share lots. Typical of premarket trades, his stop was wider than usual at $142, so Steve wasn't sweating. He believed to his core that the market makers would be selling into the opening strength this morning.

9:29 a.m.   One minute to go before opening. The market had already moved in his favor. Soon, the opening bell would ring and Steve would know one way or another whether his short would be even more successful this morning. He calmly prepared his order entry screen to exit the position at his newly adjusted stop of $140, should the market suddenly move against him. Such advanced preparation had saved Steve thousands of dollars over the years.

9:30 a.m.   Intel opens at $137½ and a huge tug-of-war is raging. The market-maker screen dances, wiggles, and jiggles as trades fly off between $137½ and $138. So far, Intel has held up pretty well. Steve can see the tension between the traders as he watches the action.

9:42 a.m.   Twelve minutes into the opening, Intel is trading close to the $139 area, but is having a tough time breaking above. Steve is taking a slightly longer-term perspective this morning, and this moderate retrace against him is just a small but expected pause in the morning's game plan. A few prints go off at $139, and a few more at $138⅞, but Intel has run out of gas! It's a wild opening today, but Steve is rather calm as he takes another sip of his Colombian blend.

Already over 5 million shares have traded. "Phenomenal volume today," Steve muses. He realizes that with the "good" news out on Intel today, he may have only a small window of opportunity to cover his short.

9:44 a.m.   Two minutes later and some profit taking starts to come in. Some of the people who have held Intel over the weekend are now beginning to sell, and the market makers are more than willing to sell right along with the profit takers. A nice sell-off (from Steve's perspective!) ensues.

10:11 a.m.   Another, weaker, retrace goes back to the 138½ level. (See Figure 1–2.) Steve feels very comfortable holding his short since this buying thrust is even weaker than before. And his patience pays off! The selling starts now in earnest, and with only one short pause, the market makers now drive the price down below 136.

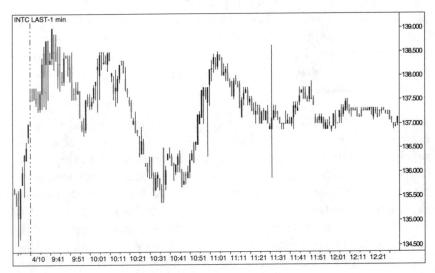

Figure 1–2 Intel 1-minute candle chart for April 10, 2000.

10:33 a.m.   Intel is now bid $135¹³⁄₁₆ × $135⅞. Steve has already made $4,000 on paper. As the selling dries up, and in light of the morning's continually hyped positive news, he decides he'd better cover.

His expectations have been more than met. Intel has closed the gap. Steve enters his buy order at $135⅞. This is not a scalping trade, and he's not trying to be greedy, so he decides to take the offer, instead of bidding for the stock. He enters his buy order, and 10 seconds later his buy is filled. He's covered. He's made $4⅛, or $4,125, in little more than an hour. After the trade is closed, he smiles, knowing that now he can relax and stop trading for the day, or he can continue to take advantage of the opportunities of today's volatility.

10:38 a.m.   Intel has already traded back through $136, and the buying pressure mounts. Steve's juices are flowing now. He's in a winning situation. He knows that the time to "press" just a little is while he's winning. (As it turns out, $135⅜ was the bottom on Intel in the early trading, which was fine with Steve. He knows that his job is not to pick bottoms and tops, but to enter low-risk trades and exit with the majority of his profit intact.) Steve has high expectations that he'll get a good bounce off this early-morning short. As the market moves up, in the direction of his new expectation, he prepares and strikes. All systems are go as he bids and is filled at 136⁷⁄₁₆. As always, Steve prepares his order entry screen with his stop order in case the market moves against him. He has chosen a ¾-point stop based on his knowledge of these mid-morning momentum plays.

10:43 a.m.   As sometimes happens, the S&P futures take a temporary turn against Steve's position, and Intel follows. With absolutely no change in his state of mind, Steve calmly prepares to stop out of his position. With zero hesitation and no emotional reaction, Steve hits the "Sell SelectNet" button and is filled by the market maker that he had identified before the market got to his stop price. In this case it was First Boston (FBCO). Steve takes a rather serene sip of his coffee, actually very satisfied that he followed his strategy. However, this momentum trade is still ripe for action, and he immediately begins the stalking process for a reentry.

10:47 a.m.   Steve watches the market-maker screen as 15 Archipel-ago traders ("Chippies") line up on the bid. Steve watches the "ask" and notices that the tiers are collapsing. Traders are now only willing to sell at higher prices.

A novice trader, of course, wouldn't even understand what Steve is thinking, but Steve knows what a collapsing tier size means. He decides to strike! It's time to go long again. Steve enters his order: Buy 1,000 Intel at $135⅜. He pays the ask price. He wants to make sure he's filled because Kernen just mentioned Intel again! David Faber is also talking it up, so Steve expects a run-up as traders learn of the "fresh" news.

Steve is filled a few seconds later. He's long 1,000 shares at $135⅜, and watches as the stock ticks up. He's not in any big hurry here; he's totally satisfied with his position.

10:53 a.m.   Intel is now $136½ × $136⁹⁄₁₆, and the trading action has paused a bit. Steve decides it's time to buy another lot. Since the pace is slower, he decides to bid at $136½. Island has huge liquidity on Intel this morning, so he bids on Island. This time his fill takes longer—about 30 seconds—as he waits for an "Islander" to hit his bid. Soon enough he's filled for 1,000 shares at $136½.

Momentum traders are now really piling on. Steve recalls from his earlier preparation that the annual high on Intel is just over $145. "Today, Intel might even take out its annual high," he thinks. "It's totally possible given this news." But Steve's not in a big hurry. He waits and watches the market-making activity. For the next couple of minutes, Intel is embroiled in a battle. Intel moves up a half point, then down a half point, but it seems that for the most part the buyers and sellers are locked in a stalemate. He reflects, "I'm in a plus position on this trade already, although not hugely plus. No need to rush. No need to dump off the shares every time it wiggles and jiggles down a bit." He's set his stop and under-stands that these "shakes" are a normal part of Intel's daily market-making and trading activity.

10:57 a.m.   Another 2 minutes have gone by, and Steve notices Goldman go high bid at $137³⁄₁₆, and Goldman is showing 2,000 size. He watches Goldman with keen interest as Goldman just sits on the bid while several thousand shares cross the tape. Goldman is buying all the shares he can at $137¾₆! Steve understands that this is the time to act. No time for hesitation now!

He immediately puts in a buy order at $137¼, upbidding Goldman by ¹⁄₁₆. This time, however, he decides to truly pyramid his position, so he adds 2,000 shares. Several traders hit his bid as it takes him another 30 seconds to get filled on his full 2,000 shares. Now Steve is satisfied. He's long 4,000 Intel at $136¹⁹⁄₃₂ net, and his game plan is to hold on as he watches Intel with the expectation that it will trade higher on the constantly rehyped news.

Based upon the volatility of Intel and Steve's intimate knowledge of its trading ranges, he selects a 1-point stop on his net position. Because of the size of Steve's account, a 1-point stop is less than 1 percent of his trading capital. This is a very comfortable stop for the 4,000 shares that he's holding. This may not be typical of all traders, but Steve is not the typical trader. At one time, Steve was very much a "beginning" trader, but over the past 2 years he's increased his account size over 700 percent. So Steve has really learned his craft well.

From this point on, Steve watches with eyes glued to the market-making screen. He pays very close attention to who the bidders are and who the sellers are. He remains alert to the action on his market-making screen. His ear is tuned to CNBC, just to make sure that any additional morning news doesn't take his beloved Intel in the wrong direction and move it against him. With his 1-point stop in mind, Steve remains positively relaxed and alert.

11:00 a.m.   Steve now watches the time & sales window flicker and flash. Time & sales shows the buys and the sells as they occur. He has become very adept at "tape reading" using this tool. He's making sure that there are no errant trades or huge block trades that might shake up or scare other traders. Steve kicks back just a little and props his feet up, comfortably crossed on his ottoman. He sips the aromatic coffee he enjoys so much, and relaxes for the few minutes as he watches Intel trade.

During this same time, Steve scans the S&P futures. He's learned through experience that Intel often trades with a very high correlation to the S&P futures contract. This morning, thankfully, the market is relatively strong, and the S&P futures are trading up in the 1,530 area. But Intel itself is even stronger because of the news.

11:04 a.m.   Steve has now been holding Intel for a little over a quarter of an hour. In that time, it has traded up toward the $139 area, but just can't get there; it has simply run out of steam. He has to ask himself the question, "Hmmm, has the whole-number theory taken the upside out of my trade?" Steve has just made one tremendous trade; in fact, it's the best single trade he's made in the past few trading sessions.

Steve knows that other traders are going to be watching Intel very closely right now. He knows the market makers on this stock like the back of his hand, and he knows they're going to be watching $139 to see if Intel can make a new intraday high. He believes that the market makers will try to run through the high, especially since the S&P futures are holding up. "Swing traders and position traders love to buy these 'new daily high' breakouts," he reminds himself. "That's one of their entry signals."

He also knows that the perfect time for "smart money" to start slowly unloading some of their shares is precisely when Intel tests this new intraday high. In fact, less than 2 weeks ago, as Intel reached its annual high, volume picked up as new traders were buying in. But 6 days after it reached its annual high, it had already traded back down almost 20 points! This is typical. Steve had seen hundreds upon hundreds of these distributions, as long-term holders sold off into the last leg of strength.

11:05 a.m.   Hesitation can kill many a good trade, and Steve knows it. Goldman again comes on the bid at $138⁷⁄₁₆, showing "200" size. Steve muses, "A very small lot for Goldman. Perhaps a head-fake? How many times have I watched Goldman try to push Intel up through a whole number, only to reverse and sell thousands of shares a few minutes later?" Steve knew the game well.

Intel is now trading $138⁷⁄₁₆ × $138½. Will it take the high out? Steve doesn't know, and he doesn't really care. "I'm getting out." He knows well that he *must* take his profits here and now. Steve puts in his sell order. Again, not getting greedy, he decides to offload 2,000 of his shares at $138⅜, which is just below the bid. Why? Because he sees a market maker bidding $138⅜ for 2,000 shares and he wants his fill. He is filled almost instantly at $138⅜. Interestingly, the market maker sits on the $138⅜ bid, but reduces the size to 1,000 shares. Happy to be filled at that price, Steve offers out his last 2,000 shares to this same market maker using a Select-Net preference, and to his delight the market maker takes his full 2,000. Steve congratulates himself, "Excellent trade!"

Steve sits back, stretches out, crosses his arms behind his head, and grins. "Good day—I've made $11,250. But I missed my tee time!"

He utters in a low tone, "I think I'll stop trading for the day. After all, I don't really want to push it too much, and I think I've already done well enough for one day." So he turns off CNBC, closes down his trading software, shuts off his computer, and strolls downstairs to the kitchen, where Nancy, his wife, is slicing some fresh banana nut bread that she has just baked.

"How's it going, honey?" she asks.

"Well, we had a pretty good morning," replies Steve. "We ended the day up around 11 grand." As the warm banana nut bread melts in his mouth, he remembers his golf game. "If you don't mind, I think I'm going to go out and play a round of golf. I'll call Al at the pro shop—he can always get me out, even when I miss a tee time. Then, when I get back, let's go over those St. Martin brochures we were taking a look at. I think next week we'll head on down to the islands for 4 or 5 days. How does that sound?"

IS A MASTER TRADER INSIDE YOU?

I certainly hope you've enjoyed this short story of Steve, the trader. I want you to know that even though our character Steve is fictional, the actions and situations depicted are real life. They are a composite of myself and other good day traders that I know. So while I've dramatized this for fun, and while the specific trades and numerical references are simply examples, the lifestyle and the type of trading that Steve does is representative of a top-notch direct-access trader.

The thing you need to know is that this type of trading and lifestyle *can* be reality for you! Although it may seem far-fetched right now, I hope that after reading this book you'll understand that you, too, could become a master trader, just like Steve. Your values, beliefs, and goals may be different from Steve's, but you can develop your own trading skills to help you live *your* dreams, whatever they may be. To make this happen, you must simply learn the methods and thought processes that Steve put into practice during our example trading day here.

Did you notice how confident Steve was? He wasn't at all nervous. Throughout his trading he was relaxed and in control of himself. Steve was confident, not cocky, and the difference is in the preparation. Steve understood that his reality, his skill as a trader, had *nothing* to do with the market or anything external to him. He understood that the promise of the life that he was living was a completely internalized experience! And that *he* created this experience. He understood these key elements and more, because he put into practice the things that we're teaching in this book.

So is a master trader inside you? I really don't know, but I do believe that if you follow the processes we teach in this book, you'll have every element that you need to create your own promise, to create your own trading business. In this way, you can live a life that is congruent with the person you are! This is one of the most exciting aspects of life! It is also one of the very best things about electronic day trading. Day trading is one of the very few occupations where you can combine all the elements of *yourself* into a harmonious lifestyle: personal integrity, self-knowledge, self-reliance, freedom—and enough money to chart your own course, day in and day out!

In the chapters that follow, Dr. Van Tharp and I will lay out in vivid detail every critical factor that we've discovered is necessary to earn financial freedom through electronic day trading. While there are some good books dealing with specific areas of electronic direct-access trading (EDAT), we know of no other work designed to take you through a total course or road map to day trading success. This book is that road map. We know that this is a huge undertaking. And we don't take the responsibility lightly.

The work in this book is the result of many years of Dr. Tharp's research into the minds of master traders. It is combined with my own profitable day trading experiences to show you how to enjoy the same. By the end of the book, you'll understand how Steve was able to make such great trades.

THE MOST IMPORTANT STEPS TO TRADING MASTERY

As you move from where you are today to your goal of becoming an excellent (and, therefore, highly profitable) trader, perhaps the key point to understand is that you can go as far as your trading psychology allows you. This book will guide you through a process that, when followed, will catapult you to your loftiest goals. The process itself is based on understanding and then improving your trading psychology:

- What you understand about yourself as a person and a trader
- How you prepare yourself
- How you think and make decisions
- How you react to both positive and negative external influences

The bottom line is this: You and you alone are responsible for your trading success. You must keep this in mind at all times! This book shows you how successful traders prepare themselves to win.

Here's how you'll step through this exciting process. You'll begin your journey to trading excellence by defining who you are. You'll develop a new mission with an emphasis on how trading fits *your* life. Next you'll gain some insight into your personal attributes—especially the ones that relate to trading. When faced with a self-assessment such as this, it's easy to pass it over and say, "Hey, I already know myself." But, remember, there are many different styles of EDAT. Choosing one that is consistent with your personality can make the difference between relaxed, profitable trading and a tortured, losing experience.

With a clear idea of where you are as a trader (through self-assessment), you need a vehicle to move you to where you'd like to be (as stated in your mission). Goal setting is just that tool. One of the characteristics shared by every trader who is profitable in the long term is a set of clear, well-defined goals. These goals will drive the rest of your trading process. And two of your most important trading-related goals will be to develop a business plan and a trading plan. The trading plan will describe in detail what your edge is as a trader and how you will systematically make money day in and day out. Your business plan will then describe how you expect to structure your trading activities so that you have the greatest chance for business success and can keep the maximum amount of money that you make in the markets.

Once you've made it this far in your journey—to the point of being committed to a set of written personal and trading goals—

you'll be ahead of 90 percent of those who trade. Keep in mind it's this same 90 percent or more who *lose* money! Next, we'll help you take care of some trading logistics:

- Choosing or upgrading your computer hardware
- Selecting your Internet connectivity routes
- Setting up your trading software

These steps will take you to the point where you are receiving the best real-time data available. We will then guide you through a detailed description of how to interpret the data that are flooding across your computer screens. This will be an intimate look into the mind of a master trader and will surely be one of the highlights of your journey to trading to excellence!

Your sojourn will then take you to a review of critical areas that every trader must master. All traders must understand the expectancy of their trading strategy. A strategy's expectancy tells how much, on average, the strategy will profit for every dollar risked. A clear understanding of expectancy is needed in order to take advantage of the position-sizing strategies. Position sizing™* is the aspect of your trading plan that tells you "how much." How many shares will you buy or sell on any given trade, based on the size of your protective stop? Position sizing is also *the* key to maximizing profitability.

Then you'll be ready to get down to the daily tasks of trading. You'll go over daily preparation—the most critical aspect of executing your trading plan. You will learn the secrets that top traders use every day to prepare themselves mentally, physically, spiritually, and emotionally. You'll find that with a consistent daily routine that is built on a solid trading plan, you can approach every trading day (indeed every trade) with the same inner confidence exhibited by Steve, our model trader.

Next, we will outline the key criteria that you'll need to build a set of specific trading rules that will guide you during each moment of decision during the trading day (regardless of the EDAT style you choose):

---

*Position sizing is a trademark of Position Sizing Technologies.

- When to pull the trigger to enter a trade
- How to determine the exact price to get out on the trades that go against your expectation
- How to exit a profitable trade

The next step in your journey to trading excellence is one that really sets top traders apart from the average trader: daily review. Successful traders know that a consistent and systematic review of their daily trading activities is the direct path to growing and improving. You'll find detailed instructions that show how to turn your raw trading data into a flexible database that you'll use to track and understand your trading results. And then we'll walk you through steps that demystify the art of keeping a trading journal. With your database and journal in hand, you'll then step through the periodic feedback process that will help you continuously refine and improve your trading plan based on your actual trading habits.

Up to now you will have traveled down a specific route that is applicable for all trading styles and should be (but usually isn't) followed by *all* traders. Given the foundation of how excellent traders structure their trading routine, you can then explore the different styles of EDAT: scalping and momentum trading. We will give you much more than just an overview. You will learn detailed strategies that market makers and top traders use every day. And more importantly, you'll gain insight into how a top trader thinks as you step through actual trades taken by my associates and me (Brian).

Last, you'll take a tour of the "minefield" of mistakes that have hindered or ended the careers of countless traders. You'll review the foundation on which every good trader stands: trading psychology, and then you'll review the characteristics that make up peak-performance trading.

And now the call to action! As you learn and internalize the knowledge revealed in this book, you'll be exposed to some of the finest wisdom in the trading world. The excellence that you achieve in *your* trading will depend on your ability to learn these successful strategies and then consistently put them into practice. Let the journey begin!

KNOWLEDGE KEYS

✓ Thorough preparation is a critical element of trading mastery.

✓ Trading one stock or a staple of "favorite" stocks will dramatically increase your profitability.

✓ Since you cannot know in advance what a stock will do, you can *only* trade your *beliefs* about a stock.

✓ Having a trading plan is another critical element of trading mastery.

✓ By defining your mission, you trade with purpose. Without a mission you trade without hope!

## CHAPTER 2

Prepare Yourself for Trading Heights

> Concerning all acts of initiative and creation, there is one
> elementary truth; that the moment one definitely commits
> oneself, then Providence moves too.
>
> *Johann Wolfgang Von Goethe*

Let's now take a look at some of the things that you will need to do
to be able to emulate Steve and what he has done. If you truly want
to move from where you are (you can start from almost anywhere)
into the position of an excellent, consistently profitable trader, there
are certain key elements that you simply must do. Otherwise you
will never achieve your dream. However, most traders skip or
ignore these essential elements, even when they're told how important they really are! The bottom line is that it all starts with . . .

THE POWER OF COMMITMENT

Jack had a successful business, but he wanted to be a trader. Never-
theless, he wasn't willing to give up his annual $100,000 salary until
he was certain that he could be successful as a trader. As a result, he
just dabbled in the markets, waiting to find the *magic secret*. He tried
different brokers, different advisers, different software programs,

and different systems. Everything he tried, however, had the same result—he never made enough money.

One day, Jack discovered the name of a trader who had made consistent and large profits in the markets for over 30 years. Furthermore, he learned that this trader would teach anyone who was willing to learn how to trade effectively. As a result, Jack packed his bags and went to visit the old man.

"I want to be a trader," Jack said. "I understand that you're willing to teach people how to do what you've been doing over the last 30 years."

"Well," responded the trader, "I'm willing to teach people, but most people don't seem to be willing to learn. I've had this offer to teach people all these years. All I ask is that they do what I tell them to do. Many people say, 'Yes, that's the life for me!' But most of them don't even carry out the first assignment. I imagine you will probably be the same. But, maybe not. Tell me about yourself! What makes you think you're a trader?"

"Let's see," explained Jack, "I've been at it for over 10 years. I keep losing money, but I still stick with it. I'll do whatever it takes to find the secret of trading successfully. I followed Guru X's advice. He was successful, but I wasn't able to make money following his recommendations. I then bought the XYZ, the RKS, and the PRT systems. I know people make money following those systems, but somehow I don't. So I came here to learn how you trade. What's your secret?"

"I'm a trader," stated the old man.

"I know that," said Jack, "but what's your secret?"

"I just told you. I'm a trader. You're not. You're just playing a game. When you decide to become a trader, to become fully committed, then you will understand. Are you willing to fully commit yourself to trading?"

"I want to make a living as a trader," replied Jack. "When I'm sure I can do that, then I'll do it full time. But every time I think I'm on my way, I suffer a major setback. Somehow I need a system that avoids those losses."

"You have to come to terms with one of the major obstacles traders face," said the old trader. "That obstacle is your losses. What if I told you that to be a trader, the best way is to take your losses and not worry about them? Just enjoy the process of trading, which involves both winning and losing. You might feel bad about losses, but notice that this is just you *feeling bad* about losses. It has nothing to do with the process of trading, which involves taking losses."

"That's fine for you to say with all your money," commented Jack, "but I don't want to lose money, and I want to be a successful trader."

"Then I think you need to make it OK to be unsuccessful," said the old man. "It's very difficult to trade if you're not willing to lose. Almost impossible. It's like wanting to be alive, always willing to breathe in, but not willing to breathe out! And you still haven't answered my question about whether or not you are fully committed to trading."

"I'm committed now," said Jack, "but I'll make even more of a commitment as soon as I know that I can be successful. Tell me your secret of success. I need to know your secret first. That's why I came here."

"I told you," the old man repeated, "I'm a trader. What I do is an art form. You can't be something else and be a trader at the same time. A trader, who knows what he's doing, trades. No one else could possibly understand. If you want to become a trader, then you should commit your life to doing it. Trading for you, as far as I can tell from our discussion, is just a dream and a struggle with something that doesn't work. You really need to go one way or the other. To go into trading saying 'I'm basically a lawyer or doctor or something else and I'll just trade on the side' is not adequate. Can you imagine this society tolerating someone who says, 'I'm going to practice brain surgery as a hobby.' When it's a hobby, there's something missing. You have to look inside yourself to find the truth. Maybe you have some inner voice in your head from your youth or a friend that says, 'Boy, I should really be a trader.' And you're convinced you should be a trader. But do you have what it takes to be a real trader? Do you really have a love for the art?" asked the trader.

"I think so," Jack answered.

"Then I'll help you trade," said the old trader skeptically. "But you must follow my instructions. First, here is a list of books I'd like you to read. Read these books and make plans to fully commit yourself to living with the markets. When you've done that, come back and we'll talk some more about trading."

Jack took the list and thanked the trader. He left the house shaking his head. "I don't want a list of books to read," he murmured to himself. "What I want is to know is how he trades. What's his secret? I guess he just doesn't want to share it with me."

THE TRUTH INSIDE YOU

I recount the story of Jack, because it had a great impact on me. Van Tharp, in volume 1 of his *Peak Performance Course for Investors and Traders*, tells this story as it relates to commitment.[1] When I first began to trade, I shared Jack's problem of poor performance.

After losing about $30,000 in my early trading, I decided that something was definitely missing from my approach! So I started reading everything I could get my hands on that related to trading. In one of the best books I've ever read, *Market Wizards*, I came across the name "Van K. Tharp." Many top traders interviewed in the book had used the coaching services of Van. I decided that if Van could help these world-class traders, he could help me too. So I contacted his company and bought the home study course.

What I discovered was that I was just playing games with the markets. I was not truly committed to trading; I had no mission, no defined purpose for pursuing a trading career. I had completed no self-assessment. I had not objectively examined my beliefs about the markets. I had not discovered how my own biases were sabotaging my trading results. In short, I had no specific goals, and I should not have been trading.

At this point you're probably thinking, "Duh, Brian! Who on earth would be stupid enough to trade like that?" The truth is, I didn't know what I didn't know. And neither do *most* people who want to trade for a living. That's precisely why the vast majority of day traders lose money! So stick with me in this process. By the time we finish this chapter, you'll know what you need to do to start trading profitably, whether you're just starting to trade or whether you're trying to dramatically improve your current results.

Needless to say, the decision to contact Van was one of the best I've ever made. Not only did I learn how to trade profitably; as a result of our friendship, Van and I are now able to bring these same concepts and strategies to you through this book. One of the most unique aspects we bring to you through these pages (and your efforts) is the melding of the best psychological practices and top-notch trading strategies and tactics!

By now you probably realize that the story of Jack could be your story. For some of you I'm sure that it is. How can I make this bold statement? Because if you knew what you needed to do, you'd just go do it! Many people who have picked up this book are in the same predicament as Jack (or me as a beginning trader); you want to trade, but "you don't know what you don't know." Well, it's time to find out!

As I've coached and counseled traders, I'm constantly amazed at how many know what they *should* be doing, and yet, for whatever reason, they will not do what they know is required! They're like Jack, and they're losing big bucks! I urge you to take to heart these suggestions and this information so that you realize your promise of trading success. Now on to . . .

THE MISSION YOU MUST ACCOMPLISH

As I said in Chapter 1, the promise of success as a trader is inside you. What does that exactly mean? It means that in order to succeed as a trader, you have to first understand yourself, *not the market*. This begins with your personal goals and mission. In other words, you have to have an overall guiding purpose in your life. Most people without any kind of a purpose in their life wander aimlessly like a ship without a rudder and are blown around every time the wind changes. If this describes you, your chances of success as a trader are limited by your lack of a defining mission in your life.

Mission statements are not fun for most people, and most aspiring traders will not examine their lives in conjunction with their trading. Instead, they'll say, "Well, my mission is to make a lot of money." A mission of making a lot of money, unfortunately, isn't a mission at all, and it's certainly not a strong motivator for most people. If making money were really a huge motivator, why are wealthy people in such a minority?

A recent study conducted for the American Association of Retired Persons (AARP) shows that making money is not that important to many people. When asked, "Would you like to be wealthy?" fully 33 percent of those surveyed said no.[2]

It's also interesting that the Executive Summary of that same study states: "The United States is enjoying one of the longest periods of economic expansion in its history. The television program *Who Wants to Be a Millionaire* has grabbed the collective American attention. *Ordinary Americans are becoming day traders.* (Emphasis added.) Yet others wonder how they will make ends meet, send the two children to ever-more costly college, and manage to retire."

This study and its conclusions are packed with information that is tremendously useful from a trading perspective. In fact, we'll revisit some of it later. But for now, just realize this—your brain has been wired by everyone (but you?) regarding money and what you should and should not do with the money you make; and maybe even with what you should and should not be doing with your life! (What! You're going to day-trade?) If you're going to take personal responsibility for your trading results, you must wire your brain the way you want it!

Learning to trade is a process. It takes a real investment of time and energy. Sometimes it can be drudgery or even painful. Without the firm foundation that a purposeful mission provides, you'll most likely stop trading before you'll endure the tough parts of learning! In short, like Steve from Chapter 1, a mission is an integral part of all successful traders. It will help you stay the course when the waters of learning become turbulent.

Your mission as a trader is totally and completely impacted by your life's mission or your life's purpose. Determining your overall life's mission is, undoubtedly, one of the most powerful and significant things you could ever do. This will help you identify the things that are most important in your life: your relationships, your roles, your interaction with other people, and the degree of self-satisfaction you have. Indeed, the degree to which you enjoy your life and live it fully is, in a very real sense, determined by what your mission is.

Dr. Stephen R. Covey, author of *The Seven Habits of Highly Effective People* (America's number one business book and a *New York Times* best-seller for 5 years), has done extensive research and writing with respect to mission. Here's an approach to mission building I've adapted from his work. Take a few minutes right now to complete this exercise. Simply take out a sheet of paper. Across the top write "My Mission." Then for the next 5 minutes answer the following questions. Do so in an uninterrupted "stream of consciousness" mode, so that what's inside of you simply flows out and onto the paper. Do it now!

- What are your guiding principles? (What beliefs do you hold in such high regard that you're unwilling to change or bend them?)
- What do you value? (*Hint:* Values can be thought of as preferences, things you like but are willing to change.)

The more closely our values align with our guiding principles, the more effective we will be. This is probably the single most critical concept for a trader to recognize. It's so critical, I'll come back to it after you've finished this exercise.

- List the most influential persons in your life. What do you admire about them?
- Detail your strengths and talents.
- What are your challenges and obstacles?
- How strong are your relationships with those closest to you? How do they currently affect your mission? How might they affect it in the future?
- Project yourself forward in time. What will your life look like in 1 year, 3 years, and 5 years?

So that you have a model to work from, look at Figure 2–1. It shows what my draft mission statement looked like after I went through the above steps.

Here are a few more questions to ask yourself when considering your mission:

- What do I want to do with my time?
- To what will I dedicate my talent?
- What principles will I adhere to?
- What kind of legacy do I want to leave?

In short, your mission statement, both your personal mission and your trading mission, will be your source of guidance when things get tough—and things will get tough. In Chapter 3 we'll work on a trading mission statement as a part of our trading plan. Coupling your personal mission statement with your trading mis-

Figure 2–1 Brian's Mission

To live my life with value, fulfillment and joy I will:

LEAD a life centered in the principles of integrity, encouragement, empowerment and excellence.

REMEMBER the things that are important in life: a personal relationship with God, my family, my friends and sense of accomplishment.

REVERE admirable characteristics in others, such as being forgiving, compassionate, courageous, and principle-centered. I will strive to implement similar characteristics in my own life.

RECOGNIZE my strengths and develop talents as a person who is articulate, imaginative, optimistic, confident, generous, and intelligent.

HUMBLE myself by acknowledging that I can be inflexible, sometimes uncommitted and a procrastinator. I will never cease in my efforts to transform my weaknesses into strengths.

sion is probably the single most important step to becoming a trader. Just like the old trader in our story of Jack, you must *be* a trader to trade like one! Your trading must be inextricably linked to who you are at your core.

You're probably reading this book either because you want to change your current career or because your current trading isn't yielding the results that you would like. In either case, that implies certain dissatisfaction with your current situation. Simply *be* a trader. Start by taking action, by determining your mission. After writing your mission, you will more easily achieve a sense of satisfaction. You'll understand much more clearly what it will take to move yourself from dissatisfaction into satisfaction and from sporadic results into consistent profits.

I'M STARTING WITH THE MAN IN THE MIRROR

The next step that we need to explore is self-assessment. During a self-assessment, you determine your strengths, your talents, and also your weaknesses. You should take these strengths and weaknesses into consideration when reviewing your overall mission statement.

Obstacles are often overlooked during self-assessment. What issues stand in your way as you map out your personal and trading plans? Although these obstacles are sometimes not pleasant to look at, it's very helpful to know what they are. For instance, I can sometimes be quite a procrastinator. Yet I know as a trader, the last thing I want to do is procrastinate when deciding to enter or exit a trade!

Many of us have trouble determining our mission, simply because we have not taken the time to ask ourselves good self-assessment questions. So why don't more traders ask powerful questions of themselves? Simple. I believe it's because they have never been taught to! So here goes . . .

THE MOST POWERFUL TRADING QUESTIONS YOU COULD EVER ASK

Powerful trading is almost all between the ears. That is, trading success is about 10 percent mechanical in nature and 90 percent psychological. Anyone can learn the mechanics of trading. Mastering the psychological is the true challenge. What questions do the top traders ask themselves? First, they start with some dynamic queries into their own nature. We cover that aspect here. Then they ask specific questions while they're actually trading. We'll examine those questions in Chapter 5.

By far, the most powerful questions stem from a complete and honest self-assessment. From a trader's perspective these questions fall into three broad categories—time, money, and talent. Just like you did with determining mission, take paper and pen, and delve into these areas. Don't rush yourself. Be very deliberate and specific with your answers. This may take an hour or two to complete the first time through. As you refine these questions further, they may take a couple of days to really examine. That's OK. Like all great endeavors, most of the work is in the preparation, not the execution! Ready? Great. Start writing!

Time

- How much time per day, week, and month can I devote to trading?
- Do I have the additional time required to prepare each day?

- Do I have 30 to 60 minutes available each day before the market opens?

Money

- How much risk capital do I have?
- How much money do I need to make each month?
- How much of this must come from trading?
- Do I have other financial resources available to me as a backup while I learn to trade profitably?

Talent

- How strong are my computer skills?
- Am I disciplined?
- Do I have strong stock market knowledge?
- Do I have many outside factors in my life that could have a negative impact on my trading?
- What is my trading "edge," or what *could* it be? (*Note:* Trading edges are discussed in detail in Chapter 3.)

If you take the time to go through these questions purposefully, you'll notice that something interesting will occur—they will evoke still more questions. Each time you ask a more defining question, you'll be forcing your mind to be ever-more specific about what *you* need to be a successful trader.

Each of you will answer these questions differently. Each trader is unique. Your unique qualities and distinctions will be the ingredients you will use to form your strategic and tactical trading plan. In other words, these distinctions will help you address many critical trading situations. For example, how will you enter and exit your positions? How will you know when to stay in your trades and when to exit? How will you be able to trade in a way that *guarantees* your profitability over the long haul? We go over all these issues in Chapter 3, so it's important to finish this assessment before you move on.

As you can see, self-assessment dovetails with the mission. Mission is what you want to be, do, or have—the person you really want to be and the accomplishments you want to achieve. Self-assessment tells you where you are today, so that you can understand the differences between the person that you desire to be and the person that you are right now. Once you understand what these differences are, then you can devise an action plan that will lead you from where you are to where you want to be!

Once you've completed the first two exercises in this chapter, you'll be well on your way to discovering yourself as a trader— well on your way to *being* a trader. Take a close look at what you've done so far. What you've really compiled is a set of beliefs—in this case, a set of beliefs about who you are and who you could become. Let's examine beliefs a bit more closely.

THE BELIEF DYNAMIC

A belief is a model of reality. We all hold beliefs because they help us interpret the world we live in. All the statements you've made in your self-assessment are beliefs about what you think is possible or impossible, about what you think you need or require in some way. Throughout the ages people have loved and hated, brought life into the world or ended life, all based upon beliefs. In some sense, beliefs underlie all psychology. Beliefs and belief systems are potent allies or weapons in the world of the trader. Look back at Steve, our trader, or Jack, our "would-be" trader. The reality both experienced was shaped and molded by their beliefs. From your perspective, you'll need to examine your own beliefs on two levels: your global beliefs about yourself (covered here) and your specific trading beliefs about the markets and the systems you trade. (These trading beliefs are developed in the section on trading plans in Chapter 3 and in the chapters on trading strategy—Chapters 9 and 10.)

IF YOU DON'T BELIEVE IT, YOU CAN'T TRADE IT

If you've been around the markets long enough, you've probably heard the saying "You cannot trade the market. You can only trade your beliefs about the market." This saying, often uttered or paraphrased by the old-timers of the market, attempts to encapsulate the twin truths of knowing yourself and knowing the market. Van Tharp's body of work suggests that the reason so many "off-the-shelf" systems fail is simple. When a system begins to generate some drawdowns, the trader who purchased the system either stops following it or alters it so that it no longer has a positive expectancy (see Chapter 5). He's found that the reason for this is that the trader *doesn't believe* the system.

This whole issue of beliefs had a huge effect on me when I reassessed my early trading performance. I went through the disciplines of building a mission statement and completing a self-assessment. I put together a business plan and a trading plan, but something was still missing. Although I didn't realize the problem at first, I soon discovered that some of the beliefs that had helped me so much in the corporate world were actually hurting me as a trader. One of the beliefs I held was that losing money was bad. Since most of us have been taught this concept from a young age, this belief probably doesn't surprise you. However, *one of the ironies of trading is that you must be ready and willing to lose small amounts of money to make significant profits!*

Since money seems to be an area of conflict for many traders, let's further explore this concept. I'd venture that you probably have a similar belief and that this belief, that losing money is bad, will trip you up on your way to trading profits if you don't learn to recognize it and deal with it now.

Let's say you have a brokerage account with $100,000 in it, but you have not touched the money for 3 years. You've put no additional money into your account; you've taken no money out of it; and because your trading has been erratic, your account balance goes up a little bit, then comes back down a little bit, but basically it's flat after 3 years. What has happened is this—you've become secure and satisfied that you have $100,000 in your trading account. However, notice you've done absolutely nothing *with* the money! Except for the feeling of security you derive, the money has no value from a practical economic standpoint. Reflect on this as much as you have to. Truly understand this. Too many traders allow conflicts with money to stand in the way of successful trading!

Now you decide to start direct-access day trading. You still have the same $100,000 in your account, and you begin to trade. After the end of the first month you've lost $10,000 and you receive your brokerage statement. You've now experienced a 10 percent drawdown. You have $90,000 in your trading account, and you become irritated or even slightly frightened. At a bare minimum you're dissatisfied. Perhaps you're feeling a little insecure; perhaps thoughts are running through your head like, "Oh my word, what am I going to do now that my trading capital has been decimated!"

I'd like to point out to you that absolutely nothing has changed other than the way you're thinking about it! Why do I make this radical statement? Because you hadn't touched your money for 3 years prior to beginning to trade. In fact, you had done *nothing* with it. The only function it performed for you (in our example) was that it gave you a feeling of security. We can see this because now that your account has drawn down 10 percent, you feel less secure. Notice, however, you still haven't spent one nickel!

I'm pointing this out because as I went through the process of building my mission statement, completing my self-assessment, and examining my beliefs, I had to come to grips with what money meant to me. The belief noted above—that I have to be ready and willing to lose small amounts of money in order to make larger amounts—helped me to deal very effectively with the drawdowns. Of course I trade to make money! But I was not fully aware of my money beliefs and how they were negatively affecting me. The bottom line is this: If you don't profoundly understand your current relationship with money, making more of it won't change anything in your life! Likewise, having less money will not change anything about you, as my story above points out. Like me, it may be necessary for you to deliberately change your money beliefs to something more empowering and useful in order to be a trader.

TO GET CLEAR ON YOUR GOALS, LINK YOUR BELIEFS TO YOUR MISSION

Let's go back to that AARP study again. You'll recall that 33 percent of the respondents had no desire to be wealthy, even when they acknowledged that more money would probably make their lives easier. But take a look at these beliefs:

- Of the 66 percent who did want to be wealthy, 81 percent thought that is was likely that "having a lot of money makes a person too greedy."
- Fully 74 percent of the same group said having wealth would likely make them insensitive to other people![3]

Do you notice the total lack of congruency in these statements? How many of the people who want to be wealthy will ever get there with such internal conflicts? My guess is darn few. (Actually I've found having more wealth has caused me to be much less greedy and much more sensitive to the needs of others.) My point here is that very few of us understand our beliefs. We are wired by everything and everyone—except ourselves! Is it any wonder so few people live to their fullest potential?

One result of these "mixed messages" is that we often confuse goals with mission. For example, when new or potential traders are talking to me about becoming a trader, I usually ask them, "What's your mission?" After a long and goofy silence or stare, they'll say something like "I want to make a boatload of money." But most people don't even want the money. What they really want is the things that money can buy! When I refine the answer of "making money" by asking them why they want to make money, I'll often get an answer such as "I want to buy a new home."

Do this yourself. Ask yourself this essential question: Do you really want more money? My guess is not really. Maybe you want to send your daughter to a top-tier college. Maybe you want to make a large contribution to a charity or your church. But the money in and of itself is virtually meaningless to most people.

Continue to refine the question and ask yourself why you want these things. You'll probably end up giving answers that get to the essence of who you are—the essence of your mission. Why do you want to have a new home? Because you expect a new home will give you a feeling of security. Why do you want to send your daughter to college? Because it will give you a feeling of inner peace to know your child has a good education. Or why do you want to give to charity? Because you'll feel immense pleasure realizing you're helping other people.

So as you continue your analysis, you'll find that your goal (which you stated as a mission) wasn't truly money at all. Your goal is some mental or emotional state. Some feeling that you derive by achieving the goal. Money is simply a means to an end. After all, a person can do absolutely nothing with money that is sitting static in a brokerage account or in the bank. It's simply a digit, a one or a zero, that sits in a computer somewhere. You receive a statement once a month that tells you how many digits you have!

As I spent time and energy discovering these secrets in *myself*, I realized that I had to link my trading beliefs to my mission. I now teach this as an essential element of trading success. I was asking myself key questions such as "Why am I trading?" "What do I want to achieve?" and "Is trading consistent with my life's purpose?" If you can answer these questions, you'll be able to iron out the rough spots in your trading that may be preventing you from achieving true success as a trader. As I was doing this, I came to a point where I realized that I had to form some core overall belief about my trading that would take me back to my life's purpose. This is a vital element, a key link, and a connection that many traders fail to make. Yet I'd bet that most excellent traders have done this either deliberately or unconsciously.

In my case, the link from belief to mission was a direct outgrowth of what I'd learned as a child. Let me tell you what I mean. We're trained from the time we are very young children, from even 1 or 2 years old, to be producers in some way, shape, or form. We're trained to become employees, and sometimes we're trained to become self-employed. But we're trained to produce something. We're trained to manufacture something, create something, produce homework, produce "good" grades, produce some kind of athletic achievement, produce results in college, and then we usually go on to some kind of an employment situation where, again, we are expected to produce—and if we don't produce, we get fired.

Here a real problem can develop, because when most people make the jump from being a producer in the marketplace to being a trader, they lose that connection between their work and their production. I know I did. Our society has taught many of us to equate trading with gambling, and we then equate trading with nonproduction. This causes huge conflicts in most of the traders that I work with, and, in fact, it was a conflict in my own psyche when I started to learn how to trade. The problem was this: I knew what my overall life's mission was, but I couldn't come up with a link that took trading back to my mission because I saw trading as largely a nonproductive activity. The exciting part is this—you really are producing something! But most people haven't taken the time to think about what they're producing. In Chapter 3, when we talk about the business plan, we're going to specifically talk about what you produce as a trader.

At any rate, I had to come up with a link between my mission statement, my business plan, and my trading plan. I had to come up with a belief system, or a belief statement, that helped me get there. I'll share mine with you so that you will begin to think about this yourself. One of my highest beliefs is that I have to produce something. One of the ways I can do this is to leave this world, if I can, a better place than when I arrived. So how does trading fit into this? Figure 2–2 shows what I came up with.

Compare my mission statement (Figure 2–1) with my belief statement (Figure 2–2). Do you see how they are congruent? By taking these deliberate steps, I eliminate any conflict. As simple as this seems, it allows me to enjoy what I do, knowing I will be less greedy and knowing I will be more sensitive to the needs of others. When I'm in the middle of a trade, I believe that I'm adding not only to my own well-being, but to the well-being of all humanity. Since I do believe this, I act differently and make better mental distinctions than if I were simply trying to make a buck. Holding onto that overall belief helps me when things aren't going well—and sometimes things don't go well.

Take the time before the end of this chapter to come up with a personal belief statement that will link your beliefs to your mission statement. Remember, you cannot trade the markets—you can *only* trade your beliefs about the markets. You need to make this mental connection or you'll have great difficulty when attempting to set meaningful goals and milestones for your trading. If your goals and milestones are inconsistent, your trading will be too!

TURN YOUR GOALS INTO ACTION

As a trader (or at least an aspiring one), you probably picked up this book chomping at the bit to make some trades. "Show me some good entries and I'll be on my way to riches that trader Steve would

---

Figure 2–2 Brian's "I Believe" Statement

I believe that I possess all of the qualities, knowledge, and skill to be a top trader. I believe that trading is an honorable and worthy profession. I believe that my trading adds to the well-being of myself, my family, my community, and the whole of humanity.

be proud of!" is a typical cry of the average would-be trader. If you are still reading up to this point, you may be one of the rare few who realizes that there is more to successful day trading than stock picking and entry signals.

Since I know you are committed to using this book as a resource to become a better trader, you've no doubt completed a few things by now:

- You have a written mission.
- You've completed a self-assessment exercise.
- And you've made a written list about your beliefs, especially as they relate to the markets and trading.

Congratulations! You deserve to reward yourself for your diligence to this point. Do something nice for yourself—right now!

Now let's continue on our journey toward trading excellence. We're going to spend some time developing goals in two broad areas: personal and trading. The same general principles apply to both, so let's review some proven goal-setting guidelines that are applicable for any area of endeavor that you choose. Here are some key areas in which excellent traders set goals:

Key Areas for Trader Excellence

1. Personal
   a. Spiritual
   b. Mental
   c. Emotional
   d. Physical
   e. Organizational (for example, time management and record keeping)
      (i) Remember to formulate a business plan for your trading business!
2. Trading
   a. Process-oriented goal areas (those things that will lead to positive results—also known as profits!)
      (i) Written trading plan
      (ii) Daily trading disciplines
         (1) Pretrading checklists (include the concepts embodied in the "Ten Tasks of Trading"[4])

 (2) Trading records
 (3) Trading journal
b. Results-oriented goal areas
  (i) Monthly profitability
  (ii) Return on investment
  (iii) Maximum drawdown
  (iv) Maximum number of losing months per year

Notice that these goal areas aren't necessarily the ones most people would associate with trading excellence. Of course, the specific trading goals are easy to see. The personal goals are more difficult to accept until you realize that your body, mind, and spirit are all individual members of an interconnected whole. To be a successful trader for the long term, you must balance all these areas of your life with your trading activities.

Since this book was written to guide you toward becoming a successful direct-access day trader (and not to make you a master of the finer points of goal setting), the following section is only an overview of the goal-setting process. For a more detailed look at setting and achieving goals, especially personal goals, please see the following references:

Anthony Robbins, *Awaken the Giant Within*

Brian Tracy, *Maximum Achievement*

Van K. Tharp, *Peak Performance Course for Investors and Traders*[5]

HOW TO DEVELOP POWERFUL, ACTION-ORIENTED GOALS

Take a moment right now to review your mission and your beliefs. Together, these tell you two things: where you ultimately want to be and what your guiding principles are. Now close your eyes and imagine that you are living your ideal life right now. What does it look like? How does it feel? Are there any sounds or scents connected to your dreams and desires? Try to distinguish every possible detail that you can and write them all down. Be sure to dream big here. Don't be afraid. It's your dream, so anything goes. The whole purpose of this exercise is to help you destroy any limiting beliefs you may have and to help you nurture and strengthen your useful beliefs. (Remember my limiting belief that trading was somehow nonproductive? I had to permanently annihilate it.) If you make any mistake here, it will simply be that you failed to dream and plan big enough. So set your standards high. Make your goals worthy of your time! Once you've done this, you'll have some excellent internal ideas and images of where you're heading in the very near future.

Next, go back to your self-assessment answers. Take a moment to reflect on them once more. Do they still make sense? Are they still congruent with your mission and belief system? Your purpose in this review is to help you understand your current situation. It will give you a starting point for identifying the goals that will take you from where you are to where you want to be.

Now choose one specific area where you desire change, improvement, or growth. Use the list "Key Areas for Trader Excellence" above as a starting point or guideline. Pick an area that is most important to you right now. Brainstorm this one subject by writing down everything that you'd like to *be, do,* or *have* in this particular area. Write nonstop for 5 minutes—never let your pen leave the paper. Write down every thought that pops into your head—nothing is too trivial or grandiose. Let yourself be creative—be a kid again. Be outrageous—dream big! The important thing is to get ideas on paper. After you brainstorm, ask yourself the following questions:

- If I had only 6 months to live, would I add (subtract?) any items to (from) the list?
- If I received $1 million tax-free, would I add (subtract?) any items to (from) the list?
- If I set one goal in this area and knew *I could not fail,* what would that goal be? Add it to the list.

Take your list and prioritize it. Mark any goal that will directly affect achieving your mission a "1." Mark any goal that will not directly affect your mission but is still important to you a "2." Mark the rest of your goals and ideas a "3." Assign a time frame for completion to every item that is a 1 or a 2 (in months or years). Be aggressive but realistic. Remember that you don't need to know how you're going to accomplish the goal at this point; you just need to make your best guess at how long it should take.

Now go back to the "Key Areas for Trader Excellence" list, select the next area you wish to focus on, and repeat this same brainstorming exercise. If you're like me, you'll find this process exhausting and exhilarating at the same time—exhausting because this does take some real energy to complete, and exhilarating because once done, you'll be more clear on your goals and objectives than you've ever been. Not to mention that you'll also be more clear than 90 percent of all other traders! Completing this assignment will, in fact, give you a huge edge over almost all other traders!

THE MOST CRITICAL GOAL-SETTING SECRET

Here's where goal setting breaks down for most people. You have a great set of prioritized objectives—probably too many. To stay focused on only the most important ones, you must now pick the single most important objective for each goal. This is the one that excites and energizes you the most, the one that once accomplished will make you feel like your whole year was well spent. Do this right now. For each area, what is the single most important objective?

The final step is to develop a written action plan for that goal, including:

- Your motivation for achieving the goal (what excites you about getting it done?).
- What you need to learn or find out to achieve this goal.
- The obstacles to achieving this goal. What personal issues or beliefs might impede your progress? What external issues such as people, events, or other factors might impede your progress?
- The resources you will need—time, other people, equipment, capital, etc.

Write out a step-by-step plan for achieving each objective. Make sure each step has a time frame for completion.

Now take action! Do something—anything! Regardless of how small the step may seem, make something happen *today* toward the achievement of one of your goals. I suggest you start on your highest-priority goal. The secret to attaining your life's dream of being a trader is to take action now and then remain on a steady course toward its achievement. In other words, take action each and every day until you've achieved your objective. This keeps your mind tuned in and your subconscious working toward your goal. It's so easy to be distracted by letting your mind wander to less productive areas.

Few things in life can top the feeling of accomplishing a challenging and meaningful goal. And as strange as it may seem, you get almost the same feeling just by going through the act of setting the goals. If you don't have that feeling right now, don't read any further! Go back and do the exercises in this section again. The road to successful day trading leads directly through a set of well-planned goals. In particular, your goals need to include the completion of a strong business plan and a thorough trading plan. Guidelines for producing these critical plans lie straight ahead in the next chapter.

While I don't profess to be an expert on psychology, I do know what works when trading. Fortunately, many different approaches work. You don't have to share my beliefs or use my system to make money in the markets. *But whatever your mission, beliefs, and goals, they must be consistent with one another and congruent with who you are.* That is the *magic secret* to ascending the trading heights!

KNOWLEDGE KEYS

✓ The most important element of trading is understanding your personal mission and how it relates to trading.
✓ To trade profitably and consistently over the long term, you must understand both the distinctions and connections between your personal mission and your trading mission.
✓ Self-assessment is a critical part of trading mastery.
✓ Your personal belief systems will impact your trading—positively or negatively.
✓ Creating a useful set of personal and trading beliefs is essential to trading.
✓ Goals are the bridge between your mission and your day-to-day trading execution.
✓ You need to have a well-balanced set of written goals.
✓ Your personal goals will impact your trading life.

CALLS TO ACTION

✓ Make sure that you are deeply committed to trading before you risk large sums of money in the markets.

✓ Follow the exercises in this chapter to firmly establish both your personal and your trading mission. Make sure these are in writing so that you know beforehand where you're heading as a trader.

✓ Go through the self-assessment actions as outlined. Define where you are currently in terms of time, money, and ability.

✓ Examine your personal and trading beliefs. Are they harmful or useful as a trader? Work on gaining useful beliefs and eliminating harmful beliefs. Go through the belief material in this chapter.

✓ Based upon the above action items, take whatever time is necessary to firmly establish, in writing, your personal and trading goals. Be sure to include any and all areas that impact trading. Aspiring traders often overlook mental, spiritual, emotional, physical, and organizational issues.

✓ Make sure all your goals have a time frame for completion and a measurable outcome.

✓ Take action now!

NOTES

1. While Jack is fictional, the trader is one of the world's top traders. This story was relayed to Van Tharp in an interview with this trader who was in his forties at the time of the interview.

2. Survey conducted on behalf of the AARP. This national survey of 2,366 adults over age 18 was conducted by phone during January and February 2000. The full report can be found on the Web at http://www.research.aarp.org/econ/money_1.html.

3. See note 2.

4. The "Ten Tasks of Trading" are daily self-examination, daily mental rehearsal, developing a low-risk idea, stalking, action, monitoring, take profits, abort, daily debriefing, and periodic review. See *Peak Performance Trading (Home Study) Course*, volume 1, by Van K. Tharp.

5. Van Tharp's *Peak Performance Course for Investors and Traders* concentrates on integrating personal and trading goals to achieve higher profits and more consistent results. Van's success in coaching several world-class traders attests to the wisdom of this integrated approach.

## CHAPTER 3

Design a Plan Even Goldman Sachs Might Envy

A good plan, executed now, is better than a perfect plan next week.

General George S. Patton

Imagine that you have several friends and they know someone who started up a neighborhood grocery store, and the person is making a killing. That sounds good to you, and you've always craved the independence of working for yourself, so you decide you're going to start a brand-new grocery store business. But you need to borrow some money to get things going. You call a few suppliers and find out how much your inventory is going to cost (stuff like milk, bread, eggs, and butter). There's a small store on a nearby corner for rent, and you figure you can rent the building pretty cheap.

Armed with this knowledge, you go to your bank and you say, "Ms. Banker, there are little grocery stores everywhere, and I think I can make money in the grocery store business, too. After all, I can buy lots of basic staple items. Sometimes I can buy them for less than my competition; sometimes I have to pay a bit more. The bottom line is I think I can sell them for more than I pay for them. After all, that's how you make money, isn't it? Also, I can rent this little building down on the corner near my house. My overhead will be pretty low because the rent is cheap and I won't have to drive very far to work. I just need some shelving, a cash register, a cooler, and a telephone line. Add in some paper bags with my store name on them, and I'll be ready to go. What I'd like to know is, would you please loan me $100,000 so I can open my grocery store?"

What do you think the chances are of the bank loaning you the money based upon your "business plan"? Good? Not so good? If you have any business experience at all, you'll understand that the banker is probably going to laugh you right out of the door. Not only will she not give you the loan, but she'll probably strongly suggest that you stop wasting your time and hers. No banker will loan money for a poor, sloppily planned, totally off-the-cuff "business idea." And yet that's how most aspiring day traders approach their business.

They see mesmerizing ads on television, where everyone, including the kindly granny next door, is making (it seems) a killing by day trading. They may have a friend who has done a little online trading. They have a little bit of money to trade, maybe $10,000, maybe $20,000. They can easily download the trading software through the Internet. It's pretty simple to open up a trading account. So, enthralled by the promise of easy riches, they open up a trading account and deposit $20,000 and they're in business!

Little do they realize that they've just set themselves up to compete against some of the best-financed and best-managed trading companies in the world—companies such as Merrill Lynch, Goldman Sachs, and Morgan Stanley. Not to mention the fact that they'll also be trading against many highly skilled private market makers and traders.

Now put yourself in this situation. What do you think your chances as a trader are against that kind of competition? Do you think your chances of survival are good or not? If you think that your chances are good and that you're going to make money, why do you think that?

You probably realize how ridiculous this proposition is. Even if you have very little practical business experience, you intuitively know that this kind of "plan" is going to fail. Your new store is going to get crushed by the competition. Yet primarily because of "success stories" (a buddy knows a buddy who's made some money) and because of advertising and the fact that the media have so convinced you that it's easy to trade, you think you're going to open up your little trading shop and compete with Goldman Sachs. Well, I can tell you that you're not. At least you're not going to make any money, not at first anyway—and especially not without a business plan and a trading plan that clearly define and explain exactly how you'll thrive in the face of such fierce competition.

HOW TO CREATE A DYNAMITE PLAN

One of the things that I've found is that many people really don't understand the function of a business plan. So before we talk about what a business plan is, let's talk about what it is not. A big misconception I often hear is that a business plan is about some new and brilliant idea, an idea that will revolutionize or change the marketplace in some way. It isn't. We've all heard countless stories of clever people inventing new products or services and becoming hugely wealthy through this new idea. More often than not, hundreds or maybe even thousands of people have already conceived the same idea. While it's fine to have a good idea, that isn't the most important part of the plan. What is most important is the execution of the idea. And that's what a business plan really is—a written document that shows *how to turn any idea or concept into a profitable venture.*

Trading is one of the oldest concepts on the planet, and that's an advantage to your new business. You don't have to reinvent the wheel. What you have to do now is create a written set of instructions for your brain, instructions that will turn your concepts into cash. Think of your business plan as *Cliff Notes* on how to make money by trading, because that's what it will be once it is completed. Since only the best traders have the discipline to make such a plan, you'll have one of the "edges" you need to compete alongside the top market makers and traders.

For most people, writing a business and a trading plan is about as much fun as having a root canal. Another issue is that most traders have very little if any business school or business background. If this describes you, you may not have been exposed to the disciplines of writing a business or a trading plan. And you may consider it pure drudgery!

But before you despair, remember that these plans are vital guides along the path to long-term profitability. Also focus on the fact that even though some traders have a trading plan, which dictates what they do day in and day out, they can't distinguish between trading daily and running their business profitably. They are so close to the trading activity that they can't see the big picture. The problem is, they never step back and get a large enough perspective to see where the trading is taking them from a business standpoint and how their trading fits into their overall mission.

The purpose of the rest of this chapter is to relieve the anxiety about writing trading and business plans. To get started, take a look at Figure 3–1. It shows an outline of a good business plan for your trading business. This plan is very similar in structure to many excellent business plans you might find in business schools or corporations, large and small. It includes *all* major areas for planning and running any profitable business. *Notice that it goes far beyond a typical trading plan.* In fact the "trading plan" is only one subset of the overall business structure. Most business plans would include a section on strategy and implementation. Such a section might include the following subtopics: market opportunity, business strategy, and service implementation and marketing strategy. Since the strategy and implementation section of a business plan is all about income production and a trading plan deals with the same issues, a trader would substitute "trading plan" for "strategy and implementation." In essence, what business planning for a trader really boils down to is shown in Figure 3–1.

STEPPING THROUGH YOUR OWN BUSINESS PLAN

Executive Summary

Even though it comes first in the outline, the executive summary is usually the last section written. This allows you to review all the content in the other sections and then present the key points to make this an effective section. Here are a few points to consider when compiling your executive summary:

- Executive summaries usually describe the objective of the business plan, whether it is written to secure financing or to provide operational guidance. Most business plans for traders are for operational guidance.
- The executive summary doesn't have to cover every section of the business plan, but it should touch on key

1. Executive summ
2. Business descri
   a. Mission
   b. Overview and
   c. Products and
   d. Operations
   e. Organization, r
3. Industry overview
4. Trading plan
   a. Low-risk ideas
   b. Strategic concep
   c. Implementation
      i   Entries
      ii Exits
      iii Stops
   d. Strategic alliances
   e. Skill maintenance
5. Financial information
   a. Budget
   b. Cash flow statemen
   c. Profit and loss state   ...ome statement)
   d. Balance sheet

Figure 3–1 Business plan outline for traders.

personnel, reasons why the business will succeed, and the timetable for key financial goals.

Business Description

Mission

Before you begin writing your business plan, go back to your personal mission. Reflect on how your trading business's mission will tie into your broader personal mission. Reflect for a few moments on the goal-setting work you completed in Chapter 2. Take a moment to review the goal-setting rules. Remind yourself of your goals. One of your trading goals should be to make money. How far have you drilled down? Are you willing to lose one-half or even three-quarters of your money in order to end up winning in the long run? Are you willing to lose 25 percent of your capital to double your money over the next year? Did you complete all your exercises from Chapter 2? Do you have your goals in writing? What are you doing or what have you done so far to achieve your goals? Make sure that your goals are very succinct and that you can put them in writing in one or two sentences. If you haven't probed these issues deeply enough, designing a business plan will be quite difficult.

This may be one of the toughest areas of the business plan for you to complete. If you are not naturally a reflective person or just don't do much contemplative thinking, it's hard to start from scratch! To help you along, here are some questions that will serve as a general guide for you:

- What will your business do to support your broader personal mission?
- What is the primary purpose or objective of the business?
- Will one of its main objectives be to generate cash?
- What are the key values that the business will embrace as it operates?

Please note that this list is by no means exhaustive—it is provided to get you started, not to limit you!

Overview and History

This section is actually much more critical in a business plan that will be used to secure outside financing for a business, but it is still useful for a trader's operations-oriented plan. Here are some thoughts on what you can include in this section:

- Your personal history and trading background
- A brief overview of your trading strategy

Products and Services

There are many services that traders provide to the marketplace. But perhaps you haven't given this much thought. One of the key services provided is liquidity. It's one of the most important aspects of today's sophisticated markets. In this respect, one of your roles as a day trader is strikingly similar to that of a market maker.

If you were trading, or were involved in any other way with the markets, on April 14, 2000, you'll remember that it was a tremendously volatile day. The Dow sold off over 625 points, and the NASDAQ sold off 355+ points. It was one of the largest sell-off days in recent history, though not comparable on a percentage basis to October 1987. (I'm sure it may have felt the same to many traders.) However, this huge sell-off was very different from October 1987's "Black Monday." During the October 1987 fiasco there were simply no buyers around to take the sell orders. Some brokers were not even answering their phones! In fact, this "stonewalling" by the brokers on Black Monday was one of the key events that gave birth to EDAT. Because of consumer outrage, the Securities and Exchange Commission made rule changes over time that have allowed individual traders to compete on a tick-by-tick basis with the institutions. Contrast the incredible lack of liquidity that plagued the markets in October 1987 with the liquidity on April 14, 2000, and you'll note that as bad as the selling was, there still was liquidity on the buy side. This, in my opinion, is one of the factors that prevented a repeat panic on the scale of the October 1987 debacle. This new liquidity is one of the reasons that the markets are able to rebound so quickly after severe sell-offs. For example, on April 17 and 18, the next two trading sessions, the Dow, the NASDAQ, and the S&P had already recovered more than 50 percent of their April 14 losses.

For additional examples of the liquidity effect, take a look at stocks such as Qualcomm, Inc. (QCOM) (Figure 3–2) and JDS Uniphase Corporation (JDSU) (Figure 3–3). From approximately March 1999 through March 2000, JDSU moved from the low $16s to over $153 per share, and QCOM went from about $21.5 to $200 per share! The only way that this can happen is through tremendous liquidity. In the current market environment, individual traders are providing more and more of this liquidity.

Another vital service provided by individual traders is capital creation. Admittedly, this may be a tad harder for you to see. Nonetheless, it is an essential element of American and worldwide enterprise. This capital is the fuel that businesses need to expand and grow. Of course, as long as we as traders are providing our cap-

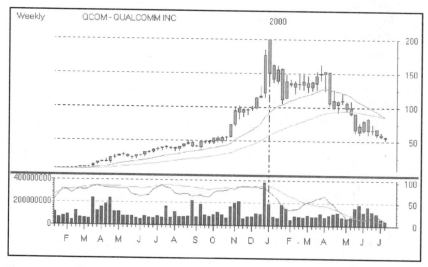

Figure 3–2 Liquidity drives Qualcomm higher last week of 1999.

ital to the marketplace, we are doing our part to enable business expansion. Expanding businesses hire new people, who in turn demand even more products and services from the economy. So when we're willing to invest and trade risk capital, an entire chain of economic events occurs.

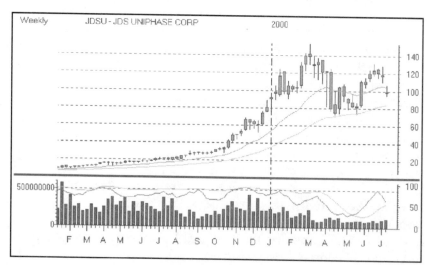

Figure 3–3 Liquidity drives JDSU higher late February 2000.

Of course, we want to make a profit from our risk capital, and we don't put our risk capital up with the idea that we're going to lose money. However, the fact is that whenever we subject our capital to risk, there is a possibility that we will in fact lose some of that money. For this reason, standard economic models demand that we earn a return on our risk capital. Because we traders take comparatively large risks, we expect a fairly substantial rate of return on our risk capital. Throughout the past few centuries, whenever risk capital has been put to work, the owners of that risk capital required a much higher rate of return than did the holder of a secured instrument such as a bond or mortgage. The same is true for traders.

So you can see the value that traders bring to the market. Their services are instrumental to commerce. This neural connection between risk and reward is a distinction that many marginal traders fail to make. Consequently, as we discussed in Chapter 2, they are conflicted with the issue of "gambling" and being personally nonproductive. However, when we view trading as a business, it's easy to see the connection between the risk associated with trading and the high levels of return that you can make for accepting that risk. This is no small connection! It's vitally important to understand the risk-reward connection of trading in order to be congruent in your beliefs. When traders realize that taking profits is their reward for the risk they accept, for the liquidity they provide, and for their contribution to free enterprise, then they can feel good about trading. Instead of perceiving themselves as gamblers or bandits, they are captains of commerce who are rewarded for adding to the greater good.

Operations

As mentioned above, almost all business plans for trading are written to provide operational guidance. While the detailed day-to-day trading tasks are covered in the trading plan section, there are some other issues that you will want to cover under this broad category.

One area to consider is site selection. You have two broad choices—should you trade from home, or is a trading room more suited to your needs? If you trade from home, you'll need to find a quiet, comfortable spot that can accommodate lots of electronic equipment and meet your needs for personal comfort. If you choose a trading room and you're in a large metropolitan area, such as New York City, you have several trading rooms to select from. If you're in Elkton, Maryland, I doubt that you have one. In this case, your only meaningful option (short of moving) is probably to trade from home.

Each option has its advantages and disadvantages. The primary disadvantage of trading from home is that you have no one to model. This can be especially detrimental to a new trader. Trading is like any other skill that has a kinesthetic element. You need to watch and repeat the actions of someone more skilled than yourself. If you're going to be a brain surgeon, you simply must model another skilled surgeon. There's no way to consistently perform the surgery without first watching someone else do it many times. Slowly, your mentor will allow you to take over portions of the surgery until, over a period of time, you can successfully complete the surgery on your own.

Piloting an airplane is another great metaphor. When I'm teaching students to fly, one of the first skills I teach is just to taxi the plane. Once students can taxi, I allow them to place their hands gently on the yoke while I do the takeoffs and landings. With their hands on the yoke and feet on the rudders, they begin to build neural pathways between their eyes, hands, feet, and brain. The actions they perform, when properly reinforced, become habitual and instinctive. Eventually, through repeated practice, they learn the proper procedures. When I believe they're ready, I allow them to both taxi and take off. It's easy to take off. The plane wants to fly naturally. Just point the nose down the runway and give the plane fuel; once the plane has gained enough speed, it takes off. However, one of the last things I allow students to do is to land, since under normal operating conditions, that's the most complex piloting operation.

Think about this from a trading perspective. It's easy to trade. You want to buy stock—just click on the "Buy" button. You can buy stock anywhere, anytime, anyplace, at any price—it's very simple. Selling and making a profit is the most difficult part. One of the most complex tasks you have as a trader is to figure out how to consistently get out of the trade with a profit.

So if you decide to trade from home, I highly recommend that you arrange for training or mentoring. Attend seminars and get either personal one-on-one coaching or mentoring over the Web or telephone. But make sure that you're coached until you can get into and out of your trades profitably. Be sure you can take off and land without crashing and burning—without destroying your capital.

Some of the advantages to home trading are that it gives you tremendous personal freedom and control over your environment, especially ergonomics. While I'm on this subject, make sure you get a comfortable place from which to trade—a room where you can adjust the brightness and the contrast of the lighting, depending upon the amount of daylight you have. One of the casualties of trading may be your eyes. Sitting in front of computer monitors for hours on end can produce a tremendous amount of eyestrain, so lighting is important. Temperature control is also important. And get a good chair—the best you can afford. You do want to be very comfortable, as comfortable as possible.

The whole idea here is to make sure your environment is set up so that your body isn't screaming at you about your sitting position, the temperature of the room, the amount of light in the room, the amount of oxygen available, the amount of water available, and all the other things that your body requires to be in top form. Make sure your body isn't screaming for attention, because you want your attention to be focused on the trading process itself.

Let's talk now about trading from a trading room. I've investigated many trading rooms and have spent a lot of time in various trading rooms. However, I have never actually traded from a trading room. Given what I know now and the money that I initially lost learning to trade from home, I wish I had started my trading career from a trading room.

One of the biggest advantages of locating in a trading room is that, especially if you're in a career transition, you'll feel a sense of continuity. You'll still have the routine of taking your shower, getting out the door, and physically going somewhere. This reinforces the fact that EDAT really is a profession.

Before you commit to a particular room, you'll want to examine several factors. Of course, check out the management, trading rules, and commission structures. But don't forget the ergonomics. I have to say, after seeing many trading rooms, some are well designed and well run and others are . . . well, they're not! Take a look at the physical arrangement of the workstations. Are the traders packed in like sardines? Is there elbowroom and personal space between you and the trader sitting next to you? Are television monitors well placed? Can you control the audio? Is the lighting adequate? Try to find a trading room that will come as close as possible to the physical comfort that you'd normally have at home.

Another advantage you're likely to find in a trading room is the camaraderie—the interplay with other passionate traders. Trading is in the air. It's talked about from early in the morning until late at night. So you'd be totally immersed in the trading environment.

If you're lucky, there's one other advantage to a trading room that could possibly outweigh all other considerations. You may be able to find and establish a mentoring relationship with the top traders in the room. If you could accomplish this, it would be powerful. Now, I have to tell you, some of these guys are very guarded about how they trade and what they do. So there's no guarantee, even if you sit next to them, that they will share information. Top traders tend to come from both ends of the communication spectrum. Some are very open about what they do and how they do it—and they're happy to share it. Others are almost paranoid about their trading systems and will not share their information with anyone.

Another area you can cover in the operations section is your trading equipment. This issue is critical to an EDAT trader. You'll find some useful discussion on equipment in the "Effectively Marshaling Your Resources" section later on in this chapter and in Chapter 4. The information on equipment that you should include in the operations section should focus on what you are doing or will do to ensure that you have proper uptime (redundant equipment, etc.) and that you will be set up to operate efficiently. Obviously, if you will be working from a trading room, you will spend time working on the equipment requirements.

Organization, Management, and Employees

Since most trading businesses are single-employee operations, this section really boils down to organizational issues. However, you may choose to include your biographical information in this section instead of in the overview and history section. The selection of organization structure really centers on the issue of legally minimizing the amount of taxes you pay. This is because taxes will be one of your business's biggest expenses.

So make sure that you pay close attention to taxes. For instance, if you've chosen to trade individually (under your own name as opposed to a corporation), you'll want to make sure that you seek tax status as a professional trader. You'll also want to elect the marked-to-market method of accounting. This is something that a good CPA will be able to help you with. IITM also covers this topic in their Infinite Wealth Seminars.

If you haven't paid close attention to taxes, April 15 can be painful! The biggest thing you need to know is that if you don't take the right elections, then your losses will likely be subject to what are called "passive loss limitations." At the time of this writing the passive loss limitation is $3,000, which means that even if you lost $10,000 or $50,000 or more, you could write off only $3,000 of those losses. As you can see, you could end up with a losing trading year but still owe a huge income tax bill simply because you didn't pay enough attention to your tax trading status. Don't let this happen to you!

Later down the road, when you become highly profitable, you need to give some thought to the type of entity you choose as your trading vehicle. My guess is that most EDAT traders simply select individual trader status. In other words, they trade under their own name and their own tax ID. But as you become more sophisticated and more profitable, you may not want to trade under your own name because there are some potential tax advantages to trading through either a limited liability company or a corporation. Once you're consistently profitable, or, better yet, even before that, you should be discussing your situation with a tax professional well versed in trading taxation.

Industry Overview and Competition

The hope is that while reading the introduction to this chapter, you gained some appreciation for the trading industry and the competition that awaits you. For a trading business, this section doesn't require a great deal of verbiage. What it does require is a great deal of research on your part. Know whom you are trading against. The market is not one big group hug; every transaction has a buyer and a seller. Two ticks later, someone has made money and someone has lost. This section of your business plan should indicate that you are a serious student of the market and of the competition that exists there.

Show Me the Money or Why Have a Trading Plan?

Now we've come to the area that truly sets a trading business apart from any other. And by more than coincidence, this is also the area that sets top traders apart from the "also-rans." One of the most important things that you can do as a trader is discipline yourself to construct a model trading plan. I use the word "model" because what you ideally want to build is a working model of exactly how you intend to trade before you actually begin. The primary reason you construct a model or a simulation is so that you'll be mentally and physically prepared to react appropriately to any situation that confronts you.

Modeling and simulation are standard operating procedures for pilots, and they should be for traders too. When I became a pilot, I flew a simulator of the actual aircraft I was learning to fly. I'd spend several hours in each type of aircraft that I wanted to pilot. Along with an instructor, I practiced what happened when one engine quit and what happened when two engines quit. I practiced what happened when we got into a steep dive or a very steep climb. I simulated what happened when we got into really bad weather such as severe thunderstorms. I practiced all these strategies and tactics so that if I did encounter these situations in flight, I would know instinctively how to react. On more than one occasion, this simulation and modeling literally saved my life. As a new direct-access trader, one of the very best ways to save your financial life is to model and simulate both your trading strategy and that of other successful traders prior to actual trading.

So let's start. You will construct your simulation around a trading plan that specifies many components including setups, entries, stops, profit-taking exits, and position-sizing rules. Each of these areas is designed to preserve your capital and maximize your returns.

Van Tharp teaches a 12-step method for creating a trading plan:

1. Inventory your market and trading beliefs.
2. Gather market information.

3. Determine your objectives.
4. Determine your time frame and trading style.
5. Find the best historical patterns in your time frame and determine what they have in common.
6. Understand the concepts behind the historical patterns and determine how you can potentially identify them in real time.
7. Determine your stops and transaction costs.
8. Develop a profit-taking exit scheme and find your expectancy.
9. Look for large R-multiple trades.
10. Increase your profits with proper position sizing.
11. Constantly look for ways to improve your results.
12. Plan for worst-case events and then mentally rehearse.

I have taken Van's steps and modified them slightly to be congruent with the fast-paced world of a direct-access trader. I'm not going to go through each step of the planning process since Van's book *Trade Your Way to Financial Freedom* covers each area in great detail. Instead I'm going to drill down in those areas that need amplification for the direct-access trader. These are the "hot" topics that I've found to have the most dramatic impact on your results.

Make an Inventory of Your Market and Trading Beliefs

In Chapter 2 we spent quite a bit of time on your personal beliefs. Now we're going to focus on your market and trading beliefs and make sure that they are congruent with your personal beliefs. If this seems a little difficult to understand at first, don't worry. We'll work on it a bit in this section, and I'll share some of my trading beliefs with you in Chapters 9 and 10.

Taking inventory of your beliefs may be difficult at this point since, as a trader new to direct-access day trading, you may not have formed many beliefs. Or if you have trading beliefs, you may wonder if those beliefs are applicable to this style of trading. It's kind of like the question about the chicken or the egg. You might say, "I've never done this so can I have valid beliefs? How do I get started?" Fortunately, the answer is simple—find someone who's already getting the results you desire. In other words, find somebody who's already making money trading. Find someone who's already trading in a style similar to the style that you think might fit you. In this case, because you're reading this book, you've already taken this step. By completing the exercises I've given here, you'll be modeling me. And to reiterate, I've spelled out several of my market and trading beliefs in Chapters 9 and 10.

I believe that if you could model exactly what I do and simulate my exact mental trading processes, then you would get exactly the same results that I get. Think about that for a minute. Why does Coca-Cola protect its secret formula? Why does Kentucky Fried Chicken guard its secret recipe so closely? Because they recognize a basic fact—once someone has the recipe, it's very easy to duplicate. In fact, this belief is one of the underlying assumptions of Neuro-Linguistic Programming (NLP). There is a key distinction to make here: To successfully duplicate my results, you have to duplicate my complete trading process. You have to know my beliefs, my mental strategies, and my mental states that allow me to trade through drawdowns and come out the other side sticking with the strategies and continuing to make money. You can't just copy my entry techniques and hope to trade profitably. Said another way, you can't duplicate the unique taste of Kentucky Fried Chicken if you only know about and use 3 of their famous 11 herbs and spices! Now we both realize that short of doing a brain transplant, you'll never be able to duplicate me exactly, but you should be able to come close—close enough to learn to trade profitably! That's one of the reasons you should commit to *doing* this book versus reading this book. *Do* this book!

On the other hand, you may already have quite a bit of experience in day trading, online trading, or even direct-access trading, but find you're not getting the consistent profits that you want. If this is the case, I hope you'll be able to take some of my beliefs and a couple of my basic trading strategies and apply them to what you're already doing. I'm not asking you to totally change everything you're doing. Simply look at areas where my distinctions are very different from yours and try to model those things.

And here's an important point to note: Often these distinctions are not in the mechanics of trading, but lie rather in the "soft" areas that most unsuccessful traders avoid—mission, beliefs, business plans, and trading plans. Think about this for a minute—these unsuccessful traders don't have a mission, a business plan, or a trading plan, and they're losing major bucks. On the other hand, most of the traders that I know who are successful and consistently profitable do have a mission, a business plan, and a trading plan. So that might be a clue to how important these areas really are!

Now back to the issue of making your personal and trading beliefs consistent with each other. I've made this point earlier, so let me give you an example. Say you have a belief that you're a fast thinker and you can act and react quickly when information meets your eyeballs. This would be a useful global belief if you direct-access-trade, because you'll need to react and to make decisions very quickly. On the other hand, if you believe that you are slow and plodding and you need to take a lot of time to make decisions, then you're going to find direct-access trading to be a totally frustrating experience. Something has got to change with your beliefs or you won't be able to direct-access-trade and make any money.

Ya Gotta Have an Edge

Here's a belief for you to contemplate. To be a successful trader, you have to have an edge. Do you think it's true? Do you hold this belief? I do. To me, one of the most important things you can do right out of the gate is to define what your edge is going to be. What is it that's going to make you successful in the market? Your edges can be very specific, or they can be very broad. For most traders they're a combination of both.

So just what is an edge? When we think about edges, oftentimes we conjure up visions of some skill or some unique "angle" that no one else in the world possesses. This viewpoint has been popularized in television and movies, particularly in stories about gangsters and gambling. Somehow, these guys have some edge, some secret that no one else on the planet knows, and they're "gonna make a killin'."

This is not what I mean by an edge. It is not something that you and only you possess. That's the wrong way to think about an edge in the market. *An edge is a skill or a belief that you have that enhances your probability of making money.* Many traders may share the same edge and all still profit. For example, almost every winning trader shares the ability to cut losses short and let profits run (trite but true). Yet they all profit from this edge.

What are edges then? Some are surprisingly simple. For instance, many times patience can be an edge. Reading this book, doing the exercises, and adopting the beliefs will give you an edge, particularly the material on expectancy and position sizing. Why are these edges? Because they are the key "secrets" to massively expanding your profits. Perhaps your edge could be your ability to deeply understand and read a Level II screen or a time & sales screen. There are countless possible edges. To get you started in defining yours, refer to the "Calls to Action" list at the end of the chapter.

As you develop your trading knowledge and skill, you'll discover that you have more than one edge. It's also important that you define, right now, as succinctly as you can, what your edges are—or at least what you think they might be.

Once you've taken inventory of your beliefs (both personal and trading), and once you have worked on defining your edges, it's time to . . .

Choose Your Trading Styles and Time Frames

Trading style is a big factor in determining your profitability as a direct-access trader. I've divided trading style into three broad groups: market making, momentum, and swing. In actuality there is a wide spectrum of direct-access styles. In addition, within each style there are many strategies and tactics.

Later I present a basic market-making strategy and a basic momentum strategy. I also show you one set of trading rules for each strategy. However, in my actual arsenal of trading, I have several sets of trading rules (specific strategies or execution plans) for each trading style. The trading rules presented are designed to get you started—to give you a model to follow. Ideally, you should test these models against your own beliefs, objectives, and edges. If they fit, use them until you've gained some experience with them and can trade them profitably. At that point you can put your own imprint and personality on them, seeking to improve your results. You should not blindly follow these trading rules. Make sure they are congruent with who you are. Remember, if you don't believe them, you will not be able to trade them!

Are You a Natural Market Maker?

Market makers have traditionally traded the spread. They buy on the bid, sell on the ask, and pocket the difference. As recently as 2 years ago, direct-access traders, dubbed "scalpers," would exploit the wide spreads (that have mostly disappeared) by stepping in front of market makers, bidding ⅟₁₆ more, and offering out for ⅟₁₆ less. By doing this they were often able to make huge piles of cash. Unfortunately, this strategy isn't that effective any longer. As is the case with almost all arbitrage opportunities, this one also eventually evaporated as the spreads decreased under the ever-increasing competition aimed at capturing those lucrative wide spreads. So I've expanded the definition of market making somewhat to describe any nontrending trading strategy, where the stock is trading in a definable channel. I also include certain types of "day holds" under the market-maker strategies. Perhaps the terminology isn't perfect—but it *is* useful.

Scalping requires excellent execution skills including the ability to manipulate a mouse and keyboard very quickly and to act ruthlessly to enter and exit positions. If you're scalping, you may be making 20, 50, 100, or perhaps even more trades a day. I know some scalpers who make 400 to 500 trades a day. So it's extremely intense. The duration of your trades will most likely be anywhere from 5 seconds to 2 minutes. If you're not wired to put up with that kind of intensity, then maybe you're not going to want to scalp.

Are You a Born Momentum Trader?

Momentum trading is primarily news-driven, and the trading strategies tend to be discretionary as opposed to being technical analysis–based. There are several fine distinctions that you need to make in order to momentum-trade. One is the ability to quickly form trading expectations based upon news. It's also helpful if you are comfortable with high levels of uncertainty. By definition, the momentum stocks tend to be pretty volatile, and volatility means uncertainty. A momentum trader is looking for larger moves than the scalper is. Depending upon personal preferences, market conditions, liquidity, and a host of other factors, if you momentum-trade, you're likely to hold your positions for between 2 minutes and 2 hours. On occasions you may be in your trades for most of the day.

Swing Trade for a Slower Pace

Swing trading requires still another set of skills. Normally you'll hold your positions for between 2 trading days and 7 trading days, so you have to put up with perhaps even more uncertainty because you're subject to the vagaries of overnight gapping. Just as stocks can gap in your favor, stocks can gap against you. I've had stocks gap 20 points against me on swing trades. I've also had them gap 20 points in my favor, but the point to recognize is this—if you don't have the stomach for large adverse moves, you probably don't want to be a swing trader.

Various Time Frames and Styles

Even within a given style, there are various time frames you can choose to trade. Take a look at Table 3–1. You can see that some scalpers trade 1-minute bars and some trade 2- or 3-minute bars.

The same is true with momentum traders. Some trade 2-minute bars, some 5-minute bars, and some 15-minute. All these traders are

TABLE 3–1

Trading Styles and Time Frames

Style	Primary Charting Time Frames	Typical Holding Period	Critical Skills and Abilities Required
Swing	Daily	2–7 days	Good technical analysis (TA) skill, high tolerance for ambiguity
Market maker I Day holds	15 and 30 minute, 1 hour	1–6 hours	Ability to combine TA with "market pulse." Fortitude to trade with convictions.
Momentum	2, 5, and 15 minute	2 minutes– 1 hour	Less TA required, but Level II and tape-reading ability a must.
Market maker II Scalpers	1, 2, and 3 minute	5 seconds– 3 minutes	Highly skilled in Level II, tape reading, and lightning fast execution. Must be able to stop out.

momentum traders, but they're all trading different time frames. The time frame that they trade helps define and dictate the rest of their trading rules, what their setups look like, what their stop losses look like, what their profit-taking exits look like, and if or how they'll scale in and scale out. So trading style and time frame become critical factors in determining how you're going to trade.

Implementation

Entry Strategies and Stops

One of the most critical things you can do as a direct-access trader is define your trading rules. These rules govern your *entry, stop losses, reentry, profit-taking exits,* and *position sizing.* You should treat these five areas as sacrosanct. Don't trade without them under any circumstances. Other rules to consider relate to pyramiding (or scaling) into and out of a position and to handling overall portfolio management; these, however, are beyond the scope of this book and will only be covered briefly.

The setups and entries for electronic day traders are generally much more discretionary than for pure position trading. Most material in the marketplace dealing with entries uses either chart pattern recognition or technical analysis, or a combination of both. And while many of these entry strategies are good, most are not designed for direct-access traders. To work for direct access they need to be adapted quite a bit. It's this discretionary adaptation of technical entries that gets many newer traders into trouble. They have not had enough experience to recognize when to use those setups and when not to.

Much of the art of direct-access entry is based upon understanding and interpreting Level II data. Unfortunately, there are very few mainstream sources today that describe entries based upon Level II interpretation. Those sources that are available are "underground" and have to be obtained from another direct-access trader or in some cases on the Internet. Just remember, to trade using my tactics, you'll need to develop entry rules that recognize the huge importance of Level II. When you read the strategic chapters, you will see that my entries rely heavily upon Level II data and interpretation.

Your trading plan should address both phases of entry. These are commonly called the setup and the entry. A common misconception is to lump these two steps together and ignore the roles that each plays. Let's examine the distinctions and why it's important for a trader to recognize them. Before you pull the trigger to take a position, you consciously or subconsciously look for certain conditions to exist. This "prequalification" is commonly referred to as the trade setup. For your trading plan, you need to understand your setup for each strategy. Think of your setup as that part of your trading method that tells you to start looking for an entry. By default, if there is no setup, there is no entry! A setup can contain multiple parts. For example, your trading strategy may require a certain time of day, a particular move by a selected technical indicator, and a certain level of volume. However, simpler is almost always better.

The second phase of entry is usually referred to as just the "entry." The entry defines the exact moment at which you'll click the button to establish a position. At this phase of the trade, simplicity is almost a necessity. Complexity can lead to indecision or other forms of delay. For many EDAT strategies, a signal of strength in Level II in your intended direction of trade is all that is required. As with all phases of developing your trading plan, you can refer to the model trading plan at the end of the chapter to help clarify these steps.

Let's move on to the area of stop losses. Many formulas for stop losses tell you to stop out based upon either a trading stop or a money management stop. What do I mean? Say you enter a stock as a *position* trader, and you buy ABCD at $48 on a breakout. ABCD's 50-day moving average is $46½, and your stop rule tells you to stop out if ABCD trades below this price. This is a trading stop.

A money management stop, on the other hand, would be when you place your stop based upon the amount of your portfolio that you're willing to put at risk. For instance, let's say you have a $100,000 account and you've decided as part of your trading rules you'll risk 1 percent of your capital on any one trade. By definition then, you can lose $1,000 on any given trade. Let's say you own 100 shares of a stock. That means you can take a 10-point move against you before being stopped out (100 times $10 is $1,000). This is a money management stop.

The point of the matter is that sometimes you will use trading stops and sometimes money management stops, depending upon the situation at hand. Critical to your success is that you define both the trading stops and money management stops now before you ever put even one measly buck at risk. When we get into the strategy chapters, I'll go through some examples of how I use both types of stop loss.

Reentry

I really enjoyed *Apollo 13*. What a great movie! After I watched it a couple of times, it hit me—reentry is life and death to a direct-access trader. You will be stopped out—many times. But it's what you do after you're stopped that will determine your success. You must have rules for reentry. One of my favorite tactics is to short a "high-flying pig." The problem is that even pigs can remain aloft, given enough fuel and hot air. Tactically, what happens many times is that I will attempt to short a stock off a pivot point (see Chapter 9), but the short turns against me. The solution? Stop out. Again, I'll attempt the short, at an even higher price. Again, I'm stopped. Sometimes I'll stop out three or four times while attempting to nail down a low-risk entry, each time losing ⅛ or ¼ point. If my expectations are correct, that is, pigs can't stay aloft for long, my fourth or fifth short will be tremendous, good for a profit several times larger than the sum of the small losses I took on the stops. This is powerful, though it's not easy for most traders. But if you have the constitution and the proper belief system, using a reentry technique will make you some serious cash when incorporated into a well-defined trading plan. If you can't hack the idea of reentry, you should probably go back to the self-assessment exercises before continuing.

Where the Money Is Won or Lost—Profit-Taking Exits

I cannot overemphasize the importance of learning when to exit a profitable trade! Along with keeping your risk at 1 R (in other words keeping your stops), this is the part of your strategy that determines your R multiples. And as you'll find out in Chapter 5 on expectancy, R multiples determine your profitability. The question is this: Are you letting profits run or not? Since it's much easier to enter a trade than to exit it profitably, many people simply avoid this discussion.

If you're a pure scalper, this part of your trading plan is much more mechanical. Because scalping trades tend to occur in channels, you simply place your exit order slightly in front of the congestion near the channel boundaries. For example, assume you're trading DELL. You notice that during the last hour it's been in a channel between 43⅛ and 43⅝. This type of situation is not rare for DELL. As DELL approaches the lower price boundary, you place a buy order at, say, 43³⁄₁₆. You're filled, and a few minutes later DELL is heading back toward the high price boundary. Say, it's trading 43⁷⁄₁₆. In this case, you'd immediately offer out in the 43½ to 43⁹⁄₁₆ area. Do not wait for the stock to actually get to the high price boundary. You're scalping, remember? On occasion, DELL will actually take out the higher price, but most of the time, it will stay in the channel as other traders attempt to get out at 43⅝. If you haven't predetermined your exit, you'll very likely be run over by sellers once ⅝ is hit and the price starts to reverse. Many aspiring scalpers will let their profit disappear into a loss. Don't let this happen to you.

When determining your exit strategy for profitable trades, you'll want to consider your time frame. If you're trading 1-minute bars and your profit target has not been hit within about 2 minutes maximum, you should more than likely flat the trade. Just get out. As a rule of thumb, when scalping or momentum trading, I'll give each trade up to 2 times my trading time frame to move in my direction. If it hasn't moved in my direction, I stop out. If I'm trading 1-minute bars, I give the trade 2 minutes, max. If I'm using 2-minute bars, then I give it 4 minutes, max. This will save your rear end many times over. And it will more than make up for what it costs you in lost opportunity!

If you decide to use a momentum or swing trading strategy, executing consistently effective exits will make a much bigger impact on profits than fancy stock-picking or entry strategies. In these (relatively) longer time-frame strategies, profit-taking exits become more of an art form. The more you trade, the better you should become at determining your momentum and swing exits. Here are some guidelines to get you started.

Swing traders will probably do well with picking a target and sticking with it. I know some swing traders who choose a 7 percent,

10 percent, or even 20 percent fixed profit level. If their stock trades to their fixed profit level, they're out. A fixed dollar profit also works. As the stock approaches their profit target, these traders tend to use a trailing stop to protect their profits. Timing the exit, using Level II, or using some other tool is not critical since swing traders typically manage their positions on market open or market close.

For the momentum trader, choosing an appropriate profit target is a more subtle challenge. Time frames become a much larger issue. Will you momentum-trade 5-minute, 15-minute, or 1-hour holds? Will you do day holds? Generally the longer your holding period, the larger your stop loss should be. The same holds true for profit exits. You can, like the scalper, simply predetermine your exit and get out before the crowd. But you'll often be cutting your profits short if you do this. As you know with momentum trades, sometimes these stocks really take off. You don't want to liquidate too early, because you'll have endured most of the risk without reaping the appropriately large reward.

I suggest using a trailing-stop methodology for momentum trades, based upon the stock's recent price range or volatility. Assume you're trading Intel using a 5-minute bar and that today's 5-minute bar range is about 3 points. In other words, if you captured 100 percent of the move in a 5-minute time frame, you'd make 3 points. Now, you're *not* going to get 100 percent of the move. But 50 percent is realistic. So your initial profit target would be 1½ points. Here's how I'd initially set my stops and exits:

- I would set my initial stop loss to achieve a 2- or 3-R multiple based upon the range. If I'm trading for a 2-R gain, my stop is ¾ (1.5 divided by 2). If I'm trading for a 3-R gain, my stop is ½ (1.5 divided by 3).
- When the stock moves in my direction by the amount of my initial risk, I would adjust the stop to break even. In other words, if my risk (or stop loss) is ½, once the stock moves ½ in my favor, I would move my stop to my entry price.
- As the position continues to trade in my direction, I would simply continue to move my profit-taking exit, using a factor of my initial risk. Here's where the "art" comes in. Sometimes the factor will be ½ my initial risk, and other

times it may be as much as 2 or 3 times my initial risk, depending upon how far the position has moved, the current market conditions, and the current trading profile of the stock.

A few words on phasing out of a position. Many position and swing traders will phase out of a position as it moves in their favor. For example, say that they're long 1,000 shares of ABCD and that their initial risk was 1 point. Since entering, the stock has moved 2 points in their favor. So they sell 500 shares, pocket their initial $1,000 risk, and have (mentally) a "free ride" on the other 500 shares.

To the plus side, this does lock in some profit, and it does eliminate further risk, assuming they move the stop to break even on the rest of the position. Now I'm all for managing risk. And this might be OK (I'm not totally sold!) for a position or swing trader. But it also reduces the expectancy of the trade, meaning you'll win less for the dollars you have at risk. Additionally, it increases the risk-to-reward ratio—just the opposite of what you'd like to do! Here's why: You hold 100 percent of your stock during the highest-risk portion of your trade, before you've made any money, and you hold only 50 percent of your stock during the highest-reward portion of your trade—after it's already making money for you! Are you sure you want to do this?

I've found that your best risk management strategy, as a direct-access trader, is simply to keep your stops: both stop losses and profit stops. Use your mental toughness and the great technology that you have as an edge.

Does Size Really Matter?

If there is a magic ingredient in trading, if there's one element that will boost your profits beyond all expectations, that element is position sizing. Position sizing answers the question "How much?" or said a bit differently "How many shares should I buy of a particular stock?" Position sizing has nothing to do with taking on large positions. As a matter of fact, most of the time it means *not* having large positions! Newer traders tend to buy too much and too often. They tend to overtrade, and they tend to take on much more risk than they should for their portfolio size. I've been guilty of this myself. So you've been warned! Read on so that you can avoid this costly error of poor position sizing and instead reap the rewards offered by proper position sizing.

When you think position size, think about having positions that are appropriate both for your personal comfort level and for the mathematical side of your risk management strategy. Most master traders suggest never risking more than 1 percent of your portfolio (or risk capital) on any one position. In fact, many believe that even this is too much.

Another factor for determining your position-sizing rules is if, when, and how you should scale or pyramid your positions. There is not a consistently profitable trader (long term) who doesn't understand the power of pyramiding and scaling. And this knowledge is rarely discussed outside the ranks of top traders. Yet scaling and pyramiding are ways to massively increase your profits.

A quick clarification here. I call adding to a profitable position "pyramiding." When a position moves in my favor and I add to it, I'm pyramiding. When a position moves (slightly) against my position and I add to it, I call this "scaling." Many people might disagree with my definitions; I use them just to keep my strategies straight. However, please note: Don't ever scale a position unless you're a very experienced trader and you have a phenomenal reason for doing so!

All except the most sophisticated traders often think of pyramiding as very risky. Why? Let's look at the way a typical swing trader manages his position. A swing trader, for the most part, manages positions once a day, maybe twice a day. He might look at his positions in the morning at market open and make a buy or sell decision. He may then make another decision on market close. He'll do a bunch of number crunching and analysis in the evening. But he's not immersed in the market minute by minute or tick by tick.

Some position traders manage their portfolio only once a week, and some less frequently than that. I personally find that hard to fathom in the current market environment, but that's how they do it. They have different rules, rules that I haven't internalized. Under these circumstances I, too, would be fearful of pyramiding my positions, because I don't have enough information at my disposal to know when I should or shouldn't pyramid.

However, when I'm in the market every day, literally trading minute by minute, I'm very comfortable adding to my positions as they move in my favor. I often do this with Intel. I buy 1,000 shares and it moves up ⅛ of a point. Level II indicates there's still strong buying (and little selling), and so I add another 1,000 lot. If it continues to move, I add another lot. Some traders will wait for a ¼- or even a ½-point move in their direction before they'll pyramid their position. Because I'm trading 1-minute bars, that's too long to wait. I just let it move ⅛, or even 1⁄16, in my direction, and if there is still strength in my direction, I'll add shares.

You need to determine for yourself if a pyramiding strategy is right for you. But if it is, using this technique can radically increase your profits when the position is moving in your favor. Since this is an advanced technique, I suggest you avoid it until your execution skills are razor sharp. You must get some experience (6 months to a year), or you must model and trade with somebody who can teach you how to do this. If, however, you've been trading successfully for a long time and you're looking for the best way to rocket your profits, look intensely into position sizing and pyramiding. These areas have the highest potential to really launch your profits.

The More Tools the Merrier

Regardless of your preferred trading style, you'll want to remain flexible to maximize your profits. The more tools you have, the better you're going to do. So learn to scalp, learn to trade momentum, and learn to swing-trade.

Learn the art of reversing on a position. If short, learn to cover and go long. If long, learn to reverse and go short. Excellent traders are just as proficient at shorting as they are at going long.

Our huge bull run over the past few years has biased many traders to favor long positions. Some of these people are tremendous traders. Nonetheless, I know many traders who were totally wiped out during the relatively short period from March to May 2000. Several crashed because they had never really learned to trust or trade the short side. They have no tools, tactics, or trading plans for bear markets—or to trade from the short side. They've never trained themselves to know what to do in a down market. They've never learned how to short.

Shorting is one of my specialties, one of my edges. I take pride in my ability to profit from the short side. Several of my trader friends have commented that I tend to short even more than I go long. And my trading records support their observation. I'm fairly good at recognizing the mania and the froth, and one of my edges is my ability to read Level II and the time & sales tape. Therefore, I've developed the skill of knowing when and how to get short. I'm not trying to bolster myself by making these distinctions. My goal is to burn into your frontal lobe the importance of being well rounded. You never know where the markets will trade today or tomorrow. Be sure that your trading plan includes knowing how to handle down markets. Know when to short. And devise these strategies and tactics before you'll need them.

Before I conclude this section, here are a couple of insights. When you are momentum trading in a raging bull stock (or a raging bull market), don't go short. You don't want to be short in this type of market unless buying becomes hysterical. The time to get short is once the hysteria subsides a bit. When it does, panic selling almost always follows.

In a very slow market—a nontrending market—don't try to momentum-trade. Why? You're subjecting your capital to needless risk where there's very little opportunity for commensurate rewards. Momentum-trade when some news "engine" is driving a stock in a decided direction—when a stock is being driven in an orderly manner. I have a special play called a "stair master" that takes advantage of this phenomenon.

Some of these tactics are very advanced and are not covered in this book. However, at the back of this book you'll find a request form for some of these advanced strategies. Simply mail in the form and we'll send you this advanced play, free and without obligation.

Final Countdown

So wrapping up this whole area of the trading plan, it really boils down to a few key points:

- Number one—know your beliefs. If you don't have beliefs, model someone else's until you make the beliefs your own.
- Until you're skilled and profitable, do not make the mistake of jumping from one style and/or time frame to another. You will totally confuse yourself and never develop a knowledge base from which to grow.

- There is no "right" system. Pick one and stick with it until you make it your own. Make it your belief.
- Don't take every ounce of capital that you have available, every nickel that you have on the planet, and keep it in trading positions. That's a recipe for disaster. Make excellent position sizing a part of your arsenal.

Once you've achieved these milestones, you can start imprinting your own personal style upon your trading strategy. At that point, you can really start to refine your trading plan into something that is as comfortable to you as an old pair of jeans, something you trust and believe in. At that point, you can make a tremendous sum of money that will allow you to live a lifestyle that few people ever achieve. I live a lifestyle that most people only dream about. I'm not bragging about this—it's just a statement of fact. And I do so because over time I've tried a lot of different trading methodologies, and I've tried them until I made them my own, and then I refined them to imprint my personal style on them. I've also been flexible enough to know that only one style, only one strategy, isn't enough to be profitable long term.

Know your beliefs, pick a trading plan, and then stay with it until you learn it. Make it your own belief system and then alter it to fit your own style. If, because of lack of experience, you haven't done this, find someone to model. You don't have to invent the recipe to enjoy the benefits. You, too, can buy a franchise, make Mrs. Fields' cookies or Kentucky Fried Chicken, and enjoy all the benefits by simply knowing what the recipe is. You don't have to invent it from scratch. Get something, whether it's this book or another book, whether it's my styles or somebody else's styles and strategies, stick with what you've chosen, and follow it. If you can learn to duplicate that recipe, and I know you can learn to duplicate the recipe, then you're going to make tremendous sums of money and have tremendous enjoyment and personal fulfillment as a result of doing so.

So, let's go on now. We've finished our trading plan. Again, I've included for your review a copy of a concise trading plan at the end of this chapter. Simple is best when we're starting, so this example is an excellent place to start. Take a close look at this well-thought-out plan; it is an actual trading plan for a strategy that we call the "gap and trap," and it's one that D. R. and I actively trade. We'll refer to it in other sections of the book as well. Your business plan is almost complete. Let's finish by addressing the financial statements that you will use to track the fiscal health of your business.

Financial Information—The Numbers Don't Lie (Mainly Because They're Inanimate Objects)

The remaining sections of a trader's business plan are a delight for number junkies and a terror to those unfamiliar with the world of financial reporting. But fear not! The process is really quite simple. We'll demystify the elements of the main financial statements that every business should have. All you'll need is a touch of discipline to get started and then to update them periodically. And the payoff is great: You'll always know where your business stands—are you in trouble or in great shape? Better yet, having up-to-date financial statements can help you see trouble coming before it arrives. Are you constantly over budget in your expenses? Are you short on the revenue side again? Financial statements show the way. Don't let a few little numbers scare you—let's get started!

Budget

Let's start with an often-ignored area—start-up costs and budgeting. Here's the usual start-up plan for many traders: They're watching the Super Bowl or the World Series when an Ameritrade, Datek, or E*Trade commercial comes on (we're not playing favorites—insert your preferred online broker *du jour* here!). They have a friend who's made a few bucks trading. They already own their own computer. They've been thinking about "trying their luck" at trading anyway, so after seeing the online broker's ad, they open a trading account and fire up their computer. They're now officially a trader! I actually know several people who've done this. They put much more effort into planning their vacation! They totally ignore start-up costs and budgeting or any other semblance of a plan that could lead to success.

Perhaps one reason many of us ignore budgeting is that we don't like it very much. Who wants to be on a budget? Not I. I want to have plenty of cash available, so at the suggestion of a friend I started calling my budget my MAP—my *money* *a*vailability *p*lan! Everyone loves to have plenty of money available. With a money availability plan I have a treasure MAP to my gold doubloons. What fun!

Table 3–2 shows the expense side of a basic MAP. It displays both start-up and ongoing expense areas. I give both a high and a low figure. Your actual expenses may vary widely, but most EDAT traders whom I know spend somewhere in the range given. For instance, you can definitely buy a basic computer, suitable for trading, for $1,500. And although you may have more than $100,000 available as risk capital, I suggest that you use this number as an upper limit until you can trade profitably. In addition to this chart, at the end of the chapter you can look at the Budget section of the model business plan. You may not have all the categories listed in the table, and you may have others. But you can use the basic struc-

TABLE 3–2

The Expense Side of a MAP

	Start-Up	Recurring	Low	High
Base capital	Yes		$10,000	$100,000
Computer hardware	?	Yes	$1,500	$10,000
Computer software	?	Yes	$200	$20,000
Other equipment				
Copier	?	Yes	$200	$1,500
Fax	?	Yes	$200	$1,500
Data feeds	Yes	Yes	$600	$3,600
Seminars	?	?	$500	$50,000
Books	Yes	Yes	$200	$2,500
Magazines	Yes	Yes	$100	$500
Subscriptions	Yes	Yes	$100	$3,000
Travel	?	?	$500	$10,000
Office rent	?	?	—	$18,000
Telephone	Yes	Yes	$600	$3,000
Taxes	No	Yes	?	?
Misc. supplies	Yes	Yes	$500	$1,200
Totals			$15,200	$224,800

ture along with any spreadsheet program to start the process and create your own MAP. Now let's get into a more detailed discussion of a trader's expenses.

Expenses

Business people know that they should try to maximize their revenue. That's the "top-line" growth we hear of so often in the markets. After all, one of your goals is to maximize revenue through successful trades. However, while you're concentrating on the top-line income, how often do you consider the bottom line by including those evil expenses? How hard do you try to limit those expenses?

When I first started trading, I hadn't made many distinctions about what I needed and what I didn't need, and so I bought almost everything that there was available to buy. I bought books, magazines, newspapers, white papers, "special reports," and fax services. I subscribed to so many Web sites and chat rooms that I lost count. I bought so much software that I ended up pitching most of it out. Don't get me wrong. Many of these services are great. In fact, I still use several. Unfortunately, though, far too many are junk! And a beginner has no good way of discerning the good from the bad.

Besides that, all the advertising is designed to push all your buttons. So when you pick up *Stocks and Commodities* magazine or *The Wall Street Journal* or *Investor's Business Daily*, you see advertising for countless products and services and your head swims with dreams of riches. You page through the ads, and literally hundreds of stock trading systems scream out to you, "Buy my system and make over $1,000,000 per year!" or "Subscribe to my system. I'm up 2,000 percent. Just take my trades and you could be up over 2,000 percent too!" You don't know what's good and what isn't.

Stock trading Web sites abound, so you subscribe to a few of those. Most are only $29.95 a month, and so you think, "What the heck. It's just $30 a month, and it might help me." Before you know it, though, you've subscribed to 10 of them. Now you're shelling out another $300 per month, and you're not even using most of the Web sites!

Besides the software, publications, and Web sites, other areas of expenditures include continuing education, seminars, coaching, conventions, airfare, hotel, car rental, and meals. All these are expenses that you will incur during a trading career. Of course, they're all totally deductible if you set up your trading business correctly.

We've tried to outline very carefully those tools that you need to have to trade profitably. Be judicious about spending money beyond that. Start slowly, and after you've gained some experience, you'll be better able to determine if a software system, a publication, or a Web site is a good fit for you and your trading style.

You're also going to need a telephone, fax, printer, television, cable connection, at least one ISP, and miscellaneous supplies including paper and pens. Add all these items to your MAP. I suggest that you keep very close track of these expenditures for a couple of reasons. First of all, they're expensive; they add up and affect your net profits. But second, and more importantly, the more you treat your trading like a business, the more likely you are to profit. There is no such thing as accidental profits on a long-term basis. You may accidentally have a few good trades, or even a good month, but you're not going to accidentally make profits over the long run. Trading without putting together a business plan and a MAP is like buying a lotto ticket. You're just not going to hit that lotto every month.

Cash Flow—The Lifeblood of Any Business

Tens of thousands of small businesses start up every year. And fully 80 percent are out of business within 12 months. What is the number one reason they don't last? A failure to manage cash flow. A business can have a great product or service, customers beating down the door, and the brightest of futures. But even with all these things in its favor, if it can't manage cash flow, the doors will close, and sooner rather than later. Fortunately, as a trading business, your cash flow picture is much simpler than that of most businesses— especially those that have outside financing, intricate payroll requirements, and extensive accounts payable and accounts receivable. We have assumed that you have no outside financing; your payroll is yourself (for the current time)—and the great thing about trading is that when you earn income, you get it the same day!

Take a look at the cash flow statement in the model business plan at the end of the chapter—it really is quite basic. It only deals with money in and money out—it's not complicated by tax rules that say some items count and others don't. Now look at an income statement. The bottom line on the income statement is different from that of the cash flow statement because the income statement concerns itself with the tax treatment of your business. The two statements diverge in this way: The cash flow statement just counts dollars that come in and go out. The income statement determines the tax ramifications of those dollars. For a well-structured business, the two statements should be quite different, reflecting your ability to take advantage of opportunities provided by the tax code and increase your cash flow! Since we covered the expense side of the equation quite thoroughly in the "Budget" section, let's look a little more closely at a trader's income before we move on.

Income

One of the critical questions during your business planning is how much money will you make? This is no trivial question. All too often, however, new traders will not think deeply or clearly enough about it. When I ask aspiring traders how much they want to make, they give me a flip answer like, "Well, I want to make $100,000 a year." For some reason, $100,000 seems to be the magic number. Practically all the traders I've ever talked to want to make $100,000 a year from trading. But when I dig below that superficial answer, it's clear that not much thought has gone into determining either the number or the methodology that will get them there.

How much money are you going to make per hour? Have you thought about that? Do you have a plan for that? Say, you're currently making $40 an hour, which is equal to $80,000 a year. You're interested in transitioning out of that position into a full-time trading position. How much are you really going to have to make per day in order to replace that income, including all the employee benefits you had, like medical insurance? It's important that you think about that.

While you're pondering this question of equivalent incomes for a self-employed person versus an employee, you can refer to Table 3–3, which shows the amount of net income you're deriving and then calculates your profit per hour. This assumes that you're working on your trading business 8 hours a day. How does this compare with what else you could be doing in the marketplace?

TABLE 3-3

Daily Income/Hourly Wage Conversion

Daily	Hourly
$100	$12.50
$200	$25.00
$400	$50.00
$700	$87.50
$1,000	$125.00

Keep in mind that the average wage in the United States today is about $15 to $20 an hour, based on the Bureau of Labor Statistics.

Although there are other factors to consider when transitioning to a new career, such as personal enjoyment, personal freedom, and the amount of time you have available for your family and for yourself, you most certainly will want to gauge how much money you're making per hour as a result of your trading endeavors.

Let's take a look at some realistic potential income figures. One of the benefits of this book is that we've developed a financial model that will help you achieve your income goals. We present this model in Table 3–6. It actually tells you, based upon any given expectancy,[1] how many trades you have to take in order to make a given annual income. This information is priceless. But for now, let's just take a look at what your profit potential might realistically be.

Are you going to shoot for daily, weekly, monthly, or annual profits? In Table 3–4, you'll see potential profits broken down daily, weekly, monthly, and annually. For instance, if you want to make $100 a day, in round numbers (assuming 250 trading days) that's about $25,000 a year. If you want to make $1,000 a day, that's roughly $250,000 a year.

These numbers are very straightforward. But in order to understand whether they are realistic or not, you have to examine how much capital you have. I'm talking about risk capital, the amount of money that you can totally put at risk without jeopardizing your lifestyle—without jeopardizing your ability to buy

TABLE 3–4

Income per Day, Week, Month, and Year

Daily	Weekly	Monthly	Annually
$100	$500	$2,150	$25,800
$200	$1,000	$4,300	$51,600
$400	$2,000	$8,600	$103,200
$700	$3,500	$15,050	$180,600
$1,000	$5,000	$21,500	$258,000

your groceries, make your mortgage payment, or pay your other monthly obligations.

Table 3–5 shows the annualized rates of return required to yield any given annual income. When you examine the table, you'll notice that the horizontal axis contains the amount of risk capital that you have available, and the vertical axis is the amount of annual income you want to make. The intersecting grids show the annualized returns you'll need to enjoy for any given income.

Let's say, for instance, you have $50,000 in risk capital and you want to make $25,000 a year. You can see from the table that in order to do that, you'd have to be making 50 percent annually on your money. If you had $50,000 in risk capital and you wanted to

TABLE 3–5

Annualized Rates of Return

	$10,000	$25,000	$50,000	$100,000
$25,800	258.00%	103.20%	51.60%	25.80%
$51,600	516.00%	206.40%	103.20%	51.60%
$103,200	1032.00%	412.80%	206.40%	103.20%
$180,600	1806.00%	722.40%	361.20%	180.60%
$258,000	2580.00%	1032.00%	516.00%	258.00%

make $100,000 a year, you have to be making 200 percent a year on your money. Again there's nothing fancy here; it is simple linear mathematics. But you need to ask yourself, do you really think it's realistic for you to make $100,000 a year based upon $50,000 in trading capital, keeping in mind that that's a 200 percent return? Consider the returns on the Dow, the S&P, and the NASDAQ. Consider what top professionally managed mutual funds have done. Last year (1999) the NASDAQ turned in one of the most impressive results in history by ending the year up 80 percent. In 1998, it was up "only" 20 percent. So is a 200 percent return realistic in an environment where the major averages are not doing nearly as well?

By now I've probably put a little bit of doubt in your head. Good. I've got you thinking seriously now. My desire is not that you doubt yourself, your ability, or even the ability of day trading to return these kinds of monies. You may be able to enjoy yields this high. A handful of traders far exceed even these lofty numbers. That's the exciting part of day trading. What I am trying to show you is that it takes work, preparation, diligence, and an investment of many hours to make these kinds of returns.

When you're day trading, you're trading against some of the sharpest minds in America—people who work savagely hard, long hours, some of them working 12, 16, and 18 hours a day—brilliant people with IQs of 140, 150, and 160. These are the people you're competing against. So if you want to make 100 percent or 200 percent a year, you've got to pay the price.

If you're already making $150,000 a year, why on earth would you possibly want to day-trade full time unless there was something else motivating you? Perhaps one of your motivations would be the freedom to control your own time. Perhaps one of the motivations would be that you'd like to be able to retire in 10 years, so you want to prepare a path along the way. Those are valid reasons for doing so. On the other hand, if you're pumping gasoline for a living making $6 an hour, then $50 an hour looks like an absolute fortune to you. I would point out, however, that to go from pumping gasoline to making $100,000 a year is going to take some quantum leaps in the way you're thinking, and that's what we're trying to do with this book. And it's important to understand that going from your $150,000-per-year job to consistently successful day trading will also take some other, perhaps different leaps in your thinking. Do you see how your mission statement and your life's purpose now start to enter into the trading equation?

How Many Trades Should You Take?

Often newer traders have no idea how many trades they should take to achieve a given annual income. The best answer, of course, will be a direct result of the system you are trading, your expectancy, and the position size that you take. All these issues are addressed elsewhere in this book. However, to help you during your planning process, take a look at Table 3–6.

Table 3–6 shows another informative way to look at your trading activity. The chart gives you the number of times you'll need to trade per trade day to achieve a given daily profit target. Once you've determined your desired profit target per day (see Tables 3–3 through 3–5 to provide a "reality check" for your goal), Table 3–6 allows you to determine the frequency with which you'll need to trade given the expectancy of your trading strategy. (Chapter 5 gives a detailed discussion of how to determine expectancies for a given system.) As you would expect, trading strategies with lower

TABLE 3–6

Trades Required per Day to Achieve Given Daily Income
(R = $500 or 1% of a $50,000 account)

$ per Day Desired	Expectancy							
	0.05	0.1	0.25	0.5	0.75	1	1.25	1.5
100	4	2	1	1	1	1	1	1
200	8	4	2	1	1	1	1	1
300	12	6	3	2	1	1	1	1
400	16	8	4	2	2	1	1	1
500	20	10	4	2	2	1	1	1
600	24	12	5	3	2	2	1	1
700	28	14	6	3	2	2	2	1
800	32	16	7	4	3	2	2	2
900	36	18	8	4	3	2	2	2
1,000	40	20	8	4	3	2	2	2

expectancies (such as market-making strategies) will require you to trade more frequently than higher-expectancy strategies (such as momentum strategies) would to reach the same daily profit target. You should note that the expectancy of your strategy *must* include trading costs such as slippage and commissions. Minding your trading costs is important in any time frame; it it critical for the EDAT trader. It doesn't take a rocket scientist to figure out that if you're trading 20 times a day and ignoring $50 of slippage and commissions per trade, you'll find yourself short $1,000 per day versus your projected profits!

Balance Sheet Basics

A balance sheet is another straightforward yet important financial statement. It's simple to think about: The business is balancing the stuff it owns (assets) against what it owes (liabilities) plus the value of what the owners contributed (owners' equity). That's it! Again, take a look at the model business plan at the end of the chapter for some guidance.

EFFECTIVELY MARSHALING YOUR RESOURCES

You've seen an excellent outline for a business plan (Figure 3–1). We have also provided a sample business plan at the end of this chapter that you can use as a template and a starting point for your own plan. Now let's look at some specific areas that will help a trader flesh out a useful plan. In order to effectively run any business you have to marshal resources. You have to command and control the resources that are at your disposal. So what are the resources that you have as a trader? There are really four, and they're the same four resources that any business might have: time, equipment, capital, and talent.

The first resource you have is your time. Every business has to concern itself with the proper management of its time and the time of its employees. If you're going to run your own day trading business, then you have to manage your own time effectively. If you would like to upgrade your time management skills, an excellent resource is *First Things First* by Stephen Covey. But for now, step though the exercise below to see how important time management is for a trader.

Here is an instructive exercise for every trader. First, determine how much time you spend every day working at your "job" of trading. How much time do you spend watching financial news? How about reading financial periodicals or books on trading or the markets? How many hours do you spend on premarket preparation and postmarket debriefing? Tally up the total hours per week and multiply times 50 to annualize it. If you're just starting up, add in the time spent developing and testing your trading strategy. And then add all the time spent on all the other start-up tasks, such as opening brokerage accounts, learning EDAT software, etc. Now take this total and divide it into your net annual income from trading. Some might do better on a per-hour basis working at a fast-food joint! But there are two points to be made here: First, every hour you spend is valuable. Manage your time wisely and your return per hour goes up (not to mention the fact that you have more time to spend with your family, your golf clubs, etc.); second, a minimum wage job is a minimum wage job—whether you're flipping burgers or trading stocks.

My rule of thumb is that you will spend as much time in daily preparation as you will actually trading. So if you trade (or intend to trade) 2 hours a day, you're going to need another 2 hours a day for preparation. If you're trading 4 hours a day, you're going to be preparing another 4 hours a day. If you decide that you want to work 4-hour days, then you'll need to trade 2 hours and prepare 2 hours. The real magic of this rule is that it recognizes the importance of research and preparedness.

How much of your time you actually spend in your trading pursuits is up to you. But most top traders pursue their craft with a passion. They work just as hard as anyone else involved in an entrepreneurial enterprise. They work 8, 10, 12, or 16 hours a day. I tend to work 8 to 10 hours a day trading. I physically trade 3 or 4 hours each day, and I spend another 4 to 6 hours in daily preparation.

This book is all about making sure that your expenditure of time results in profitable trading. Taking shortcuts in this process may seem expedient at the time. But if you crave the reward of consistently profitable trading, you have to spend your time wisely—both at the start-up of your business and on the day-to-day operation. As you work on your business plan, be sure to analyze your expenditure of time. The operations section is a good place in the business plan outline to address this critical resource.

The second resource that you have is your equipment. It's important to discuss equipment separately, particularly in trading, because equipment is a critical aspect of direct-access trading. In fact, equipment is the EDAT trader's only real-time link to the markets and the outside world. Unfortunately, today's technology is in its infancy in many respects—it is far from perfect. This means there are several technology risks associated with your equipment, and your income will depend upon the technology you choose. These technology risks and equipment selection are discussed in detail in Chapter 4. For the purposes of building a business plan, you need to understand that there will be days that your technology keeps you from trading (best case) or leaves you blind in the middle of a trade with potentially thousands of dollars at risk. Your business plan needs to address how you will minimize this risk. Again, the operations section of the business plan is a logical place to address these equipment issues.

The purchase of your equipment should also be discussed in your business plan. Your budget section should address this, and of course all equipment that you own should be captured as an asset in the balance sheet portion of the plan. There are many innovative ways that traders can use to acquire and/or upgrade their equipment that will minimize the tax impact of such purchases. Filing your taxes under trader status or using a corporate structure will allow you to immediately write off a large portion of your equipment purchases. Consult your tax professional on how you might save hundreds or even thousands in tax liabilities.

The third resource that you have to manage effectively is your capital. The first question everyone asks is, "How much capital will I need to trade? Is $10,000 enough? $20,000? How about $50,000 or $100,000?" Have you deeply considered this issue? As you know, this book is geared toward people who are already direct-access trading (but would like to dramatically improve their results) or those who are professionally involved in another career and are considering making a transition into direct-access trading. In general, $50,000 is a good starting point. In certain cases, this may not be enough; in others it is more than sufficient. But for the purposes of a broad generalization (which is usually dangerous!), if you don't have at least $50,000 of risk capital to commit, you are probably undercapitalized.

In trading, we tend to think of capital as being just the money in our trading account, but actually the capital goes well beyond that. If you discipline yourself to run monthly profit and loss statements, you'll be amazed at how much money you really spend on trading—money for data feeds, software, publications, ISPs, training, and a host of other issues that you have to account for before turning a profit.

Each business will use this capital differently. Obviously, if you're opening a grocery store, you're going to use your money a whole lot differently than if you're trading. When you're trading, you must maintain "core equity." This is an amount of capital that you will never go below. Actually, core equity is important for any business, but many businesses ignore it because the way that the business world is wired, you can actually operate on a shoestring for a very long time and still stay in business. However, you can't do that when you're trading. Lack of core equity shows up *immediately* when you're trading—if you wipe out your account balance at 10:00 a.m., you'll be out of business at 10:01 a.m. (at least until you recapitalize your account). You won't need a bankruptcy court to tell you that you're out of business. The rules of the game take you out.

You will address the issues associated with your capital resources in the four subsections of the financial information portion of your trading plan. Again, you can reference the sample business plan at the end of this chapter. If you're not familiar with these standard business formats or financial statements, pay particular attention to how they interact with each other and how the money coming into your business (income or revenue) and the money going out of your business (expenses) flows through the various statements. Cash flow is the lifeblood of any business; if it stops flowing, the business dies. Having a well-developed business plan will help you to understand this critical element of your business and to keep more of the cash that flows your way!

The fourth resource is talent—your personal abilities and skills, in addition to those of partners, customers, suppliers, clients, and employees. The CEO of any business has to concern herself with training and the proper matching of people to positions. Most trading businesses are one-person operations. However, if you lack expertise or experience in a particular area of your business, don't hesitate to do what the big fish do—contract out the work! Do you hate keeping records? Perhaps hiring a local bookkeeper for an hour or two a week would save you lots of headaches and protect you against mistakes that could cost you big bucks in unnecessary taxes. Perhaps you could avail yourself of the tax advantages of hiring family members or friends to take care of some of the tasks you don't like or don't do well.

One area that traders have to pay particular attention to is that of maintaining, or better yet, improving, their level of market knowledge. You have to manage your own training. To stay current in the marketplace you should constantly read trading and stock market publications. Attend seminars. Read the best books, both the market classics and the current best thinking. Find a group of like-minded people that you can bounce ideas off. There are many ways to build your market and trading knowledge. But it's entirely up to you. Be a strict but fair manager of your key employee—yourself!

You must also be vigilant to make sure that you're being most effective at any given time. For instance, are you a morning person? If you're the kind of person who thrives during the early part of the day, then you're probably better suited to day trading than if you're a night owl and can barely prop your eyes open until noon. The reason for this is, of course, that some of the best trading opportunities occur between 9:30 a.m. and noon Eastern Time in the United States. If at that time you would naturally rather be sleeping, chances are you won't be a peak performer. To make matters worse, you'll be competing with people who are at their peak during that time frame. This is just another nuance of trading, and one that is often overlooked. For your business plan, you have a choice of places where you'll write about yourself in glowing terms. You can include your background in the overview and history section, or you could opt for the organization, management, and employees section.

To wrap up this business-planning marathon, let's do a quick review. A business plan is a well-thought-out written document that deals with the marshaling of four primary resources—time, equipment, capital, and talent. Constructing the plan involves taking an inventory of your resources and then describing in detail how you're going to use those resources to generate cash flow. And remember, having a working business plan will put you in the elite company of the top traders who are already living their promise.

Business Plan
D. R. Barton, Jr.
Electronic Day Trading
June 30, 2000

1) Executive Summary

   a) This business plan will serve as an operating guide for the Electronic Direct Access Trading (EDAT) business. The business will start as a sole proprietorship and transition to a corporate structure. A well-qualified trader is running the business. It will succeed because it will take advantage of the "edge" the company has developed in the market, using a disciplined approach to apply proven trading practices. The business requires no initial outside funding, and it will be cash flow and income positive in its first reporting period.

2) Business Description

   i) Mission

      (1) This trading business exists to honor and glorify the Lord. To best accomplish this primary purpose, this principle-centered business will be run with the highest integrity and will give 10 percent of all income before income tax to Christ-centered ministries. The business's main operation is the Electronic Direct Access Trading of stocks. This activity generates substantial profits and cash flow for the business owner and the ministries it supports. This business will strive to constantly improve its trading proficiency and to be a model of the best trading practices in action.

   ii) Overview and History

      (1) D. R. Barton has a broad trading background. He has been an active trader in the commodity and equity markets since 1986. In addition to his B.S. in Chemical Engineering and an M.B.A., D. R. has studied extensively with Van Tharp and Brian June, is a contributing author to the EDAT industry's premier "how-to" book, and is currently developing several EDAT training products.

iii) Products and Services

    (1) This trading business provides two essential services to the capital markets: liquidity and capital generation.

iv) Operations

    (1) This trading business will be operated from a home office properly equipped for trading. The key elements represented by this home office setup are proper ergonomics, redundant connections, and redundant essential equipment.

    (2) The business will trade primarily momentum strategies, the first of which is outlined under the "Trading Plan" section. By the end of the year, the business will have a portfolio of strategies that it incorporates according to market conditions and opportunities. All of these trading strategies will be described in detail in the trading plan before the business will trade them.

    (3) Time Management: Initially, less than 10 hours per week will be spent actually trading. In addition, 25 hours per week will be spent in trading preparation, 5 hours in post-trading journaling and record-keeping, and 15 hours per week will be spent in active learning. This learning time will be spent with my coach, reading market periodicals and books and on system research.

    (4) Disaster Plan: This portion of the business's operation attempts to capture the major foreseeable problems that could adversely affect the business's day-to-day operations. Longer-term issues, such as legislative changes that have the potential to impact the business, are not addressed at this tactical/execution level.

        (a) Power outage—An appropriately sized Un-interruptible Power Supply (UPS) is installed and maintained so that the business will have a minimum of 20 minutes to exit any existing positions in the case of power outage. The phone used for trading does not require AC power to operate.

        (b) Phone outage—A charged cell phone and extra batteries are available at all times.

(c) Internet outage—A redundant ISP is kept to provide an alternative route to the Internet. Should the Internet connection or computer problems prohibit direct-access trading while a position is on, the position will be exited via telephone. No positions will be held if direct access to the trading account is lost.

(d) Family emergency—If a family member or neighbor has a medical emergency that does not allow for a timely exit from existing positions, all positions will be exited via a cell phone call to the broker at the earliest possible time. The broker's trading desk number is programmed into the cell phone. People are always more important than money. However, good judgment will be used. If the emergency response can reasonably wait 30 seconds, all positions will be exited via EDAT in the fastest possible manner.

v) Organization, Management, and Employees

(1) The business will start as a sole proprietorship with a "trader election, marked-to-market." The structure will transition to a corporation within the first 6 months of operation. Therefore, the pro forma financial statements in this business plan reflect ongoing operation under a corporate structure.

3) Industry Overview and Competition

a) EDAT trading is still in its infancy. Since the regulatory changes that made EDAT trading possible are only a few years old, the competition represented by individual traders has not reached even a fraction of its potential size. Government studies estimate that there are approximately 15,000 to 20,000 active EDAT traders. In addition to these traders, institutional traders and market makers are significant and strong competitors in this field. So while there is significant individual and professional competition, the EDAT market is still many years (perhaps decades) from maturity.

4) Trading Plan (See Attachment)
   i) Low Risk Ideas
   ii) Strategic Concepts and Beliefs
   iii) Implementation
      (1) Entries
      (2) Exits
      (3) Stops
   iv) Strategic Alliances
   v) Skill Maintenance and Coaching
5) Financial Information
   i) Budget

Trading Budget

Item	Monthly Cost	Comments
Tithe for Ministries	$ 519	
Data Feed	—	Free after 50 trades
ISP	20	
Satellite Feed	40	
Redundant ISP	10	
Telephone	115	Second phone line + Long distance
Seminars	400	Prorated to monthly basis
Equipment Lease	200	Computers, printer, fax, etc.
Office Supplies	20	
Computer Misc.	50	Soft/hardware upgrades & maintenance
CPA + Legal	100	
Subscriptions	20	
Cable TV	20	Incremental cost for trading
Cell Phone	20	Power/phone outage backup
Total	$1,534	

ii) Cash Flow Statement

Cash Flow

Item	Monthly Cash Flow	Comments
Net Income	$6,000	Net commissions
Interest Income	200	Interest on core equity
Expenses	(1,534)	From trading budget
Approx. Taxes	(433)	Corporate rate
Net Cash Flow	$4,233	

iii) Profit & Loss Statement (aka Income Statement)

Income Statement

Item	Monthly Income	Comments
Trading Revenue	$6,000	Net of commissions
Interest Income	200	Interest on core equity
Trading Expenses	(1,534)	From trading budget
Operating Income	4,667	
Gen'l & Admin. Expenses	(2,500)	Empl. benefits, salary, etc.
Income before Inc. Tax	2,167	
Provision for Inc. Taxes	(433)	Corporate rate
Net Income	$1,733	

iv) Balance Sheet

Balance Sheet

Item	Monthly Income	Comments
Current Assets		
Cash	$50,000	Trading equity
Prepaid Expenses	1,200	Subscriptions, leases, etc.
Total Current Assets	$51,200	
Property & Equipment	3,500	Furniture, computer, etc.
Other Assets	—	Currently none
Total Assets	$54,700	
Current Liabilities		
Accounts Payable	$ 500	Software, other misc.
Current Debt	—	None
Total Current Liabilities	$ 500	
Long-Term Debt	—	None
Total Liabilities	$ 500	
Owners' Equity	54,200	
Total Liab. + Own. Eq.	$54,700	

Trading Plan
D. R. Barton, Jr.
June 30, 2000

Trading Goals

1) Become an excellent trader. (Process Goal)
   a) Connect to Mission:
      i)   This goal empowers me to achieve Trading Goals 2 & 3 below. (Results-Oriented Goals)
      ii) It enables me to teach and coach others
   b) I follow a well-devised written Trading Plan.
   c) I am disciplined in obeying my trading rules.
   d) I follow the "Ten Tasks of Trading" (Tharp's Home Study Course, Volume 1).
   e) I learn from every trade.
2) I know that I am an excellent trader because of the results that I generate. (Result Goal)
   a) Connect to Mission:
      i)   This is the key indicator that I am trading well
   b) No more than one down month per year
   c) Maximum of 25 percent drawdown
   d) Return on equity of 100% per year
3) Generate cash flow that will sustain family income. (Result Goal)
   a) Connect to Mission:
      i)   This cash flow is one of the streams that I will use to fund ministries.
      ii) The cash flow generated by my trading efforts is one of the means by which I serve my family.
   b) $4,000/month rate ($200 per day) before tax, net of other trading expenses by 12/31/00
   c) $10,000/month ($500 per day) by 12/31/01

My Edge

I have identified three areas that combine to create my edge in the market.

1) I model the best trading practices. This helps me build and maintain a winning trading psychology.
   a) I use the "Ten Tasks of Trading" (Tharp's Home Study Course, Volume I).
   b) I receive coaching from a top trader so that I can model his success elements.
      i) I model his trading beliefs.
      ii) I model his trading strategies.
      iii) I model his mental states.
2) I use a trading coach to guide me through new or difficult areas and to push me to higher performance.
3) I use well-developed trading strategies.
   a) I thoroughly research the past performance of the strategies.
      i) I understand the limitations of back testing.
      ii) I understand the limitations of my particular method(s) of testing.
      iii) I do not allow research results to take the place of a comprehensive understanding of the trading strategy.
         (1) The market psychology of the strategy
         (2) The fundamental basis for the strategy
         (3) The technical support for the strategy
   b) I use this preparation to give me utmost confidence when trading the strategy.

Trading Strategy

My Trading Plan contains strategies for different market conditions (i.e., different times of the day and different macro market conditions). My primary trading strategy for market openings is the Gap & Trap.

Gap & Trap Basket Strategy

Strategy Overview (My beliefs about why the strategy works):
This strategy fades the opening gap for selected stocks (i.e., a basket of stocks) based on their expected best direction for trading. The expected best direction is established by historical testing. Some stocks react best to shorting opportunities for these opening gaps, others for long entry opportunities.

1) <u>Market psychology</u> for this strategy is based on overreactions of the public to news on well-known stocks, the technology sector, or the market in general. This causes the stock's price to climb too high on good news or fall too low on bad news. Market makers take advantage of the overreaction and trade on the opening in a manner that increases the gap before they fade it (hence the strategy name). To avoid curve fitting the back-testing results, all stocks in this basket use the same stop loss of ¾ point.

2) The <u>fundamental basis</u> for the strategy relies on the fact that heavily traded stocks overreact to news or even general movement in the sector or market direction. In other words, the stock price must react beyond what the fundamental picture of the news will support. By definition, the high-profile stocks in this strategy will usually overreact relative to the rest of the market, forming the fundamental grounding for the strategy.

3) The <u>technical support</u> for the strategy lies in the old adage, "Gaps are always filled." I do not believe they are *always* filled, but I do believe that the probability for filling the gap is high. This is supported by research (Connors & Rashke, Babcock, Larry Williams, etc.), including my own.

Setup: An "Opening Gap" that meets the following direction and gap size targets:

Stock	Gap Directions	Gap Size Target
DELL	Down	0.75
MSFT	Up	1.00

Entry: Enter when the Level II screen indicates definitive movement in the direction of the fade. This entry is indicated and bounded by the following conditions:

1. Entry is during the first 15 minutes of regular trading hours. After that, the trade is aborted.
2. As a guideline, the trade is entered on the "fade side" of the daily opening price. This means that I enter the trade after the price has

started moving in my direction. However, significant Level II discretion is allowed: If tiers are collapsing, my entry is immediate and I wait for no other price action. But I don't step in front of freight trains! This means that when initial price movement continues strongly in the direction of the opening gap, I wait for definitive indication of a turn before entering (I use any one of three indications: a pivot top (or bottom), a stochastic crossover, or moving average crossover. I strive to keep it simple!)

3. Enter with supporting or neutral S&P futures (1st forward contract) direction. (DO NOT enter these basket stocks directly against the S&P.)

4. For entry, I need to see collapsing levels on the L2 screen in the direction of the trade. Strength on my side of the trade is also preferable, but not a necessity. However, with no tier collapse, there is no entry (due to the fading nature of the trade). Again, this helps to keep me from the business end of freight trains.

Stop Loss: 0.75 points from entry. If my entry is significantly better than the stock's daily open price (i.e., higher for an up gap or lower for a down gap), the stop loss amount can be reduced.

Reentry: After being stopped out, one reentry attempt is allowed if the setup and entry criteria from above are still in place. This means that I am still within the first 15 minutes of the trading day.

Profit-Taking Exit: Use a trailing stop. Initial trailing stop is 0.375 points after 0.75 points of profit.

1. The trading window for this strategy is 60 minutes maximum. One hour after the open of the regular trading session, tighten trailing stop to 0.25 points. This allows me to continue to ride any uptrend but then close out before any significant retracement takes place.

2. Exit immediately on stock-specific or significant market news against my position—if any reaction is noted in the Level II screen or the S&P futures (1st forward contract). I make the market tell me the news is against me.

3. Be aware that there is a high probability for a rapid change in direction after the initial fade. Be ready to exit immediately if tier support in my direction weakens significantly. This means that I still use a trailing stop (so I don't get unduly whipsawed), but I stay ready to exit because of the tendency for quick reversals at this time of the trading day.

4. If stock starts to trade in a channel before the end of the first hour, exit ASAP at the favorable end of the channel. (A channel indicates that this is no longer a momentum trade!) When classifying a developing channel, I make sure that I'm not observing a key direction change (i.e., "V" bottom or top)! In the case of a "V" bottom (or top), I get out immediately. I recognize the "V" visually (as opposed to using technical analysis). A severe reversal (especially an island reversal—a bar with a gap on both sides—or any reaction turn after a parabolic move in my favor) tells me to exit as fast as possible: give up the spread, give an extra $\frac{1}{16}$ or even $\frac{1}{8}$ away if necessary! I don't want to be on the wrong side of a fast-moving market at this time of day.

Position Sizing: Since this is a high-probability trading strategy (60 percent or greater), I am slightly more aggressive with position sizing. (For definitions of terms used, see Chapter 6.)

1. Use a "Total Equity" model.
2. Use a 1.5 percent risk level in a "Percent Risk Model."
3. Use additional risk allocation of 5 percent of the market's money.
4. Scaling (in or out) is not addressed at this time.

KNOWLEDGE KEYS

✓ It's essential to have a business plan as a part of your trading career.
✓ The business plan should encompass both your personal and your business missions.
✓ It's vital to clearly understand the services that you offer to the marketplace through your trading business.
✓ Your business plan should encompass the marshaling of resources that include time, talent, capital, and equipment.
✓ The type of entity you choose as a trader could critically impact your net profits.
✓ When constructing your trading plan, it's important to identify your edges in the marketplace.
✓ Clearly understand both what an edge is and what it is not.
✓ Your trading style is an important part of your trading plan.
✓ Trading rules are an important part of your trading plan, but they are often ignored by all except the best traders.
✓ Your own personal likes and dislikes, your own personal style, can have a large impact on your bottom line.
✓ A trading plan should tell you what market conditions are applicable for your type of trading.

CALLS TO ACTION

✓ Discipline yourself to complete a written business plan. Refer to the outline we provide in Figure 3–1.
✓ Be sure to include your business mission and tie this to your personal mission.
✓ Include the following key factors: site selection, start-up costs, budgeting, ongoing costs and cash flow analysis, type of entity, organization of work area, record-keeping, and taxes.
✓ Be sure to include start-up and recurring expenses when constructing your budgets.
✓ Construct your trading plan based upon your overall business plan, your beliefs, and your mission.
✓ Pay special attention to, and define, your competitive advantages and edges.
✓ Identify those trading styles that are most suited to your personality.

✓ Clearly define the trading system that you will use, including setups and entries, stop losses, profit-taking exits, scaling, and position-sizing algorithms.
✓ Make sure your trading plan also contains the market conditions under which a particular trading system will be used.
✓ Finally, be absolutely sure that your trading plan is consistent with your personal beliefs and personal trading style.

NOTES

1. R multiple refers to a multiple of the initial risk. See Chapter 5.

## PART TWO

Putting the "Laser-Guided Rocket" Together

(Some Assembly Required)

You can think of Part One as "soft mechanics," dealing with your own behaviors and planning. This section deals with the "hard mechanics" of trading. These issues include hardware, software, and the mechanics of various trading screens. In fact, we've gone to great lengths to dissect the actual screens you'll use to trade. Trying to trade without this knowledge is like trying to drive while your windshield is covered in mud! You can do it, but not without serious risk of injury or death!

We've also disclosed, in layperson's terms, the money-making secrets of the masters: They are R multiples, expectancy, and position sizing. This material will radically change your thinking about being "right" and "wrong." It will also show you how big money is won and lost in the markets (again—it's probably not what you think!). Understanding this material is one more step toward reaping long-term consistent profits! It takes some time and effort to put all these elements together. But the effort will greatly maximize your profits. Read on!

## CHAPTER 4

The Trader's Toolkit

Essential Secrets for Getting the Most from Your Hardware and Software

> To the man who only has a hammer in the toolkit, every problem looks like a nail.
>
> *Abraham Maslow*

When I first started direct-access trading in 1997, I remember being very frustrated searching for all the tools that I needed. There were few Web sites for traders, and there were no electronic day trading books around. As a result, it was very difficult to find the kind of information that I needed to put together a "trading toolkit"—the best trading hardware and software. Once I found the tools, it was even more difficult to determine how best to use them for maximum trading profits—this, despite the fact that I had an overexposure to technology from my prior careers.

My first career was as a flight instructor. I taught scores of people how to fly fixed-wing aircraft (airplanes). Flight is filled with technology, from weather systems to aircraft systems and from air traffic control to instrumentation systems. Later, I was the CEO of a company that designed and coded software for interactive voice-response systems. Eventually, we switched to Web-based programming as the Internet overtook interactive voice-response systems. No need to explain how technology is related here!

As a result of my jobs, I learned a tremendous amount about technology along the way. But even with all this background in software and computers, I was still pretty frustrated about what I needed as a trader. Interestingly, much of this confusion still exists today, despite how direct-access trading has caught on in the marketplace. My goal in this chapter is to clear some of this confusion up for you—fairly quickly. It's not all that complex; it's really rather simple.

So what are these tools? You need a computer and some peripherals like a printer and a data backup system. You need an Internet service provider (ISP) and the hardware to connect to it. You need the trading software itself, and you need to understand the difference between direct-access trading software and Web-based systems.

As background information, before we discuss hardware and software basics, you need to understand that there are risks involved with technology. If you trade long enough, I guarantee that some of these technology risks are going to tap you on the shoulder, if not knock the wind right out of you! I've had both happen to me on more than one occasion, despite my best efforts to have the proper systems and to be properly prepared.

Once you have all the technology side out of the way, the "tools" in the trader's toolkit, you still need to understand how to read the gauges. But first let's answer . . .

HOW MUCH COMPUTER DO YOU NEED?

First, you need a base computer system with a fast CPU, a large hard drive, and as much memory as you can possibly afford. For now, just understand that the faster the computer, the better; the more hard drive, the better; and the more memory, the better. Fortunately, prices today are low enough that you can purchase a top-of-the-line system for approximately $3,000 to $3,500. If you cannot afford that, then you cannot afford to do direct-access day trading.

The Base Computer

Begin with a 500- to 650-megahertz computer. That's the fast CPU part. These computers process 500 million operations per second or faster. The nice thing is that these are now second-generation machines to the 1-gigahertz computers that have come out, so they're more affordable than they used to be. A base 500- to 650-megahertz machine is probably going to run about $2,500.

Second, you need a lot of memory—RAM. Memory is really the lifeblood of a computer, because if there's not enough memory, the computer has to take time to make extra reads and writes to the hard drive. Since the drive is the slowest part of your computer system, this can really slow you down when trading. More memory will result in fewer reads and writes to the drive. I recommend 128 to 512 megabytes of RAM. Again, more is better.

The third part of your base computer is the hard drive. Here you want a 10- to 30-gigabyte hard drive.

Summing it all up, here's your base computer. It has at least a 500-megahertz processor, at least 128 megabytes of RAM, and at least a 10-gigabyte hard drive.

SWEAT THE SMALL STUFF

Pay attention to the "small" details. For instance, don't get a cheap keyboard. Get a good keyboard that's going to hold up well. You can buy a keyboard for $10, or you can buy one for $100. Generally, you get what you pay for. The more expensive board is going to hold up better under a trading environment where you're banging on the keys. If you buy a system similar to those we recommend, it will typically come with a good keyboard. Make sure you stay with that one and don't try to substitute a cheaper keyboard to save a few dollars. Here's what can happen.

One day while I was trading with my backup computer system (which had a "low-end" keyboard), one of the keys totally froze and stopped working. It happened to be the F-9 function key that I needed to kill a trade. I kept hitting the F-9 key like mad, but it wouldn't cancel the trade! I had to call my broker to get me out of it. Unfortunately, the trade moved against me by a half point or so in the time it took me to get the broker on the phone. A half point on 1,000 shares is $500. Thus, using a cheap $10 keyboard on my backup system cost me the price of five top-end keyboards. Lesson learned.

Monitors

I also recommend as part of the base system the largest monitor you can possibly afford. Big monitors are better, because they allow you to get more information on your screen at higher resolutions. That means the monitor will be easy on your eyes. You're going to spend many hours in front of your computer day trading, so it's important to have a high-quality monitor with crisp resolution. The resolution is generally referred to as "dot pitch." The higher the dot-pitch number, the worse the resolution will be. Thus, a 0.25 dot-pitch monitor is clearer than a 0.29 dot-pitch monitor.

A serious day trader needs to have at least two monitors, and most that I know have three or four monitors on their desktops. Some traders even have three or four monitors on their *backup* computer system.

Why do you need so many monitors? When you trade, you filter information to decide which stock is appropriate to enter and when. This is not necessarily the most important aspect of trading, but you'll probably spend the most time doing it. Later in this chapter we'll go through some specific screens, and you'll see that there's no way that you can keep all these screens on just one or even two monitors easily. Thus, more monitors allow you to configure your trading desktop so that you can see all the screens: market maker, time & sales, charts, and other "minor" screens. You also can keep a chat window open; plus you can keep some Web browsers open to do some quick, fundamental analyses, and even a window for your news feed. Some traders I know even have a PCTV built into their computer and watch CNBC cable on another monitor! I recommend four monitors.

I also have a preference for flat-screen plasma monitors. Why flat-screen monitors? First, the screen resolution is good. Second, they take up much less space. You can actually put four 18-inch flat-screen monitors on a desktop. And most important, they generate much less heat. Four CRT-type monitors will generate a tremendous amount of heat. If you're in a closed or even semiclosed environment, you're going to find yourself getting very, very warm, particularly in the summer months. When I first started with four such monitors, I had trouble keeping my trading room below 95 degrees in the summer, even with air conditioning. Sweat would drip off my brow and drip onto the keyboard. Not a good environment for making huge financial decisions!

Additional Equipment

First, you'll want to consider a printer. We strongly recommend that you print out your notes and screen shots of the trades you've taken. Print the chart, the time & sales window, and the order entry screen. Do this at the end of each trading day. If you're just starting out, print these screens and the market-maker window just before you enter and exit trades. *Note:* Do this as a simulated trade only! We don't recommend that you try to print screens *during* your actual trades! (This is also a great review and practice technique for seasoned traders.) This will help you create a notebook of your trades so that you can do a daily debriefing. This is one of the key tasks that you'll want to do as a trader, and we discuss it more extensively in Chapter 12.

You'll also need some kind of a backup system for your hard drive. Hard drives do crash. In fact, every hard drive ever made, *every one,* someday will stop functioning. The only question is when. Will it fail in 1 month, 6 months, 1 year, or 10 years? If you follow our advice in this book, you'll have very specialized screen setups. You'll have saved a lot of data, including trading records, specialized screen shots, and specialized templates used for trading. One morning you'll turn on your computer and it will not boot because your hard drive has fried. In fact, the heads, which are mechanical devices, will have scraped across the plates of the hard drive, eradicating the data. You can jump out of the window, or you can replace your hard drive. You'll feel like doing the former, but the only one that's useful is the latter—you're going to have to replace your hard drive.

When your drive does fry, replacing it doesn't solve the problem of lost data. While there are services that attempt to recover lost data, this can cost thousands of dollars, and even when successful, they seldom recover 100 percent of your data. As a result, you must get a backup device such as a Zip drive, an optical drive, or a read-write CD-ROM. When you do this, you may only lose a half day's or a day's worth of data. The bottom line is that missing data are very expensive in lost opportunity, to say nothing of trades on which you might end up taking a loss just because your computer is down. Back up your hard drive regularly! I suggest not less than once a week.

The final peripheral that I absolutely, positively recommend is a UPS, an uninterruptible power supply. A UPS keeps your computer running for some period of time in the case of a power outage. Many places have regular blackouts (no electricity) or brownouts (reduced electricity). When these happen, they might destroy your computer system. You don't want that to happen. Instead, if you have a UPS, it will detect a brownout or a blackout and keep your computer running at full power for a period of time. The amount of time depends upon the size of the UPS (a very good utility for sizing a UPS based on your system parameters can be found at www.apc.com). You'll need one that will operate your system for about 15 minutes so that you can get out of trades and shut everything down before any damage occurs.

INTERNET CONNECTIVITY—GET A BIG (BROADBAND) PIPE!

Once you've solved your computer hardware and peripheral problems, it's time to face the real challenge of the day trader, the issue of connectivity. I can think of no other area that will add to your frustration, delight, profits, or losses than the whole area of connectivity. Frankly, in my opinion, the Internet just isn't all that it's cracked up to be yet. And depending upon where you live, whether or not you are surrounded by trees, whether you have exposure to the southern sky, whether you are close to a telephone central office, whether you have cable in your area, and more—all these issues will come to the fore as you decide to become a pioneer in electronic direct-access trading.

Given the kinds of risks you face in just getting connected to the Internet, what is the very best way? The answer is that there is no one best way for you. It's going to depend upon your situation—where you're located and what kind of services are provided in your area.

With those restraints, you absolutely want the very fastest, most stable connection that you can get. You want fast, but fast without stability is worthless. For instance, it might be better to go with a very reliable 56K analog connection if all your other broad-

ONE TRADER'S "ADVENTURES IN CONNECTION LAND"

I started to learn direct-access day trading in mid-1999. I started with a 56K analog modem, but found that I was getting data 7 to 10 seconds later than those who have more bandwidth. I sometimes traded with a friend by calling him on the phone. When I'd talk to him about his trades, I couldn't see what he was seeing. Sometimes, I'd get filled at a certain price, but I wouldn't see the stock reverse on me until 15 to 20 seconds later. Therefore, when I was long and had to sell, I'd be selling into a falling market. This isn't much fun when you are competing with others who have up-to-the-millisecond information.

My next step was to call the local telephone company to upgrade to DSL. However, the phone company said that I lived so far from one of its switches that it didn't think DSL would be reliable. In fact, the company refused to install it.

Now, I was really upset, so I decided to try a cable connection. However, my cable company didn't have an Internet service in my area. I did finally find a second-tier provider (called a CLEX, competitive local exchange carrier) for DSL, only to find that the provider basically resells the Bell Atlantic DSL system. The provider agreed to install it for $550 in about 4 weeks. The monthly fee would be about $65, which didn't seem too bad. However, when the installer finally came out, he was able to get a signal but not one that would get 640K bandwidth. So he kept downgrading the connection until he found a speed where the Cisco router would talk to the central office. We had to go down to 256K, which is still much better than my 56K analog modem, but less than what one would hope for with DSL.

After agreeing to that arrangement and getting everything up and running, the data coming from the broker servers were still lagging by 3 to 4 seconds. True, it was no longer 7 to 20 seconds, but 3 to 4 seconds can be an eternity when you're trading. While working with the broker and some of the broker's computer geeks, we found that the problem was a bottleneck in the server bank of the ISP that the CLEC was using, a problem not easily fixed. The CLEC told me it was hoping to fix the problem in the next 3 to 6 months, but it was not a viable option for trading.

So once I found out that DSL was not going to work, I tried a DirecPC satellite connection. Now, satellite connections bring broadband data into your computer (downstream), but they take instructions from your computer through a standard 56K modem and ISP (upstream). I figured that since most trading data are downstream, this would be OK.

The easiest way to buy DirecPC is through a local store such as Circuit City or Best Buy. The store I chose told me that it installed its satellites within 1 week, so I thought, "Great, I can be up and running in 1 week." So I bought my satellite hardware for about $150. I also paid $100 for installation.

The store where you buy your dish (and pay for installation) is not the installer. The store sends your order to a national wholesaler of installation, who then calls a local installer, who then usually subcontracts the job out to an independent contractor. Thus, the accountability for installation has many places to break down. Finally, 3½ weeks after I bought my satellite, someone showed up at my door to put it on my roof. And the only reason it happened that quickly was because I tracked down the people at the national level who handled the account and talked to them directly.

Once my satellite was installed, we found out that my signal was too weak to run at top speeds. I was able to get maybe 100 to 150K broadband. As a result, I had to bring out a tree surgeon to trim some trees in the backyard to the tune of another $150. A clear exposure to the southern sky is required. By now, I've spent about $1,000 trying to get a strong, high broadband connection. You have to really want to do this to go as far as I did!

At this point, with the tree trimming and a little bit of redirecting of the satellite, I'm now up to a perfect signal. So I'm trading the first day on my broadband, and all of a sudden, my signal disappears completely. I was in the middle of a trade, which was going very well my way. I had to call up my broker, find out what the best bid and ask were, and get out of the trade. In order to get out, I had to enter an order that got me out at a slightly less favorable price, only to find out that the market was still moving my way. That little incident with that trade probably cost me about $700.

I called up DirecPC to find out what happened, and the first gentleman didn't know. As a result, he had me reinstall my whole connectivity software package. That took about 2½ hours because he was not very competent. Later, when I still wasn't getting a signal, I called back and found out that the gateway was brand new and the company was having stability problems. So the 2½ hours that I spent trying to reinstall hardware and software were unnecessary. It was really a problem on the company's end, which continued to last for about a week. So, as you can see, all the technology options come with their own baggage and potential problems. The good news is that I do finally have a fast, reliable connection to the Internet!

band solutions are very unstable. This is going to vary from area to area. You can look at Table 4–1, which we've organized in terms of speed from the slowest connection to the fastest connection available. The Internet access speeds noted in the table are theoretical maximums; because of such issues as Internet congestion and latency, actual results may be lower. Where more than one speed is listed, the figures indicate the lowest and highest offerings for that type of service.

Notice the newer service—fixed-point wireless—in the table. In some areas it's called terrestrial wireless, which is really a combination of wireless and T1. In my particular area, this gives me a minimum—a guaranteed minimum—of 1.544 megabytes per second in both directions, and the company guarantees 99.9 percent uptime, which is highly stable. At one time, I had a hard-wired T1 connection to my home. It cost about $1,200 per month. The new fixed-point wireless system, in contrast, costs $2,000 for installation and $250 a month for the service. I currently use fixed-point wireless. It is awesome!

WHERE CAN YOU RENT THAT BIG PIPE?

Your ISP is the first link between you and the Internet. An ISP comes in all kinds of flavors—from national providers, such as Sprint, down to local mom and pop operators. You can think of the ISP as the software side of the solution. On the most basic level, it provides you with your e-mail and keeps the physical layer running for you.

If you have a choice, use a national ISP as opposed to a local provider. The national companies usually have bigger backbones, meaning they have more bandwidth. They're running on major circuits as opposed to smaller circuits. They have more staff, more technical ability, and more financial wherewithal to solve whatever kind of problems you may be having.

TABLE 4-1

Routes to the Internet

Type	Estimated Installation and Monthly Cost	Infrastructure Requirements	Available Speed: Download, Upload
56K analog	Up to $25, $19 a month for ISP	POTS (plain old telephone service) line, modem	56, 33.6
ISDN	$50–$300, $20 a month	POTS, ISDN terminal adapter; maximum distance from the central office: 18,000 feet	128, 128
xDSL	Up to $500, $38–$840 a month	POTS, DSL modem, or router; maximum distance from the central office: 12,000–18,000 feet	144 (min.)– 7,270, 90 (min.)–1,536
Cable	Up to $175, $39–$49 a month	Access to cable TV service; maximum distance from the service provider: 30 miles	384 (min.)– 4,096, 128 (min.)–2,560
Satellite	$300–$800, $20 a month (25 hours)	Unobstructed line of sight to the south; satellite dish, modem	400, 33.6
Fixed-point wireless	Varies	Wireless router/modem; choice of transmission technologies: microwave, RF, infrared	128 (min.)– 1,536, varies
T1 (DS-1)	Varies	Router, data service unit (DSU)	1,536, 1,536

If you want the fastest connection to your broker, you should find out the name of the backbone provider for your broker. For instance, if you trade with MB Trading, its backbone is provided by U-U Net. Therefore, if you want the fastest possible connection between you and MB Trading, you should buy your ISP service from U-U Net also. When you do so, you never have to go outside of the U-U Net network to get a connection from you to MB Trading. Theoretically, you would be within the same network and, therefore, should have the fastest connection time. I suggest this even though you may not always get the fastest connection, even using the same backbone, due to technical and physical properties of the Internet.

One problem that might occur with this, unfortunately, is perhaps your broker's backbone provider doesn't offer ISP service in your area, or if it does, you cannot get access to it. You might be too far from the central office, for instance. Let's say you have cable in your area. Generally speaking, cable modems are very compatible with trading. However, the cable providers (@Home and Roadrunner) offer their own ISP services. Very few brokerage companies are connected directly to a cable provider. Most are connected via one of the primary telephone providers, such as Sprint, MCI, or U-U Net. So some trade-offs are involved here. In this particular case, I suggest you rely primarily on your cable and get the telephone provider as your backup ISP provider.

KEEP THAT CONNECTION CONNECTED!

You should also consider purchasing and installing some utilities that will help you determine how good your Internet connection is. This can be very valuable during your trading session when you're trying to determine if your data feeds are up to speed or not. Three of the most useful are Ping Plotter, Net.Medic, and Swatch.

Ping Plotter is a utility that uses both a trace route utility and a ping utility. It shows you graphically how fast the connection between you and your server is. It also shows you hops—the number of routings that you have to go through to get where you're going, the number of turns that you have to make. When you are driving a car, if you have to go through 20 intersections to get where you're going, that's going to take a whole lot longer than if you go on the interstate, where you have no intersections to go through. If you do use the same backbone provider between you and your ISP that your broker uses, you're much more likely to have very few hops between you and your broker, perhaps as few as two or three.

Ping Plotter will display graphically the entire route, and tell you what your round-trip time is in milliseconds (1 millisecond =

$\frac{1}{1,000}$ second). Generally for trading, you want 200 milliseconds or less. Anything more than that and you're starting to get time degradation due to problems along the route. Another term for this delay is "latency." With terrestrial wireless, the latency is generally 20 milliseconds or less. Speed is very important when you're trading.

Net.Medic, another great utility you should have, shows you the actual speed you're receiving downstream and upstream—in other words, the bytes per second for both your download and upload streams. It also shows you how fast your connection really is. You might be connecting with a 56K modem, but only connecting at 28.8K. Net.Medic will tell you that.

The third utility you need is called Swatch. Swatch uses university or military timeservers to keep your computer time synchronized to the atomic clock. Therefore, if you keep Swatch running all the time, your computer clock will never be out of sync with the atomic clock. That's the clock used by the New York and NASDAQ exchanges. You'll find this very helpful, because it's very disconcerting to have your clock be a minute or two ahead of, or behind, the real New York time. For instance, your clock might say that it's 3:58 p.m. So you think you have 2 minutes to get out of a trade during normal market hours, but, in fact, the market's closing in 10 seconds. Swatch is the utility that will prevent this from happening.

TECHNOLOGY RISKS—THE DIRTY LITTLE SECRET OF TRADING

The best artisans empower themselves with the very finest tools. As a top trader, you'll need the best trading tools you can find. Without them, you may come close to excellent trading, but you'll never quite achieve the pinnacle of your trading ability. The tools you'll need fall into these broad categories: computer hardware and peripherals, connectivity tools, and software. These are the technologies associated with trading. And while the larger issues are normally addressed, the granular detail is often overlooked! Does this matter? Only if you want to avoid crashes during a trade! I call these risks "technology risks" or "technology costs." What I'm really talking about here is technology downtime. Before we close this section, it's important for you to recognize the time and energy required to manage the technology end of the business, and then be prepared for the downtime associated with the technology. Downtime can come from many sources, starting at your end and working toward the NASDAQ and NYSE computer systems:

1. Electricity
2. Nontrading software (e.g., Windows, modem drivers, etc.)
3. Trading software
4. Computer hardware
5. Peripheral hardware
6. Phone lines
7. Broadband technology (some are more robust than others)
8. Broadband provider (servers and other bottlenecks)
9. ISP provider (not necessarily the same as number 8)
10. Broker's servers
11. ECN servers
12. NASDAQ servers

Any one of these can keep you from trading. And they can keep you "out of business" for several days at a time! There are costs (out-of-pocket and opportunity costs) associated with maintaining them and with living through the glitches (in the middle of a trade!) and the downtime. These risks are simply a cost of trading; you'll never solve them all, but there are ways to mitigate several problems.

INTEGRATED TRADING SOFTWARE—THE HEART OF YOUR TRADING PLATFORM

Let's move on to the real heart of trading, the software. By software, we mean the direct-access trading software that actually allows you to connect to a broker and trade. First, you must understand the difference between trading online through a broker interface and direct-access trading. Browser-based systems give you access to your broker's computer systems, allowing you to place trades through a computerized trading desk. In this respect, you're really trading just like you used to when you called your broker to place a trade. The only difference is that you use the computer rather than the phone to communicate with your broker. It's basically a glorified e-mail system! This description is a bit of a simplification, but we hope it will help you understand the contrasts between Web-based systems and direct-access systems.

A direct-access system is directly connected to the markets, usually via your broker's computers, but it bypasses your broker's trading desk. Instead your orders are placed directly into the market right alongside the bids and offers of major institutions and market makers. This allows in many cases for "instant" fills, since no human touches or even sees your order—you can be filled before your finger has left the "Buy" or "Sell" key! Recapping, the connectivity issues we discussed extensively a bit earlier would not be so critical if you are just doing Web-based trading. However, when you are direct-access trading, you must know what is happening tick by tick, making a fast, stable connection absolutely necessary.

A direct-access system is a software system built on what's called "client-server" technology. This means that the entire application software is running on your computer. You actually download or install from a CD-ROM an application program. It's loaded onto your computer, and that software knows how to communicate directly with your brokerage company and the NASDAQ and the NYSE servers. It's an integrated trading environment where, on your desktop at any time, you can see any or all elements at once. That is, you can have market-maker screens, time & sales windows, charting, order entry screens, and fundamental screens, all on your desktop at the same time, and all live, with live, automatically updating data.

Not all real-time data are the same. There are real-time dynamic data, which change as they occur. All direct-access systems have dynamic data. This means not only are the data real time, but the data themselves update on your screen as they occur, assuming no data lags from your ISP. You can have a real-time system, however, which is not dynamically updated. Those systems are real time, but you have to continually do screen refreshes in order to get the true data. For the most part, these are browser-based systems in which the actual software running the trading desk is not on your computer but on the brokerage's computer. The system is called browser-based because you use your browser to access the trading software.

For direct-access trading, which is the topic of this book, you must have a direct-access system. A Web-based system simply will not allow you to trade the very fast-moving market-making strategies and momentum strategies we talk about later on. While they may be very good systems for certain position or swing traders, Web-based systems, such as those offered by DLJ Direct, Ameritrade, etc., are simply not adequate for direct-access trading.

There are three major integrated trading systems you should consider—RealTick (www.realtick.com), CyberTrader (www. cybercorp.com), and TradeCast (www.tradecast.com). All three systems are what I'd term heavy-duty, industrial, direct-access trading systems. While they each claim to have their own unique features and functionality, a trader can trade profitably using any of them. In fact, the distinctions are so small between them that the platform itself makes no difference. Just use a top-notch platform, and any of these three fits the bill.

CyberTrader, in particular, has some very good order handling routines. It allows you to place stop orders on a NASDAQ stock by keeping it on your computer until the stop price is hit. It then transmits the order—as either a limit or a market order. RealTick Version 7 includes this similar functionality. Neither of us has used TradeCast, so we are unfamiliar with how it handles such orders.

In any case, either as a fledgling or an experienced direct-access day trader, you'll be more than satisfied with CyberTrader, RealTick, or TradeCast. CyberTrader has been acquired by Schwab and is quite inexpensive. At the time of this writing, CyberTrader costs an active trader about $100 a month, compared with approximately $250 a month for the RealTick system. In fact, if you trade enough, even this pricing is irrelevant since both companies rebate the software and data fees, assuming you meet their minimum trade requirements. Visit their Web sites on a periodic basis to make sure you're staying current with the best software and the best pricing available in the marketplace.

READING THE GAUGES—THE MOST IMPORTANT TRADING SCREENS

Now that you understand the hardware, connectivity, and basic software issues, let's roll up our sleeves and dig into the actual trading screens. It's very important that you understand these screens because these screens are the basis of all the direct-access trading methodologies described in this book. These are part of the tools you will need to be a sound trader.

The Market-Maker Screen

The heart of modern direct-access trading systems is the Level II screen. A day trader *must* understand Level II (L2) inside and out to be profitable on a consistent basis. At first, the screen may look somewhat complex, but it really is quite simple. In fact, most of my entry and exit techniques rely heavily upon knowledge and interpretation of the market-maker screen. I'd estimate that as much as 70 percent of my actual entry and exit decisions are based upon the market-maker screen alone.

I've divided the screen into several main components. Here we'll dissect the main elements. A thorough understanding of this information will be required as we discuss specific strategies and tactics in Chapters 9 and 10.

Let's now examine the Level II screen. Since this is your trading "radar screen," it is imperative that you understand it completely. Figure 4–1 is a screen shot of Qualcomm (QCOM) showing most of the relevant information available on better trading platforms. I've labeled the key features and provided a succinct definition for each. It's hard to believe, but this information is not easy to find! For instance, several software users' guides tell you that these features exist, and some even tell how to get your software to display them—but amazingly they don't tell you what the various components are or what they mean to a trader! The official name of Level II is "NASDAQ Level II Quotes Montage."

Level II Display

The Level II montage in simplest terms displays the current bids and offers of all market participants for the stock being traded. Market participants include market makers, electronic communications networks, and now you. The screen updates dynamically, in real time, as the market participants change both their price and transaction size. Depending upon the stock, news, time of day, momentum, etc., the screen will be gyrating wildly, at a dead standstill, or somewhere in between.

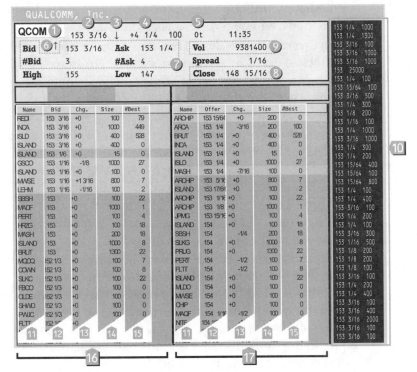

Figure 4–1 NASDAQ Level II (L2) montage.

While the screen shot in Figure 4–1 is typical, it's important to note that various software packages will display this information in a slightly different manner.

1. *Symbol.* The symbol of the stock. Three-letter symbols are NYSE stocks (e.g., AOL). Four- or more-letter symbols are NASDAQ stocks (e.g., QCOM or ERICY).

2. *Last sale.* Here you'll find the price, number of shares, and time of the last sale. QCOM traded 100 shares at 153³⁄₁₆ at 11:35 Eastern Time.

3. *Tick arrow.* Often misunderstood, this arrow shows the direction of the last actual trade. It will point in an up direction if the last price is unchanged or is higher than the previous trade. This is an "uptick." Often the arrow will be green on an uptick. If, however, the last sale was lower than (or equal to the last lower price) the

immediately previous trade, the arrow will point down
and usually will be red. This is a "downtick."

4. *Change from previous close*. This displays a "+" indicator if
   the stock is up or a "–" if the stock is down from the
   previous trading session. In addition it will show the
   magnitude of the change (e.g., +4¼). It is usually green, if
   up, or red, if down.

5. *Exchange*. Most often, one of four symbols will show here:
   (1) "Ot," or less frequently "Os," for NASDAQ national
   market stocks; (2) Kk, meaning a NASDAQ "bulletin-
   board" stock, sometimes also called "pink sheets"; (3)
   "M" for NYSE stocks; and (4) "N" for stocks on the
   AMEX. (These last two may seem counterintuitive! They
   are, however, the symbols that are used.)

6. *Bid arrow*. Often confused with the tick arrow, it is *not* the
   same! The bid arrow displays the direction of the last
   bid. If the last bid is equal to or higher than the previous,
   this arrow will point up and is displayed in green on
   many software platforms. If the last bid is lower than or
   equal to the immediately previous bid, the arrow will
   point down and will usually be red.

7. *Inside market*. This shows the "best" bid and offer, also
   known as the "inside market." The best bid is the most a
   buyer is willing to pay for a stock. The best ask or offer is
   the least amount a seller will accept for a stock. When
   you get a quote from your broker, you're quoted the
   inside market. On some systems you'll also see here the
   "#Bid" and "#Ask." This is the numerical count of the
   participants willing to buy or sell at the inside market.
   This is also referred to as the "depth" of the inside
   market.

8. *Close*. The closing price from the previous day's regular
   trading session. This price does *not* reflect any pricing
   during extended trading hours.

9. *Volume*. The current day's total trading volume. This
   volume number *does* include trades made during
   extended trading hours, therefore reflecting all trades
   made between 8 a.m. and 8 p.m.

10. *Dynamic ticker.* Displays actual sales as they occur. Also known as the "prints" or "tape." Normally will show the price, time, and size of the last sale. However "irregular" trades are *not* reported. Many traders, myself included, prefer the more advanced time & sales window. One great use for the dynamic ticker is to use it in conjunction with the time & sales window to determine slow or missing data.

11. *Market participant.* A four-letter acronym identifies the market participant willing to buy or sell stock. Normally you will see market makers and ECNs here. Some of the better know market makers are GSCO (Goldman, Sachs), MLCO (Merrill Lynch), and BEST (Bear, Stearns). The better-known ECNs are ARCA (Archipelago), INCA (Instinet), ISLD (the Island), and REDI (Redibook).

12. *Bid-ask price.* The current price at which the market participant is willing to buy or sell shares. A market maker must honor the current bid or ask in the size he displays. However, as a practical matter this rule is almost impossible to enforce for the NASDAQ. Once a market maker has filled orders in the size displayed, he is free to change his quote, both price and size, at will. Unfortunately, market makers do occasionally back away from their unfilled quotes. Traders must be aware of this.

13. *Change.* This shows the changes in the market participant's most recent quote. Are participants willing to pay more or sell for less? This will give a short-term indication. A "+" indicates an increase from the most recent price displayed by a specific participant, while a "−" indicates a decrease. Most systems will also show the amount that the quote has been raised or lowered.

14. *Size.* The number of shares being bid or offered at the displayed price. Most systems will display actual size; however, some will show a multiple of 10. On such a system, for example, a size of 100 will mean 1,000 shares.

15. *Number best.* The number of times that a market participant has been the *only* participant left at any given price level. In other words, the number of times he has

been willing to buy for more, or sell for less, than any other participant. This is fantastic information for helping to determine who the ax is. See Chapter 8 for a more detailed discussion.

16. *Bid book.* The left side of the montage shows all the market participants currently offering to buy stock. The highest price is at the top, with all other bidders sorted by price in descending order. The bid book can also display information such as change, size, and number best, as discussed above. The books are color-coded to make it easy to see the various price levels, or "tiers." An astute day trader will pay special attention to the depths of the various price tiers. However, the colors themselves have no particular meaning. They simply make it easier to read the screen.

17. *Offer book.* The right side of the montage shows all the market participants currently offering to sell stock. The lowest price is at the top, with all other bidders sorted by price in ascending order. The offer book can also display information such as change, size, and number best, as discussed above. Just like the bid books, the offer books are color-coded to make it easy to see the various price levels, or "tiers." And as he would with the bid books, an astute day trader will pay special attention to the depths of the various price tiers. Again, the colors themselves have no particular meaning. They simply make it easier to read the screen.

Bulletin-Board Stock

From time to time, you'll see an L2 screen that looks similar to the one shown in Figure 4–2. It is a "bulletin-board" stock. Although you can get quotes and see the Level II information, you can't trade it electronically. Due to certain structural differences, the NASDAQ prohibits electronic trading in bulletin-board issues. If you *must* buy or sell a bulletin-board stock, you'll have to call your broker. Bulletin-board stocks are easy to identify by the "Kk" indicator circled in Figure 4–2.

Name	Bid	Chg.	Size	#Best		Name	Ask	Chg.	Size	#Best
POOS	4.7500	+.3750	500	0		FLTT	4.8750	+.0000	500	0
HRZG	4.5000	+0	500	0		ALWC	5.0000	+.1250	500	0
WEN	4.5000	+0	500	0		HRZG	5.0625	+0	500	0
NAB	4.3750	+0	500	0		NTE	5.1250	+0	500	0
NTE	4.3750	+0	500	0		SHRP	5.2750	+0	500	0
FLTT	4.3750	-.1250	500	0		WEN	5.2750	+0	500	0
PGON	4.2500	+0	500	0		HLL	5.0075	-.1250	500	0
SHRP	4.1250	+0	500	0		PGON	5.2500	+0	500	0
ALWC	4.1250	+.1250	500	0		GVRC	5.5000	+0	500	0
HLL	4.0625	+.1250	500	0		NAB	7.0000	+0	500	0
GVRC	2.0000	+0	500	0		FLL	7.0000	+0	500	0
FLL	2.0000	+0	500	0		POOG	7.0750	+.3750	500	0
NATC	2.0000	+0	5000	0		NATC	0.0000	+0	0	0

SREP

"Kk" Indicates Bulletin Board Stock

SREP 4.7500 ↑ -.0625 1000 (Kk) 11:39

Bid	4.7500	**Ask**	4.8750	**Vol**	7000
#Bid	0	**#Ask**	0	**Spread**	.1250
High	5.0000	**Low**	4.5000	**Close**	4.8125

Figure 4–2 Bulletin-board stock L2 screen.

Let me stress the critical importance of L2 once more, because you'll have to go through a learning curve to master this important tool. At first, the data seem complex and sometimes bewildering. After some practice and practical experience, you'll get to know the components and their meanings without thinking about it. It's at that point that you're ready to learn how to trade!

Knowing the layout and meaning of the data is one of the first steps to successful trading. Understanding how to interpret, use, and trade on the Level II is the next step.

Time & Sales Screen

Time & sales (T&S) data (see Figure 4–3) are vital to interpreting the trading activity in any stock. Together the T&S screen and the Level II screen form the backbone of direct-access day trading.

'INTEL CORP

Date	Time	Price	Volume	Exch	Type	Bid	BSize	BEx	Ask	ASize	AEx	Cond
3/30/2000	16:10				Best Ask	127 3/16	500	NAS	127 1/2	100	NAS	down
3/30/2000	16:10	128	100	NAS	Irg Trade							
3/30/2000	16:10	127 1/2	100	NAS	Irg Trade							FormT
3/30/2000	16:10				Best Bid	127 3/16	500	NAS	127 1/2	100	NAS	
3/30/2000	16:10				Best Ask	127 3/16	500	NAS	127 3/8	5000	NAS	down
3/30/2000	16:10				Best Bid	127 3/16	500	NAS	127 3/8	5000	NAS	
3/30/2000	16:10				Best Ask	127 3/16	500	NAS	127 3/8	5600	NAS	down
3/30/2000	16:10	127 1/2	100	NAS	Irg Trade							FormT
3/30/2000	16:11				Best Bid	127 5/16	5300	NAS	127 3/8	5600	NAS	
3/30/2000	16:11				Best Ask	127 5/16	5300	NAS	127 9/16	2500	NAS	up
3/30/2000	16:11	127 3/8	600	NAS	Irg Trade							FormT
3/30/2000	16:11	127 3/8	5000	NAS	Irg Trade							FormT
3/30/2000	16:11				Best Bid	127 3/8	300	NAS	127 9/16	2500	NAS	
3/30/2000	16:11				Best Ask	127 3/8	300	NAS	127 9/16	2500	NAS	up
3/30/2000	16:11				Best Bid	127 5/16	5300	NAS	127 9/16	2500	NAS	
3/30/2000	16:11				Best Ask	127 3/8	5300	NAS	127 9/16	2500	NAS	down
3/30/2000	16:11				Best Bid	127 3/8	400	NAS	127 9/16	2500	NAS	
3/30/2000	16:11				Best Ask	127 3/8	400	NAS	127 9/16	2500	NAS	up
3/30/2000	16:11				Best Bid	127 5/16	5300	NAS	127 9/16	2500	NAS	
3/30/2000	16:11				Best Ask	127 3/8	5300	NAS	127 9/16	2500	NAS	down
3/30/2000	16:11				Best Bid	127 3/8	400	NAS	127 9/16	2500	NAS	
3/30/2000	16:11				Best Ask	127 5/16	400	NAS	127 9/16	2500	NAS	up
3/30/2000	16:11				Best Bid	127 5/16	5300	NAS	127 9/16	2500	NAS	
3/30/2000	16:11				Best Ask	127 3/8	5300	NAS	127 9/16	2500	NAS	down
3/30/2000	16:11				Best Bid	127 3/8	500	NAS	127 9/16	2500	NAS	
3/30/2000	16:11				Best Bid	127 3/8	500	NAS	127 9/16	2500	NAS	up
3/30/2000	16:11				Best Ask	127 3/8	500	NAS	127 5/8	1000	NAS	up

Figure 4–3 Intel time & sales (T&S).

I continually monitor the T&S window to help me glean the current action in a stock. The data shown here are usually referred to as "prints." These are the actual trades, normally as they occur, as reported by the clearing firms. Questions such as "Was the last print at the bid, ask, or somewhere in between?" can often help you determine a directional bias for a stock. It can also help you determine if a short-term reversal or "pivot point" is near. Other useful information such as "out-of-sequence" trades can be seen, as well as block trades and trades significantly above or below the current market. For instance, if a trade was above or below the market, was it an actual real-time trade, or was it a print of an earlier transaction? Prints of earlier trades are designated in the type column as "Irg Trade," meaning irregular trade. As seen in the examples below, time & sales offers the trader much more information than the simple "dynamic print ticker."

Intel Time & Sales Window

As you can see in Figure 4–3, most of the columns are easy to understand. For clarity, however, let's go through a few of the more important identifiers in the figure:

- *Trade.* If "Trade" appears under the "Type" column, this indicates that a regular trade occurred at the date, time, price, and lot size reflected in the associated row.
- *Irg Trade.* Again under the "Type" column, this shows an irregular trade. More than likely, an irregular trade is a trade than has been reported out of sequence, or a trade that occurred prior to or after regular trading hours.
- *Exch.* The exchange where the trade occurred. These are again pretty simple: NYS is the New York Stock Exchange, and NAS is the NASDAQ. Regional exchanges may also be shown.
- *Best Bid–Best Ask.* This is also found under the "Type" column. Whenever a market participant displays a price that changes the inside market, "Best Bid" or "Best Ask" will be displayed. Either the price or the size or both have changed.
- *Form T.* A trade that occurs either premarket or postmarket will display Form T.

America Online Time & Sales Window

AOL is a "listed" stock. As you can see in Figure 4–4 the T&S information is very similar to that for Intel. I've noted below the main differences.

- *Bid-Ask.* When a specialist changes his price or size, but no accompanying trade has occurred, you'll see a price accompanied by a "Bid" or "Ask" identifier.
- *Sold.* A trade that occurred 20 minutes or more before the "print."
- *Closing/Opening.* Matched or crossed trades during the opening or closing when the specialist pairs off as many trades as possible. This yields the opening or closing prices for "market-on-open" or "market-on-close" orders.

The 1-Minute Candle Chart   Take a look at the 1-minute chart in Figure 4–5. The 1-minute chart is really the heart of charting for the momentum and market-making strategies described later in this

*AMERICA ONLINE

Date	Time	Price	Volume	Exch	Type	Bid	BSize	BEx	Ask	ASize	AEx	Cond
3/30/2000	16:03				Bid	63 15/16	100	BSE	65 5/16	100	BSE	
3/30/2000	16:03				Ask	63 15/16	100	BSE	65 5/16	100	BSE	
3/30/2000	16:03	64 5/8	2200		Trade							
3/30/2000	16:03	64 5/8	1000		Trade							
3/30/2000	16:04	64 5/8	4000		Trade							
3/30/2000	16:04				Bid	64 9/16	20000	NYS	65 3/16	100	BSE	
3/30/2000	16:04				Ask	64 9/16	20000	NYS	64 11/16	20000	NYS	Closing
3/30/2000	16:04				Bid	63 15/16	500	PSE	64 11/16	20000	NYS	
3/30/2000	16:04				Ask	63 15/16	500	PSE	64 3/4	500	PSE	
3/30/2000	16:04				Best Bid	64 7/16	100	PHS	64 3/4	500	PSE	
3/30/2000	16:04				Best Ask	64 7/16	100	PHS	64 3/4	500	PSE	
3/30/2000	16:04				Bid	63 15/16	100	BSE	64 3/4	500	PSE	
3/30/2000	16:04				Ask	63 15/16	100	BSE	65 1/4	100	BSE	
3/30/2000	16:05	64 5/8	100		Trade							
3/30/2000	16:05	64 5/8	100		Trade							
3/30/2000	16:05	64 3/4	1000		Trade							
3/30/2000	16:05	64 5/8	4900		Trade							
3/30/2000	16:05	64 5/8	500		Trade							
3/30/2000	16:05				Bid	63 15/16	500	PSE	65 1/4	100	BSE	
3/30/2000	16:05				Ask	63 15/16	500	PSE	64 11/16	1100	PSE	
3/30/2000	16:05				Best Bid	64 7/16	100	PHS	64 11/16	1100	PSE	
3/30/2000	16:05				Best Ask	64 7/16	100	PHS	64 11/16	1100	PSE	
3/30/2000	16:05				Bid	63 15/16	100	BSE	64 11/16	1100	PSE	
3/30/2000	16:05				Ask	63 15/16	100	BSE	65 3/16	100	BSE	
3/30/2000	16:08	64 5/8	17500		Trade							
3/30/2000	16:08	64 5/8	200		lrg Trade							Sold
3/30/2000	16:11				Bid	64 7/16	100	NAS	65 3/16	100	BSE	
3/30/2000	16:11				Ask	64 7/16	100	NAS	64 13/16	100	NAS	MMMcl

Figure 4–4 America Online time & sales (T&S).

book. Approximately 70 percent of my entry and exit decisions are based upon the market-making screen, while another 10 to 15 percent of my decision making comes from the daily chart.

  The 1-minute chart I use is overlaid with three studies—a 20-, 50-, and 200-period moving average. We also color the candlesticks

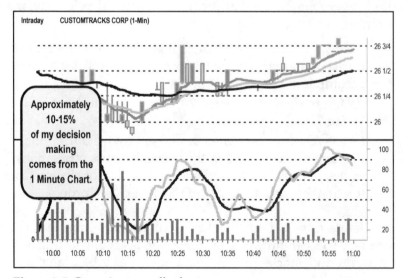

Figure 4–5 One-minute candle chart.

either green for an up candle or red for a down candle. In an environment that requires quick decision making, this makes it easy to discern the difference between an up and a down candle.

In addition, notice that a volume study is included at the bottom of Figure 4–5 with a fast and a slow stochastic. The stochastics are an additional guide to the timing on the entry and exit.

The Daily Chart   The daily candle chart is useful to determine major support and resistance areas. It also clearly shows whether the stock is generally in an uptrend or a downtrend or if it's consolidating. A sample daily chart is given in Figure 4–6. Notice that the same technical setups are used in the daily chart as are used in the 1-minute chart. This is because these moving averages (20, 50, and 200) and the stochastics tend to be good, that is, reliable across various time frames. I've found them to be just as useful on a 1-minute chart as they are on a daily chart.

Broad Market Charts   Broad market charts are great for an overall sense of market direction. Figure 4–7 shows the Dow Jones Industrials. The Dow Jones Industrials are the most commonly quoted index worldwide. A common symbol for many data feeds is $INDU. Figure 4–8 shows the NASDAQ composite. On most data

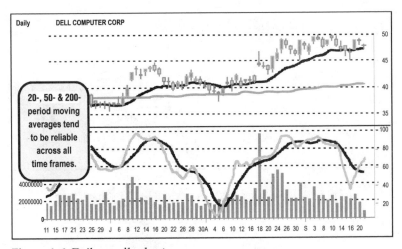

Figure 4–6 Daily candle chart.

feeds, the symbol is $COMPX, or sometimes it's $COMP.X. Again, on all these charts, consider using the same moving averages and the same stochastics so that they're consistent. When you do that, you won't have to stop and reflect on what the specific meanings of the indicators are, because they will be consistent across time frames and symbols. You'll have a congruent foundation to work from.

When you are looking at a particular stock, you'll use these charts to discern when that stock is strong or weak against a broader market. Let's say you are trading Intel. The NASDAQ is capitalization-weighted, and Intel is a very large-capped stock on the NASDAQ. Intel should be moving with the NASDAQ, or you have a major divergence. Let's say the NASDAQ composite is going up, but Intel is down a half point on the day. It doesn't need to be down a lot, just a little, especially if the major average is up strongly. The point is that on that day, Intel would be very weak against the NASDAQ composite indicator. When you see that kind of divergence, one strategy might be to short the highs on Intel. When we get into the trading chapters, we'll discuss these concepts a bit more thoroughly.

When you keep your symbols in a minder window, you can simply drag the symbol up into a chart and get a very quick look at the market's behavior. If you only have one or two monitors, this is

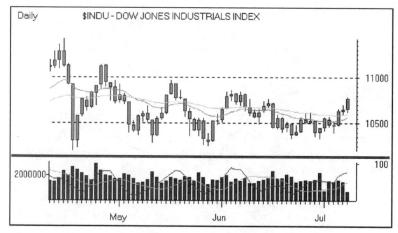

Figure 4–7 Dow Industrials daily.

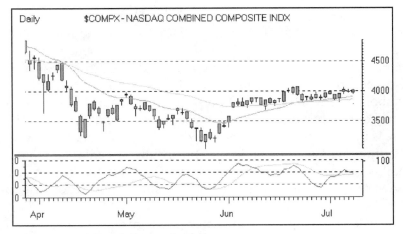

Figure 4–8 NASDAQ Composite daily.

an easy way to organize your layout just to get a quick glance at where the market is at any given time.

Figure 4–9 shows a broad market window setup that I keep with the S&P futures, $TICK, $TRIN, and Dow Industrials. For the futures, I keep both the Globex session and the normal CME ses-

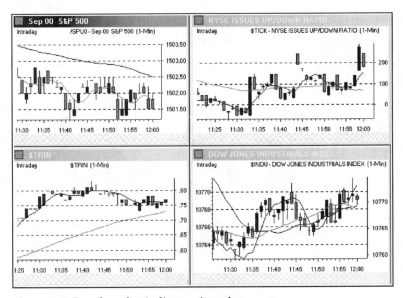

Figure 4–9 Broad market indicators intraday.

sion symbols. In addition, I keep the NASDAQ futures symbol, and I keep the New York TICK and the TRIN. I keep these in a special minder window showing the last price, the change, the percent change, the high, the low, the open, and the close from yesterday. I also keep the total volume, which is useful for individual stock symbols but, with the exception of the Dow Industrials, is not an accurate number for the broad market indicators. Again, the idea here is that at a glance I can know where the market is. And by simply dragging a symbol up into a chart, either a 1-minute or a daily chart, I can see where the market has been over the last few days and where it has been over the last 5 minutes, 15 minutes, or hour.

TICK Indicator   The TICK indicator (see Figure 4–10) measures the number of advancing versus the number of declining stocks on the New York Stock Exchange (not the NASDAQ) at any given moment. $TICK is frequently the symbol on data feeds. The TICK baseline is zero, meaning that advancing and declining stocks at that moment are equal.

When the TICK is largely positive, say plus 500, meaning we've got 500 more issues trading up than we do down, then we would expect to see the broader market moving up too. The con-

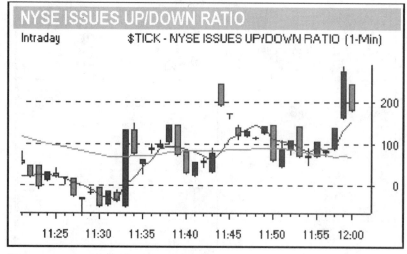

Figure 4–10 NYSE $TICK indicator intraday.

verse is also true—if the TICK is negative 500, we would expect to
see that the broader Dow measure is down.

TICK extremes are often useful as a reversal indicator. For
instance, if we were to see the TICK at a plus 800 to a plus 1,000, or
a minus 800 to a minus 1,000—conditions that are rarely seen in the
marketplace—then we have an excellent chance of a market reversal, at least in the short term. Thus, if you see the TICK up near plus
800 to plus 1,000, begin to look for the market to sell off in the next
5 to 15 minutes.

The Arms Index   The Arms Index, also known as the TRIN
($TRIN) (see Figure 4–11), was named after its inventor, Richard
Arms. In this case, the formula involves both the volume and the
price of advancing and declining issues. The baseline of the TRIN
is 1, meaning total quiescence. The market is moving totally sideways. In a strongly positive market, the TRIN would be a high plus
number, while in a very negative market, the TRIN would be a very
low number or even a number that approaches zero.

The point that I really want to make about the TRIN is that it's
a very good contraindicator. Like the TICK, when the TRIN reaches

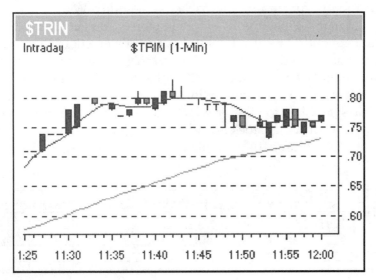

Figure 4–11 The Arms Index ($TRIN) intraday.

extremes, a market reversal is indicated. It would be an aberration for the TRIN to move beyond a positive 3, for instance. So when I see the TRIN move this high, I might prepare myself mentally and begin to look for good short opportunities. The converse is also true; a TRIN near zero may clue me to look for short-term long plays.

Consider configuring your screen like that shown in Figure 4–9 so that you can see all the broad market indicators at the same time. This will keep current market conditions in the forefront of your thoughts throughout the trading day.

Order Entry Screen   It's very important that you understand the order entry screen. Order entry screens are specific to the trading software that you use. Misinterpreting the information on these screens can cause immediate damage to your trading capital. Carefully review any and all documentation covering the order entry methods for your particular trading platform.

Boomers and Busters   The last window I use to sort my stocks is a filter for boomers and busters. I'm looking for stocks that are up 20 percent or more on the day (boomers) or down 20 percent or more on the day (busters). I sort the symbols according to total volume, because low-volume stocks can easily be boomers or busters and yet be unsuitable for trading due to lack of liquidity. With low-volume stocks, I may not get my fill—or even worse, I do get filled but then cannot get out! Thus, even if a stock is up 20 percent or more on the day, if it has traded only 10,000 shares, I'm going to ignore that stock as a potential trade because there's not enough liquidity in it.

After I do my filtering to find the daily boomers and busters, I put the symbols into minder windows to show me throughout the day how a particular stock is trading. In Figures 4–12 and 4–13, you can see the column titles, which are fairly self-explanatory. The

Boomers									
Symbol	Bid	Ask	Last	Change	Net Chg. %	High	Low	Open	Tot. Vol.
XOMA	7	7 1/32	7	+2 3/4	+64.71	7 5/16	4 31/32	5 1/8	12264500
OAOT	5 15/16	5 31/32	5 15/16	+2 1/8	+55.74	6 1/4	5 1/2	5 3/4	2202000
ATON	131 1/8	131 1/16	131 1/64	+30 5/64	+29.80	134 3/16	111	112 31/32	4233800
PBSC	22 1/4	22 3/8	22 3/8	+4 1/8	+22.60	23 1/4	19 1/4	19 3/8	933300
APCS	22 9/16	22 5/8	22 1/2	+4 1/16	+22.03	23 7/8	18 1/4	18 7/16	328900

Figure 4–12 Boomers watch list.

Busters								
Symbol	Bid	Ask	Last	Change	Net Chg. %	High	Low	Open	Tot. Vol.
ISCA	34 5/16	34 3/8	34 3/8	-8 5/8	-20.06	36 1/16	34	35 5/16	3584600
ASPT	19 7/8	19 15/16	19 15/16	-23 15/16	-54.56	21 5/8	19 7/16	21 1/8	14168200
PCLE	9 15/32	9 1/2	9 1/2	-13 1/8	-58.01	10 1/4	8 13/16	9 7/8	16998000

Figure 4–13 Busters watch list.

most important column to me is the one showing the net percent change. This is the change from the previous day's close (normal trading session, not the extended hours) and tells me at a glance which stocks are up or down by the largest percentages.

KNOWLEDGE KEYS

✓ Your choice of a computer can have a dramatic impact on your trading profits.

✓ One of the biggest challenges you'll face is finding and maintaining a superfast and reliable connection to the Internet.

✓ There is a huge difference between the quality and reliability of Internet service providers. Choosing an inexpensive solution can cost you big money.

✓ Don't underestimate the technology risks (and inherent downtime) involved when trading. Have backup systems and a plan to deal with technology risks.

✓ Use only an "industrial-strength" trading platform. There is a real difference between competing products.

CALLS TO ACTION

✓ If you don't have a computer that meets minimum direct-access trading requirements, get one! Then set it up according to our recommendations.

✓ Research the best broadband connectivity available to you. Get it installed and tested.

✓ Select a high-quality Internet service provider. The provider may be the same company that provides your broadband, but will not necessarily be. Make sure your primary connection is fully operational.

✓ Select and install a backup ISP.

✓ Select and install your direct-access trading software. Test it for proper functionality.

✓ Take the time to totally understand the operation of your trading platform.

✓ Set up your trading screens according to the recommendations in this chapter.

✓ Understand both the function and the interpretation of the trading screens.

✓ Review, understand, and comprehend the operation of the NASDAQ Level II montage. This is the heart of direct-access trading.

✓ Review, understand, and comprehend the operation of the time & sales screens. This is the lifeblood of direct-access trading.

✓ Determine all your technology risks and develop backup systems and backup plans to deal with a crisis should one occur.

## CHAPTER 5

Understanding the Golden Rule of Trading—R Multiples and Expectancy

When you make the finding yourself—even if you're the last person on Earth to see the light—you'll never forget it.

Carl Sagan

In order to be successful as a trader, you must make several paradigm shifts, or major changes, in your thinking. It means you must get out of the box you are in (i.e., your current perspectives) and determine what is possible from other perspectives. If you understand the power of paradigm shifts, you can begin to understand what it is to be a genius. You can create money out of nothing. You can accomplish miracles. You can become a very successful electronic day trader.

The first one of these shifts that you must make is to understand that *making money in the market has nothing to do with predicting the market or picking the right stock.* Instead, one of the major keys to trading success is the *golden rule of trading*—cutting your losses short and letting your profits run. If you understand this rule, along with the powers of expectancy, opportunity, and position sizing, then you can earn a tremendous living as an electronic day trader. Furthermore, you can probably do it while seldom having a losing month. It *is* possible, and you'll learn the logic behind it in Chapters 6 and 13.

THE GOLDEN RULE OF TRADING—CUT YOUR LOSSES SHORT AND LET YOUR PROFITS RUN!

Most people do just the opposite of the golden rule. They allow their losses to grow, hoping those losses will turn around and become profits. For example, if you hate to take a loss when you are down by $1, then it will be even more difficult when you are down $2, and still more difficult at $5. Many short-term traders turn into long-term investors because they cannot take a loss.

Similarly, these same people cut their profits short just to be sure that they keep them. In other words, as soon as they have a profit, they want to take it. Thus, they might buy a stock at $50 and sell at $50.50 just to be sure they have a profit. So most people's behavior is to let losses run and cut profits short. These people might end up being right 60 percent of the time or more, but they seldom make money from this venture. Why? The reason is because their net losses are greater than their net profits.

If you are like most people, you are probably thinking, "How can I make money if I am not right and if I don't predict the market?" We are not talking about perfectionism here, which is the primary focus of most traders—being right most of the time. Instead, we are talking about making a lot of money when you are right, instead of trying to make money on every trade.

Let us give you an example of how it works. One way to trade is to look for the fastest movers, stocks that are making new highs and taking off dramatically. You buy these stocks with the hope that they will move 10 to 20 points (or more) in your favor during the day. However, as soon as one of them starts to turn into a loss, you get out immediately. Note that this strategy is similar to a momentum technique described in Chapter 10.

Are you predicting the market in this example? No, you are not. *You've simply selected stocks that have some potential for a huge move.* In fact, if you find one that has such a move in your favor 20 percent of the time, you'll probably be very happy with your trading.[1] As a result, you are not predicting anything, since you only expect to meet your objectives 20 percent of the time or less. With this kind of trading, you're not even "right" most of the time. Instead, what you get from this kind of trading is steady profits. Very few traders actually trade strategies that are only 20 percent accurate. However, we hope that this illustration will help you adjust your mindset, your beliefs about trading, away from high accuracy and toward high expectancy.

To understand how these high-expectancy profits are achieved, you must understand three cardinal principles of good trading: (1) knowing your risk when you enter the market, (2) making your profits large multiples of that initial risk, and (3) knowing the expectancy of your system. Actually, there is a fourth principle—sound position sizing—but we'll save that one for Chapter 6.

KNOWING YOUR INITIAL RISK: BEGIN WITH THE END IN MIND

When you enter the trade, you must know the point at which you will get out to protect your capital. While all traders and investors should follow this rule, it is especially important for day traders. You must determine your initial stop-loss point when you get into the market. This point is your initial risk. *This principle is so important that if you cannot follow it, then you might as well give up the idea of electronic day trading right away.*

We will define your initial risk as being 1 R no matter where you set your stop. If you set your stop at 5 points, then 5 points is 1 R. If you set your stop at 2 points, then 2 points is 1 R. If you set your stop at ½ point, then ½ point is 1 R. Once again, the idea here is to always have a stop when you enter the market. This stop point is your 1-R risk. While this stop may be a mental stop or one actually placed in the market via your EDAT software, you want to make sure you obey that stop and you don't take 2-R or 5-R risks if you can avoid it.

Let's look at an example. Suppose you buy 100 shares of JDSU at 120. The stock is moving up quickly, and you expect it to move at least 10 more points today. You decide to sell the stock if it moves against you by 1 point. The bid-ask spread is currently ½ point. Now let's think about your situation here. Your stop loss is 1 point. If you get stopped out, you will lose $100 plus commissions and slippage—$1 times 100 shares. Thus, your risk, R, is $1 per share.

You might believe that a $1 stop is ridiculous when you only have a ½-point bid-ask spread to begin with, because you could easily stop out. However, this thought has to do with the belief of not wanting to be wrong. It has no meaning if your profits sometimes can be transformed into very large R multiples of your initial risk.

Think about the following example: What would get you wetter—99 drops of rain or jumping in the swimming pool? Jumping in the swimming pool because it's a huge experience of wetness. What you want as a trader is a huge experience of winning. You can have a lot of little "raindrop" losses if you have a "swimming pool" experience of winning.

Making Your Profit a Large R Multiple

One reason for having tight stop-loss points is that they make huge gains possible, with respect to your initial risk. For example, notice that your potential gain on the stock in our example is $10 per share. Since your probable loss is only $1, your potential gain is 10 times as big—or 10 times R, or 10 R. Let's say you took your minimum loss five straight times. At this point, you will have taken five 1-R losses, with a total loss of 5 R. On the sixth trade, your trade takes off as expected and you obtain your 10-R profit. What is the net result? You have a total profit of 5 R. You've been wrong five trades out of six, and yet you still have a total profit of 5 R. If you could do this twice each day, you would have a total profit of 10 R—despite being correct on only 18 percent of your trades. Thus, if R is equal to $1 per share, you'll make $10 per share per day.[2] Think you could live with that?

Using this example, let's restate the golden rule of trading in terms of R multiples.

The golden rule of trading is to keep losses at a level of 1 R as often as possible and to make profits that are high-R multiples.

Notice that in our original example, 1 R was $1 per share and a 10-R gain was $10 per share. If your initial risk was $2 per share, then you would have had to produce a $20-per-share profit to earn a 10-R profit. On the other hand, if your initial risk was only ⅜ of a point, then you would only need a $3.75 move in order to make a 10-R gain. So the farther your stops are placed from your entry point, the harder it is to make large-R gains. And the tighter your stops (i.e., cutting your losses really short), the easier it is to have large-R gains.

If you understand the golden rule of trading in terms of R multiples, then you have made an immense breakthrough that most day traders fail to make. It means that you no longer have to focus on predicting the markets, picking the right stocks, and/or being right. Instead, it means that you can now focus on your exits. It means that you can now determine how good your system is in terms of expectancy and that you can make money through the proper application of position sizing. It means that you have a chance at making a consistent three-digit rate of return in the market.

If you understand the importance of large-R-multiple trades, then you can understand why good trading has little to do with predicting the markets. Yet most people believe that successful trading comes from successful prediction. Traders are always asking, "What is the market going to do?"

Wall Street analysts are paid six-figure salaries to simply predict the earnings and future price of stocks. Yet I've never met an analyst that I would consider a top trader. In fact, without having at least some of the skills covered in this book (understanding expectancy, position sizing, and judgmental biases to name a few), most of them would fail miserably. If analytical or predictive skills were important to trading, you would expect most of these analysts to do very well in the trading arena. Yet they don't. The reason is simple. You don't have to predict the market to make money. Instead, making money comes from controlling your exits and using logical position sizing.

Take another look at the example given above. You made a 5-R total profit after being right only one time out of six trades. This had nothing to do with predicting that the stock was going to go higher. At best, you just picked an overall stock that was in an uptrend and assumed that the overall trend would continue.

Does this mean that you don't focus on entry at all? Of course not! When you momentum-trade, you want to look for stocks that have huge potential moves. These might be stocks that are going up with huge momentum, or they might be stocks that are just bouncing off the bottom of their trading range. When you buy a stock like that, you are not predicting the markets at all. You're just saying that this stock is a good candidate to have a big move. However, that's not *predicting* when you are right 50 percent of the time or less.

At this point, you might be saying to yourself, "How can I make money on a stock if I'm not right more than 50 percent of the time?" It's simple; what you are looking to do is make money overall. You want to know for certain that you'll make money after 10 trades or, at least, after 50 trades. *You don't need to make money on the trade you are taking right now.* You simply need to focus on your rules for exiting the trade, whether it is profitable or not, according to your rules for losses and profits. The need to make money on every trade is a sure-fire path to disaster. Instead, to make consistent profits you simply need a trading system with a solid positive expectancy.

KNOWING THE EXPECTANCY OF YOUR SYSTEM—WILL THIS DOG HUNT? OR WHAT KIND OF RETURN CAN YOU EXPECT FOR YOUR RISK?

What is this thing called expectancy? It just sounds like a complex mathematical term. How is it useful to me as an electronic day trader? How do I calculate it? And why should I bother to calculate it at all? Simply put, expectancy is your average return per trade. In the previous example the expectancy would be 0.83, which is merely the 5-R net return divided by the 6 trades you took. This tells you that a system like this will return 83 cents for every dollar risked. (Of course 6 trades is hardly adequate to calculate an accurate expectancy, but we'll get to that.)

This means that expectancy is a way to compare the merits of various trading systems that might fit you. It's that simple. A higher-expectancy system will generally return more money than a low-expectancy system. And the expectancy of the system must be positive in order to make money, because negative expectancy systems by definition only lose money.

Your system's expectancy tells you how much you can expect to make on the average, with respect to your initial risk, over many trades with your system. For example, a system with an expectancy of 0.5 will return 0.5 R per trade, as an average, over many trades. Similarly, a system with an expectancy of 0.8 will return 0.8 R per trade, on average, over many trades. Thus, over the same number of trades, system 2 is four times as good as system 1. It's useful information to have. Don't you agree?

DEFINING AND CALCULATING EXPECTANCY (RELAX, THE MATH'S EASY)

Expectancy can be defined and calculated three different ways.

Method 1

In its most simplified form, expectancy is the *probability of winning* times the *average amount won* less the *probability of losing* times the *average amount lost*. For example, if you have a system that wins 60 percent of the time that simply wins or loses 1 R, then it would be simple to calculate the expectancy of the system using this method. You'd just plug in the numbers and get the expectancy: 0.60 (probability of winning) times 1 R minus 0.40 (probability of losing) times 1 R = 0.20 expectancy.

Thus, in this example, you'd have an expectancy of 0.20. This means that you'd make on average 20 cents per dollar risked. That is, if you risk a dollar, you'd keep your dollar and make 20 cents on average over many, many trades.

An expectancy of 0.20 also means that you'd make 0.2 R per trade on average over many trades. Thus, if you happened to risk 1 percent of your equity per trade, you'd make 0.2 percent of your equity per trade, on average, over many trades.

Most trading is not as simple as winning or losing 1 R and being right 60 percent of the time. Instead, in real trading you tend to have a wide distribution of positive and negative R multiples. Thus, you need a better way to calculate the expectancy of your system. So we devised Method 2.

Method 2

You may also calculate expectancy by multiplying *each R multiple* by its *probability of occurrence* and then summing all the *products*. Of course, to do this, the probabilities of your R multiples must add up to 100 percent. That is, you must account for every R multiple (that is, every trade).

For example, suppose you have a system that gives you the following distribution of R multiples over 100 trades[3]:

- 1% 30 R
- 2% 20 R
- 5% 10 R
- 12% 5 R
- 15% 2 R

- 10% 1 R
- 35% –1 R
- 15% –2 R
- 5% –5 R

Notice that all the percentages add up to 100 percent. You have 45 percent winners and 55 percent losers.

Now let's multiply each R multiple by its probability:

$$30 \times 0.01 = 0.3$$
$$20 \times 0.02 = 0.4$$
$$10 \times 0.05 = 0.5$$
$$5 \times 0.12 = 0.6$$
$$2 \times 0.15 = 0.3$$
$$1 \times 0.10 = 0.1$$
$$-1 \times 0.35 = -0.35$$
$$-2 \times 0.15 = -0.30$$
$$-5 \times 0.05 = -0.25$$

When we add all of these up (i.e., subtracting the losers from the winners), we end up with a total expectancy of 1.3. That means that, on average, over a long number of trades, you'll make 1.3 R per trade (or $1.30 per dollar risked).

Notice that this system is right only 45 percent of the time, while the last system we talked about was right 60 percent of the time. Yet this system makes a $1.30 per dollar risked while the other system, the one that was "right" more often, only made 20 cents per dollar risked. Think about that—could you afford to be wrong more often? Especially if it paid better? Are you starting to understand why many successful traders say, "Would you rather be right or make money?"

Method 2, though, has some drawbacks when it comes to analyzing real trading. Most trades are not nice, whole-number R multiples like 10 R. Instead, the R multiple might be something like 8.31. Thus, if you have 100 real trades, you might have 80 different R multiples. How do you decide where to put a 7.8 R-multiple trade? Is it more like a 5 R or a 10 R? And if you categorize it as either one, aren't you losing too much information?

Yes, you are losing a lot of information. You might be willing to do that just to simplify things. However, if you'd like to be more accurate, then you'll need to use the third method to calculate expectancy. In addition, methods 1 and 2 both require you to filter out the effects of position sizing by dividing your actual profit or loss by the number of shares purchased in order to get your R multiple.

Method 3

Method 3 allows you to calculate the ongoing expectancy of your system without much hassle. I recommend that all day traders calculate their ongoing expectancy in this manner. It simply requires a spreadsheet and a few automatic calculations. You can do it at the end of each day.

Keep a daily spreadsheet with some simple information on it. You only need five basic columns: (1) an identifier column—what trade was it and when; (2) the number of shares you are buying; (3) your entry risk, which is equal to the difference between the entry price and the initial stop times the number of shares purchased; (4) the total gain or loss when you sold the stock (yes, you can figure in commissions); and (5) the R multiple, which is column 4 divided by column 3. You might want other columns such as the entry price and the exit price and the % risk taken on the trade. However, these columns are not critical to obtain the R multiples and the expectancy of your trades. Table 5–1 shows such a table composed of scalping trades taken by Brian June on a single stock. These trades come from the strategy similar to the one suggested in Chapter 9.

When you do such an exercise, you gain incredible information. *First, you force yourself to write down and know where your initial stop is.* There is no cheating when you do this. You must know where your stop is. Just doing this exercise alone will save you money because it will force you to have a stop and it will show you whether you are paying attention to it or not. If most of your trades are showing up on the spreadsheet as less than 1 R, you are paying attention. If most of your trades are larger than 1 R, then you are not paying attention to the stop or you are trading instruments that are so volatile that you cannot possibly expect to get out at those stop levels.

The second thing this exercise forces you to do is *define what 1 R is in each trade in the simplest way possible.* You're asking yourself, "What is my total, worst-case risk going into this trade?" and you're

TABLE 5-1

A Set of Scalping Trades

Trade	Ticker	Strategy	Qty	Price	Initial Risk	Gain/Loss	R Multiple	% Wins
1	XCIT	Short	400	44.375	100	550.00	5.50	1.000
2	XCIT	Short	400	40.688	100	125.00	1.25	1.000
3	XCIT	Short	400	40.188	100	400.00	4.00	1.000
4	XCIT	Short	400	40.375	100	200.00	2.00	1.000
5	XCIT	Short	400	34.500	100	275.00	2.75	1.000
6	XCIT	Long	500	35.500	125	-156.25	-1.25	0.833
7	XCIT	Short	500	28.500	125	1,906.25	15.25	0.857
8	XCIT	Short	500	30.125	125	-531.25	-4.25	0.750
9	XCIT	Short	500	26.625	125	-125.00	-1.00	0.667
10	XCIT	Short	300	23.563	75	150.00	2.00	0.700
11	XCIT	Long	400	28.000	100	125.00	1.25	0.727
12	XCIT	Long	400	30.000	100	-450.00	-4.50	0.667
13	XCIT	Long	961	26.297	240.25	480.50	2.00	0.692
14	XCIT	Short	400	27.625	100	-200.00	-2.00	0.643
15	XCIT	Long	1,000	27.813	250	-62.50	-0.25	0.600
16	XCIT	Long	300	41.906	75	-121.88	-1.63	0.563
17	XCIT	Short	500	40.625	125	31.25	0.25	0.588
18	XCIT	Short	500	42.000	125	-31.25	-0.25	0.556
19	XCIT	Short	300	37.563	75	0.00	0.00	0.526
20	XCIT	Short	500	38.496	125	-60.55	-0.48	0.500
21	XCIT	Short	300	35.125	75	9.38	0.13	0.524

Trade	Ticker	Strategy	Qty	Price	Initial Risk	Gain/Loss	R Multiple	% Wins
22	XCIT	Short	300	34.000	75	412.50	5.50	0.545
23	XCIT	Short	300	33.250	75	−93.75	−1.25	0.522
24	XCIT	Long	300	37.875	75	−37.50	−0.50	0.500
25	XCIT	Long	400	29.188	100	175.00	1.75	0.520
26	XCIT	Long	400	28.313	100	200.00	2.00	0.538
27	XCIT	Long	400	29.484	100	−193.75	−1.94	0.519
28	XCIT	Long	400	31.188	100	−200.00	−2.00	0.500
29	XCIT	Short	100	35.063	25	−37.50	−1.50	0.483
30	XCIT	Long	400	33.813	100	−200.00	−2.00	0.467
31	XCIT	Long	400	33.000	100	75.00	0.75	0.484
32	XCIT	Short	500	34.063	125	125.00	1.00	0.500
33	XCIT	Long	500	35.625	125	125.00	1.00	0.515
34	XCIT	Short	500	35.125	125	156.25	1.25	0.529
35	XCIT	Long	500	35.563	125	187.50	1.50	0.543
36	XCIT	Short	500	33.875	125	281.25	2.25	0.556
37	XCIT	Short	600	32.188	150	262.50	1.75	0.568
38	XCIT	Short	450	34.000	112.5	84.38	0.75	0.579
39	XCIT	Long	600	34.125	150	150.00	1.00	0.590
40	XCIT	Short	500	33.184	125	−169.92	−1.36	0.575
41	XCIT	Long	500	44.625	125	0.00	0.00	0.561
Expectancy							0.75	
Total profit/loss						3,815.66		

writing it down on paper. Again, this value is the *entry price* less the *stop price* multiplied by the *total number of shares* purchased. Here 1 R is combined with position sizing, but it is also included in the profit or loss, and so position sizing cancels out.

Third, this exercise forces you to *calculate your R multiple for each trade*. When you close out the trade, you compare it with the initial risk. Is it bigger or smaller than the initial risk—and by what magnitude? When you look at this information, it can be very valuable. What you actually have is an ever-growing sample of the R-multiple distribution of your system. This is very useful, and as we will see in Chapter 6, it also allows you to simulate your system.

Last, this exercise *provides an easy way to calculate the expectancy of your system on an ongoing basis.* You simply add up your *R multiples for all your trades* and divide the total by the *number of trades.* The resulting value is the current expectancy of your system. It's easy to calculate, and by doing this exercise you'll know where you stand every day. You'll know the expectancy of your system—how much you'll make per trade on average as a function of your initial risk—and you'll know why it changes.

When Brian first explained his system to me, he described it as a 60 percent system that risks $\frac{1}{16}$ of a point on 1,000 shares to gain $\frac{1}{16}$ of a point—in other words, a 60 percent system with winners and losers that are both 1 R. He even wrote an article in our newsletter, *Market Mastery,* describing it as such. And the fact that the distribution of his R multiples was quite different from his target again shows why this is such an important exercise. Many traders don't understand the expectancy of their strategies, and they find out the systems are actually breakeven or have a negative expectancy when closely examined. Brian was probably being overly conservative in the original characterization of his strategy (which is the opposite of the tack taken by most traders!).

While he was right about the system being correct 60 percent of the time, he was wrong about the R multiples. Half his profit comes from one single trade. And although only 41 trades are given in the sample, I expect that the sample is pretty typical of his trading.

There are several other interesting pieces of information in the data. Notice the losses on trades 27 through 30. We have four losers in a row,[4] all of which are 1.5 R or bigger. You also have six losers in eight trades. These are nasty contingencies that one might have to contend with while trading such a system, even though the system has a reliability of 56 percent.

The losses of 2 R and greater were all *psychological mistakes* in which the author did not take his stops in hopes that the trade would turn around. This is also good to know, because you can potentially eliminate them and improve your expectancy dramatically.

The expectancy of the system is 0.75, which is excellent. You get to make, on average, 0.75 times your risk for every trade you make. Notice how easily expectancy is calculated when done in this manner.

Last, let's look at a distribution of the R multiples. They are given in Table 5–2. Notice that five of the losing trades, over 10 percent, have a negative R multiple of 2 or more. Fortunately, ten winners have R multiples of 2 or more, and six of those are bigger than 2 R. This tells you a lot about the strategy.

Let's also look at a sample of R multiples from a momentum strategy similar to one we'll be describing in Chapter 10. Again, these are real trades made using this kind of strategy. These are shown in Table 5–3.

Notice that in this particular set, there are no negative R multiples of 2 or worse, which usually means bad gaps against you or psychological mistakes. In addition, in this set there are 11 winners (52 percent) and 10 losers. However, at least 7 of the winners (63 percent) are 2 R or bigger. None of the losers is bigger than 1.28. And notice that the expectancy of this set of trades is nearly twice the size of the scalping trades.

The expectancy of this system, at least what we can ascertain of it from this small sample, is a very nice 1.29. This means that for every trade, on average, you will gain 1.29 times your initial risk. This, of course, is an average over many trades.

Also notice that the largest entry risk taken is $305. If this were on a $50,000 account, it would mean that the trader managing this account never took an initial risk bigger than 0.6 percent of her account. This is outstanding risk control for this type of trading. But notice that she never purchased more than 65 shares so that she could keep her risk level low.

TABLE 5 – 2

R Multiples Sorted

15.25
5.50
5.50
4.00
2.75
2.25
2.00
2.00
2.00
2.00
1.75
1.75
1.50
1.25
1.25
1.25
1.00
1.00
1.00
0.75
0.75
0.25
0.13
0.00
0.00
−0.25
−0.25
−0.48
−0.50
−1.00
−1.25
−1.25
−1.36
−1.50
−1.63
−1.94
−2.00
−2.00
−2.00
−4.25
−4.50

Total expectancy = 0.75

TABLE 5–3

Momentum Trade R Multiples

Shares	Trade #	Symbol	Price	Stop	Entry Risk	Gain/Loss	R Multiple	R Multiples Sorted
50	21	CHKP	196⅝	191¼	270	–281.25	–1.04	7.34
55	20	SONE	138⁹⁄₁₆	133	305.93	–357	–1.17	6.18
53	19	HGSI	188⅙	183	270	–429	–0.16	6.00
50	18	CKFR	94½	90	225	287.5	1.27	4.38
50	17	CREE	191¹¹⁄₁₆	188	184	–43.5	–0.23	2.94
45	16	INFY	260	255	225	1,350	6.00	2.18
55	15	INFY	627	623	220	440	2.00	2.00
60	14	INSP	194³⁄₁₆	190	251.25	–251.25	–1.00	1.81
47	13	CREE	150⁷⁄₁₆	147	164.5	358.37	2.18	1.27
55	12	GSPN	222	218	220	–265	–1.20	0.50
50	11	INSP	183.56	181	100	–128.125	–1.28	0.37
60	10	BVSN	164	160	240	90	0.37	–0.16
65	9	GSPN	210⅞	207	195	–70	–0.35	–0.23
50	8	CREE	147	144	150	–175	–1.16	–0.34
50	7	GSPN	178⁵⁄₁₆	174	215.62	634.375	2.94	–0.35
55	6	WVCM	127½	125	137.5	68.75	0.50	–1.00
48	5	INSP	152⁵⁄₁₆	148	207	1,281	6.18	–1.04
45	4	SNDK	145	142	180	–61.87	–0.34	–1.16
45	3	TXN	135	131	180	326.25	1.81	–1.17
30	2	GSPN	161⅝	157	120	881.25	7.34	–1.20
50	1	HLIT	111½	106	225	987.5	4.38	–1.28
Expectancy							1.29	1.29
Total profit/loss						4,643		

Our sample represents about a month of trading, so this trader made 9.3 percent in a month while never risking more than 0.6 percent of her account for any one trade. This shows the power of position sizing, which we'll discuss more extensively in Chapter 6.

THE OPPORTUNITY FACTOR

Expectancy is not the only factor in determining how good your system is. Your system's profitability also depends upon how many trading opportunities it gives you in a specific time frame. For example, suppose one system gives you 0.3 R per trade while another system gives you 1.2 R per trade. You would assume, just by expectancy, that system 2 was about 4 times as good as system 1. This is actually a correct assumption over the same number of trades—that is, over 1,000 trades, system 2 is four times better than system 1.

However, the missing factor is the number of trades per given time frame. Suppose system 1 gives you 50 trades per day, while system 2 gives you only 5 trades per day. You need to multiply the expectancy times the number of trades in a particular time period to determine how much the two systems will make. For example, system 1 will generate an average of 15 R each day (i.e., 0.3 times 50), while system 2 will generate an average of 6 R each day (i.e., 1.2 times 5). Given these conditions, system 1 will actually generate 2½ times as much profit each day as system 2, despite having an expectancy that's only ¼ as big.

As an electronic day trader, you'll have a great advantage over most other traders simply because of the potential number of trades you can generate—your opportunity is huge! For example, if you could duplicate system 2, making 6 R each day on average, you'd seldom have a losing day, much less a losing week. And as you'll see from Chapter 6 on position sizing, if R represents 0.25 percent of your equity (i.e., 0.0025), you'd have a daily gain in your account of 1.5 percent per day. Think about what that would mean on a yearly basis!

Is this possible? You've just seen how it's possible from real trading data. Is it likely to occur? There will be limits to how much size you can trade, thus restricting your ultimate growth. (But I think we'd all like to worry about how to continue to grow after we exceed

$10 million in trading profits per year!) In addition, as illustrated in Chapters 11 and 13, psychological factors can stop you in your tracks. If you make mistakes, your expectancy will probably become negative. And that's where the dark side of opportunity shows up. Negative expectancy with a lot of opportunity behind it can totally wipe out an account. And day traders, more than anyone else, have the chance (and unfortunately the historical tendency) to overtrade. Once again, the importance of knowing yourself and having and following a written trading plan comes to light! Preparation takes your positive expectancy system and puts it into a framework that changes trading opportunity (or frequency) from a dreaded enemy to an amazing ally!

KNOWLEDGE KEYS

✓ Making money in the market has nothing to do with predicting the market or picking the right stock.

✓ The golden rule of trading is: Cut your losses short and let your profits run.

✓ When you enter a trade, you must know the point at which you will get out to protect your capital.

✓ The golden rule of trading restated in terms of R multiples is: Keep losses at a level of 1 R as often as possible and make profits that are high-R multiples.

✓ You don't need to make money on the trade you are taking right now to make money in the markets.

✓ Expectancy tells you how much you can expect to make with your system, on average, per dollar risked, over many trades.

CALLS TO ACTION

✓ Know what your exit is before you enter your trades.

✓ Review your trading strategy to determine which method you should use to calculate its expectancy.

✓ Calculate the expectancy of your strategy as you know it today (using your trading log or back testing).

✓ Calculate the profit of your strategy per day, week, or month using its expectancy multiplied by its trading opportunity.

✓ Keep a log of your trades so that you can calculate your R multiples and expectancy.

NOTES

1. You might enter the same stock three or four times in the same day in an attempt to do this.
2. The exact amount represented by R will vary from trade to trade since it depends on your initial risk setting. In Chapter 6, you'll learn how, through position sizing, you can equate your initial risk despite having R be different for different trades.
3. Using 100 trades will give you a good sample of your universe of possible R multiples. Generally, the more trades you have, the more representative your sample will be of your R-multiple population.
4. We could easily have seven to eight losers in a row in a big enough set of trades.

CHAPTER 6

Position Sizing

The Key That Makes It All Work for You

I took the one [road] less traveled by, and that has made all the difference.

Robert Frost

Position sizing is the most critical part of your system. It makes the difference between making and losing money or between no significant losses and huge losses. Consequently, it is a topic that you must understand as a trader.

I generally play a game in my workshops to illustrate the importance of position sizing. The participants and I simulate a trading system that is right 60 percent of the time and wrong 40 percent of the time. In this game, 55 percent of the trades are 1-R winners, and there is a 5 percent chance of a 10-R winner. Similarly, 35 percent of the trades are 1-R losers, and there is also a 5 percent chance of a 5-R loser. The R-multiple distribution of this game is actually similar to the R-multiple distribution of the trades in the scalping strategy described in Chapter 5 and presented in Table 5–1.

In the game, the trades are all randomly selected from that R-multiple distribution by drawing marbles out of a bag and then replacing them. We generally start the game with everyone having $100,000 and then simulate 50 trades. Since the trades are randomly selected, with the marbles being replaced, all 50 trades could be winners or losers. Generally, however, the trades are usually pretty close to the distribution of the marble bag. In fact, we seldom have a game that doesn't have a positive expectancy at the end of the 50 trades.[1]

What is fun about this game is that it is very much like real trading. As a result, when you understand the game and all its implications, it usually has a huge impact on your trading. Here are the major observations that we see most often when we play the game.

First, in an audience of 100 players, we will usually have 100 different ending equities, except for those who go bankrupt. The final equities might range from a high of $5 million or more to those who go bust. Now think about this finding for a minute and let it sink in. Everyone gets the same trades, but most people end up with different equities. Why? It certainly has nothing to do with prediction or trade selection skills. The trades are randomly selected marbles and everyone gets the same trades. It certainly isn't due to luck, because, once again, everyone gets the same trades with the same expectancy. Only two significant factors remain—psychology and position sizing. In other words, *the emotions of the players and "how much" they risk per trade are the only key factors in this game.*

Second, the objectives of the game are biased toward making a lot of money, because I usually give a prize to the person who has the highest equity at the end of the game. With those instructions, in an audience of average people, about a third of the room goes bankrupt. Another third of the room loses money. And the final third makes profits. However, I can control this distribution by giving people other objectives and incentives to help them meet those objectives. For example, I might tell one group that their only objective is not to lose money and that if more than two people in the group lose money, then no one in that group can win the prize.

The key here is that your objectives strongly influence what you do through position sizing. Objectives and position sizing go hand in hand. In fact, position sizing might be described as the major factor in determining whether or not you meet your objectives. And the normal objectives of the game are to win the prize or go bust trying. *Most electronic day traders who are trying to make a killing usually go bust trying.*

Last, we notice that emotions run very high during the game despite the fact that the prize might only be a $30 book. People groan with each loss and cheer 10-R winners as if their lives depended upon them. These emotions often cause serious errors in how much the players might be willing to risk. For more on how psychological factors influence peak performance trading, refer to the last chapter (Chapter 13) of the book, where it is covered in detail.

So what might you learn from the game? Let me summarize the key learning objectives one more time:

- Despite having a positive expectancy system, 100 people getting the same trades could easily get 100 different results with final equities ranging from bankrupt to 50 times the initial starting equity. This is all due to position sizing and psychological factors.

- The objectives given for the game have a lot to do with the results people get. In other words, you achieve your objectives through position sizing. And if you are trying to win really big, you have a good chance of going bankrupt if you don't know what you are doing.

- Last, the psychology of the individual tends to influence his position-sizing strategies.

Position sizing is that part of your system that tells you how much you are going to risk on any given trade. In addition, there are as many potential systems for position sizing as there are systems for picking stocks—only position sizing will have much more of an impact on your bottom line than stock picking. If you remember one statement from this book, remember that last one—*position sizing will have much more impact on your bottom-line results than stock picking ever will.*

When you have a positive expectancy system and can take plenty of trades, then with discipline and proper position sizing, you can make substantial returns in every 200-trade block. If those 200 trades happen to occur in a single week, then you may never have a losing week. However, you must be disciplined and apply the concepts given in this chapter.

Let's say your trading has the exact distribution of R multiples as in Table 5–1. We ran 5,000 simulations of that trade distribution with tests of 50, 100, 150, and 200 trades. Based on the results of that simulation, we discovered that with 50 trades you have a 96 percent chance of getting a positive expectancy. Thus, if your system had this distribution and you made 50 trades per week, you'd probably have only two losing weeks each year. With 100 trades, the chance of a getting a positive expectancy increases to 99 percent. Thus, if you made 100 trades each week with that distribution, then you'd probably have only one losing week every two years. When you reach 150 trades each week, the probability of a losing week approaches zero.

While these numbers may seem incredible, they also depend on an accurate assessment of the R-multiple distribution of your system (a topic covered in Chapter 5), the use of sound position-sizing techniques (the major topic of this chapter), and the discipline to carry all of it out (the major topic of Chapter 13). One major mistake in any of these three factors and the expected result of consistent winners will change to one of a financial disaster.

Before we talk about position-sizing techniques, I want to reemphasize what position sizing is not and what it is. First, it is *not* any of the following:

- It is *not* that part of your system that dictates how much you will lose on a given trade.
- It is *not* how to exit a profitable trade.
- It is *not* diversification.
- It is *not* risk control.
- It is *not* risk avoidance.
- It is *not* that part of your system that tells you what to invest in.

Instead, position sizing is that part of your trading system that answers the question "How much?" throughout the course of a trade. "How much" essentially means how big a position should you have on at any one time during the course of a trade.

The purpose of position sizing for you as an electronic day trader is to tell you how many shares of stock you should buy and should maintain at any given time, given the size of your account. For example, a position-sizing decision might be that you don't have enough money to put on any positions for a given scenario because the risk is too big. It also helps you equalize your trade exposure in the elements in your portfolio. Lastly, and perhaps most importantly, the position-sizing strategies that we will talk about in this chapter equate to a 1-R risk across all trades.

So let's take a look at a position-sizing strategy that will work well for you as a day trader.

POSITION-SIZING TECHNIQUES THAT WORK

Martingale versus Antimartingale Strategies

Professional gamblers will tell you that there are two primary position-sizing strategies—martingale and antimartingale. Martingale strategies will increase your bet size during a losing streak or as your equity gets smaller. Antimartingale strategies, on the other hand, will increase your bet size as your equity increases or during winning streaks.

People have a bias toward martingale strategies because they like to risk more when they are down. The assumption is "We've just had a losing streak and I'm down, but if I risk more I'll catch up quickly." That assumption just doesn't work because you never know how long a streak is going to last or how big it will be.

If your risk continues to increase during a losing streak, sooner or later you will go bankrupt. And even if your bankroll was endless, you would be using risk-reward strategies that no person could withstand psychologically. For example, if you were to bet on black at a roulette wheel and double your bet each time, you'd eventually win a dollar when the losing streak ended. But after 10 straight losers, which are quite possible, you would be risking a loss of over $8,000 (i.e., with the odds slightly against you) just to be ahead by a dollar at the end of your streak.[2] Those are not very good odds. In fact, your odds are excellent that this event will happen well before you've accumulated $8,000 in winnings.

Antimartingale strategies, in contrast, do work—both in gambling (if you can figure out how to have a positive expectancy game) and in investing (where we've already shown you how to have a positive expectancy game). They work because they call for larger risk during a winning streak. Smart gamblers know to increase their bets, within certain limits, when they are winning. And the same is true for trading or investing. Position-sizing systems that work require that you increase your position size when you make money.

The Best Position-Sizing Strategy for Electronic Day Traders: Risk a Percentage of Your Equity (Don't Bet the Farm, Just a Hog or Two)

You've seen the importance of having a bailout point when you enter into a trade—your 1-R loss—in Chapter 5. If you still don't understand the importance and implications of a 1-R loss, then go back and reread that chapter until you do. Let me repeat, don't read any further until you thoroughly understand the importance of pre-defining, before you enter into a trade, what your 1-R loss will be.

What we are going to do now is make 1 R a percentage of your total equity. Here's how it works. Let's say you have a $50,000 account. You want to buy LU at 71.375,[3] and your stop will be 70.875. Thus, your 1-R risk is $0.50 per share. Your position-sizing decision is how much to buy. How much risk to your portfolio are you willing to take on this position on LU? Let's say you decide to take no more than 1 percent risk per trade. One percent of $50,000 is $500. You are willing to risk $500 on this trade, so how much can you purchase if your 1-R risk is 50 cents? You simply divide your 1 percent risk (i.e., $500) by your 1-R amount, and your result is 1,000 shares.

Notice here that you are buying 1,000 shares of a stock that's priced at $71.375. That means you are buying $71,375 worth of stock. Is that your risk? No! It's not your risk unless Lucent goes completely bankrupt in the 15 minutes that you'll be in the trade. It's also not your risk because you will keep to your predetermined 1-R loss of 50 cents. The main reason you keep a 1-R stop is to preserve your capital. Thus, your risk in this situation is $500, or 1 percent of your portfolio. If you didn't get out at $70.875, then your risk would be bigger. For example, if you exited at $70.375, then you would have lost $1,000, or 2 R. And as a day trader, you want to avoid risks bigger than 1 R at all costs.

Let's do one more example. Suppose you want to buy QCOM at 141.75. The bid-ask spread when you buy it is ¾ point. You want to give it a little room beyond the spread, so you set a mental stop at 139.75, or 2 points. Thus, a 1-R risk on QCOM for this trade is $2 per share. You now have a position-sizing question—how much should you buy? Let's say your account is now worth $52,000 and you still plan to risk 1 percent of your account. One percent of $52,000 is $520. Since 1 R is 2 points, you divide $520 by 2 points and get your answer of 260 shares. In this case, you are buying

$36,855 worth of stock, but that is not your risk. Your risk, as long as you keep your stop, is $520, or 1 percent of your account.

Notice that in each example, you determined what 1 percent of your account was in terms of dollars. This value is what you have determined your position sizing will be. Now you must divide that value by 1 R (i.e., your risk per share) to determine how many shares to buy. Thus, each of our two examples represented a 1 percent risk in your account. In the first example, with R being 50 cents, you bought 1,000 shares. In the second example, with R being $2 (and 1 percent now being $520), you purchased 260 shares. Notice that in the second example, R was 4 times as big so you are basically exposing yourself to one-fourth as many shares.

Notice what you've done by risking 1 percent of your account. First, your position-sizing algorithm has the same impact on your account regardless of the characteristics of the stock you are buying. Second, your position size is the same (i.e., X percent of your account) regardless of what 1 R is for the stock you are buying. Thus, if the expectancy of your system is 0.3, it means that after 100 trades you can expect to be up by about 30 R. If you've equated R through using a 1 percent risk position-sizing algorithm, then after 30 trades you can expect to be up by about 30 percent.[4]

In each of these examples, we used a 1 percent risk for ease of calculations. However, until you become very seasoned at what you are doing as an electronic day trader, I recommend that you not risk more than ¼ percent of your account per trade. Don't move to higher levels until (1) you are sure of the expectancy of your system and are making money regularly and (2) you know that you seldom make psychological mistakes (see the material in Chapters 11 and 13). Once you've done that, you might move to as much as a 1 percent risk per trade.

Now, let's do five more examples, only you work out what the position sizing will be. In each case, assume you have a $100,000 account. You will be risking ½ percent of that account, or $500. Based on the given R, determine how many shares of stock you will be buying.

1. You are scalping TXN 68.125, and a 1-R loss is 12.5 cents.
2. You are doing momentum trading with HLIT, buying at 141.375 with a ⅜-point stop.

3. You are trading AMZN at 68 with a 2.375-point stop.
4. You are trading JDSU at 288.875 with a 6.5-point stop.
5. You are trading IBM at 98.5 with a $\frac{1}{16}$-point stop.

Now calculate the position size for each of the examples. Are there any cases where the position size is "too big" even though you are only risking 0.5 percent of your account? Give at least two reasons why the position might be too big despite the fact that your risk is only a small percentage of your account. The answers will be given at the end of the chapter.

SIMULATING YOUR SYSTEM TO DETERMINE WHAT'S POSSIBLE

When you have your R-multiple distribution—which you might get from filling out spreadsheets of your trades, like those shown in Tables 5–1 and 5–3—then you can simulate your system with various position-sizing strategies. You can do the simulations in several ways.

The simplest way is to determine the R-multiple distribution and make up a bag of marbles with the same distribution. You can then draw marbles randomly, with replacement, and get an idea of what it would be like to trade your system. For example, you might have a system that has an expectancy of over 1.0 but that is right only about 35 percent of the time. When you simulate such a system, you'll learn what it feels like to have 10 to 15 losses in a row and still get good returns simply because the 16th trade might be a 30-R winner that totally makes up for the rest of the losses. It's important to know such information, because you must live through such events if you are to trade your system.

Incidentally, IITM, Inc., has developed a five-level computer game that is designed to teach the importance of expectancy and position sizing.[5] The last level of the game allows you to input your own R-multiple distribution and simulate your system trade by trade.

The second major way of simulating your system is through automatic computer simulations. You could design such a simulator using Excel that would allow you to run 500 simulations of 50 trades each with various position-sizing strategies. The net result of such simulations would be a global comparison of various position-sizing strategies so that you would know the average return, understand what could happen with respect to drawdowns, and even compare strategies. The results could be very interesting. However, such computer simulations do not give you the feel of living through each trade as do the marble simulations.

In order to help you understand both the power of position sizing and the way to do simulations, we've done a number of them for you using the data given in Table 5–1—the 41 scalping trades using the methods recommended in Chapter 9. Remember that these trades contain two 4-R losses, which represent either psychological errors (such as a stop that wasn't kept) or hugely unanticipated market moves.

First, we ran 5,000 simulations of 50 trades each with this R-multiple distribution. We found that the probability of a positive expectancy was 0.885. In other words, if 50 trades represented a week of trading, you would have winning weeks 90 percent of the time.

Next we ran 200 simulations of 40 trades each with five different position-sizing algorithms, ranging from 0.1 percent risk to 1.0 percent risk. We assumed that the trader was making 40 trades each week with a $100,000 account.

Table 6–1 shows the results of this simulation. Notice that the 0.25 percent risk per trade, which best represents the way one of the authors trades his account, returns an average of 4 percent a week, or 16 percent per month. It's possible to have returns that are much higher with more risk, but a risk as high as 1 percent is very hard to do with tight stops, as you will see from the answers to the problems later in this chapter. Also notice that the key to these returns is the expectancy (i.e., keeping losses to 1 R) and the position sizing.

Table 6–2 shows what might occur on a monthly basis. Here we are doing 200 simulations of 150 trades each.

Notice the implications of Table 6–2. Assuming that you could maintain the distribution of trades given for the scalping system and risk 0.25 percent of your equity per trade, your average monthly return would be about 16 percent and you'd have an 80 percent chance of having at least a monthly gain of 10 percent. These are amazing results, but quite realistic because the data included several large losses that were due to psychological mistakes.

TABLE 6-1

200 Simulations of 40 Trades with Scalping R-Multiple Distribution

	0.1% Risk	0.25% Risk	0.5% Risk	0.75% Risk	1.0% Risk
Avg. final equity	$101,866	$104,020	$107,848	$112,822	$118,416
Probability of 2% drawdown	0%	3%	7%	9%	12%
Probability of at least break even at end	89%	88%	88%	91%	87%
Probability of 10% gain	0%	4%	32%	56%	65%
Minimum final equity	$98,293	$95,747	$91,553	$84,072	$83,367
Avg. % gain	1.9%	4.0%	7.8%	11.5%	18.4%
Min. % gain	−1.7%	−4.3%	−8.4%	−12.6%	−16.6%

Also notice that the maximum monthly drawdown from these simulations was 7.7 percent, even though the probability of a 2 percent drawdown or more was only about 2 percent. Such drawdowns can be psychologically devastating for people when they occur and may result in many psychological mistakes that can make the drawdowns much worse.

At 1 percent risk, the gains become huge, averaging 84 percent per month. However, with scalping trades this level of risk would be very unrealistic because you would constantly be exceeding the margin of your account. Also notice the huge drawdowns that are possible, although unlikely, at this level of risk.

The hope is that by now you can understand the importance of simulating various position-sizing strategies. It is critical both to trade properly and to understand your trading system as an electronic day trader.

POSITION-SIZING MISTAKES YOU MUST AVOID

Position sizing is your key to making a great living as an electronic day trader. However, position-sizing mistakes can also lead to dis-

TABLE 6-2

200 Simulations of 150 Trades with Scalping R-Multiple Distribution

	0.1% Risk	0.25% Risk	0.5% Risk	0.75% Risk	1.0% Risk
Avg. final equity	$106,499	$116,270	$134,770	$155,870	$183,622
Probability of 2% drawdown	1%	2%	2%	2%	2%
Probability of at least break even at end	99%	98%	98%	98%	98%
Probability of 10% gain	8%	80%	94%	96%	97%
Minimum final equity	$96,892	$92,292	$84,863	$77,656	$70,789
Avg. % gain	6.5%	16.3%	34.8%	55.9%	83.6%
Min. % gain	–3.1%	–7.7%	–15.2%	–22.3%	–29.2%

aster in your trading. When people lose everything in their trading account, it is usually because of position-sizing mistakes.

Mistake 1: Having Your Largest Position on the 1-R Losses

One of the biggest mistakes traders tend to make is to begin with a large position, say a 1 percent risk, and then eliminate it gradually as the price of the stock rises. For example, you might start with 1,000 shares of QCOM and then take quick profits on 500 shares when you can raise your stops high enough to assure that you won't have a loss. You might then take off another 250 shares after a 2-R profit and just hang onto the remaining 250 shares for your maximum gain. What's wrong with this sort of trading? After all, you make sure that you keep a profit as quickly as possible, don't you?

The problem with this strategy is that you guarantee that you have your largest position size, 1,000 shares, when you have the highest potential for a 1-R loss. If you made a 10-R profit, you'd do it with only 250 shares, or a quarter of your starting position. This would only be equivalent to a 2.5-R profit with a full 1,000 shares. Can you begin to see the problem? When you do this, you

are effectively cutting your profits short through position sizing.
You are doing the opposite of the golden rule of trading.

Mistake 2: The Gambler's Fallacy

The gambler's fallacy is the next mistake that people make with
position sizing. Imagine that you have $10,000 and that you want
to double your money. You have a 60 percent system, and you basically win or lose 1 R. On the first try you risk $1,000 and lose. You
do this three times in a row. You now have $7,000 left after three
straight losses. You are thinking, "Wow, I should be right 60 percent of the time, and I've had three straight losses. I must be overdue for a win. I think I'll risk $4,000 on this one." You now have
your fourth loss, and you are down to $3,000. You decide that you
are really overdue for a win, and you risk the balance of your
account. The fifth trade is the same as the others, a loser, and you
are now broke.

After a set of loss. Although it might seem unlikely to lose five straight times in a
60 percent system, such a streak is quite likely to occur when there
are enough trades. Furthermore, it might occur just when you get
into this type of thinking. If you have a 60 percent system, then the
chances of a win are 60 percent on any trade. The odds do not
increase after a set of losing trades. They are still 60 percent. Making an assumption that the odds of a win go up after a losing streak,
could result in your financial downfall, and it does for many
traders.

Mistake 3: Not Enough Money

You've seen from some of the examples in this chapter that risks of
0.25 percent of your equity per trade are quite reasonable for electronic day traders. Risk rates above that (for example, 1 percent)
can result in huge returns, but they also make it possible for huge
drawdowns to occur.

Remember that our examples came from a $100,000 account.
Notice that a 0.25 percent risk in this size account is only $250.
Now, if your account is as small as $10,000—which it often is for
many beginning electronic day traders—then your $250 risk would

amount to a risk of 2.5 percent. You would probably run into margin problems. Furthermore, if you didn't run into such problems, you would still be risking the possibility of huge losses.

Frequently, day traders tell me about how much money they've been making in the markets, except for today when they lost more than half of the value of their account. When I hear a story like this, I automatically know what the problem is—the trader's position sizing was way too big or her account was way too small.

ANSWERS TO THE POSITION-SIZING PROBLEMS

1. You are scalping TXN $68.125, and a 1-R loss is 12.5 cents.

In this example, you must divide your ½ percent risk of $500 by R, which is 12.5 cents in this case. The result is 4,000, so you can buy 4,000 shares. Notice that 4,000 shares at $68.125 would require $271,875 of capital, and you only have $200,000 when fully margined. Thus, although your risk is only $500, you could not do this trade at that risk level.

2. You are doing momentum trading with HLIT, buying at $141.375 with a ⅜-point stop.[6]

In this example, you must divide your ½ percent risk of $500 by your 1-R value of 0.375. The result is 1,333 shares. Thus, you could buy 1,333 shares of HLIT at this risk level. Those 1,333 shares would cost you $187,578 at $141.375 per share. You could do that with margin in this account.

3. You are trading AMZN at $68 with a $2.375-point stop.

In this example, you have to divide your risk of $500 by 2.375 to determine the number of shares you could buy. The result is 210 shares, which would cost $14,280. You could do that easily in this account.

4. You are trading JDSU at $288.875 with a $6.5-point stop.

In this example, you must divide your $500 risk by your 1-R risk of $6.5 to determine the number of shares. The answer is 76 shares, which would cost you $21,954.50.

TABLE 6-3

Answers to Problems

Trade	1-R Value	Number Shares	Percent Risk	Total Cost
TXN at $68.125	12.5 cents	4,000	0.5%	$275,875
HLIT at $141.375	37.5 cents	1,333	0.5%	$187,578
AMZN at $68	$2.375	210	0.499%	$14,280
JDSU at $288.875	$6.50	76	0.494%	$21,954.50
IBM at $98.5	6.25 cents	8,000	0.5%	$788,000

5. You are trading IBM at $98.5 with a 1/16-point stop.

In this last example, you must divide your $500 risk by your 1-R risk of 1/16 of a point, or 0.0625. Thus, in this example, you could buy 8,000 shares, which would cost you $788,000—obviously, you'd have some margin problems with a $100,000 account.

Table 6–3 describes all five trades in terms of R, number of shares, percent risk, and total cost involved. You should understand every aspect of this table before you move on to Part 3 of this book. Note that trades 1 and 5 are too big for your account size. More importantly, trades 1, 2, and 5 are probably too big to execute using the techniques we've suggested in this book.

KNOWLEDGE KEYS

✓ Most electronic day traders who are trying to make a killing usually go bust trying. The reason is that they risk too much on each trade.

✓ Position sizing will have much more impact on your bottom-line results than stock picking ever will.

✓ Position sizing is that part of your trading system that answers the question "How much?" or "How many shares?" throughout the course of a trade.

✓ The best position-sizing strategy for direct-access traders is to risk a small (1 percent or less) percentage of your equity, per trade. To do so, figure out what that percentage of your account is and then divide that amount by R to determine your position size.

CALLS TO ACTION

✓ Simulate your system using various position-sizing strategies to determine not only what is possible, but also what may even be probable given a large number of trades.

✓ Avoid the position-sizing mistakes as outlined in this chapter.

✓ Do have your maximum position size when a trade is moving in your direction.

NOTES

1. Based upon Monte Carlo simulations of 5,000 runs of 50 trades each, the actual probability of getting a losing expectancy in 50 trades with this R-multiple distribution is about 0.115.

2. This also assumes that the casino doesn't have minimum and maximum bets, but all of them do.

3. Notice how much the price of a volatile stock can change between the time this chapter was written versus when you read it.

4. And if you risked ½ percent per trade, you'd be up by 15 percent. If you risked ¼ percent per trade, you'd be up by 7.5 percent. While these lower numbers will give you smaller returns, they also expose you to much smaller losses should you have a bad losing streak.

5. The game is available by calling 919-852-3994.

6. Ironically, within a few months of the initial writing of this chapter, HLIT dropped to $23 per share. This clearly shows the importance of stops to preserve your capital.

## CHAPTER 7

Prelaunch Preparation—Your Daily Routine

People only see what they are prepared to see.
Ralph Waldo Emerson

We've already talked about overall preparation for trading through the development of a comprehensive business plan and a strategic trading plan. No trading should begin until these plans are in place. However, daily preparation is equally important. The purpose of this chapter is to cover the steps that you should take on a daily basis to make your trading more effective. I'll also give you specific illustrations of what I do in my daily trading.

THE POWER OF SIMPLICITY

One woman we know says that she has made hundreds of thousands of dollars through day trading stocks. She describes her daily preparation as follows: "I pray to God for guidance for the day. I then get together my watch list of stocks. I scan these stocks throughout the day, buying the stocks that are really going up. If they go against me, I get out quickly. Otherwise, I just stay with them until the end of the day." While we think this is probably an oversimplification of what she does, it definitely describes the essence of successful trading: (1) being prepared, (2) having an exit and entry methodology, (3) cutting losses short, and (4) letting profits run.

START YOUR DAY THE EVENING BEFORE

There are thousands of stocks that you could trade, and so a key task for a direct-access trader is to develop a "watch list" of stocks that might be in play. You could do this very early in the morning. However, it usually takes some time, so I recommend that you do it the night before. Here's how my typical night goes from the standpoint of preparation.

I begin by running my scanning software, looking for potential setups for the following day. I use two pieces of software—VectorVest ProGraphics and AIQ Trading Expert Pro. Other software packages may be just as good, but I'm used to running these. I've set the software to run automatically. At approximately 8 p.m. Eastern Time, the software downloads data from that trading day and runs through its scanning techniques looking for certain technical setups. Each software package then generates a list of potential plays. In addition, each program ranks the generated plays according to a scoring system. Perhaps once a week, both packages will signal the very same trade. When that happens, of course, I pay special attention to those situations.

There's also a second source for tomorrow's trading—the trades I was doing (or looking at) today. In other words, if I was trading boomers or busters today, then tomorrow I might be looking to trade the double boomers or the double busters. Another potential source for tomorrow's trading is the volume breakouts and stocks making new 52-week highs or lows today.

These scans will produce a list of perhaps 50 or so stocks. For each of these, I look at a daily chart. This gives me a very good feel for (1) support and resistance areas and (2) whether the stock is in an uptrend or a downtrend. I know if it has recently broken through a 52-week high or 52-week low. And I know if it has broken through a 20-, a 50-, or a 200-period moving average. After I'm done running through the charts, I cull the original list, ending up with perhaps as many as 20 stocks. I place these into a minder window in my trading software, ready for the next morning.

This whole process takes me less than an hour to do, once the scanning software has run. This may or may not be feasible for you, depending upon when you can actually download data and run scans.

T MINUS 2 HOURS AND COUNTING

I also strongly recommend that you have a daily procedure in the morning for reviewing your stocks and preparing to trade. Let's review what my morning looks like:

I have a checklist I use to prepare to trade that day. If I don't follow that checklist, I won't trade.

1. Review the Previous Evening's Stock Lists   I start by reviewing the daily charts for the stocks on my screening lists one more time. All these stocks go into a market-minder screen. Most of them will fit into either a boomer or a buster minder, although I do sometimes create these minder windows on the fly, which you can do in either CyberTrader or RealTick (or in most other direct-access software packages). I put my stock symbols into the minder screen so that during the trading day I can watch these stocks constantly. I also have certain stocks that I trade, day in and day out. I call these my basket stocks. In addition, I do a chart review of the momentum trades that are in play that day, as described below.

2. Look for News-Driven and Momentum-Driven Stocks   Next I look for potential momentum trades from two sources: CNBC and trader chat rooms. First, let's talk about CNBC. I begin watching CNBC normally at 7 a.m. Eastern Time. Joe Kernan and David Faber have a "Stocks to Watch" segment. The actual "Stocks to Watch" segments on CNBC are at 5 and 35 minutes after the hour starting at 6 a.m. Eastern Time. They air at 6:05, 6:35, 7:05, 7:35, 8:05, 8:35, and then 9:05. At the 7:05 news brief, they cover any early-morning breaking news and what's happened overnight. At 8:05, they start covering that day's press releases. This keeps me pretty well posted on what's happening marketwise. I do not get up for the 6:05 or 6:35 segments. If, for some reason, I can't actually watch the other segments, I tape them for review prior to trading.

My next source is the Web sites and chat rooms that feature momentum-driven trading. My favorite chat room is Daytraders .org.[1] My favorite Web site is briefing.com. These sources give me a lot of potential momentum trades.

Finally, I look through stories and stock charts in *Investor's Business Daily* and/or *The Wall Street Journal.* (If you can receive the current issue of either paper early in the morning, skim the main news stories and the recap of the previous day's market.)

From these sources I build my daily watch list. For each stock I make an initial assessment (based upon the news or the technical indicator) of which direction I expect the stock to trade. I build a "short" and "long" market-minder screen from each of these sources. You can do these all in one minder screen if you want to—especially if you have limited monitor space. However, I find it useful to put them into separate minders, because in my post-trade review (see Chapter 12) I can make some useful distinctions about how good these trades were and the validity of various setups.

The news-momentum setups are an art form. You have to be able to interpret the news you get from CNBC and from the chat rooms. In Chapter 8, we show a system and a tracking spreadsheet (Table 8–5) for grading the news on a scale of 1 to 5. Also, a much more comprehensive discussion of interpreting news is given there. This type of tool will give you a starting point for improving your ability to discern whether the news will have a positive or negative effect on the stock in question.

3. Interpret the Momentum Stocks   The real job in the morning is to interpret that day's news and to determine whether the stock has a directional bias (and how much it might be) based upon the news. Once I have done so, I again put that information into a minder and watch for trading activity.

Sometimes, your assessment of the news might have such a high probability that you'll want to trade right away. An example would be where "good" news comes out on a basket stock or a momentum stock you are watching closely. The type of news I look for has little chance for impacting the company fundamentals— some call this "fluff" or "weak" news. Typically on this type of news, in the premarket the stock just overreacts to the upside. Often, by reading the time & sales window premarket, we're able to actually nail a short very near the high of the day or buy a bottom (on "bad" news) near the day's low.

You can see that the stock selection process is really not that difficult. It's rather perfunctory and mechanical, with the exception of the experience required for interpreting the news. Figure 7–1 shows a recap of this process.

Stock Selection Checklist

Evening Preparation
8:00–8:30 p.m.

Run software scans
    Mechanical setups (from AIQ and Vector Vest)
        Select top 10 +/–
        Analyze daily charts for each stock selected
        Put selected stocks in "software scan" minder
        window

Morning Preparation
7:00–8:30 a.m. (1½ hours)

Find and interpret news (see Chapter 8)
    CNBC
        "Stocks to Watch"—7:05 a.m. and every half hour
        thereafter until 9:05 a.m.
    NewsWatch
        Keyword search
    Briefing.com
    Put all selected stocks in "news/momentum" minder window

Scan for gap and traps on basket stocks
Scan for boomers and busters
    Put prescreened stocks in "boomers and busters" minder
    window

Premarket Trading
8:00–9:30 a.m. (1½ hours)
    Trade boomers and busters based upon news aberrations

Figure 7–1

APPLIED BEHAVIORAL FINANCE—KNOW THYSELF

The bigger area of preparation that traders have to face each day is the internal mental and psychological issues dealing with trading. Here, we get into the soft areas that are often ignored by traders, but are really important. This is the notion of psychological preparation each day. You might call this daily preparation "applied trading psychology" or "applied behavioral finance."

Much of our discussion so far in this book has been geared to preparing yourself on a global basis. It has included defining who you are and what your mission is. It also has included developing objectives that are congruent with your mission. Now we're becoming more focused and doing the daily preparation that is necessary to prepare you to trade, or to determine if you're ready to trade. We've categorized these as physical, mental, and spiritual, or body, mind, and spirit. Let's go through these elements by looking in detail at my daily preparation.

Get Your Body Ready to Trade Every Day—Broken Cars Don't Win Races

The brain loves oxygenated blood. The more oxygenated blood you have pumping through your system, the better your brain will function and the better trader you will be. Aerobic exercise is vital—running, jogging, doing jumping jacks, riding a bicycle, or operating a stationary bike are all great ways to oxygenate your blood.

I exercise using a treadmill when I first get up. My typical morning exercise is 30 minutes on the treadmill. During that time, I try to get my heart rate up to 80 percent of my peak rate. Your peak heart rate is determined by the formula (180 − age).

Another fantastic way to supply oxygen to the brain is by simply drinking plenty of water. Many physiologists suggest a minimum of eight glasses of water daily. I do admit to having some difficulty drinking this much water every day. Especially since I must be able to sit at my computer for extended periods of time while trading. A half gallon of water filtering through my kidneys is not exactly helpful in this regard! Nonetheless, I do try to drink as much water as I can.

Proper nutrition is important also. I personally like fruits, and my wife is kind enough to keep the house stocked with bananas, Granny Smith apples, and oranges, which I eat after I exercise. Then I shower, and I'm ready for my trading day.

I want to emphasize the importance of doing these things. Remember, mind, body, and soul are connected, and your health (or lack of health) will show up in your trading results. You are the most important factor in your trading results. And if you don't do everything you can to keep yourself in peak physical condition, then you are not doing everything you can to help yourself perform at a peak level. Van Tharp's *Peak Performance Course for Investors and Traders* is a good source for material that will help you perform at a peak level. While an in-depth discussion of this topic is far beyond the scope of this book, his work has really helped me in these areas.

Get Your Mind in the Game, Too

Control of your mental state is the essence of discipline. Each task that you perform during the day requires a particular mental state for optimal performance. You need to practice this sort of control in order to be a peak performance trader. Here, we're really talking about taking responsibility for your life. Taking responsibility for what happens in your life is your maximum form of control over it. You can learn from your mistakes and not repeat them. But more importantly, you can shape your destiny. It all starts with selecting the frame of mind that you're going to be in for the day. Here's what I find most useful in this critical area of mental preparation.

I have learned over many years to live in a joyful state. I'm still learning—so I can't say I'm totally there. But I constantly use several techniques to help me maintain a state of joy. I've done a lot of work that gets into coaching issues and spiritual issues. In one sense, this work is the sum of my life. So I'll simply give you a short summary that deals only with trading. Here's how I do it. I have an attitude and belief that says, "I'm a good trader. I enjoy life. I'm happy with what I do. I'm fulfilled in what I do. I'm bringing positive fruits and results to myself, my family, and the world." When I maintain that joyful state, I'm connected to my mission, and it shows up almost every day on my bottom line. When I'm not connected— if I'm physically very tired or ill or I have some other problem that's weighing on me—that too shows up on my bottom line. Unfortunately, it shows up negatively. What I've learned to do, however, is to control my state.

Here's a technique for doing this: Let's say you've done your other preparation in terms of stock screening and physical preparation. You now ask yourself how you are feeling, and you find that you are not that happy or joyful—you feel down. One technique that works for me is simply to enumerate all the things that I have to be happy and joyful about that day. These are really simple things. I might look outside and the sun might be shining. If the sun's not shining and it's raining, I might think of my wife and my daughters and the love that we share. I might think of my friends or the nice thing that a friend did for me the day before or the week before. Or I might think of a nice thing that I did for one of my friends. I might think about the blessings that I have and the fact that I'm not hungry. I might think about the fact that I have abundance and more than I need. Simply by thinking about these things, I'm able to move myself into a state of joy because there are many, many things to be joyful about.

Here's another technique I sometimes do, called "positive self-talk." Spend a few minutes noticing your dialogue within your mind. When you hear something negative, like calling yourself an idiot, think again. For example, I would rephrase that to say, "I just made a mistake, and I'm grateful that I get to learn from my mistakes." Tony Robbins's book, *Awaken the Giant Within*, contains a whole chapter devoted to the vocabulary of ultimate success. That chapter is well worth reviewing for the purposes of upgrading your own self-talk and therefore upgrading your trading practice.

Another part of my mental preparation is visualization. Visualization is hugely important to successful trading. I tend to go to the visualization steps when there's some other problem that seems to be blocking me. For example, if I've been making errors, I'll see myself in that same situation as if I'm actually there, but instead of taking the trade and making errors, when I rerun the tape in my visualization, I do it correctly. I reinforce the proper process by doing it over and over and over correctly in my head, and that way, the next time I actually experience the same situation, I should do it correctly.

Feed Your Soul before You Trade

Remember our example of the woman who had made a lot of money day trading? She began her day by simply giving thanks and turning her trading over to God. That's an example of spiritual preparation, and for some people that may be enough.

A famous trader once told one of the authors a personal story. He said that every day he had to commute to his downtown trading office by train. He said that one day he decided to show his thanks by giving a nice donation (about $20) to a beggar at a train station. Suddenly, his trading became hugely successful. That continued each day until one day the beggar disappeared. That day, perhaps by coincidence but perhaps not, was his first losing day in months. You might consider giving a daily gift as a way of saying thanks. There are many ways to say thanks and to prepare yourself spiritually. I don't insist that you follow my beliefs or preparation routine, but I do believe that to be the best trader you can be, you have to provide yourself with proper spiritual preparation. This is a very personal area, but to get you started, here's how I approach my daily spiritual preparation.

Every day I give thanks to God for the joys and the blessings I have in my life. For the most part, those joys tend to be people— I don't focus on money. Although I'm thankful for food and money and physical things, I'm even more thankful for the people that I have in my life—they are a joy and a blessing. So I offer a prayer of thanks. I specifically ask for God's blessings on my trading that day. Just as an interesting aside, on those days when I forget to do this, I tend not to do nearly as well as the days when I remember. Perhaps He is reminding me that He is my ultimate source. Even if your beliefs are different from mine, I believe you'll find that giving thanks is a wonderful thing. It helps bring joy to your life. Another thing that you can do when you pray before you trade is to ask to use your gifts and talents to your best ability.

That's it for an overview of the preparation that leads to consistent profits. After completing your pretrading countdown, you're ready to trade. So let's get to the launch pad—we're T minus 1 minute and counting. The trading day is about to begin!

KNOWLEDGE KEYS

✓ Realize the importance of daily trading preparation.
✓ A key to trading success is creating your watch lists the day before you actually trade.

✓ Understand the components of preparation: (1) your own physical, mental, and spiritual wellness and (2) stock selection.

✓ Most unsuccessful traders underestimate the impact that physical, mental, and spiritual well-being have on their trading results.

CALLS TO ACTION

✓ Create your own a daily countdown checklist.

✓ Be sure to create a basket of favorite stocks that you learn well. Examine these basket stocks daily for trading opportunities.

✓ Build a daily watch list.

✓ Create a complete, well-defined list of expectations for each stock that you trade during the day.

✓ Have a written checklist for your daily physical, mental, and spiritual preparation.

✓ Know what you need to do daily to work on yourself and then do it!

NOTES

1. Found on irc.othernet.org.

## PART THREE

Launching Your Trading Rocket

Hint: This Is the Stuff Almost All Traders Want Right Away, but Most Trading Careers Crash Because They've Skipped the Important Preparation!

When most people approach direct-access trading, this is the material they want right away. "Tell me, how do you pick stocks?" or "How do you know exactly when to buy (or short) a stock?" or "How do I keep from getting whipsawed?" If someone is making money in the markets, everyone else wants to know how that person is doing it. It's not that this information is not important—it is! It's just that many people put the cart before the horse. If you want to know how and when to buy, it's easy: Point, click, and buy. Or call your broker. But if you want to know how to trade for financial freedom, then you're going to have to ask yourself very different questions.

In this section, we do answer many of the "How do I buy?" and "How do I sell?" questions, but we go far beyond that. If you've read this far, you know we advocate an all-encompassing approach to trading that goes far beyond what most people will ever do (because most people want all the success and none of the work or discipline required to achieve it). If you're willing to put in outstanding efforts, you'll enjoy outstanding results. It's a natural law. Read on! We'll uncover not only the strategies and tactics, but also the secrets to keeping those profits once you've made them.

## CHAPTER 8

The Trading Day Liftoff

Navigating Trade by Trade

We are what we repeatedly do.
Aristotle

Three . . . two . . . one . . . zero . . . we have liftoff! The trading day has begun! We've covered a tremendous amount of material up to this point. And if you've understood the knowledge keys at the end of the first seven chapters, your knowledge exceeds that of most direct-access traders. In addition, if you've completed the action items thus far, you're just about ready to begin trading for profits! Research indicates that very few, 5 percent or less, will actually attain this profit orbit!

But before you actually begin to trade, there are a few finesse steps that, once mastered, will assure that you stay in that profit orbit once you attain it. These are complete mastery of Level II interpretation and order entry selection. We'll cover these in the first part of this chapter and then move on to trade-by-trade execution.

NASDAQ LEVEL II—YOUR BOOSTER ROCKET TO TRADING ORBIT

Back in Chapter 4, we dissected the Level II montage (L2) with the goal of understanding all its component parts. Here we'll take a closer look, our goal being to understand how to use it during your trading day. At first, you'll just want to understand the dynamic nature of Level II from the viewpoint of supply and demand. These concepts are easy to grasp, since the supply and demand model is intuitive and mechanical in nature. Next you'll want to find the deeper secrets of Level II, and understand how to use it to glean the near-term direction of a stock. You'll do this by learning to spot market-maker activities and tactics.

THE SUPPLY AND DEMAND MODEL

The most conventional interpretations of stock movement are based upon the old economic laws of supply and demand. Simplified, this "supply and demand model" says essentially three things: (1) If demand for a product or service is greater than its supply ($D > S$), the price will tend to increase. (2) If supply is greater than demand, $S > D$, the price will tend to decrease. (3) If demand and supply are in balance ($D = S$), the price will tend to remain stable; that is, the price will tend to remain where it is. With this model in mind, let's examine some L2 screens, looking for evidence of all three of these economic conditions.

Demand Greater Than Supply ($D > S$) (see Figure 8–1)

1) More bids than offers.
2) More shares bid than shares offered.
3) Power bar skewed to the right side of the screen.

In powerful moves, tiers collapse on the offer, and the power bar slides to the far right.

Supply Greater Than Demand ($S > D$) (see Figure 8–2)

1) More offers than bids.
2) More shares offered than shares bid.
3) Power bar skewed to the left side of the screen.

In powerful moves, tiers collapse on the bid, and the power bar slides to the far left.

Demand Equals Supply ($D = S$) (see Figure 8–3)

1) Bids and offers about the same.

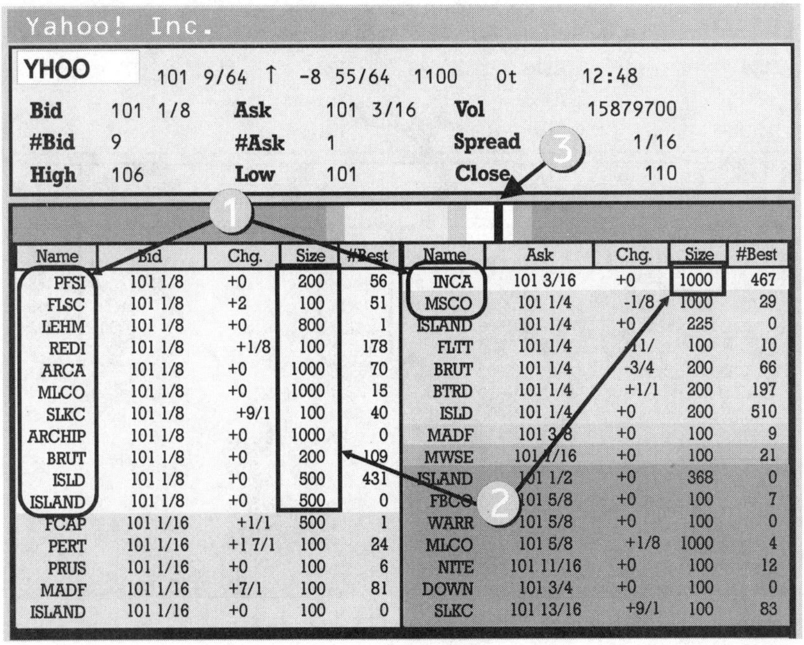

Yahoo! Inc.

YHOO 101 9/64 ↑ -8 55/64 1100 0t 12:48

Bid	101 1/8	Ask	101 3/16	Vol	15879700
#Bid	9	#Ask	1	Spread	1/16
High	106	Low	101	Close	110

Name	Bid	Chg.	Size	#Best	Name	Ask	Chg.	Size	#Best
PFSI	101 1/8	+0	200	56	INCA	101 3/16	+0	1000	467
FLSC	101 1/8	+2	100	51	MSCO	101 1/4	-1/8	1000	29
LEHM	101 1/8	+0	800	1	ISLAND	101 1/4	+0	225	0
REDI	101 1/8	+1/8	100	178	FLTT	101 1/4	11/	100	10
ARCA	101 1/8	+0	1000	70	BRUT	101 1/4	-3/4	200	66
MLCO	101 1/8	+0	1000	15	BTRD	101 1/4	+1/1	200	197
SLKC	101 1/8	+9/1	100	40	ISLD	101 1/4	+0	200	510
ARCHIP	101 1/8	+0	1000	0	MADF	101 3/8	+0	100	9
BRUT	101 1/8	+0	200	109	MWSE	101 [illegible]/16	+0	100	21
ISLD	101 1/8	+0	500	431	ISLAND	101 1/2	+0	368	0
ISLAND	101 1/8	+0	500	0	FBCO	101 5/8	+0	100	7
FCAP	101 1/16	+1/1	500	1	WARR	101 5/8	+0	100	0
PERT	101 1/16	+1 7/1	100	24	MLCO	101 5/8	+1/8	1000	4
PRUS	101 1/16	+0	100	6	NITE	101 11/16	+0	100	12
MADF	101 1/16	+7/1	100	81	DOWN	101 3/4	+0	100	0
ISLAND	101 1/16	+0	100	0	SLKC	101 13/16	+9/1	100	83

Figure 8–1 Demand greater than supply (D > S).

2) Shares bid are about equal to shares offered.
3) Power bar is near the center of the screen.

Study these examples carefully. Spend as much time as possible just watching stocks trade on L2. Learn to recognize instantly what different situations look like—they will be critical to your entry and exit timing and to your decision to "pass" on a trade. Fortunately, trading some stocks will be this simple. You just determine whether the stock is rising or falling in the near term and trade with the trend. We'll show you some examples of this in Chapter 9, "Market-Making Strategies." Unfortunately, just when you think you've got this all figured out, a little wrinkle arrives on the scene and you get whipsawed out of your position! That little wrinkle is often . . .

THE AX

Many EDAT traders, especially newer traders, don't even know that she exists. Surprisingly, even some seasoned traders, who know all

Cisco Systems, Inc.

CSCO	62 9/16 ↑ -9/16	200	0t	12:42
Bid 62 9/16	**Ask** 62 5/8	**Vol**		16926700
#Bid 5	**#Ask** 5	**Spread**		1/16
High 64 9/16	**Low** 62 1/2	**Close**		63 1/8

Name	Bid	Chg.	Size	#Best	Name	Ask	Chg.	Size	#Best
BTRD	62 9/16	+2 7/1	800	186	BEST	62 5/8	+0	1000	16
NITE	62 9/16	+1/1	100	122	PRUS	62 5/8	+0	1000	23
DBKS	62 9/16	+1/1	100	9	RAMS	62 5/8	-1/1	1000	46
PERT	62 9/16	+1/1	100	21	INCA	62 5/8	+0	8000	235
ISLD	62 9/16	+0	1500	51	ISLD	62 5/8	-1/1	1000	362
MONT	62 1/2	-1/2	1000	1	ISLAND	62 5/8	+0	2000	0
ARCHIP	62 1/2	+0	2000	0	NITE	62 11/16	+0	100	113
SBSH	62 1/2	+0	1000	10	WCAI	62 11/16	+0	100	32
GSCO	62 1/2	+1/1	1000	27	ISLAND	62 1/16	+0	3100	0
NTRD	62 1/2	+0	400	9	RSSF	62 3/4	-1/8	100	10
MWSE	62 1/2	+0	4700	27	SBSH	62 3/4	+0	1000	1
ISLAND	62 1/2	+0	200	0	SLKC	62 3/4	+1/1	1000	29
HRZG	62 1/2	+0	200	27	DEMP	62 3/4	-1/8	100	9
WCAI	62 1/2	+0	100	20	REDI	62 3/4	+0	1000	230
ARCA	62 1/2	+0	2100	78	DIBOOK	62 13/16	+0	1000	0
ARCHIP	62 1/2	+0	100	0	DLJP	62 7/8	-3/4	1000	1

Figure 8–2 Supply greater than demand (S > D).

about the ax, totally ignore her actions. I certainly don't, and neither should you. Who is the ax? She is the market maker who *at a given time* is controlling most of the trading in a particular security. It's important for you to understand that the ax can and does change week to week, day to day, and sometimes even hour to hour.

Many times a particular market maker is the ax simply because of institutional orders. Say, for instance, that Fidelity Magellan wants to buy 400,000 shares of Microsoft. Fidelity may call Goldman Sachs (GSCO) and say, "I want to buy 200,000 MSFT at $72 net. Can you do it?" Microsoft has been trading, let's say, in a range of $71 to $73 per share over the last few days, and so Goldman accepts the order and is very happy. Likewise, Fidelity calls Morgan Stanley (MSCO) with the same order, and again Morgan Stanley obliges with a smile. Goldman doesn't know about the Morgan order, and Morgan doesn't know about Goldman. And it would be a violation of the law for them to disclose to each other that the order even exists, much less the details such as the buyer or the price of the order.

JDS Uniphase Corporation

JDSU		98 5/8	↑ +2 15/16	200	0t	10:06	
Bid	98 9/16	**Ask**	98 5/8	**Vol**		5427000	
#Bid	4	**#Ask**	4	**Spread**		1/16	
High	98 7/8	**Low**	95 15/32	**Close**		95 11/16	

Name	Bid	Chg.	Size	#Best	Name	Ask	Chg.	Size	#Best
ARCHIP	98 5/8	+0	1100	0	MLCO	98 5/8	+0	1600	7
ARCHIP	98 5/8	+1/8	500	0	FBCO	98 5/8	+0	2500	5
ARCHIP	98 5/8	+0	100	0	SNDV	98 5/8	+0	500	13
ISLAND	98 5/8	+0	2950	0	REDI	98 5/8	1/8	100	73
ARCHIP	98 9/16	+0	700	0	SELZ	98 11/16	-3/8	100	1
ARCA	98 9/16	+1/1	700	49	JPMS	98 11/16	+1/1	100	0
INCA	98 9/16	+0	4000	73	CIBC	98 3/4	+1/2	100	4
ISLD	98 9/16	+0	2800	131	WCAI	98 3/4	+1/4	500	21
REDI	98 9/16	+0	100	81	MONT	98 3/4	+1/4	100	4
ISLAND	98 9/16	+0	800	0	INCA	98 3/4	+0	2000	73
ARCHIP	98 1/2	+0	1000	0	MWSE	98 3/4	+1/8	400	1
NITE	98 1/2	+1/1	500	38	BRUT	98 3/4	+1/1	3000	21
ARCHIP	98 1/2	+0	300	0	ISLAND	98 3/4	+0	250	0
MWSE	98 1/2	+0	100	6	ISLD	98 3/4	+0	200	101
ARCHIP	98 1/2	+0	1000	0	GSCO	98 13/16	-3/8	500	14
ISLAND	98 1/2	+0	1700	0	SLKC	98 13/16	-1/4	100	2
HRCO	98 7/16	+1/8	100	15	MASH	98 13/16	+0	100	23
MSCO	98 7/16	+1/8	200	19	ISLAND	98 27/32	+0	500	0
ARCHIP	98 7/16	+0	100	0	HMQT	98 7/8	+1	100	4
ISLAND	98 7/16	+0	800	0	ISLAND	98 7/8	+0	500	0

Figure 8–3 Demand equals supply (D = S).

Now all day long both market makers "work" the order, each attempting to purchase 200,000 shares at a price somewhat less than $72 per share. If they are successful, they are able to buy for less than $72 and sell to Fidelity for $72, pocketing the difference (subject to some legal limitations). And they are very happy indeed! *The extent to which an ax can handle large institutional orders without greatly affecting a stock's price is the measure of her skill.* Since market-making firms go to great lengths to obtain institutional business and since the institutions want to enter and exit positions as undetected as possible (to get the best prices possible), market makers will go to very great lengths to conceal their true intentions. This concealment takes the form of many tactics. This keeps the institutions happy and placing orders, it keeps the market-making firm happy, it keeps the market maker's boss happy, and it keeps the market maker herself happy. The only person who may be unhappy is you if you get caught in one of her tactics! (Now remember what I said about how "easy" it is to interpret a L2 screen?)

OTHER MARKET MAKERS KNOW THE AX

Institutional orders are only one of the many elements that give the ax her power. Another is simply that other market makers know who she is, and they often try to trade in "lockstep" with her! In addition, seasoned traders have also learned to spot the ax rather quickly, and this too adds to her might. These market makers and seasoned traders, knowing the power of the ax to move a stock, have taken to the habit of shadowing her actions.

Here's how I do it. If I can determine with a high degree of confidence that a specific market maker is a net buyer, I simply try to buy along with, or slightly in front of, her. If I determine that's she's a net seller, again I'll try to go short along with her sales, or try to step in front of her. Now just to make this easy to explain, I'm simplifying this quite a bit—so don't blindly use this technique, as it has several potential pitfalls and could hurt your ego and account equity if you don't know what you're doing!

There are really three conclusions to draw here. One, with so many traders following the ax's actions, her actions to move a stock up or down often gain greater magnitude than they otherwise would. Two, she knows that everyone is trying to "key" on her and tries very hard to disguise her intentions, especially when working a large institutional order. Finally, because she does know her power, she deliberately tries to fool other traders by using several tactics that we discuss in Chapter 10.

TO SAVE YOUR ASK, FIND THE AX!

Now that you know why you have to identify the ax, let's discuss the "how." You'll be delighted to know that this is getting much easier as trading software continues to advance in sophistication. In the "old" days, prior to 1999, you had to be very diligent and determined and had to be willing to spend a lot of time staring at *each stock* to determine who the ax was. The method required careful observation—watching a stock trade and paying strict attention to which market maker seemed to be bidding or offering the most stock, and how often they did so. Most seasoned traders would also watch to see if a particular market maker would "sit on the bid or ask," meaning that once she bought (or sold), she would refresh her quotes in such a way as to remain at the inside (best) bid or ask. While this skill is still an art form (and very useful), it is now much easier to find the ax. And even though the market makers don't like it, modern software is making it harder for them to hide their intentions. Take a look at the screen shown in Figure 8–4.

The better trading platforms will have a column called "#best" or sometimes "hammer." It is important that you understand what

Sun Microsystems, Inc.								
SUNW	94 3/3	↑ +1		500	0t		11:54	
Bid ↓	94 5/16	**Ask**	94 3/8	**Vol**		5217100		
#Bid	1	**#Ask** 4		**Spread**		1/16		
High	94 1/2	**Low**	92	**Close**		93 3/8		

Name	Bid	Chg.	Size	#Best	Name	Ask	Chg.	Size	#Best
AGIS	94 5/16	+0	100	68	ISLAND	94 95/256	+0	400	0
ARCHIP	94 9/32	+0	200	0	NITE	94 3/8	-1/1	100	71
ISLAND	94 9/32	+0	200	0	PRUS	94 3/8	+0	100	15
ARCA	94 1/4	+0	200	83	SLKC	94 3/8	-1/4	100	72
MADF	94 1/4	+0	200	14	ISLAND	94 3/8	+0	1200	0
MSCO	94 1/4	+0	1000	18	ISLD	94 3/8	+0	1600	355
BRUT	94 1/4	+0	200	56	BRUT	94 7/16	-1/1	100	40
ISLD	94 1/4	+0	500	429	INCA	94 7/16	-1/1	200	256
ISLAND	94 1/4	+0	300	0	GSCO	94 1/2	+1/8	1000	3
JPMS	94 3/16	-1/8	100	5	MWSE	94 1/2	-3/4	200	4
RAMS	94 3/16	+0	1000	11	HRZG	94 1/2	+0	1600	7
DIBOOK	94 1/8	+0	100	0	MLCO	94 1/2	+0	1300	5
MRZG	94 1/8	+1/8	700	19	DLJP	94 1/2	+1/8	200	3
MEED	94 1/8	+0	100	1	BEST	94 1/2	+0	100	5
PWJC	94 1/8	+0	100	16	MADF	94 1/2	+0	1100	9
REDI	94 1/8	+0	100	181	PWJC	94 1/2	+0	700	3
PRUS	94 1/8	+3/4	100	15	AGIS	94 1/2	+0	100	69
CANT	94	+1/4	100	3	MSCO	94 1/2	+0	1000	16
BARD	94	+0	100	1	ISLAND	94 1/2	+0	102	0
ISLAND	94	+0	0	0	MASH	94 1/2	+0	300	52
MLCO	94	+2 1/2	1000	7	SBSH	94 1/2	+1	700	6
LEHM	94	+0	100	0	FBCO	94 5/8	+0	100	4
SHWD	94	+0	100	270	DIBOOK	94 5/8	+1/8	1300	0
ASSF	93 15/16	+1/4	100	18	DSKS	94 5/8	+1/8	200	3
MASH	93 15/16	-3/8	100	0	COST	94 5/8	+0	100	17
ISLAND	93 7/8	+0	100	10	ISLAND	94 5/8	+0	400	0
GSCO	93 7/8	+1/4	1000	0	COWN	94 5/8	-3/8	100	1

Figure 8–4 Using #best to determine the ax.

this means. Many traders mistakenly think that the "#best" is the number of times a market participant has gone best bid or best ask—meaning the participant was "outbidding" or "outoffering" the competition. This is *not* the case! As I described in Chapter 4, the *#best* (number best) *is the number of times a market participant remains the best bid or ask, after every other participant has left that tier level.* This means that a participant was willing to buy more (or sell more) than any other participants at that price tier. In other words, she was a significant purchaser (or seller) at that price. The more times that a participant remains at the inside market, after everyone else has gone, the more likely that she is the ax. Thus the #best, although not perfect, is the best tool available to determine who the ax is. To do this most effectively, to cover your ask, so to speak, you must know who the participants are.

WHO'S PLAYING POKER?

Study Tables 8–1 and 8–2 carefully. They will give you a good overview of the "poker players"—the market makers, the customers

TABLE 8-1

Market Participants

Market Participant	Role	Participant Symbol*
Professional trading groups	Firm's capital is traded for profit.	JPMS, MLCO, FLTT, DBKS
Market makers	Firms registered with the NASD. They must provide liquidity and make a two-sided market. Often trading institutional orders.	MSCO, WARR, HRZG, GSCO
Retail brokerages	Fill customer orders.	DEAN, LEGG, DLJP, MLCO
Order flow market makers	Pay brokers for order flow and fill customer orders.	NITE, SLKS, HRZG, MASH
Institutional ECNs	Electronic trade matching for large institutions such as banks	BTRD, INCA

*These are by way of example only. There are hundreds of market participants. See www.nasdaqtrader.com for a full list of current participants.

TABLE 8-2

Electronic Communication Networks

Full ECN Name	ECN Participant
Archipelago, L.L.C.	ARCA
Attain	ATTN
B-Trade Services, L.L.C.	BTRD
The BRASS Utility	BRUT
Instinet Corporation	INCA
The Island ECN	ISLD
MarketXT	MKXT
NexTrade	NTRD
Spear, Leeds & Kellogg	REDI
Strike Technologies	STRK

they may be trading for, and other players (participants) in the game. Except for the ECNs, which are all included, we've only included the "heavyweights" in the other categories. This may help you to determine who the ax is, and for whom she may be trading. Of course, these pigeonholes aren't perfect. Like everything else in trading, they require some application of skill and common sense. Here's my schematic for determining the ax from what we've covered so far.

1. Look for the highest #best on both sides of the market. The ax on the bid may be different from the ax on the ask.

2. If the #best is a retail ECN, especially ISLD or ARCA, ignore it! Island and Archipelago are *not* the ax!

3. If the #best is a professional trading group, a market maker, or a retail brokerage, that's the one I classify as the ax at that moment.

4. When order flow market makers and institutional ECNs are #best, the situation is a bit harder to get a read on. You'll have to study their actions carefully to determine if they are truly acting as the ax. Perhaps there is simply a lot of retail order flow at that time. Small retail orders are not strong enough to significantly move a liquid stock. Institutional buying or selling is required to move a stock significantly.

5. Finally, if INCA is #best, I pay special attention, since many times market makers of every persuasion will use INCA to buy or sell large quantities. They often do this to cloak the identity of the buying or selling market maker. They don't want to show their hand!

Once you've determined who the ax is, you can use that knowledge in at least two ways. First, if you determine that the market maker is involved in tactical maneuvers such as head-fakes or short squeezes, you can simply elect to stay out of her way. Or if you find an ax who is obviously a net buyer or net seller, you can often shadow the ax and trade along with her. We'll cover these tactics more deeply in Chapters 9 and 10.

CHIPPIES ON THE BID—WHAT DOES IT MEAN?

Besides the market makers, there are two groups of traders you'll want to pay special attention to: (1) traders on Archipelago (ARCA), also know as "Chippies," and (2) traders on the Island ECN (ISLD), known as "Islanders." Take a look at Figure 8–1 again, and you will see them. Remember that both ARCA and ISLD are retail ECNs. But even more important is that together these two ECNs match the overwhelming majority of direct-access trades. That is, most direct-access volume is traded on either ARCA or ISLD. Making the situation even more alluring is the fact that most Chippies and Islanders have relatively little trading experience and are not particularly astute traders. This is no reflection on either system or the traders themselves. It is more a matter of the infancy of direct-access trading. Reflect upon this for a moment. Assume that you are an astute trader and that you know where the beginners are—this just might give you a few trading ideas. Perhaps, even an edge or two! Now let's take a look at Figures 8–5 and 8–6 to see what Chippies or Islanders on the bid (or ask) might mean.

Figure 8–5 illustrates few Chippies on the bid.

1) One or two Chippies or Islanders on bid
2) Several market makers (MMs) on ask
Situations similar to this often indicate that the stock is headed lower in the near term.

Cisco Systems, Inc.								
CSCO	66 1/2	↑ +2 5/8	100	Ot	11:09			
Bid ↑ 66 7/16	**Ask** 66 1/2	**Vol** 22631200						
# Bid 4	# Ask 5	**Spread** 1/16						
High 67 1/16	**Low** 63 7/8	**Close** 63 7/8						

	Name	Bid	Chg.	Size	$Best		Name	Ask	Chg.	Size	$Best
P	ARCHIP	66 1/2	+0	100	0		ISLAND	66 15/32	+0	542	0
O	SELL	66 7/16	+0	100	18	O	RAMS	66 1/2	-1/1'	1000	41
O	REDI	66 7/16	+1/8	1000	168	O	CEUT	66 1/2	-1/8	100	22
O	INCA	66 7/16	+0	12200	170	O	MWSE	66 1/2	-3/8	2000	21
O	BTRD	66 7/16	+1 15/	1000	181	O	DEMP	66 1/2	-1/8	100	14
	DIBOOK	66 7/16	+0	1000	0		ISLD	66 1/2	+0	1200	216
O	GSCO	66 3/8	+1/1'	1000	24		ISLAND	66 1/2	+0	1200	0
O	NITE	66 3/8	+0	100	7	O	MSCO	66 9/16	+1/1'	1000	7
O	MDLD	66 3/8	+1/8	100	5	O	GSCO	66 9/16	+0	1000	5
O	ISLD	66 3/8	+0	1600	271	O	HMGT	66 9/16	+1/1'	100	3
	ISLAND	66 3/8	+0	1500	0		ARCA	66 9/16	-1/8	500	77
O	DBKS	66 5/16	+0	1000	5		ARCHIP	66 9/16	+0	500	0
O	ARCHIP	66 5/16	+0	1000	0		ISLAND	66 9/16	+0	1708	0
O	MADF	66 5/16	+0	2000	18	O	INCA	66 9/16	+0	1400	147
	DIBOOK	66 5/16	+0	1000	0	O	MADF	66 5/8	+1/8	200	29
O	ARCA	66 5/16	+0	1000	118	O	MONT	66 5/8	+1/8	1000	5
O	KCMO	66 1/4	+0	1000	2	O	SBSH	66 5/8	-1/8	200	8
O	ARCHIP	66 1/4	+0	500	0	O	BRUT	66 5/8	+0	1000	90
O	FBCO	66 1/4	+1/4	100	0		ISLAND	66 5/8	+0	1100	0
O	SBSH	66 1/4	+0	1000	6	O	ARCHIP	66 11/16	+0	500	0
O	SHWD	66 3/16	+0	100	14	O	RSSF	66 11/16	-1/8	100	7
O	RSSF	66 3/16	+0	100	5		ISLAND	66 11/16	+0	1000	0
O	PWJC	66 3/16	+0	100	6	O	BTRD	66 11/16	+0	2000	144
O	COWN	66 1/8	+0	100	0	O	NTRD	66 3/4	+0	800	5
O	PRUS	66 1/8	+0	100	27	O	ARCHIP	66 3/4	+0	200	0
	DIBOOK	66 1/8	+0	5800	0	O	JPMS	66 3/4	+0	100	3
O	HMGT	66 1/8	+1/1'	100	0	O	SHWD	66 3/4	-1/4	500	12
O	MONT	66 1/8	+1/8	1000	22	O	RAJA	66 3/4	+0	1000	12

Figure 8–5 Few Chippies on the bid.

Figure 8–6 illustrates many Chippies on the bid.

1) Many Chippies or Islanders on bid
2) Few MMs on ask

This situation often indicates that the stock is heading higher in the near term.

THE SECRET OF COLLAPSING TIERS

You now have several of the ingredients needed to correctly discern the immediate price action in a stock: (1) supply and demand, (2) knowledge of the ax, and (3) the meaning of Chippies and Islanders in both high- and low-liquidity situations. One of the final secrets to discerning near-term stock direction is the "secret of collapsing

Cisco Systems, Inc.

CSCO	66 1/2	↓ +2 5/8	2300	Ot	10:55
Bid ↑ 66 7/16	Ask 66 1/2	Vol 18192300			
# Bid 9	# Ask 3	Spread 1/16			
High 66 3/4	Low 63 7/8	Close 63 7/8			

Bid side:

	Name	Bid	Chg	Size	$Best
P	ARCHIP	66 17/32	+0	200	0
P	ARCHIP	66 1/2	+0	1000	0
P	ARCHIP	66 1/2	+1/1i	200	0
P	ARCHIP	66 1/2	+0	800	0
P	ARCHIP	66 1/2	+0	1000	0
P	ARCHIP	66 1/2	+0	500	0
	ISLAND	66 1/2	+0	2900	0
	DIBOOK	66 31/64	+3/3:	1000	0
	ISLAND	66 15/32	+0	1000	0
	DIBOOK	66 29/64	+3/6:	3000	0
	ISLAND	66 29/64	+0	1300	0
	ISLAND	66 113/25	+0	200	0
O	BTRD	66 7/16	+1/1i	1000	148
O	SELZ	66 7/16	+1/4	100	4
O	DLJP	66 7/16	+0	1000	3
O	BRUT	66 7/16	+1/1i	900	76
	DIBOOK	66 7/16	+0	1430	0
O	GSCO	66 7/16	+1/1i	1000	19
O	DEMP	66 7/16	+1/8	100	12
O	INCA	66 7/16	+0	3200	140
O	ISLD	66 7/16	+0	7200	223
O	REDI	66 7/16	+0	1000	136
	ISLAND	66 7/16	+0	1400	0
O	JOSE	66 3/8	+0	500	1
	DIBOOK	66 3/8	+0	400	0
O	SLKC	66 3/8	+7/8	1000	23
O	SHWD	66 3/8	+0	100	9
O	WCAI	66 3/8	+0	100	3

Ask side:

	Name	Ask	Chg	Size	$Best
P	ARCHIP	66 1/2	+0	34	0
O	HRZG	66 1/2	+0	900	16
O	MWSE	66 1/2	+0	4800	16
O	PWJC	66 1/2	+0	1000	8
O	FOOL	66 9/16	+0	100	20
O	NFSC	66 9/16	-1/4	500	8
O	BEST	66 9/16	+1/1i	1000	10
O	JEFF	66 5/8	+1/4	100	0
O	PURE	66 5/8	+0	100	7
O	NTRD	66 5/8	+1/8	500	4
O	MADF	66 5/8	+1/8	600	21
O	SHWD	66 5/8	+0	100	12
O	WCAI	66 5/8	+1/8	1000	5
O	BTRD	66 5/8	+0	200	118
O	ARCHIP	66 5/8	+0	1400	0
O	ARCA	66 5/8	+0	1400	62
O	BRUT	66 5/8	+0	1300	71
	ISLAND	66 5/8	+0	1900	0
O	ISLD	66 5/8	+0	1900	185
O	RSSF	66 11/16	+1/8	100	7
	ISLAND	66 45/64	+0	300	0
	ISLAND	66 23/32	+0	120	0
O	CWCO	66 3/4	-1/8	100	1
O	NEED	66 3/4	+3/4	100	0
O	ARCHIP	66 3/4	+0	100	0
O	NITE	66 3/4	+0	1600	36
O	DBKS	66 3/4	+1/4	100	2
O	AGED	66 3/4	+1/4	100	1

Figure 8–6 Many Chippies on the bid.

tiers." It is truly amazing how few traders understand this. That's why we call it a secret. The best traders, of course, already know of and use this technique. Let's study Figures 8–7 through 8–10.

As you can see in Figure 8–7, the buyers and sellers are pretty much head to head. The stock is not really moving at the moment. However, now look at Figure 8–8, taken 30 seconds later. Notice that while the inside bid and ask are essentially the same, the tiers underneath the inside quote have changed rather noticeably. At the second and third tiers several bidders have stepped away and either are no longer bidding or are bidding at a lower price. Notice also that these bidders tend to be market makers.

Now take a look at Figure 8–9. This shot was taken just another 30 seconds after Figure 8–8. Here even more tiers have disappeared.

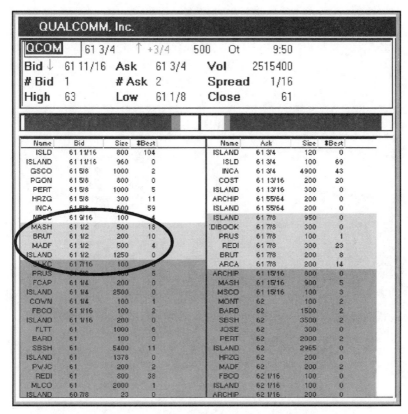

Name	Bid	Size	$Best		Name	Ask	Size	$Best
ISLD	61 11/16	800	104		ISLAND	61 3/4	120	0
ISLAND	61 11/16	960	0		ISLD	61 3/4	100	69
GSCO	61 5/8	1000	2		INCA	61 3/4	4900	43
PGON	61 5/8	800	0		COST	61 13/16	200	20
PERT	61 5/8	1000	5		ISLAND	61 13/16	300	0
HRZG	61 5/8	300	11		ARCHIP	61 55/64	200	0
INCA	61 5/8	600	59		ISLAND	61 55/64	200	0
MSCC	61 9/16	100	4		ISLAND	61 7/8	950	0
MASH	61 1/2	500	18		DIBOOK	61 7/8	300	0
BRUT	61 1/2	200	10		PRUS	61 7/8	100	1
MADF	61 1/2	500	4		REDI	61 7/8	300	23
ISLAND	61 1/2	1250	0		BRUT	61 7/8	200	8
SLKC	61 7/16	100			ARCA	61 7/8	200	14
PRUS	61 3/8		5		ARCHIP	61 15/16	800	0
FCAP	61 1/4	200	0		MASH	61 15/16	900	5
ISLAND	61 1/4	2500	0		MSCO	61 15/16	100	3
COWN	61 1/4	100	1		MONT	62	100	2
FBCO	61 1/16	100	2		BARD	62	1500	2
ISLAND	61 1/16	200	0		SBSH	62	3500	2
FLTT	61	1000	6		JOSE	62	300	0
BARD	61	100	0		PERT	62	2000	2
SBSH	61	5400	11		ISLAND	62	2965	0
ISLAND	61	1378	0		HRZG	62	200	0
PWJC	61	200	2		MADF	62	200	2
REDI	61	800	38		FBCO	62 1/16	100	0
MLCO	61	2000	1		ISLAND	62 1/16	100	0
ISLAND	60 7/8	23	0		ARCHIP	62 1/16	200	0

Figure 8–7 Qualcomm is head to head, but the ax (MASH) is bidding only ½.

And while the bidders are about the same, a few more sellers are on the ask. In the next few seconds this stock is heading down.

Now take a look at the final shot in the sequence (Figure 8–10). At 9:54 a.m., 2 minutes after the lower tiers started to collapse, the stock is trading 1¼ points lower! This is the secret of collapsing tiers! Yet many traders make the mistake of concentrating all their effort at the inside market. They might as well be trading using only Level I!

The next series of shots (Figures 8–11 through 8–13) shows what happens when the lower tiers collapse on the ask side. Study them and commit this pattern to memory. You will see this happen many times each and every day. Here a few minutes later Altera has risen about ⅝ of a point.

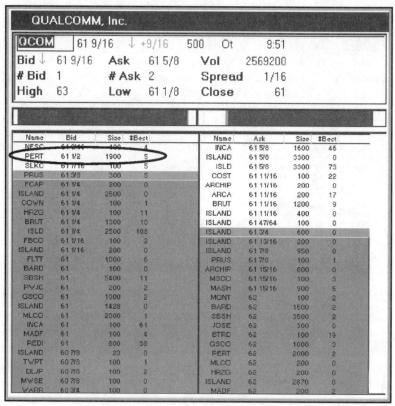

Figure 8–8 Thirty seconds later several bidders have disappeared, including the ax.

Use This Secret as a Timing Device!

While I do not use collapsing tiers as my only entry or exit signal, I do use this technique to tell me the exact time to buy or sell short when trading one of my playbook setups. Using this technique will often get you in or out ahead of the crowd, simply because the crowd does not know how to evaluate what's happening. In fact, I often hear comments such as "The Level II is jumping around erratically, so I don't know what to do!" Many times this erratic behavior is simply the result of tiers collapsing underneath, where the trader is not looking! Before you actually trade, there's one more knowledge area to address—how to get filled when it counts, when you'll have the highest probability of making a profit! Let's take a look at . . .

QUALCOMM, Inc.

QCOM	61 11/32 ↓ +11/32	400	Ot	9:52

Bid ↓	61 1/4	Ask	61 5/16	Vol	2604000
# Bid	1	# Ask	1	Spread	1/16
High	63	Low	61 1/8	Close	61

Name	Bid	Size	$Best	Name	Ask	Size	$Best
COWN	61 1/4	100	1	ARCHIP	61 1/4	500	0
ISLAND	61 1/4	260	0	ARCHIP	61 1/4	100	0
FBCO	61 1/16	100	2	INCA	61 5/16	5300	49
NFSC	61 1/16	100	4	ARCHIP	61 3/8	2000	0
ISLAND	61 1/16	700	0	ARCA	61 3/8	2000	18
ISLD	61 1/16	700	110	ISLAND	61 13/32	200	0
FLTT	61	1000	6	ARCHIP	61 13/32	200	0
BARD	61	100	0	BRUT	61 7/16	200	11
SBSH	61	5400	11	ISLAND	61 7/16	800	0
PWJC	61	200	2	ISLD	61 7/16	1000	75
GSCO	61	1000	2	REDI	61 1/2	400	23
MLCO	61	2000	1	DIBOOK	61 1/2	400	0
MADF	61	400	4	ISLAND	61 9/16	1600	0
REDI	61	800	38	NITE	61 5/8	100	11
BRUT	61	2000	10	ARCHIP	61 41/64	200	0
ISLAND	61	1578	0	COST	61 11/16	100	22
INCA	61	100	61	ISLAND	61 11/16	200	0
ISLAND	60 7/8	23	0	ISLAND	61 47/64	100	0
TWPT	60 7/8	100	1	ISLAND	61 3/4	600	0
DLJP	60 7/8	100	2	ISLAND	61 43/64	1000	0
MWSE	60 7/8	100	0	ISLAND	61 13/16	2000	0
HRZG	60 7/8	100	11	ISLAND	61 7/8	950	0
SLKC	60 13/16	100	5	PRUS	61 7/8	100	1
VARR	60 3/4	100	0	MSCO	61 15/16	100	3
GKMC	60 3/4	100	0	MASH	61 15/16	900	5
COST	60 5/8	200	5	MONT	62	100	2
PGON	60 5/8	100	0	BARD	62	1500	2

Figure 8–9 The bid tier has collapsed.

UNDERSTANDING ECNs AND ORDER ROUTING— GETTING FILLED WHEN IT COUNTS!

The first ECN was Instinet (which displays as INCA in your L2 window), introduced in 1969 as a method for institutions to display bids and offers and execute transactions, thus providing a medium of exchange. At the outset, Instinet was only a medium of trade between institutions. It later allowed brokerage firms to participate in the use of its network. A major drawback of Instinet was its attempt to exclude all other users except institutions and brokerages. Until recently, Instinet was not a route in your day trading software. [To be exact, you may have been able to trade via Instinet either by being filled through INCA when using ARCA or by pref-

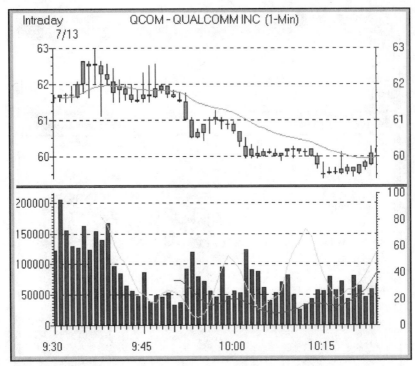

Figure 8–10 Two minutes after the bid tier collapsed, Qualcomm is trading 1¼ points lower.

erencing (PREF) INCA with SelectNet.] Now the better trading platforms are including an "Instinet" button, allowing you to execute directly via Instinet.[1] You may also trade via Instinet by calling your broker to place a trade.

In January 1997 an event occurred which opened the door to modern-day day trading. The SEC order-handling rules were implemented to provide traders with limit order protection, thus allowing them to participate in and trade in the NASDAQ market on a level playing field with institutions and brokerages. ECNs' bids and offers are displayed on NASDAQ terminals. The effect of this is to allow individual traders to make a market in NASDAQ stocks. The introduction of ECNs has given individuals the ability to conduct trades in the market the same way market makers do without incurring the costs or having to meet the rigorous requirements of becoming a registered member of the NASDAQ exchange.

Altera Corp.									

ALTR 124 3/32 ↑ +13 1/32 200   Ot   9:39
Bid ↑ 124 5/16 **Ask** 124 3/8 **Vol**   2319900
 # Bid 6   **# Ask** 1   **Spread**   1/16
High 124 17/64 **Low** 119 1/2 **Close** 111 1/16

Name	Bid	Chg.	Size	‡Best		Name	Ask	Chg.	Size	‡Best
	ISLAND	124 3/8	+0	300	0	P	ARCHIP	124 3/8	+1/11	200	0
O	ISLD	124 5/16	+1/11	500	139	O	MONT	124 3/8	-3/8	200	5
O	AGIS	124 5/16	+0	100	10		:DIBOOK	124 3/8	+0	500	0
O	FLTT	124 5/16	+1/11	100	14	O	CIBC	124 1/2	+0	100	0
	:DIBOOK	124 5/16	+0	1400	0		:DIBOOK	124 1/2	+0	200	0
	:DIBOOK	124 5/16	+0	500	0	O	PRUS	124 1/2	+0	100	5
O	REDI	124 5/16	+0	1400	61	O	NITE	124 1/2	-1	200	2
O	WCAI	124 5/16	+1/8	1000	6	O	BEST	124 1/2	+0	100	5
O	INCA	124 5/16	+0	500	70	O	CHIP	124 1/2	+1/4	100	0
	:DIBOOK	124 1/4	+0	1500	0	O	JPMS	124 1/2	+0	100	0
	ISLAND	124 1/4	+0	300	0	O	MADF	124 1/2	+0	100	6
	ISLAND	124 13/64	+0	100	0	O	ISLD	124 1/2	+1/8	100	25
O	NFSC	124 3/16	+0	1000	17	O	REDI	124 1/2	+0	200	12
O	PERT	124 3/16	-3/8	100	2	O	WCAI	124 1/2	+0	1000	5
O	MADF	124 3/16	+3/11	200	10	O	INCA	124 1/2	+0	1200	16
O	HRZG	124 3/16	+0	100	13		ISLAND	124 1/2	+0	1100	0
	ISLAND	124 3/16	+0	1344	0	O	BRUT	124 9/16	+0	100	1
	ISLAND	124 1/8	+0	300	0		ISLAND	124 9/16	+0	1000	0
O	SELZ	124 1/8	+0	100	0	O	MSCO	124 5/8	+0	1000	1
O	TWPT	124 1/16	+13	100	2	O	SBSH	124 5/8	+3/8	200	2
O	SHWD	124 1/16	+1/11	100	3	O	ARCHIP	124 5/8	+0	200	0
O	GSCO	124	+1/8	1000	5	O	GSCO	124 5/8	+1/8	1000	0
O	MLCO	124	+0	1000	4		ISLAND	124 5/8	+0	200	0
O	MASH	124	+0	300	7	O	LEHM	124 5/8	+0	100	0
	ISLAND	124	+0	538	0	O	ARCA	124 5/8	+1/4	200	11
O	DBKS	124	+0	100	0	O	SLKC	124 5/8	+1/4	100	5
O	DLJP	123 7/8	+1/8	200	1	O	FBCO	124 11/16	+0	100	2
O	ARCHIP	123 13/16	+0	3100	0	O	ARCHIP	124 3/4	+0	100	0

Figure 8–11   Altera has an apparent deep ask tier at 124½.

ARCA, ISLD, SelectNet, and SOES are the most popular and accessible ECNs. A distinction should be made here. While Select-Net and SOES are electronic communication networks, they are not ECNs in the sense that they are not backed by a brokerage and do not have their own book.

ECNs as popularly defined are electronic communications (or commerce) networks where your order is posted to an electronic order book. This book lists all buy and sell orders for a particular stock that come in through that respective routing system. If your order matches another order on the book, it will be filled instantaneously as long as it falls within the trading range and does not lock or cross the market (i.e., is not bid at or above the offer, or offered at or below the bid). If your order is not filled, then it will post on the L2 display awaiting a matching order.[2]

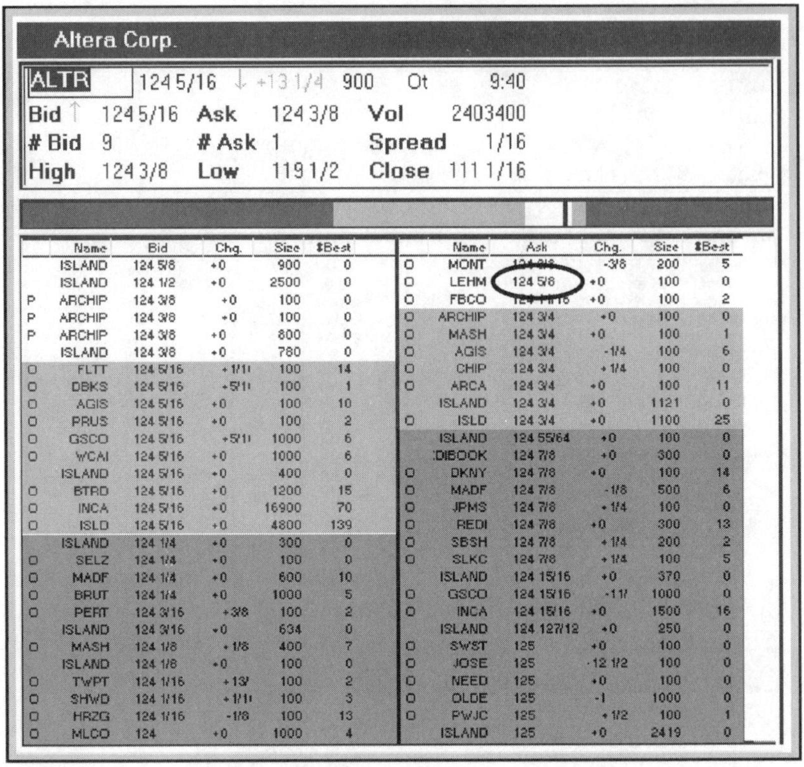

Altera Corp.

ALTR 124 5/16 ↓ +13 1/4 900 Ot 9:40
Bid ↑ 124 5/16 Ask 124 3/8 Vol 2403400
Bid 9 # Ask 1 Spread 1/16
High 124 3/8 Low 119 1/2 Close 111 1/16

	Name	Bid	Chg.	Size	$Best
	ISLAND	124 5/8	+0	900	0
	ISLAND	124 1/2	+0	2500	0
P	ARCHIP	124 3/8	+0	100	0
P	ARCHIP	124 3/8	+0	100	0
P	ARCHIP	124 3/8	+0	800	0
	ISLAND	124 3/8	+0	780	0
O	FLTT	124 5/16	+1/11	100	14
O	DBKS	124 5/16	+5/11	100	1
O	AGIS	124 5/16	+0	100	10
O	PRUS	124 5/16	+0	100	2
O	GSCO	124 5/16	+5/11	1000	6
O	WCAI	124 5/16	+0	1000	6
	ISLAND	124 5/16	+0	400	0
O	BTRD	124 5/16	+0	1200	15
O	INCA	124 5/16	+0	16900	70
O	ISLD	124 5/16	+0	4800	139
	ISLAND	124 1/4	+0	300	0
O	SELZ	124 1/4	+0	100	0
O	MADF	124 1/4	+0	600	10
O	BRUT	124 1/4	+0	1000	5
O	PERT	124 3/16	+3/8	100	2
	ISLAND	124 3/16	+0	634	0
O	MASH	124 1/8	+1/8	400	7
	ISLAND	124 1/8	+0	100	0
O	TWPT	124 1/16	+13/	100	2
O	SHWD	124 1/16	+1/11	100	3
O	HRZG	124 1/16	-1/8	100	13
O	MLCO	124	+0	1000	4

	Name	Ask	Chg.	Size	$Best
O	MONT	[illegible]	-3/8	200	5
O	LEHM	124 5/8	+0	100	0
O	FBCO	[illegible]	+0	100	2
O	ARCHIP	124 3/4	+0	100	0
O	MASH	124 3/4	+0	100	1
O	AGIS	124 3/4	-1/4	100	6
O	CHIP	124 3/4	+1/4	100	0
O	ARCA	124 3/4	+0	100	11
	ISLAND	124 3/4	+0	1121	0
O	ISLD	124 3/4	+0	1100	25
	ISLAND	124 55/64	+0	100	0
	:DIBOOK	124 7/8	+0	300	0
O	DKNY	124 7/8	+0	100	14
O	MADF	124 7/8	-1/8	500	6
O	JPMS	124 7/8	+1/4	100	0
O	REDI	124 7/8	+0	300	13
O	SBSH	124 7/8	+1/4	200	2
O	SLKC	124 7/8	+1/4	100	5
	ISLAND	124 15/16	+0	370	0
O	GSCO	124 15/16	-11/	1000	0
O	INCA	124 15/16	+0	1500	16
	ISLAND	124 127/12	+0	250	0
O	SWST	125	+0	100	0
O	JOSE	125	·12 1/2	100	0
O	NEED	125	+0	100	0
O	OLDE	125	-1	1000	0
O	PWJC	125	+1/2	100	1
	ISLAND	125	+0	2419	0

Figure 8–12 However, less than 1 minute later the ask tier has collapsed.

Archipelago (ARCA)

Terra Nova Trading, LLC, originally created ARCA, also known as the "Archipelago Book." Terra Nova is a broker-dealer and uses the ARCA internal book. As with many ECNs, many changes are afoot at ARCA. Recently Goldman Sachs made a multimillion dollar investment in ARCA and ARCA had filed to become a listed exchange. However, in the spring of 2000, ARCA withdrew its filing, and instead it has opted for a merger with the Pacific Exchange. At this time, that merger is pending regulatory approval. In June 2000, ARCA announced that it would also match listed stocks. This, in conjunction with new NYSE rules,[3] for the first time gives direct access to the NYSE via an ECN.

ARCA is more than just an electronic route through which you can buy or sell stock. It has intelligent features (and consequent drawbacks) that other ECNs do not have. By "intelligent" I mean

Altera Corp.

ALTR	125	↑ +13 15/16 100	Ot	9:41
Bid ↑ 124 13/16	Ask 124 7/8	Vol 2650000		
# Bid 3	# Ask 0	Spread 1/16		
High 125	Low 119 1/2	Close 111 1/16		

	Name	Bid	Chg.	Size	#Best
P	ARCHIP	125	+0	600	0
P	ARCHIP	124 7/8	+0	500	0
P	ARCHIP	124 7/8	+0	200	0
O	ISLD	124 13/16	+0	1000	146
O	BTRD	124 13/16	+0	1900	16
O	INCA	124 13/16	+0	14400	76
	ISLAND	124 13/16	+0	1100	0
O	NFSC	124 3/4	+1/4	100	20
O	TWPT	124 3/4	+1 1/	100	3
O	AGIS	124 3/4	+0	100	11
O	MLCO	124 3/4	+0	1000	5
	DIBOOK	124 3/4	+0	400	0
O	REDI	124 3/4	+0	400	61
O	MASH	124 3/4	+0	1000	7
O	HRZG	124 3/4	+1/8	100	14
O	FLTT	124 11/16	+3/8	100	15
O	SHWD	124 5/8	+1/8	100	3
O	GSCO	124 9/16	+1/8	1000	6
O	WCAI	124 9/16	+0	100	7
O	MADF	124 1/2	+1/4	500	10
O	NTRD	124 1/2	+2 1/2	500	0
O	BRUT	124 1/2	+0	2000	5
O	RAMS	124 1/2	+4 1/2	1000	0
O	DLJP	124 1/2	+5/8	200	1
	ISLAND	124 1/2	+0	50	0
	ISLAND	124 23/64	+0	1000	0
O	DBKS	124 5/16	+5/1	100	1
O	PRUS	124 5/16	+0	100	2

	Name	Ask	Chg.	Size	#Best
O	MONT	124 7/8	-1/8	200	6
O	SBSH	124 15/16	+1/1	200	3
O	SWST	125	+0	100	0
O	JOSE	125	-12 1/2	100	0
O	OLDE	125	-1	1000	0
O	LEHM	125	+3/8	100	0
O	PRUS	125	-1/2	1500	5
O	JPMS	125	+0	100	0
O	MADF	125	+0	900	6
O	PERT	125	+0	300	1
O	BRUT	125	+0	1400	1
O	WCAI	125	+0	100	5
O	MWSE	125	-5 13/	1200	0
O	AGIS	125	+1/8	100	7
O	NITE	125	-1/2	100	4
O	SLKC	125	+0	500	5
O	INCA	125	+0	1300	18
	ISLAND	125	+0	309	0
	ISLAND	125 7/128	+0	200	0
	ISLAND	125 1/16	+0	600	0
O	ISLD	125 1/16	+1/1	600	29
	ISLAND	125 1/8	+0	340	0
O	RSSF	125 1/8	+3/4	100	1
O	FLTT	125 1/8	+0	100	0
O	GSCO	125 3/16	+1/8	1000	0
O	HMGT	125 1/4	+5/8	100	0
O	SELZ	125 1/4	+0	100	1
O	SNDV	125 1/4	-3/8	100	0

Figure 8–13 Altera has gained more than ½ point in less than 2 minutes.

that ARCA works your order for you—it goes out to find a buyer or seller of stock. When you use ARCA without PNP (post no preference) checked in your order screen (you are selling to the best bid or buying from the best ask), ARCA goes out to each ECN or market maker to buy or sell stock for you. ARCA will attempt to "cross" an order first for speed. It will look to match your order with or "hit" another ARCA trader as its first priority. Next, ARCA will go to all other ECNs in an attempt to fill your order. If no ECNs are at the best bid or ask, ARCA will then use SelectNet to go to the most active market maker. ARCA allows each market maker up to 30 seconds to fill or pass on your order, so it can be a slow route.

ARCA, with PNP checked in your order screen, acts as a SelectNet broadcast. That is, it allows you to bid or offer stock to all market makers and ECNs simultaneously. A factor to consider here is that you cannot bid or offer at the inside market with PNP checked. If you do, your order will be canceled and a message such as "Order can-celed—would lock or cross market" will appear in your order entry screen. You have to bid either above the best bid (pay more) or below the best bid (wait to enter by offering to pay less, in which case you will most likely not be filled). Similarly, you must offer below the best ask (accept less) if you realistically want to be filled when selling or above the best ask (look to accept more, in which case you will most likely not be filled).

ARCA shows up as ARCA in your L2 window. If you have full access to the ARCA book and have "Show All NASDAQ Exchanges" checked in your setup, each price tier in the full ARCA order book will show as ARCHIP. This is significant in your trading. You have the advantage of seeing the ARCHIPs, or Chippies, piling on the bid, scrambling to get in when they think a stock is trending up (and they want to go long or cover), and piling on the ask, scrambling to get out when they think a stock is trending down (and they want to sell or short). If you are not bidding or offering, but simply using ARCA to sell at the bid or to buy at the ask, you will not show up in the L2 window.

When ARCA uses SelectNet PREF (if you have full access to the ARCA book), you will see ARCHIP in your L2 screen with a "P" in the status column if you have "status" checked in your L2 setup. This tells you that your order is being preferenced to a market maker. During this time you can't be hit by another ARCA trader. While in this mode, if you are filled by certain market makers, you will be charged extra (usually around $0.015 per share), but it is much better to get filled and pay an extra surcharge than to miss being filled at your price.

Useful ARCA Facts

- When bidding or offering stock using ARCA, you are not SOESable. (SOES section, see below.) Unlike a registered market maker, you have no obligation to fill an order and you may cancel it at any time.
- When bidding or offering stock using ARCA, you cannot do AON (all or none). While partial fills are possible, they are less likely to happen with ARCA for the reason stated above and because you would not use ARCA to get a fill on a fast-moving stock.

- While your order is live, all partial fills are charged as one ticket (one commission) by most brokerages. In a slow or moderately paced stock, if you wait, your order will usually be completed in one fill.

- For reasons stated above, ARCA is best used to trade a slow-moving stock. As ARCA works for you, it is also very good for trading larger orders of stock.

- When you are bidding or offering stock in an attempt to get a better price or get a fill when market makers won't trade with you via SOES or SelectNet, you are less likely to get a fill than if you were to simply use ARCA to buy at the ask or sell at the bid.

- The maximum position size (shares per trade) is 10,000 shares per order. This is more than sufficient for 99.9 percent of your EDAT needs.

- ARCA allows you to trade premarket and postmarket. However, all live orders are canceled 2 minutes after the market close. You may then reenter your order and continue to trade in the "evening" session using ARCA.

- Used properly, ARCA will help you increase your exposure to the NASDAQ market. This is good, as it helps minimize partial fills. ARCA's consequent downside is that it is slow and should not be relied upon to trade a fast-moving stock. Using ARCA in a fast-moving issue can lead you to either end up chasing the stock or not getting filled at all (the lesser of the two evils!).

The Island (ISLD)

Datek, Inc. created the Island Book (ISLD). Datek is a broker-dealer, and ISLD is its ECN or internal book. ISLD is not as intelligent as ARCA and allows trades only between ISLD traders, but it doesn't have many of the restrictions of ARCA, thereby making it a very powerful medium of exchange. ISLD has no size or time restrictions. You may trade any number of shares at any time of day, though at the time of this writing, you probably won't find anyone to trade with before 8 a.m. or after 8 p.m. Eastern Time. ISLD offers the benefit of what is known as Island "divergence." This is a fancy word that means that all orders entered on Island will be matched with equivalent Island orders, thereby giving the trader the tremendous advantage of instantaneous fills and potential price improvement. These advantages result from the large volume of traders that use the ISLD ECN to trade. For example, if you enter a limit buy[4] for a particular stock at 14⅞ and an ISLD order is on the book to sell the same stock at 14⁷⁄₁₆, you will receive not only an instantaneous execution but also a ⁷⁄₁₆ price improvement. On a fast-moving stock you can often receive price improvements when entering and exiting a position. Like ARCA, the Island has taken initial steps toward becoming a registered stock exchange. However, at the time of this writing, the Island remains an independent ECN.

Useful ISLD Facts

- It allows limit orders.
- It does not allow market orders.
- You can bid or offer stock to other ISLD traders and be hit (filled) by a market maker or trader executing a SelectNet preference (PREF).
- You cannot hit a market maker's bid or take her offer using ISLD. If you try, your order will cancel with the message "Order canceled—would lock or cross market." (This is an example of a locked market.)
- Limit orders stay live outside the best bid or ask.
- Orders bid as the best bid are acceptable as long as they are less than the best ask. (This would *not* lock or cross the market.)
- Orders offered out at the best ask are acceptable as long as they are more than the best bid. (Nor would this lock or cross the market.)
- ISLD allows you to trade outside market hours.
- It does not allow you to preference market makers.
- It allows odd lots[5] (not divisible by 100).

Small Order Execution System (SOES)

NASDAQ introduced electronic execution when it developed the Small Order Execution System in 1985. SOES is a mandatory execution system that allows traders to buy or sell up to 1,000 shares of stock. SOES was fully implemented in 1988 when the SEC required all market makers to participate in the use of the system. The requirement was a direct result of the market makers' actions during the market crash of 1987. During the crash, market makers were not answering their phones, and, therefore, not honoring their quotes. Traders could not get orders executed. Once market makers were required to participate in SOES, traders could execute orders with market makers electronically, without having to call them on the phone.

SOES is theoretically a mandatory execution system. Market makers must honor their quoted sizes and prices. This does not mean, however, that you will get a fill at the quoted price for the reasons stated below.

Market makers have opposed SOES since it was introduced. It is my experience that you will rarely get a good fill using SOES, at least not without superb timing. Market makers can sit on the inside market and not trade with you. They have 15 seconds to refresh their price before deciding to move to a new level. In addition, they are required only to honor their quote at the SOES tier size. This means that once they have filled even one order, they are free to change their quote. If a market is moving down and you're trying a SOES sell, the only way you'll get filled is if you're first in line—a rare occurrence. The converse is true for a buy. If the stock is moving up rapidly, getting a SOES fill is nearly impossible. The only practical exceptions to these two situations are if you're willing to pay too much or sell for too little in relation to where the market maker thinks the stock is heading. Of course in these situations, she'll gladly give you a SOES fill—but do you really want it?

SOES trades in lots (share sizes) known as tiers. These are stock-specific and are usually 200, 500, or a maximum of 1,000 shares. NASDAQ sets a stock's tier size. The tier size for a stock can usually be determined by watching the time & sales screen or the predominant "size" in your L2 window. Most brokers also incorporate a "look-up" feature in their EDAT software that will tell you the SOES tier size for any NASDAQ stock.

SOES has what is known as the "5-minute rule." This rule restricts a trader from buying or selling a stock twice within 5 minutes. Consecutive orders to buy or sell a stock in which the total amount of shares exceeds the stock's tier size must not occur within a 5-minute time period. In addition, if you receive a partial fill with

SOES, your broker may further enforce the 5-minute rule by not allowing you to buy the remainder of your order within 5 minutes using SOES. This rule does not prevent you from both entering and exiting a position via SOES, so long as the total shares do not exceed the tier size limit. For example, you could use SOES to buy 1,000 DELL and use SOES to sell 1,000 DELL within 5 minutes. But you could not then reenter DELL via SOES until 5 minutes had expired from your exit.

Short selling on SOES must be done on an uptick. This "uptick rule" seriously limits a trader's shorting ability, as it forces a trader to wait for an uptick in the print. This narrows a trader's window of opportunity to get a short order filled and forces a trader to eat the spread. Once short at the bid, a trader is already down the amount of the spread.

Useful SOES Facts

- SOES executes *only* to market makers, thereby limiting your chance of being filled.
- SOES facilitates limit and market orders up to the stock tier size.
- You cannot bid or offer (play market maker) using SOES.
- Limit orders are not permitted outside (above, below) the best bid or ask.
- SOES trading is restricted to market hours.
- You may not preference ECNs with SOES.
- SOES does allow odd lots (lots not divisible by 100).
- SOES does not allow AON (all or none) orders.

SelectNet

NASDAQ expanded electronic execution when it introduced the SelectNet system in 1990. SelectNet orders are similar to ECN (ARCA and ISLD book) orders except for one very important distinction. SelectNet orders are not broadcast to the ECNs, only to market makers. You must PREF (preference) an ECN if you wish to trade with it via SelectNet.

SelectNet orders may be broadcast (displayed to all market makers at once), or preferenced to a specific market maker or ECN by selecting the PREF checkbox option on the order entry screen. Preferencing a market maker can be a powerful order execution technique, as she is theoretically obligated to give you at least a partial fill. If a market maker does not fill your order, she is said to be "backing away," which is in direct violation of NASDAQ's firm-quote policy rule. This is difficult to prove, however, and if the market maker can show that she just filled an order at that price and was in the process of refreshing the quote, she is not obligated to fill your order.

Useful SelectNet Facts

- SelectNet allows for limit orders, which are only seen by market makers. Orders preferenced to market makers via SelectNet do not appear in the L2 montage. They are therefore not seen by other traders or market makers (assuming you're not using a "broadcast"). However, market makers are not obligated to fill your SelectNet limit order unless it is the same as the market maker's displayed price.
- SelectNet orders stay live 10 seconds before they can be canceled.
- SelectNet does not allow market orders.
- SelectNet allows you to bid or offer stock. It accepts orders at the inside market or between the inside market.
- SelectNet allows you to trade outside market hours. However, all live orders are canceled 2 minutes after the market close.
- SelectNet will allow you to enter new limit orders 30 minutes prior to the market open and 30 minutes after the market close.

EXECUTION STRATEGIES—WHEN TO USE EACH ROUTE

Use ARCA When You:

- Are trying to move a large number of shares on a slower-paced stock.
- Want to bid or offer with greater exposure.
- Want to trade outside market hours.

- Want to trade outside the best bid or ask.
- Are a beginner, trading slow stocks, since ARCA automatically "works" your order.
- Are an advanced trader and want to trade against beginners! This is an *edge!*

Use ISLD When You:

- Are trying to move smaller shares or odd lots on any paced stock (slow, medium, or fast) to other ISLD traders.
- Want to bid or offer on a fast-paced stock.
- Want price improvement due to divergence.
- Want to trade outside market hours.
- Want to detect a stock trend since ISLD traders are usually most active (at the best bid or ask) at the bottom and top of stock movements.
- Want to unload odd lots if you get an odd-lot fill.
- Are an advanced trader and want to trade against beginners! This is an *edge!* (It is my experience that the ISLD traders are the least experienced traders on the ECNs.)

Use SOES When You:

- Want mandatory automatic order fills (with superb timing).
- Want to unload odd lots if you get an odd-lot fill.

Use SelectNet When You:

- Want limit order fills at the inside market (at or between the best bid and ask) with PREF checked. Since SelectNet orders can only be seen by the market maker you're currently preferencing, both you and the market maker can trade without "showing your cards."
- Want to bid or offer at the inside market on a slow- or medium-paced stock.
- Want to get out of a stock moving against you without using a market order.

SelectNet Disadvantages

As mentioned, SelectNet orders stay live 10 seconds before they can be canceled. And 10 seconds can seem like a lifetime to an EDAT trader! Hence, it is best used on a slow-paced or moderately paced stock. The 10-second factor can be frustrating on a stock that suddenly gains momentum. For example, you have just placed a limit order to buy or sell at your desired price, the stock moves against you, you hit the "Cancel" button, nothing happens, and you get filled anyway. Major frustration!

In addition, SelectNet orders sometimes get stuck in the electronic pipeline. I have been filled on SelectNet orders up to 2 minutes after canceling the order. I called the broker and was told "That's part of the game. Deal with it!" The moral of the story? Use SelectNet judiciously when buying!

SOME FINAL WORDS ON ORDER ROUTING

See Table 8–3 for a compact summary of order routing. However, bear in mind that the area of order routing is changing rapidly. Consolidations, mergers, and regulatory issues will keep the entire arena very dynamic for the foreseeable future. To keep up, visit www.nasdaqtrader.com frequently. You should also visit ECN Web sites and your own broker's Web site regularly. Now that you understand the routing issues, let's tackle an issue of primary importance to anyone who has ever entered an EDAT trade—getting filled in a fast market.

HOW TO GET FILLED IN A FAST MARKET: HE WHO HESITATES IS LOST

Many of the newer trading platforms have "smart" order routing systems that are designed to make many, if not every, order routing decision for you. These systems have merit, especially for the newer trader. However, they also have some drawbacks, the largest of which is the time it takes for the system to choose and execute your order using the "best" (according to the software) route. These drawbacks really show up in a very fast stock. In these cases the software will preference several market makers automatically and in a predetermined sequence (similar to ARCA). Each market maker has up to 17

TABLE 8-3

Order Routing at a Glance

	ARCA Archipelago	ISLD Island	SNET SelectNet	SOES Small Order Execution System	ISI Listed Stocks
Exchange	NASDAQ, NYSE, AMEX	NASDAQ	NASDAQ	NASDAQ	NYSE, AMEX
Executes to	All ECNs and market makers	ISLD ECN only	INCA and market makers only	Market makers only	SuperDOT
Limit orders	Yes	Yes	Yes	Yes—up to stock tier size	Yes
Market orders	Yes	No	No	Yes—up to stock tier size	Yes
Can bid or offer	Bid or offer appears as ARCA	Bid or offer appears as ISLD	Yes	No	Yes
Limit orders outside best bid or ask	Yes	Yes	Yes	No	Yes
Trade outside market hours	Yes	Yes	Yes	No	No
Can preference market makers	Yes	No	Yes	No	N/A
Can preference ECNs	Automatic	No	Yes	No	No
Odd lots (not divisible by 100)	Yes	Yes	Yes	Yes	Yes
IOC—immediate or cancel orders	Yes	Yes	Yes	No	Yes
GTC—good 'til cancel orders	No—day only	No—day only	GTC—stays live until close Day—stays live 99 min	No—day only	Yes
Stop orders	Yes	No	No	No	Yes
AON—all or none orders	No	No	Yes	No	Yes

seconds to either accept or reject your order. This can obviously take a very long time, especially if several market makers decline your offer. Some software packages will wait the entire time for a fill or rejection before moving to the next market maker. Other packages will move on right away, but because of the SelectNet cancellation rules, you may actually be filled multiple times on the same offer and not even know it until a minute or two later! Hence, you should use the "smart" features judiciously! Read your software manual carefully, especially the order execution rules. If you're still not sure, call your broker and ask (and keep on asking) until you completely understand how your system works.

That said, there is still at least one other reason to completely understand the "old-fashioned" manual execution methods where *you*, as opposed to your software, choose the route. The reason is this: With practice, you can choose your route almost automatically, without even thinking about it. This is an edge. Often, your ability to select your execution route with split-second efficiency will get you filled ahead of the crowd. You certainly don't have to wait to decide whom you'd like to execute against. You can simply choose your counterparty and "ask" him to trade with you.

From a practical standpoint, you'll be dealing with only three situations when trying to get filled: (1) You're bidding or offering, or (2) you "must" buy, or (3) you "must" sell.

To simplify a bit, you should only bid or offer when you don't care if you're filled—this is when you'd like to buy or sell stock, but only on your terms. Why else would you bid or offer? If you really want the fill, simply take the offer when buying or hit the bid when selling. Of course, this can be a bit tricky in a fast-paced market—and that's where intimate knowledge of both the L2 screen and order routing comes into play (see Figures 8–14 to 8–16).

THE MYSTERY OF HIDDEN AND RESERVE ORDERS

One more factor may come into play when trying to get filled (buy or sell) in a fast market—hidden and reserve orders. Hidden orders, as we're discussing them, mean those orders that the market makers have, but that you can't see. The main functional difference between a Level II screen (that you have) and a Level III screen (that the market maker has) is the "auto refresh" feature. The auto refresh allows the

Intel Corporation			

INTC	140 1/2	↓ -11/16	1000	Ot	10:08
Bid ↓	140 1/2	Ask	140 9/16	Vol	3757700
# Bid	4	# Ask	1	Spread	1/16
High	141 5/8	Low	140	Close	141 3/16

Name	Bid	Size	$Best		Name	Ask	Size	$Best
SHWD	140 1/2	100	5		SLKC	140 9/16	100	28
GSCO	140 1/2	1000	14		ISLAND	140 5/8	600	0
ISLD	140 1/2	1100	160		ISLD	140 5/8	600	151
INCA	140 1/2	1300	93		ARCHIP	140 11/16	1400	0
ARCHIP	140 1/2	200	0		:DIBOOK	140 11/16	1000	0
ISLAND	140 1/2	100	0		REDI	140 11/16	1000	62
RSSF	140 7/16	100	1		ARCA	140 11/16	1400	62
FCAP	140 7/16	100	2		SBSH	140 3/4	100	2
BRUT	140 7/16	200	12		COWN	140 3/4	100	1
ARCHIP	140 7/16	200	0		:DIBOOK	140 3/4	6000	0
ARCA	140 7/16	200	35		INCA	140 3/4	2000	113
ISLAND	140 7/16	200	0		PRUS	140 13/16	100	3
CIBC	140 3/8	100	0		NITE	140 13/16	100	34
MLCO	140 3/8	1000	2		:DIBOOK	140 13/16	2900	0
DBKS	140 3/8	1000	6		LEHM	140 7/8	100	0
BTRD	140 3/8	100	45		DLJP	140 7/8	1000	5
COST	140 3/8	100	8		PWJC	141	100	0
NITE	140 3/8	500	3		CANT	141	100	0
ISLAND	140 3/8	100	0		:DIBOOK	141	3000	0
HRZG	140 5/16	100	2		GSCO	141	1000	4
JPMS	140 5/16	100	0		MASH	141	100	12
WARR	140 5/16	100	1		NFSC	141 1/16	100	8
NFSC	140 5/16	100	3		MSCO	141 1/8	1000	5
SWST	140 1/4	100	0		MADF	141 1/8	100	1
SNDY	140 1/4	100	0		PERT	141 1/8	500	1
FLTT	140 1/4	100	0		RAMS	141 3/16	1000	3
BEST	140 1/4	500	1		FCAP	141 1/4	200	0

Figure 8–14 Fast market "buy" conditions.

market maker to "hide" shares. For example, when a market maker has 20,000 shares to sell, but doesn't want to tip the market, he can, in effect, set his total size to 20,000 and his "displayed" size to 1,000. This is what allows a market maker to "sit on the ask" showing 1,000 shares, but selling as much as he can. And while we've used 20,000 shares in our example, in reality there is no limit on the number of shares that a market maker can transact this way. It's simply a matter of his personal choice and trading style.

Another type of hidden order is simply traders or investors sitting on the sidelines waiting for a specific price or type of market action, prior to actually entering their order. This phenomenon often occurs near whole numbers. As a stock trades nearer to the whole number, bids or offers appear on the L2 screen, as if by magic. Often

Cisco Systems, Inc.

CSCO	65 3/8	↓ +1 1/2	600	Ot	10:40
Bid ↑ 65 3/8	Ask 65 7/16	Vol 13250800			
# Bid 2	# Ask 11	Spread 1/16			
High 65 29/32	Low 63 7/8	Close 63 7/8			

	Name	Bid	Chg.	Size	$Best		Name	Ask	Chg.	Size	$Best
O	MLCO	65 3/8	+1/11	1000	19	O	DEMP	65 7/16	-1/11	100	11
O	INCA	65 3/8	+0	1000	119	O	FCOL	65 7/16	+1/11	1000	19
O	JPMS	65 5/16	+2 15/	100	1	O	CEUT	65 7/16	-9/11	100	14
O	FCOL	65 5/16	+0	100	18	O	MWSE	65 7/16	-2 15/	1500	10
O	BRUT	65 5/16		1000	56	O	REDI	65 7/16	-3/11	200	82
	DIBOOK	65 5/16	+0	3300	0		DIBOOK	65 7/16	+0	200	0
O	GSCO	65 5/16		1000	16	O	MDLD	65 7/16	+0	1000	2
O	REDI	65 5/16	+0	3300	103	O	RSSF	65 7/16	+0	1000	6
O	MASH	65 5/16	+0	1600	11	O	ARCA	65 7/16	+0	1000	49
O	BTRD	65 5/16	+0	1400	116	O	MASH	65 7/16	+0	1200	74
O	ISLD	65 5/16	+0	500	184	O	ARCHIP	65 7/16	+0	1000	0
	ISLAND	65 5/16	+0	500	0		ISLAND	65 7/16	+0	2985	0
O	DLJP	65 1/4	+0	1000	0	O	BTRD	65 7/16	+0	400	104
O	SBSH	65 1/4	+0	1000	4	O	ISLD	65 7/16	+0	2900	152
	DIBOOK	65 1/4	+0	100	0	O	FBCO	65 1/2	+1/4	100	3
O	RAMS	65 1/4	-1/11	1000	27	O	OLDE	65 1/2	+1/8	1100	2
O	MWSE	65 1/4	+2 7/8	900	9	O	ARCHIP	65 1/2	+0	500	0
	ISLAND	65 1/4	+0	1100	0	O	SBSH	65 1/2	+0	1000	3
O	MDLD	65 1/4	+0	100	5	O	ARCHIP	65 1/2	+0	400	0
O	MADF	65 1/4	+0	100	11	O	HRZG	65 1/2	+0	5300	13
	DIBOOK	65 3/16	+0	2000	0	O	RAJA	65 1/2	+0	1500	10
O	ARCHIP	65 3/16	+0	200	0	O	ARCHIP	65 1/2	+0	100	0
O	FLTT	65 3/16	-1/8	100	7	O	NTRD	65 1/2	+0	1600	2
O	MSCO	65 3/16	-1/11	1000	9	O	BRUT	65 1/2	+0	3700	55
O	SHWD	65 3/16	+0	100	6	O	GSCO	65 1/2	-3/8	1000	1
O	ARCA	65 3/16	+0	200	73	O	MLCO	65 1/2	+0	2100	7
O	MONT	65 1/8	+1/8	1000	15	O	ISLAND	65 1/2	+0	3409	0
O	CHIP	65 1/8	+1/4	100	0	O	MADF	65 1/2	+0	16000	15

Figure 8–15 Fast market "sell" conditions.

these are limit orders, stop orders, or simply retail customers, entering or exiting upon some predetermined criteria.

The bottom line is that if you're not aware that these situations are occurring or are likely to occur, you're going to be very frustrated in your attempts to read and interpret L2. Fortunately, if you have access to the full ARCA order routing system, you now have a way to fight back—with reserve orders.

ARCA RESERVE ORDERS

One of the newer (and nicer) enhancements to ARCA is the ability of traders to use their own "hidden" orders, since the ARCA "reserve" order works in a remarkably similar way to the auto refresh system

Oracle Corporation

ORCL	75 3/4	↑ +1 1/16	20000 Ot	11:30
Bid↓ 75 11/16	Ask 75 3/4	Vol 10239300		
# Bid 5	# Ask 10	Spread 1/16		
High 76 5/8	Low 75	Close 74 11/16		

	Name	Bid	Chg.	Size	$Best		Name	Ask	Chg.	Size	$Best
O	WARR	75 11/16	+1/4	100	9		ISLAND	75 11/16	+0	100	0
O	DLJP	75 11/16	+0	100	2		ISLAND	75 18 1/25	+0	100	0
O	SLKC	75 11/16	+0	100	6	O	WARR	75 3/4	+0	1000	13
O	NITE	75 11/16	+1/16	100	43	O	SHWD	75 3/4	-3/8	100	29
O	ISLD	75 11/16		100	218	O	DLJP	75 3/4	+0	100	4
O	MSCO	75 5/8	+1/16	1000	6	O	SLKC	75 3/4	+0	100	34
O	PRUS	75 5/8		100	10	O	HRZG	75 3/4	+0	200	17
O	PERT	75 5/8	+1/8	100	1	O	NITE	75 3/4	+0	100	40
O	RSSF	75 5/8	+1/8	100	7	O	INCA	75 3/4	+0	73800	146
O	SHWD	75 5/8	+0	100	29	O	ISLD	75 3/4	+0	1300	229
O	HRZG	75 5/8	+0	300	18	O	REDI	75 3/4	+0	5100	100
	ISLAND	75 5/8	+0	100	0	O	BTRD	75 3/4	-1/4	1000	38
O	SBSH	75 9/16	+0	500	25		DIBOOK	75 3/4	+0	5100	0
	ISLAND	75 9/16	+0	100	0		ISLAND	75 3/4	+0	200	0
O	COWN	75 1/2	-1/4	100	1	O	ARCHIP	75 25/32	+0	200	0
O	JPMS	75 1/2	+1/8	100	0		ISLAND	75 25/32	+0	200	0
	ISLAND	75 1/2	+0	1180	0	O	ARCA	75 13/16	+0	200	75
O	MWSE	75 1/2	+0	900	12	O	BRUT	75 13/16	+0	200	32
O	MASH	75 1/2	+0	100	24	O	MSCO	75 7/8	+0	1000	2
O	GSCO	75 1/2	+0	1000	19	O	AANA	75 7/8	-1/4	100	0
O	BRUT	75 1/2	+0	400	21	O	PWJC	75 7/8	+0	1000	1
O	FBCO	75 7/16	+1/4	500	2	O	GSCO	75 7/8	+1/16	1000	9
	ISLAND	75 7/16	+0	100	0		ISLAND	75 7/8	+0	300	0
O	PIPR	75 7/16	-1/4	100	3	O	KCMO	75 7/8	+1/8	100	4
O	LEHM	75 3/8	-1/8	100	9		ISLAND	75 15/16	+0	1000	0
O	NFSC	75 3/8	+0	100	6	O	BEST	75 15/16	+0	1000	12
O	INCA	75 3/8	+0	6000	148		ISLAND	75 127/12	+0	700	0
O	SEL2	75 5/16	-3/8	100	1	O	COWN	76	-1/4	100	5

Figure 8–16 Using SelectNet preference.

that market makers have. Using this feature, you're able to buy or sell up to 10,000 shares "in reserve." For instance, you might decide to sell out your long DELL position, but not want to scare the bejeebers out of everyone else in the process. So you use an ARCA reserve order to show 500 shares with 9,500 in reserve at the same price. Guess what? You now get to play exactly the same game the market makers have been playing ever since the advent of Level III! Your order will show up on L2 as 500 shares to sell and will automatically refresh 500 shares each time you sell your lot until the whole 10,000 shares are liquidated. Of course, whether you'll actually be filled for the whole order depends upon the market conditions at that time, but, boy, this is a nifty edge, isn't it?! As an added bonus, all the shares that are filled on a single ARCA reserve order are charged just one commission.

SPEAKING OF EDGES

Back in Chapter 3 we spoke rather extensively about edges. We discussed both what edges are and what they are not. The edges we talked about then tended to be global edges that were useful while developing your business and trading plans. Let's briefly revisit edges from a tactical standpoint. These are the specific edges that you can employ to enter, monitor, and exit your trades. We've already mentioned a few in this chapter:

- Being able to read and interpret L2
- Identifying the ax
- Understanding market-maker tactics such as the head-fakes, the fade, and the short squeeze
- Recognizing collapsing tiers
- Correctly interpreting ECNs on the bid and offer
- Routing your trades correctly to get the best fills
- Knowing about and using ARCA reserve orders

In addition to these, look over the edges in Figure 8–17. Here we've described some additional trading edges and have divided them into six sections. The placement of an edge under a specific heading is for its potential usefulness only. Most of these edges could just as easily be placed in any of the other sections or in all of them. You might review these edges periodically as a part of your daily trading preparation.

DEVELOP EXPECTATIONS FOR YOUR TRADING DAY

Now comes the day you've been waiting for—trading day. If you've been diligent, you spent the last evening in preparation for today (see Chapter 7). Let's now walk through the final launch checklist. These are the actual steps I take daily, just before the open. During this time I review my work from the prior evening, and I also establish my early expectations for the trading day. As a review, here briefly is what I do the evening before: (1) I run scans for mechanical and technical setups; (2) I pare the list down to the "best" 10 or so stocks; (3) I study the daily charts for each of these stocks; and (4) I put each stock symbol into my trading software (a minder or blotter window) ready for the next morning.

Setups and Entries
Taking all your entry setups

Stops
Keeping your stops

Profit-Taking Exits
Understanding expectancy and using it

Position Sizing
Understanding and using position sizing

Execution Skills
Using CNBC as a trading tool
Correctly interpreting news
Correctly interpreting upgrades and downgrades
Using Level II
Using T&S
Using the S&P futures correlation to specific stocks
Accessing chat rooms (especially useful for fading)
Accessing ECN limit books
Knowing support and resistance levels

General
Doing daily mental and physical preparation
Being able to control your mental and emotional states
Not having to trade
Trading with the expectation
Trading with the trend
Having patience

Figure 8–17 Trading edges.

On the morning of the trading day, I complete the stock selection process (see Chapter 7) by doing the following: (1) I find and interpret the morning and overnight news; (2) I scan for "gap and trap"[6] plays on my basket stocks; and (3) I scan for boomers and busters.[7]

One of the primary reasons that I do all these things is to form tradable expectations. Earlier, we said that it is impossible to trade the markets. The only possibility is to trade your expectations (i.e., beliefs) of the markets. This idea, common to master traders, recognizes our inability to predict with total certainty what a stock (or market) will do. Because we can't know what a stock will do, we can only place our trades based upon what we think or expect will happen. So forming tradable expectations is one of the most critical steps to profitable trading.

Underlying the idea of tradable expectations is a core belief of mine. That is, absent any reason to move, a stock will not move (Isaac Newton had similar thoughts about our physical universe). Stated another way, a stock must have a catalyst to cause it to move. Absent this catalyst, it will move sideways. The catalyst can be technically based, fundamentally based, or very often news-based. More often than not, the catalyst for the pure direct-access trader will be news. Therefore, the art and craft of interpreting the news becomes paramount to a direct-access trader's success.

THE ART OF INTERPRETING NEWS

The One Most Important Question

Most tradable news is released either postmarket or premarket. Earnings announcements, for instance, tend to come out after the closing bell, while mergers and acquisitions tend to be announced prior to the open. Of course, some news does come out during the day, and sometimes "breaking" stories (big news) will come out during trading hours. But my guess is that because CEOs and the press know that "breaking news" can have large and often unpredictable effects on a stock, stock-specific news is most often released during nonmarket hours, while news and rumors of war (or the Fed[8]) can happen at any moment.

When we interpret the news, we're really trying to discern whether the news will be good, bad, or neutral for a stock or the market in general. In this regard you'll become quite adept at assessing the news if you first remember this fundamental question regarding any news release: "Will the facts upon which this news is based affect either the top-line revenue growth or the bottom-line earnings of this company during the next two quarters?" The answer to this single question can make you untold sums! The reason is simple. In the near term, most traders do not ask this question! Markets and stocks tend to overreact, sometimes violently, when news is first released. During these manias, stocks with "good" news run to ridiculous highs. Stocks with "bad" news are slammed to the pavement and below, as if they've fallen from a 20-story window! These moments of mania can last anywhere from several minutes to several months; but once sanity returns to the market, more and more traders and investors do ask this question. And when they do, the stock's price will begin to more truly reflect its value. Herein lie the trading opportunities. Once you can assess the situation and form a tradable expectation, you can often profit by trading in the direction of the mania, or fading it!

Several tactics in my arsenal are based upon these manias. Boomers and busters, discussed in Chapter 10, are two examples. The degree of the mania is also an important factor. When fading, the bigger the irrational overreaction, the better. This is because a larger mania often results in a quicker and more dramatic correction. One of the better recent manias was Qualcomm (QCOM) in the week between Christmas 1999 and New Year's 2000. During this time the stock ran from $115 to $200, presumably in anticipation of a pending December 31 four-to-one stock split. By January 28, 2000, it was back below $115, and at the time of this writing it is trading in the low $60s! While this example is dramatic, similar situations occur *daily* in the market, albeit usually (but not always) on a smaller scale.

This example also shows how crazy these manias can become when the stock in question is a "darling" or a day trader's favorite.[9] Once the fuse is lit, news spreads quickly. The general population then starts buying into the frenzy, rocketing the prices into the stratosphere. Of course, by then the most astute traders are selling into this mania! (Yes, you can call me a bit of a cynic if you must.) The important issue is that the stock has tradable expectations based upon the news. That the stock begins or ends at a certain price level or that it makes several tops and bottoms along the way is much less relevant. To a direct-access trader, these oscillations and the high volatility are simply exploitable trading opportunities.

The Second Most Important Question

The next most important question to ask when forming expectations based upon news is, "What did the market expect?" If the market was expecting the news, my belief is that the news is already reflected in the price. The trader's axiom "Buy the rumor, sell the news" is based upon this belief. Many traders are mystified when "good" news comes out on a stock (e.g., DELL meets quarterly earnings estimates) and the stock trades down. However, most people already expected the good news and bought in anticipation. Once the news is out, assuming no additional "positive" surprises, the stock will usually sell off, as there is no more "good" news to drive the stock higher! If this doesn't seem logical to you, great! You've just learned one of the secrets of understanding news in relation to stock prices—it's *not* logical! In fact, the logic is the inverse of what you might intuitively think. Take a look at Table 8–4, which shows the expected initial reaction of a stock based upon newly reported news.

As we said, news that affects either the top- or bottom-line growth of a company should have the most meaningful and therefore the most lasting effect upon share prices. Here are some news items that meet these criteria:

- Long-term contracts (with significant[10] money changing hands)
- Merger or acquisition activity (definitive, not rumors)
- New product or product line

Here are some news items that typically have a weak (or no) effect on top- or bottom-line revenue. News-driven manias based upon these are often subject to very quick reversals:

- Strategic alliances (with no dollars changing hands)
- Joint marketing agreements
- "Fluff" announcements (for example, a new contract with minuscule revenue)

TABLE 8-4

Stock's Initial Reaction (News-Driven)

	Expected	Unexpected
"Good" news	Down (or flat)	Up
"Bad" news	Flat (or up)	Down

A Matter of Degree

So far, we've asked two questions in our attempt to form a tradable expectation based upon news. And as long as the news was expected, these two questions are sufficient. But how do you handle unexpected news (aka surprises)? In this case, instead of asking, "Was the news expected?" you'll have to ask "How 'good' (if good) or 'bad' (if bad) is the news?" This question presupposes that the news was not priced into the shares. This question is really one of magnitude. It, too, is subjective. (If all this subjectivity is more than you're comfortable with, perhaps you should review the self-assessment and trading style information in the first three chapters. Some people are not wired for discretionary trading. If you're not, a purely mechanical system may be much better!) Here's what I do. I arbitrarily assign "neutral news" a value of 3. If the news is a bit stronger, I give it a 4; if much stronger, a 5. If a bit weaker, a 2; and if much weaker, a 1. Table 8–5 will clarify this.

The final tool to assist with news interpretation is a form I use to write out my evaluations and expectations premarket. I've found this invaluable in terms of helping to refine my interpretive skills. Pay special attention to the "Actual Results" column in Table 8–6. This is a reproduction of the actual log I used on February 9, 2000. Whether you trade the stock or not, fill this in every day. The result you're looking for here is how the stock behaved versus what you thought it would do based on the surprise news (the "Direction") column. Notice that my expectations were 100 percent correct on this

TABLE 8-5

Interpreting Surprise News

Degree	Good News	Bad News
Least	1	1
	2	2
Neutral	3	3
	4	4
Most	5	5

T A B L E   8 - 6

News Evaluation Form

Date	Stock Symbol	News Category	Direction (U/N/D)	Strength (1–5)	Comments	Actual Results
02/09/2000	GT	Exceeded earnings	Up	4	Surprised analysts	Up
02/09/2000	BA	Negative news	Down	4	Strike announced	Down
02/09/2000	CSCO	Exceeded earnings	Up	5	Significantly exceed	Up
02/09/2000	AIG	Upgraded	Up	3	Salomon Smith Barney	Up
02/09/2000	ALL	Missed earnings	Down	5	Significantly lower	Down
02/09/2000	HUM	Missed earnings	Down	5	Missed by a mile	Down

particular day. (I'm not always this accurate!) Even though I did not trade all these symbols, because several did not meet my entry criteria, my expectations were definitely tradable—and that's the goal. Using this tool will really build your confidence, as over time, you'll develop an uncanny ability, a "gut feeling," to sense what a stock will do, just by hearing the news. This definitely is an edge!

The last piece of the news puzzle is simply a listing of the most important news categories. Of course, there are many, but I found the ones listed in Figure 8–18 to be so reliable that they can be used in a keyword search to filter for news.[11]

STOCK SELECTION AT A GLANCE

Figure 8–19 presents the big-picture view of my stock selection process throughout the day. As you can see from the figure, I tend to use different strategies at various times of the day. This is because certain strategies have a higher probability of success at different times. The open usually is characterized by higher volatility. In fact, stocks, absent news, tend to make both their high and their low of the day during the

---

✓ Upgrade
✓ Downgrade
✓ Acquiring
✓ Acquired
✓ Missed earnings
✓ Exceeded earnings
✓ Changed management
✓ Negative news (product- or service-related)
✓ Positive news (product- or service-related)

Figure 8–18 Suggested news categories.

first 60 to 90 minutes of trading. During the middle of the day, stocks often trade sideways in "channels." And during the last 60 to 90 minutes, momentum often returns to the market as traders and investors enter and exit their positions for the day.

DIRECTIONAL BIAS

Once you understand the stock selection process, you should be able to determine an initial directional bias for each stock on your watch list. Generally you should not be trading a nondirectional stock.[12] And if you don't have a directional belief that a stock is going to move up or down, why are you entering? So how do you enter (and exit) based upon beliefs about direction?

I have a mental algorithm—a little loop—that I play over in my head all day long. I'm looking for some basic patterns—charting patterns, Level II patterns, and time & sales patterns. Both my entries and exits are based upon these visual cues. First let's look at a macro view and a micro view of the algorithm, shown in Figures 8–20 and 8–21, respectively. Next we'll examine the patterns themselves.

It's certainly possible to write an entire book that would do nothing except drill down on these stratagems. In fact, if we were to combine this drill-down with the tactics described in Chapters 9 and 10, we would have the contents of an entire course on the tactical aspects of direct-access trading.[13] But for now, just realize we have two main reasons for examining the charts on both a macro

Premarket Trading
8:00–9:30 a.m. (1½ hours)
 Trade boomers and busters based upon news aberrations
 in premarket hours.

Morning Trading
9:30–11:30 a.m.
   Setups in order of preference
   1. Gap and traps on basket (no news)
   2. Boomers and busters (news-driven momentum)
   3. News momentum
   4. Mechanical setups (day holds)
    a. Stairmasters

Mid-Day Trading
11:30 a.m.–2:30 p.m.
   Setups in order of preference
   Market-maker strategies
   1. Channel plays
   2. Stealth specialist
   Momentum strategies
   1. Volume breakouts
   2. 52-week highs and lows

End-of-Day Trading
2:30–4:00 p.m.
   Closing momentum
   1. Volume breakouts
   2. 52-week highs and lows
   3. Swing and position trading momentum
   4. Chart patterns

Figure 8–19 Stock selection process.

and micro basis. The first is to gain an overall understanding of
how the stock is behaving in recent weeks and days. The second is
to compare that behavior with what the stock is doing today. Many
direct-access traders omit these steps and as a result fall victim to
professional traders who have studied the stock's recent behavior.

Macro Picture (Using Daily Charts)

Examine daily candlestick chart.

Determine trend, if any:
Over last 1 to 3 months
Is stock heading higher?
Is stock heading lower?
Is stock consolidating?
What is angle of slope?
Gradual (30° or less)
Moderate (between 30° and 60°)
Steep (above 60°)
Hyperbolic (above 75°)

Find support and resistance areas:
Where is whole-number support and resistance?
What is previous day's high and low
What is previous day's main support and resistance?

Examine technical aspects:
Is stock moving through?
20-day moving average
50-day moving average
200-day moving average

What is the broad market doing?
Dow Industrials
NASDAQ Composite
S&P futures (forward contract)
TICK
TRIN

How does the stock compare with the broad market?
Stronger than
Weaker than
About the same

Figure 8–20 Mental chart algorithm (macro).

Micro Picture (Using 1- and 5-Minute Charts)

Examine 1-minute and 5-minute candlestick charts.

> Determine trend, if any:
>> Over last 1 to 15 minutes
>>> Is stock heading higher?
>>> Is stock heading lower?
>>> Is stock consolidating?
>> What is angle of slope?
>>> Gradual (30° or less)
>>> Moderate (between 30° and 60°)
>>> Steep (above 60°)
>>> Hyperbolic (above 75°)

> Find support and resistance areas:
>> Where is whole-number support and resistance?
>> What is the day's high and low?
>> What is main support and resistance in the last 15 minutes to the last hour?

> Examine technical aspects:
>> Is stock moving through?
>>> 20-period moving average
>>> 50-period moving average
>>> 200-period moving average

Figure 8–21 Mental chart algorithm (micro).

DECIDING TO ENTER

One of the more difficult issues for many traders is deciding exactly where to enter a trade. Yet when you understand the real purpose of picking an entry, this becomes one of the easier aspects of trading. The reason you want to be selective when choosing an entry has nothing to do with picking bottoms and tops. *A good entry is any entry that allows you to minimize your risk in a trade.* Amateur traders pick entries based upon "how much they can make." Professional traders choose their entries based upon minimizing their risk.

PULLING THE TRIGGER

As you know, we've divided all of our trading strategies into two broad groups, market-making strategies (Chapter 9) and momentum strategies (Chapter 10). Each execution tactic falls into one group or the other. And each one of the tactics has its own nuances, which we describe in those chapters. However, there are some common cues to look for when deciding to "pull the trigger." If you've been a technical or mechanical trader, direct-access setups may present a bit of a challenge to you. The reason is that as a mechanical trader, you enter (or exit) a trade based upon the occurrence of some technical event. If the event occurs, enter. If not, don't. *Direct-access setups only tell you to be prepared to enter.* If a mechanical event occurs, be prepared to enter. If not, don't. The entry and exit decision is made by relying on two additional tools: the L2 screen and the time & sales screen. Here is the decision flow:

1. Select candidate stocks (Chapters 7 and 8).
2. Complete the macro review (see Figure 8–20).
3. Complete the micro review (see Figure 8–21).
4. See (recognize) the setup (Chapters 9 and 10).
5. Scan L2 and T&S for your entry (exit) point (Chapters 4 and 8).

THE WEIGHT OF YOUR DECISION

Take a moment to review the entry decision flow I described above. Now let's go through an actual trade based upon this process. Figures 8–22 through 8–25 will give you a visual map of this same process. In Figure 8–22, I've selected my candidate based in part upon volume and a large percentage move in price. Figure 8–23 shows my macro chart scan. Next, Figure 8–24 shows the broad mar-

Symbol	Last	Change	Net Chg. %	High	Low	Open	Hist Close	Tot Vol
ARBA	131 3/16	+27 11/16	+26.75	131 1/2	120 3/8	120 1/2	103 1/2	24444500
AMCC	153 1/2	+28 1/16	+22.37	154 1/16	145 7/8	147 15/16	125 7/16	3694800
RATL	113 1/8	+20 7/16	+22.05	113 3/4	99 3/4	99 13/16	92 11/16	3787300
BBOX	55 15/16	-34	-37.80	89 7/8	52 5/8	89 7/16	89 15/16	3676400
ACOM	21 1/2	+5 11/16	+35.97	22 7/8	20 7/8	22 7/8	15 13/16	1602400
ACTU	60 1/4	+6 7/16	+11.96	60 15/16	58	58 3/8	53 13/16	1023100

Figure 8–22 Example of daily candidates.

Figure 8–23 Macro view—Ariba is breaking from a base.

ket near a pivot point, at the time I am considering an entry. Finally, Figure 8–25, the micro view, shows ARBA with a nice up-sloping trend line. Many factors went into the decision to enter exactly when I did. Once I'm ready to "pounce," I have a "scan pattern," a sequence of looking at the various screens. Most of my attention is focused on the L2 screen. I estimate that as much as 70 percent of my decision is based on information gleaned from it. The rest of my scan narrows to the T&S screen (10 percent reliance), the S&P futures chart (again 10 percent reliance), and the 1-minute candle chart (the final 10 percent). The weight that I give any of these particular elements, of course, may change. If, for instance, the S&P futures turn suddenly negative at a time when I'm stalking L2 to go long, I may turn most of my attention to the S&P screen. After considering all factors, I may even decide to abort the entry, solely based on the S&Ps.

As you can see, I tend to make my entry and exit setups very simple. I've found that simplicity works. Most master traders agree with this mindset. Since your brain can only process a limited number of information "chunks" at any one time, looking at too many indicators and filters will only result in confusion. And confusion results in inaction. You don't want to be caught like a deer in the headlights when deciding to enter or exit a trade—that will get you killed.

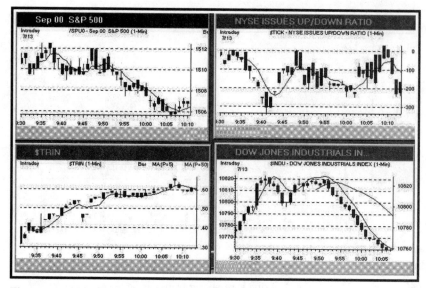

Figure 8–24 The broad market may be at a pivot, turning higher.

GETTING YOUR FILL

Once you've decided to enter, you'll need to choose a route. We've covered this material extensively in this chapter. So to review, let's walk through the route selection for a trade.

Look at Figure 8–26. You'll notice that I chose a limit order in this case. In fact, I rarely (almost never) use a market order. Be aware, depending upon the route you select, that it can sometimes take 1 minute or longer to get a market order filled. One minute on a fast-moving stock can be an eternity, or at least seem like one. In the time that it takes to get filled, you may get filled "at the market" several points away from where you thought the market was when you entered the order. Just the thought of buying or selling a stock 2 points away from your intended entry should make you cringe! Suffice to say that early in my trading I had some very bad experiences (losses) due to market orders.

NEVER ENTER A TRADE WITHOUT KNOWING YOUR STOP!

A mark of a master trader is the ability to pick a stop before entering a trade. Another is keeping that stop if it's hit. *Stops serve to preserve*

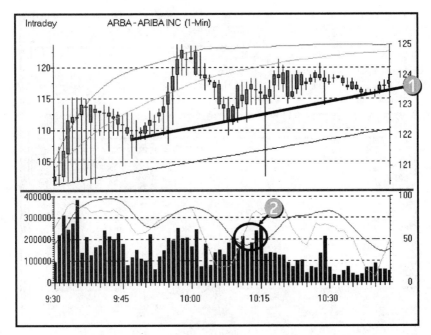

Figure 8–25 Micro view—Ariba up-sloping trend line.

your capital. For the direct-access trader there are many excellent methods of determining your stops.

I recommend that you use a "system" or "stock-specific" stop. Specific details on stops can be found in Van Tharp's *Trade Your Way to Financial Freedom.* I recommend that you study that material. Again there are many system stop tactics. Some methodologies are based on a stock's daily range, others on volatility, and still others on stops placed just above or below significant highs or lows. Trading the tactics described in this book, I advocate placing stops near short-term support and resistance (see Figure 8–27).

A SECRET FOR KEEPING YOUR STOP

Once you become proficient at selecting stops, you may face another challenge. Most traders face this challenge, especially early on. The challenge is keeping the stop once it's hit. If you discipline yourself by actually entering your stop into your software, or physically writing it down in your trade log, you'll find it much easier to take

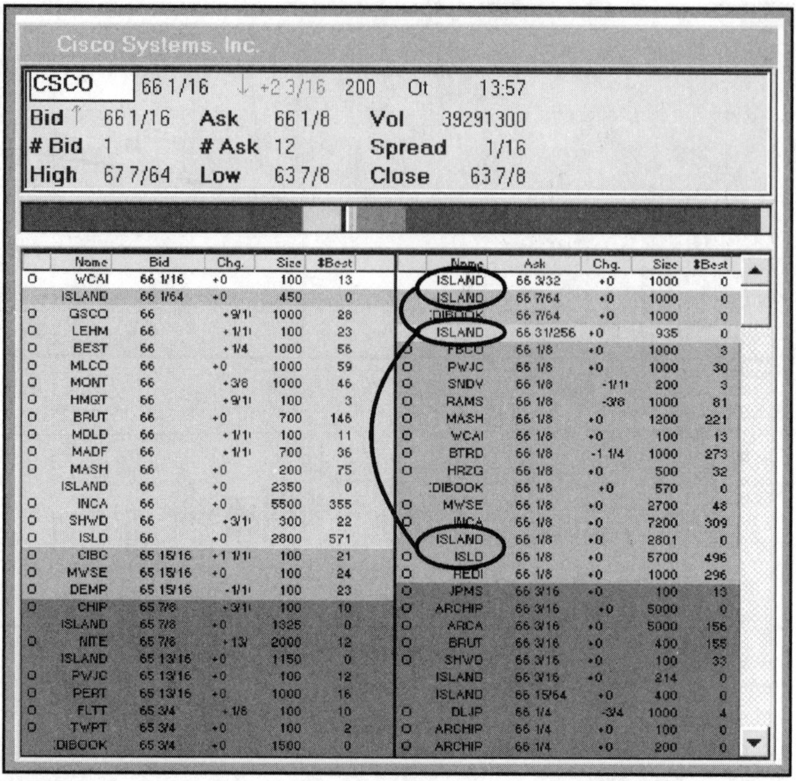

Figure 8–26 Buying Cisco at 66⅛ on ISLD.

the stop if it's hit. This may sound simple, but a good deal of research has gone into this topic. And that research shows that the simple act of writing the stop down tends to reinforce its importance. If something important is kept right before your eyes, you'll be more likely to do it.

PROFIT-TAKING EXITS

It's hard to find direct-access trading material that deals with your profit-taking exits. There's a ton of material on entries and even quite a bit on stops. But profit-taking exits? What's that about? It's about maximizing your hard-earned profits by not giving them back. I've found three types of profit-taking exits that work excel-

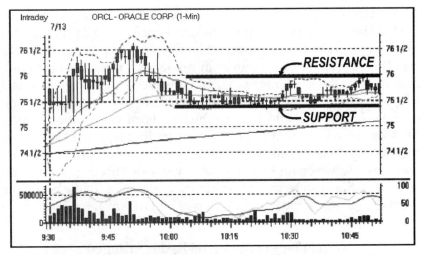

Figure 8–27 Place stops below support (if long) and above resistance (if short).

lently for the EDAT trader: (1) trailing exits, (2) profit-target exits, and (3) timed exits.

Trailing Exits (Momentum Strategies)

Most position and swing traders will be familiar with trailing exits since these exits are very common to these trading styles. They are simple, easy to understand, and effective. There are probably as many variants as there are trading styles. But in the simplest form, you pick a stop and move or trail the stop as your trade moves profitably in your favor. For example, let's say you buy 1,000 XYZ at $52⅛ with a ½-point stop. You chose ½ point because you're willing to risk $500—½ percent of your trading capital. If the stock goes to $51⅝, you'll stop out. If the stock goes to $52⅝, you simply trail the ½ point by moving your stop to break even. I'm not suggesting that you actually do this. I'm just describing the method.

The trailing stop works well for momentum strategies; however, I use a modified version. For momentum trades, I like to set my minimum profit target at ¾ point. If a stock does not present at least this much potential, I won't enter it as a momentum trade. In this situation, because I won't momentum-trade for less than an R multiple of

1.5, I'll set my stop at ½ point (0.5 × 1.5 = 0.75). If the stock gives me less than ¾, I simply keep my ½-point risk. But once I have ¾ profit, I want to keep at least half of my profit, so I tighten my stop to ⅜ (½ of ¾) and trail the stop as the stock moves in my favor. I often get taken out, only to have the stock move higher. However, when this happens, I simply implement one of my reentry strategies. When using a trailing stop, you must take into account the near-term volatility of a stock. My example above that uses a ⅜-point trailing stop works well for most of my "basket" stocks, which generally have low to moderate volatility. However, for higher-volatility stocks, I use a wider trailing stop. (Volatility can be measured in many ways. One of the best is the average true range indicator developed by Wilder.[14])

Profit-Target Exits (Market-Making Strategies)

A common trader mistake seems to be mixing trading styles. This can be very dangerous, especially when it comes to profit exits. Not only do different strategies require different entry rules, but they also require their own profit exits. When trading a market-making strategy, if you try to trail a stop, most often the stock will reverse (that's why you entered the trade in the first place!). Either you'll give back all your profits, or you'll have them turn into losses. The profit-target exit will solve this dilemma for you. *The key to making a profit-target exit work for you is to place your exit order into the market as soon as your entry is filled.* Take a look at Figure 8–28.

It's clear from this figure that the stock is trading in a very discernible channel. You don't need to be Einstein to see it, and neither does any other trader. These market-maker plays can be very profitable when traded correctly. And the correct way to trade them is to place your order to get out as soon as you get in. Here, if you wait for the top or bottom price of the channel to trade prior to trying to exit, it will be too late. Many other traders or market makers will step in front of you, preventing you from exiting with your profits. Yes, every now and then the stock will break out of the channel. And every now and then you will leave some profits on the table because of this. But it's far better, when trading channels, to take the sure profit when you can. When you're trading channels, trade channels! Don't try to change horses in midstream. Remember, you can always reenter if the setup for another strategy presents itself.

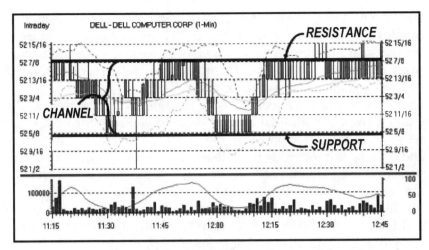

Figure 8–28 A typical channel exit prior to top or bottom of channel.

Timed Exits

Another profit exit is based upon the duration of the trade—the amount of time that your capital is at risk. This strategy is a favorite of accomplished EDAT traders. Like the other methods, there are variations on the theme. The simplest is the "day hold." To trade a day hold, when you receive an entry signal, you enter early in the trading day. And assuming that you're not stopped out, you exit at or near the end of the day. This is about as easy as it gets. I use timed exits in a slightly different manner.

You'll recall from Chapter 3 that there are several definitive time frames for EDAT traders (see Chapter 3, Table 3–1). Some traders use tick data, some 1-minute charts, some 2-minute charts, and still others 5-minute charts. One secret of direct-access trading is to remain within your own time frame. You might think of it as akin to an athletic complex with several baseball diamonds. Although everyone is playing softball, you wouldn't deliberately field a ball from a ball game on the diamond next to you.

To make sure I'm playing my own game and not someone else's, I time my exit once I'm in the trade if (1) the trade doesn't move in my direction, (2) the trade moves in my direction but then stalls for a period of time, or (3) the trade moves against me without hitting my stop and then stalls. The rule for the time stop is simple: I give the trade from 2 to 5 times my trading time frame. Since I trade 1-minute candles, I'll give the trade anywhere from 2 minutes up to (in rare circumstances) 5 minutes to stop me out or move in my direction. In all cases, if the trade stalls and goes into a consolidation for 5 minutes, I stop out and move on to other opportunities.

Take a moment to consider the reasoning (and prudence!) for a timed stop. You entered a trade because you recognized a valid setup and then got an entry signal. Now it's several minutes later and nothing is happening (or at least what you thought would happen isn't). Would you enter this trade at this instant if you weren't already in it? No! So by staying in the trade, you're just hoping— like flipping a coin to see if the stock breaks your way. Just get out and look for another low-risk entry. Naturally, I will reenter if my setup occurs again after taking a timed stop.

DON'T FORGET TO REENTER

One of the most important habits you can form to ensure your long-term profitably is the habit of reentering stopped trades. Otherwise you'll find yourself stopping out, only to be very frustrated to see the stock move strongly in the direction of your expectation after you're out of the trade. If your belief system relies on being "right," you'll most likely have difficulty reentering after you've stopped out. After all, if you had to stop out, you were "wrong," weren't you? An intimate understanding of R multiples and expectancy will help you tremendously in this area. In addition, we discuss specific reentry rules in Chapters 9 and 10.

POSITION SIZING

Don't forget to control position sizing. As a beginner, we suggest that you limit your position sizing to ¼ of 1 percent of your equity. When you are profitable for at least three straight months, then consider increasing your position sizing to ½ of 1 percent. Know and understand position sizing thoroughly before you begin trading.

TO MAKE MAXIMUM PROFITS, REMAIN FLEXIBLE

Forming tradable expectations requires significant effort. And most of us tend to attach our emotions and egos to things we've expended effort on. This ego investment can be very positive and rewarding. Consider the commitment issue we discussed in Chapter 2. Unfortunately, this ego attachment can sometimes be our undoing while we actually trade. We've formed our expectations, and we just "know" a particular stock is heading higher. It simply must! Or must it?

Master traders remain flexible. Although they, too, expend huge effort to form expectations and select candidate stocks, they remain alert to changes in the overall market or in the stock that they're trading. Master traders can easily trade both sides of the market, going both long and short. Aspiring traders often have extreme difficulty doing so. If you can't remain flexible, not only will you have difficultly trading the markets in both directions, but you'll most likely have difficulty stopping out. Reentry will also challenge you greatly.

How do you know when it's prudent to change your expectation? It's simple. If the market or stock is not doing what you expected it to do, drop the expectation. If you're not in a position, don't enter. If you're in a trade and the expectation changes, stop out. (To prevent whipsaw in these cases, I suggest you simply keep your original stop. Once you've gained more experience, you'll be able to alter this rule to fit the circumstances.) I also suggest that you spend as much time as you can studying charting patterns and technical indicators, especially those that can portend pivot points or changes in direction.

DEFENDING AGAINST WHIPSAW

Your best defense against whipsaw is to use the tools we give you in this book. Plans, beliefs, expectations, applied behavioral finance, specific strategies, and tactics—all these will help you defend against feeling like a Yo-Yo. However, it does take time to assimilate the myriad trading concepts, rules, and tactics presented into a cohesive whole that you can trade profitably. This book provides a proven road map for doing so. Make this material a part of you. Here's why. You will stop out a lot, but by following our road map you'll also frequently reenter. This is a key to big profits. Stop out to save your money. Reenter to make your money. If you understand this, you're well on your way to defeating the "Yo-Yo" syndrome. And you're well on your way to profitable trading!

Remember the purpose of entries is not to pick bottoms or tops, but to enter the position with low-risk. A practical example of this is to enter your positions so that your stop will be a bit under support (¼ point) or a bit over resistance (¼ point). In doing so, you're entering where you have a defined downside and a much bigger upside—the very definition of "low risk." This is just a rule of thumb, since many traders will set stops ⅛ of a point away from support and resistance. By giving the stop a bit more room, you're less likely to be whipsawed.

TRADING DAY QUICK VIEW

Figure 8–29 shows a total overview of my trading day. The basic divisions are preparation, morning trading, mid-day trading, end-of-day trading, and review. Notice that I choose my basic trading strategies according to what normally works during a particular time frame—momentum early and late in the day and market making during the middle of the day. Using a system similar to this will add structure and discipline to your trading, and should result in higher profits. Let's now move on to the most common mistakes that traders make—and how to avoid them.

KNOWLEDGE KEYS

✓ Basic interpretation of Level II is based upon the supply and demand model.

✓ The ax is the market maker who controls most of the trading activity in any particular stock.

✓ The ax's actions can have a significant impact on your decision to enter or exit a stock.

✓ There are many alternative routes (ECNs) to the market. Choosing the best one at any given time will make a dramatic difference to your trading profits.

✓ Archipelago and the Island are two of the most liquid ECNs.

✓ Understand the secret of collapsing tiers and how to trade using this knowledge.

✓ "Hidden" and "reserve" orders will surprise you (usually unpleasantly) unless you know what they are and how to trade in their presence.

Evening Preparation   8:00–8:30 p.m.

Run scans
    Mechanical setups
        Select top 10 +/–
        Analyze daily charts
        Put in minder window

Morning Preparation   7:00–8:30 a.m.

Find and interpret news
    CNBC
        "Stocks to Watch"—7:05 a.m. and every ½ hour
        thereafter until 9:05 a.m.
    NewsWatch
        Keyword search
    Briefing.com
    Put in minder window

Scan for gap and traps on basket stocks
Scan for boomers and busters
    Put in minder window

Premarket Trading   8:00–9:30 a.m.

    Trade boomers and busters based upon news aberrations

Morning Trading   9:30–11:30 a.m.

    Setups in order of preference
        1. Gap and traps on basket
        2. Boomers and busters
        3. News momentum
        4. Mechanical setups (day holds)
           a. Stairmasters

Mid-Day Trading   11:30 a.m.–2:30 p.m.

    Setups in order of preference
        Market-maker strategies
        1. Channel plays
        2. Stealth specialist
        Momentum strategies
        1. Volume breakouts
        2. 52-week highs and lows

Figure 8–29 Daily trading time line (*continues*).

End-of-Day Trading 2:30–4:00 p.m.

> Closing momentum
> 1. Volume breakouts
> 2. 52-week highs and lows
> 3. Swing and position trading momentum
> 4. Chart patterns

Postmarket Routine 4:30–5:00 p.m.
Daily debrief
> Calculate P&L
> Calculate expectancy
> Journaling

Figure 8–29 Daily trading time line (*continued*).

✓ You must develop daily trading expectations to win over the long run.

✓ You must form or adopt a strategy for interpreting the news.

✓ Remaining flexible throughout your trading day will allow you to change with the market, rather than fight it.

CALLS TO ACTION

✓ Learn to interpret Level II according to the supply and demand model.

✓ Know the meaning of every single element on a Level II screen.

✓ Learn to identify the ax and interpret her actions.

✓ Practice order entry using small share sizes. Try every route. Continue to use various routes (trading small shares) until you instinctively know how each works and how to use it.

✓ Make a deliberate practice of writing down your expectations for the market and stocks based upon the news. Compare your expectations with the actual results until you're proficient at interpreting the news.

✓ Know your stop before entering your trade. Once in, keep your stop.

✓ When stopped out of a trade, be sure to reenter if you get another opportunity. If you fail to do this, you will most probably not be successful at direct-access trading.

NOTES

1. Our understanding is that currently (as of June 2000) when you execute against INCA, it shows up on your broker's trading desk. Your broker must then enter the order into the Instinet machine. So in this sense you do not have direct access to Instinet.

2. Depending upon your execution software and your brokerage, your L2 montage may only display the best bid or ask. Some systems display the complete order books for the ECN routing to their system. For example, some RealTick systems display the order book for ARCA, ISLD, and REDI, in addition to the best bid and ask of other market participants.

3. In December 1999 the NYSE decided to repeal Rule 390, which restricted NYSE members from trading listed stocks off an exchange floor.

4. Island *only* accepts limit orders.

5. A trader buying from or selling to Island and wishing to get a complete order fill should be observant about the number of shares currently at the bid and ask. If there are not a significantly larger number of shares than you wish to trade, you could find yourself with a partial fill. For example, on a fast-moving stock I have put in an order to buy/sell 1,000 shares of stock only to get a fill of 727. This is not so much of a consideration when you are bidding or offering stock, but here you have to be sensitive to timing or you will get a partial fill as the stock is moving up or down a level.

6. See Chapter 3, Model Trading Plan section.

7. See Chapter 10 for a full description.

8. The Federal Reserve Board.

9. Other stocks exhibiting manias during the spring of 2000 were JDSU, PDLI, and RMBS. All were direct-access traders' favorites.

10. The larger the percentage of revenue from the new contract in proportion to the company's existing revenue, the more "significant."

11. I use NewsWatch, a program available from Track Data Corporation. This program has many powerful filtering and querying capabilities.

12. The Stealth Specialist covered in Chapter 9 is an exception to this rule.
13. Call One Minute Trader Corporation at 1-866-852-4993 for more information on our course offerings.
14. J. Welles Wilder, *New Concepts in Technical Trading Systems.*

Market-Making Strategies

Speak softly and carry a big stick; you will go far.

Theodore Roosevelt

Let's get into some specific day trading strategies and tactics. I divide all day trading into two broad strategic categories: market-making strategies and momentum strategies. This is a specific and useful way to label the systems I use that also keeps things simple. When we trade, it's easy to become lost in all the data and conflicting information, so I find a labeling system really helps me keep it straight.

This chapter covers market-making strategies and techniques. Market-making strategies are typified by the market conditions in which they are used and by the kind of R multiples (or profits) that you are targeting. Market-making strategies are used almost exclusively in quiet market conditions. This means that they are best suited for the slower mid-day time frame. Market-making strategies target smaller profits than do momentum strategies—usually a 1- or 2-R multiple. In this chapter, I'll demonstrate one market-making play for the NYSE and one for the NASDAQ. Chapter 10 covers momentum trading.

YOU CAN'T TRADE WHAT YOU DON'T BELIEVE

Before we jump into some specific strategies and tactics, we need to lay a foundation for all the trading we do in the market-making realm. As I said earlier, you can only trade what you believe. If you anticipate trading any of my market-making strategies, you have to make these beliefs your own. Understand what I mean when I say this! We both know that you can go and hit the "Buy" or "Sell" button and make market-making-type trades, whether you adopt my beliefs or not. But if you want to successfully trade these strategies for the long haul, through thick and thin, then you have to have a useful belief structure underpinning your trading. Without that belief system in place, the first time you hit a drawdown, your conviction will waver and you'll give up on the system. So make the beliefs shown in Figure 9–1 your starting point as you develop your own useful market-making beliefs.

STRATEGIES AND TACTICS

Strategy deals with your "big-picture" plan. A football coach might say, for instance, "We'll win the game by exploiting our opponent's weak defense." That is a strategy. In trading, a strategy might be: "I'll find out who the best market maker is on this stock, and I'll buy when he buys and sell when he sells."

Tactics are the specific actions we take to implement our strategy. Again, the coach might say, "Let's throw short passes up the middle—that's been open all day!" A trader might say, "I'll watch Level II because I know Goldman (GSCO) is the ax (the market maker who is controlling the stock) and a net buyer. I know this by watching how many times Goldman's been at the best bid versus the best ask and by watching the Level II. Whenever he bids, I'll upbid ¹⁄₁₆ and attempt to buy in front of him."

Trading is full of strategies and tactics. In fact, behind each trade, several strategic and tactical factors are at work.

Market-making strategies are those strategies in which we try to think and act like a market maker. Basically what we're trying to do is either make the spread or make small-R wins when a stock is trading in a channel.

Market-Making Beliefs

1. Stocks trade in an oscillating pattern.

2. Generally, the oscillations get smaller as the day progresses.

3. The oscillations resemble a sine wave.

4. Buy near the bottom (support area) of an oscillation.

5. Sell near the top (resistance area) of an oscillation.

6. Market-making strategies work best during the middle (slow) period of the day or in generally slow market conditions.

7. Market-making strategies are best suited for a stock with no significant news.

8. Market-making strategies apply to "well-behaved" stocks. This implies (a) low volatility at the time of the trade and (b) reasonable volume (I use large-cap NASDAQ stocks).

9. If you step in front of a market maker on a trade, don't upbid or downbid by more than $\frac{1}{16}$.

10. The minimum channel for these strategies is $\frac{1}{4}$ on the NASDAQ and $\frac{1}{8}$ on the NYSE.

Figure 9–1

Philosophy

The philosophy behind this strategy is quite simple and is based upon the belief that market makers are more frequently "right" than the public is. On the basis of this belief, we try to implement a game plan, which allows us to "shadow," or trade in front of, the market maker. This means that we determine who the ax is and then buy when he buys and sell when he sells.

To really get a feel for this, let's delve into one "market-maker" play that I trade frequently. Remember this is only one set of tactics that I use based upon my strategic beliefs.

I first developed my market-maker strategies out of necessity. I got caught up, like many others, in the hype and hoopla surrounding day trading. And of course, as a brand-new trader, I had no experience in trading and did not know what I was doing. The real problem was that I thought I did know! I thought (very naively) that I knew something about trading!

I was trying to emulate Serge Milman, who disclosed in an April 1998 *Forbes* magazine article that he was making over $800,000 day-trading NASDAQ stocks for "teenies" ($\frac{1}{16}$s).

Milman's methodology was to take the spread out of the mouths of NASDAQ market makers, using SOES. The basic strategy was to buy on the bid and sell on the ask. *Forbes* dubbed Milman a "SOES bandit."

At the time I first heard the term "SOES bandit," I'd been investing and trading for over 20 years. Until then I normally traded using various technical systems, most often entering swing or position trades. But I admit to being more than curious about "bandit" trading. So after doing a little additional research, I opened a new account with the specific goal of trading for teenies. I felt that with my experience, I was more than prepared to trade along, in spirit, with Serge. Within days of opening my account I was regularly losing some serious cash. Obviously I had to find a winning system or quit trading for small intraday profits. Yet for me the question nagged: "Can I really make 'big money' day-trading stocks?" So I began a quest to answer that.

MARKET MAKING—THE STEALTH SPECIALIST

One of my first lessons was that as a brand-new trader, I was trying to trade the "wrong" stocks. By that, I mean most of the stocks I was trading, while very liquid, had huge daily ranges and volatility. Because of this it was virtually impossible to trade for $\frac{1}{16}$s and keep any kind of stop. Whipsaw was my constant companion. I therefore starting looking for liquid stocks with lower daily volatility, and found that certain NYSE listed stocks were probably more suitable for me at that stage in my development as a trader.

Specifically, my observation was that high-dividend stocks (excluding the Dow 30) were less affected by random market noise. As an additional benefit, very few day traders even bother screening these stocks, much less trading them. By far, most stock day traders trade "momentum" NASDAQ stocks.

Using stock screening software, I back-tested daily and intraday data for NYSE, NASDAQ, and AMEX stocks going back to 1995. I found that dividend-paying utilities traded in a very orderly intraday manner. I began to believe I could trade utility stocks for teenies and keep a stop.

To me a "system" that only I can trade is no system at all. So I asked, "Can I trade this system for a consistent profit?" And moreover, "If I can do it, can others do it?"

The simple answer is yes. But the fact remains that most "newbie" day traders, while adding newfound liquidity to the markets, simply end up as "fish food" for the "sharks," the sharks being professional traders, specifically the NYSE specialists and NASDAQ market makers.

I use the term "sharks" as a compliment, for the shark is the undisputed ruler of sea, just as the market makers and specialists are the rulers of the trading seas. Indeed, specialists and market makers are the best-trained, best-financed, and most skilled traders in the world.

But it's also true that sharks feed on the weak and the smaller fish. And when it comes to trading, much more often than not, the new trader becomes the weaker fish, and the food, for the specialists. While hard numbers are difficult to come by, some industry experts estimate that over 90 percent of all new traders will wash out, losing thousands or tens of thousands in the process, before giving up on the business of trading.

My market-making scalping technique is one method I use to successfully trade with the sharks. This methodology was a direct result of my early losing experience and the screening and back testing that I conducted. Since systemizing the processes, I've used this method with great success. Indeed, it has allowed me to swim in the same seas with the sharks without becoming shark food! Instead it relies upon the fact that the specialists are some of the best traders. As such, my goal is to feed with the sharks and trade along with them, not against them.

My method takes advantage of the rules of the NYSE sea. I become a small beneficiary fish, feeding off the crumbs of my host, the NYSE specialist. I call this method the "Stealth Specialist."

To trade this system, it's vital that you understand the seas in which you'll be swimming. You must understand certain NYSE rules and the specific role of the specialist. If you don't understand your host shark and the water he lives in, he will eat you alive.

Every stock on the NYSE is assigned to one and only one specialist. His job as mandated by the exchange is to create and maintain an orderly market in his stock. He also must assure that all customers receive "fair" order execution. It is important to understand that all trades in a particular listed stock go through this specialist. While many investors and traders understand this, far fewer understand that the specialist is also a trader. His job and his goal are the same thing—to trade for profits. And he does this by trading against his customers. Let me emphasize this again, *he trades against his own customers.*

Many firms would prefer to spin this in any other way possible, but the fact is that *Wall Street firms make billions annually by trading against their own public customers.* See why I call them sharks? They know the seas in which they swim. Moreover, they have very deep pockets, better equipment than their customers have, and faster access to information. Until recently they also had a huge edge in order execution. (This is one area that technology has rapidly changed. With modern electronic communication networks; the field is more balanced than it ever has been.)

How then can you get an edge? How can you develop a high-expectancy system in such hostile seas? The first key to trading as a Stealth Specialist is to understand this environment. There are two critical aspects to this.

First, the specialist cannot legally front-run customer trades. That means, if he is bidding for stock and you bid for the same stock at the same price, he must execute your order in front of his, *even if he was bidding before you were.* Let that sink in a moment. You get to go first!

While it is also illegal for NASDAQ market makers to front-run customers, the NASDAQ system itself renders this rule virtually useless when trading this system. This is because there may be 20 or more market makers trading a specific stock. Since orders do not go through one specific person, and since many market-maker firms also take order flow for retail customers, it's almost impossible to differentiate between "customers" and market-making firms.

Second, because the specialist is a market of last resort, failing any customer to take the other side of a trade, the specialist will take the trade. But the key here is, he gets to take the trade at his price. And remember he is trading for a profit. Will he knowingly pay too much for a stock? Of course not!

If you truly understand these rules, and you know how to "read the e-tape," you can successfully turn this knowledge into a high-expectancy, highly profitable system.

Let's go through an actual example. In Figure 9–2, I'm trading LG&E Energy (NYSE). I'd been stalking this stock for several days. It trades in a narrow daily range and has low volatility. Another nice thing was that during the same time frame the overall market had been rotating out of technology and Internets and into cyclicals. Utility stocks were beneficiaries of this rotation.

Although I do not depend upon technicals to trade this method, confirmation helps; and in this case LGE broke out of a consolidation pattern, closing above its 20-day moving average (see Figure 9–3). Using a real-time data feed and a time & sales window, Figure 9–4 shows the current situation.

Based on my observations, I believe that the specialist is on both sides of the trade (he is high bid *and* low ask). Experience has taught me that when the trading pace is slow (1 trade every 3 to 6 minutes), the bid-ask spread is ⅛ or greater, and the size is relatively small (generally less than 3,000 shares on the bid and/or ask), the specialist is normally on both sides of the trade. This is a very desirable situation, as you'll see in a moment.

I enter an order as follows: Buy 2,000 LGE Limit 22⅝.

Remember the rule of the sea? Assuming the specialist is the

LG&E ENERGY

Date	Time	Price	Volume	Exch	Type	Bid	BSize	BEx	Ask	Asize	AEx	Cond
5/24/99	11:15				Best Bid	22 11/16	100	NAS	22 7/8	100	NAS	
5/24/99	11:15				Bid	22 1/2	100	PHS	22 7/8	100	NAS	
5/24/99	11:15	22 11/16	2200	NYS	Trade							
5/24/99	11:15				Bid	22 1/2	100	PSE	22 7/8	100	NAS	
5/24/99	11:15				Bid	22 5/8	100	NAS	22 7/8	100	NAS	
5/24/99	11:15				Best Bid	22 5/8	1800	NYS	22 7/8	100	NAS	
5/24/99	11:23				Best Ask	22 5/8	1800	NYS	22 11/16	500	NAS	
5/24/99	11:23				Bid	22 7/16	1000	NAS	22 11/16	500	NAS	
5/24/99	11:24	22 5/8	600	NAS	Trade							
5/24/99	11:24				Ask	22 7/16	1000	NAS	23	500	NAS	
5/24/99	11:24				Best Ask	22 7/16	1000	NAS	22 13/16	500	NYS	
5/24/99	11:27	22 11/16	500	NYS	Trade							

Figure 9–2 Typical time & sales.

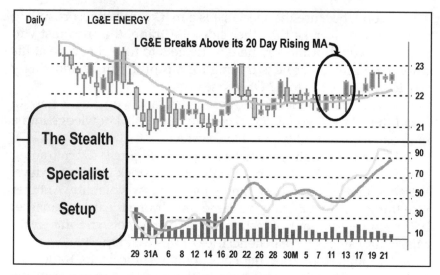

Figure 9–3 LG&E breaks above its rising 20-day moving average.

bidder, he must let me trade in front of him. Because I've used a limit order, I now become a bidder for the stock. But are there other customers in front of me? Let's watch the "e-tape." It should tell us. A second later the T&S window changes as shown in Figure 9–5.

What has changed? The exchange (Exch) has changed to NAS (NASDAQ), and the size has changed to 2,000.

Yes! The specialist was the bidder. I've now become a Stealth Specialist! I know this, because I understand the sea I'm swimming in. I entered the trade at the same price as the specialist, and he *had* to let me trade in front of him.

LG&E ENERGY						
Exch	Bid	Size	Exch	Ask	Size	Volume
NYS	22 5/8	1800	NYS	22 13/16	500	82200

Figure 9–4 LG&E time & sales—pane 1.

LG&E ENERGY						
Exch	Bid	Size	Exch	Ask	Size	Volume
NAS	22 5/8	2000	NYS	22 13/16	500	82200
NYS	22 5/8	1800	NYS	22 13/16	500	82200

Figure 9–5 LG&E time & sales—pane 2.

There are two points to note here: (1) I trade using a direct-access system to SuperDOT for very fast executions. This is *not* the same thing as "online" trading over the Internet. (2) Most orders on the NYSE from the public are "market" orders, meaning the best bidder will get the market sell orders.

Now the next market sell that comes along will be mine! I wait patiently for my fill. Depending upon the liquidity in the issue I'm trading, this could take a few seconds or several minutes. Of course, I may not be filled at all; however, this is rare.

In this case, I'm filled a few minutes later—2,000 shares at 22⅝. Figure 9–6 shows what the T&S window looks like now. This assumes, obviously, that the specialist has not changed either his bid or his ask. Although not always the case, it is often true with "slow-trading" stocks. Notice that the volume has increased by 2,000 shares. This was my buy.

Next, I immediately offer the stock I just bought. Here I'm faced with a critical decision. At what price should I offer the stock? Hard lessons have taught me not to be greedy. Except in volatile

LG&E ENERGY						
Exch	Bid	Size	Exch	Ask	Size	Volume
NYS	22 5/8	1800	NYS	22 13/16	500	84200

Figure 9–6 LG&E time & sales—pane 3.

```
LG&E  ENERGY

Exch      Bid     Size         Exch    Ask          Size    Volume
NYS    22 5/8    1800         NAS   22 11/16       2000     84200
NYS    22 5/8    1800         NYS   22 13/16        500     84200
```

Figure 9–7 LG&E time & sales—pane 4.

stocks, a relatively large ³⁄₁₆ spread will not last long in active trading. The specialist will move to tighten the spread if he perceives too much interest in the issue. So I trade the system for ¹⁄₁₆s.

Immediately after my fill, I enter the following order: Sell 2,000 LGE limit 22¹¹⁄₁₆. (See Figure 9–7.)

Again the T&S confirms the specialist was on the ask, and once again because he can't front-run my sell order, I'm first in line for any market buy orders. Now I simply wait for a buyer to take my offer. At last my sell order is filled. Figure 9–8 presents the T&S window.

PROFIT POTENTIAL

In this particular case, I was in the trade about a half hour. My profit? A cool $125 minus about $30 in commissions for a $95 net profit. Now $95 might not excite you very much. But do this successfully 8 to 10 times a day, and we're talking $760 to $950 per day, or approximately $152,000 to $190,000 per year.

```
LG&E  ENERGY

Exch      Bid     Size         Exch    Ask          Size    Volume
NYS    22 5/8    1800         NYS   22 13/16        500     86200
```

Figure 9–8 LG&E time & sales—pane 5.

This system is one of the lowest-risk day trading methods I've ever found for stocks. And I've tried plenty of methods. Regarding R multiples, I'm trading for a 1 R with a stop loss of 1 R. In other words, I'm trading for ¹⁄₁₆ and my stop loss is ¹⁄₁₆. And while I've had a few 2-R to 4-R (⅛ to ¼) losses, they have been very rare.

Why does this system work? If you've read Van's first book, *Trade Your Way to Financial Freedom* (and I recommend that you do), please note his discussion in Chapter 11, and specifically Table 11–1, "Expectancy, Cost, and Opportunity Factors for Our Four Traders." My Stealth Specialist most closely resembles Trader 4. *While the expected profit per trade is small, the daily opportunity and reliability are high.* My statistical reliability is around 70 percent. In other words I win on over 7 of 10 trades.

Also note that I personally choose to trade only part time. If you were to trade this system all day every day, I believe you could better my results.

You need to know that this system is not foolproof. You may or may not achieve results similar to mine. While I've tried to reduce this to a mechanical system, I have no doubt that part of my success is simply the result of hundreds of hours "stalking" this trade.

At times due to short-term market inefficiencies (or my own!), the trade will move against me. Perhaps the entire market turns negative, or other customer trades execute in front of me, reducing my chances of a quick favorable fill. Nonetheless, I've found the Stealth Specialist trade to be highly reliable and profitable.

Also note that I have very limited experience with this from the short side. I've tried a few shorts using this method with much poorer results. At this point I have not tried to determine why this is the case. I have simply adopted the policy of using this setup only from the long side.

Keys to trading the system include the following:

1. Learn the rules of the market you're trading. In this case the "sea" is the NYSE.
2. Deliberately trade when there is less "momentum" and therefore less competition.
3. Choose stocks that have a small daily range and low volatility.

4. Keep in mind that stocks paying large dividends tend to be less volatile.
5. Choose stocks with high institutional ownership.
6. Choose stocks that are not "headline" companies.
7. Be sure to have a fast execution system.
8. Make sure your transaction costs are low (less than $40 per round-trip).
9. Spread your feeding around. This means that if you take the trade in front of the same market maker too many times, he'll feed on you instead!

To help keep my setups clean and my trading disciplined, I have a "playbook" of my favorite trading setups and methods. This is a 3-ring binder. Each play is inserted on a single page, and setups are organized according to the type of setup and my trading objective.

Figure 9–9 shows a tear sheet of the Stealth Specialist from my playbook. As you can see, this technique is very low risk and offers scores of trading opportunities every day.

Goal	¹⁄₁₆ (1-R win)
Stop loss	¹⁄₁₆ (1-R loss)

Must-have factors to enter the trade:

Exchange	NYSE
Stock price	$10 to $25
Daily volume	50,000 to 1,000,000
Avg. daily range	⅛ to ⅜
# shares	2,000 minimum
Order type	Limit only
News	None

Optional additional factors:

Technicals	Trading just above its upward-sloping 20-day moving average

Figure 9–9 The Stealth Specialist (long scalp).

NASDAQ MARKET-MAKING SYSTEM

We'll take a look at another trading play in a moment, this time on the NASDAQ. However, there are some very large differences between the NYSE and the NASDAQ, differences that are critical for you to understand if you hope to profit consistently. Knowing the mind of the market maker is essential to successful trading.

NASDAQ stocks are not channeled through one person. Instead, there are several market makers that represent different customers and make the market. The NASDAQ allows traders many routes through which to buy and sell stock. Besides SOES and SelectNet, the NASDAQ facilitates trades through ECNs such as ARCA and ISLD. These routes all have their own unique capabilities and limitations.

The combination of several market makers competing to make a market in each NASDAQ stock, the volatile stocks that make up the NASDAQ, and numerous routes through which to buy and sell stock all make for a very dynamic and opportunistic environment. You can function as a retail customer, buying stock at the ask and selling at the bid, or you can play market maker, buying stock at the bid and offering stock at the ask. (The latter is my preferred trading method.) With a good trading system, the discipline to stick to trading rules, knowledge of trading methodologies, and good execution skills, the NASDAQ market holds virtually unlimited profit potential for traders.

Market makers perform several important functions. They provide liquidity by buying when there are no "natural" buyers and selling when there are no "natural" sellers. Of course, they do this at prices that they choose and that are beneficial to them, not you. They also provide "stabilization" functions during specific market situations.[1] Providing these services involves risk capital on their part; and of course, they intend to profit from the risks they take.

Market makers are typically acting in one of three capacities. If you can learn to spot certain of these activities, you'll radically improve your trading profits. The types of trading activity are (1) executing buy or sell orders for large institutional clients, (2) executing retail trades, and (3) trading on their own account using their own capital. In Chapter 10, I give you some specific methods to help you determine in which capacity a market maker is acting. This knowledge is indispensable when trading.

PRICE AND TRADING LEVELS

All market makers are legally required to make a two-sided market.[2] This means that while they are offering to buy stock at a certain price, they must also be offering to sell stock at a certain price. These prices or levels are different for each stock. Stocks trading with heavy volume will usually have narrower spreads (1/16, 1/8, etc.), whereas more thinly traded stocks will have wider spreads (1/4, 3/8, 1/2, etc.). For instance, if the market in DELL is 44¾ × 44¹³/₁₆ and the offers by the market makers and traders above the current offer are 44⅞ and 44¹⁵/₁₆, then the stock has levels that trade in 1/16s. These levels represent the difference in price between one bid and the next lower, or one ask and the next higher. This is particularly important, as you are concerned with the behavior that the stock is exhibiting when it is moving. See Figure 9–10.

DELL COMPUTER CORP						
DELL		44 13/16 ↑ +3 11/11 100		Ot t	11:49	
Bid ↑ 44 3/4		Ask	44 13/16	Vol 63968100		
# Bid 15		# Ask 21		Spread 1/16		

	Name	Bid	Size		Name	Ask	Size
O	MLCO	44 3/4	1000	O	NFSC	44 13/16	1000
O	GSCO	44 3/4	1000	O	SLKC	44 13/16	1000
O	HMQT	44 3/4	1000	O	SBSH	44 13/16	1000
O	JPMS	44 3/4	100	O	USCT	44 13/16	400
O	PIPR	44 3/4	100	O	DBKS	44 13/16	1000
O	COST	44 3/4	1000	O	MLCO	44 13/16	1000
O	CANT	44 3/4	200	O	LEHM	44 13/16	1000
O	MWSE	44 3/4	2700	O	BRUT	44 13/16	1500
O	FBCO	44 3/4	100	O	PRUS	44 13/16	1000
O	SHWD	44 3/4	200	O	MONT	44 13/16	100
O	ARCA	44 3/4	1000	O	MADF	44 13/16	1100
O	ISLD	44 3/4	1000	O	RAJA	44 13/16	1000
O	HRZG	44 3/4	100	O	NTRD	44 13/16	1100
O	INCA	44 3/4	8000	O	BEST	44 13/16	400
O	MSCO	44 11/16	1000	O	COST	44 13/16	800
O	BTRD	44 11/16	2600	O	MASH	44 13/16	4300
O	DEAN	44 11/16	700	O	MWSE	44 13/16	500
O	SLKC	44 11/16	1000	O	NITE	44 13/16	500

Figure 9–10 Importance of tier size—small tiers.

Stocks with less liquidity will normally trade with a greater variance between levels. For example, the price of BRCD (Figure 9–11) is 166 × 166¾, but the next higher level by a market maker or trader is 167, then 168, and so on (1-point increments). A two-level move in this stock, defined as the stock starting at the price spread of 166 × 166¾ and then trading up past 167 (the first new level) to 168 (the second level), is equivalent to a 32+-level move in the more liquid stock (DELL) with a ¹⁄₁₆ increment between levels. Thus, the ask in each stock would move up 2 points, but it would be a 32-level move in DELL and a 2-level move in BRCD.

Being aware of these levels is extremely important, because watching the Level II window requires intense concentration on how many levels the stock is moving, as opposed to how much the

BROCADE COMMS SYSTEMS INC							
BRCD		166 3/4	-2 1/4	600	Ot	t	12:00
Bid	166	Ask		166 3/4	Vol	514900	
# Bid	2	# Ask		1	Spread	3/4	

	Name	Bid	Size		Name	Ask	Size
O	DAIN	166	100	O	RSSF	166 3/4	100
O	ISLD	166	100	O	NITE	167	100
O	SLKC	165 3/4	100	O	MASH	167	200
O	ARCA	165 11/16	1000	O	DBKS	168	100
O	SHWD	165 1/2	200	O	HRZG	168	100
O	NITE	165 1/2	200	O	SLKC	168 1/4	100
O	MSCO	165 3/8	200	O	MSCO	168 3/8	200
O	REDI	164 11/16	500	O	REDI	169	500
O	INCA	164 1/4	1000	O	ARCA	169 1/2	300
O	HRZG	163 1/2	100	O	ISLD	169 1/2	100
O	MWSE	163	100	O	INCA	169 1/2	500
O	USCT	162 1/2	200	O	MWSE	169 3/4	100
O	DBKS	162	100	O	MOKE	169 7/8	100
O	MASH	161 5/8	100	O	JBOC	169 15/16	100
O	RSSF	159 3/4	100	O	USCT	170	1000
O	LHFC	158	100	O	LHFC	170	100
O	MOKE	157	100	O	SHWD	170 7/8	200
O	JBOC	153	100	O	DAIN	176 3/4	100

Figure 9–11 Importance of tier size—large tiers.

price has moved. The only way you will be able to determine these levels is by becoming familiar with how a particular stock trades, by paying special attention to the prices at which the ax is buying and selling, and by determining when the ax is the inside (best) bid or ask and how many shares are being offered.

THE AX REVISITED

Many NASDAQ stocks are controlled by a specific market maker. (The larger market-making firms are able to exert such strong influence because of a large cadre of institutional customers. By way of contrast, the smaller firms tend to trade on their own accounts or simply handle retail order flow.) The controlling market maker may handle 10 percent to 50 percent of the trades in a specific stock. Higher-liquidity stocks almost always have a "lead" market maker. He is affectionately known as the "ax." (This is because you'll have your head handed to you on a platter if (1) you don't know who he is and (2) you don't understand that he carries a *big* ax for decapitation purposes!)

The ax will frequently take positions with his own capital. He is often an underwriter (if not the lead underwriter) in a particular stock. Other market makers tend to follow his lead. He has power. In the absence of strong market momentum, the ax can dictate the direction of his stock at will. You can see why it is so important to know who he is, what he's doing, and how he's doing it.

The four largest market makers are Goldman Sachs (GSCO), Morgan Stanley (MSCO), Merrill Lynch (MLCO), and Bear Stearns (BEST). If one of these four firms is making markets in stocks you are trading, you'd better pay attention to that firm's moves. These firms will often attempt—and succeed—at deliberately driving a stock lower when filling an institutional buy or pushing it higher when executing an institutional sell. They do this, of course, to keep their multibillion dollar clients happy. Better fills equal happier clients. In Chapter 10, we cover the specifics of *how* they do this; here we are filling in the background.

Day traders often refer to the actions of market makers as "market-maker manipulation." However, I intensely dislike the term for two reasons. First, the market makers are doing their job—trading can be a poker game. And second, many traders use "market-maker manipulation" as an excuse for their own poor trading performance. Until the advent of Level II, this kind of action was totally hidden from the public and often resulted in poor fills to public customers. Now, with Level II and the knowledge of tape reading (Level II screen and time & sales prints), you can see what's happening behind the scenes and trade accordingly. Suffice it to say that many market makers would prefer that you didn't have access to Level II. They would have all day traders sitting behind a screen displaying only the inside and best bid and ask, downloading static quotes. This wouldn't just put you at a disadvantage; you would not even be in the game!

UNDERSTANDING THE MARKET MAKERS

The primary purpose of NASDAQ market makers is to trade retail and institutional accounts for their brokerage. They do this by displaying their quotes (offers to buy stock at the bid or sell stock at the ask) in their Level III software, which shows up in the market-maker window of your Level II trading software. (Level III is essentially the same as Level II, except that it allows for automatic refreshes of the bids and asks.) Market makers can also call each other on the phone to trade. However, because of the SEC's investigation into the collusion by market makers to keep spreads artificially wide, their phone calls are now monitored, and thus most market makers now execute their orders electronically using SelectNet. Market makers who are quoting a size and price of stock are expected to trade the number of shares that they are quoting. If they do not, it is said that they are "backing away" from the trade. A market maker can be fined as well as lose face among fellow market makers for backing away from a trade. Just remember, this doesn't mean it doesn't happen—it just doesn't happen often. When a market maker sells stock, he is responsible for reporting the transaction so it is printed with all the other sales on the tape.

The secondary purpose of market makers is to trade for their own accounts. Each broker usually has an extensive list of NASDAQ stocks in which it is willing to make a market. Each market maker is given a list of stocks for which he and his clerk are responsible. In addition to filling customer orders, they are also trying to make money by trading the stocks on their lists.

Market makers will speculate on future price movements of certain stocks, depending on market conditions. Each brokerage has specific risk parameters (levels of exposure it is willing to allow a market maker to assume), but most major firms have experienced traders who are knowledgeable in taking risk. With the leverage of deep pockets, expensive proprietary information systems, and inside information, many market makers can move stocks as they speculate.

The most important thing to remember about market makers when they're trading for their own accounts is that they are participating in the market for the same reason as you and I are, to make money! They will do everything in their power legally and professionally—and for some, illegally and unprofessionally—to take your money.

DIFFERENCES BETWEEN MARKET MAKERS AND SPECIALISTS

I've gone into quite a bit of detail on the NASDAQ market maker. Now let's briefly compare him to his cousin, the specialist of the listed exchanges.

The specialist must also make a two-sided market, and often trades her own account in addition to customer accounts on behalf of her brokerage firm. Although much of my discussion regarding the market makers applies to the specialist, a few distinctions are very important.

Small orders on the listed exchanges are handled on the SuperDOT electronic communications system.

Trading ahead of customer orders (front-running) is more highly monitored on the NYSE than on the NASDAQ. Therefore the rule against front-running is enforceable. Since there is no Level II, interpreting specialist quotes can be more difficult, since only the specialist sees the entire order book. Even with NASDAQ Level II, no one person sees the entire order book. For instance, while you see Goldman's best bid and ask, only Goldman knows his full order book. That said, the specialist thinks, acts, and walks like a NASDAQ market maker.

RECAPPING MARKET MAKERS AND SPECIALISTS

Market makers and specialists have several responsibilities:

- Fill orders for their brokerage firm's customers.
- Make a two-sided market.
- Trade their own account.
- Make money.

MARKET MAKING—THE CHANNEL FEEDER

With this background, let's take a look at another market-making technique, one that I trade regularly with great success. I call this the "Channel Feeder" to remind me that a critical element of this play is that the stock must be trading in a defined channel. The feeder part reminds me that this is a real "bread and butter" trade, one that can be traded almost every day.

Like the Stealth Specialist strategy, I'm looking for a stock that has little volatility at the time I intend to trade it. This can occur during slow periods of the day, even if the stock otherwise may have good volatility.

Unlike the Stealth Specialist, I'm looking only at NASDAQ stocks, and, further, only stocks with very high daily volume. Figure 9–12 shows my choice stocks for applying this play. You'll notice that these are all NASDAQ large-cap stocks. The reason that I like these is precisely because of the huge daily volumes they generate. For every seller there are many buyers, and conversely for every buyer there are many sellers. In other words, the price tiers are normally very deep at any given level.

One advantage of this trading depth is that it is normally very easy to get out at any given price tier, meaning it's pretty easy to keep your R losses to a minimum by keeping your stop price without incurring much (or any) slippage. Slippage is the difference between the price at which you'd like to get filled and your actual fill price.

Let's go through this trade step by step.

On March 16, 2000, Intel (INTC) began trading by gapping up approximately 3 points. Since INTC is one of my basket stocks, I already had a chart up. See Figure 9–13.

Cisco	(CSCO)
Dell Computer	(DELL)
Intel	(INTC)
Microsoft	(MSFT)
Sun Microsystems	(SUNW)
MCI WorldCom	(WCOM)

Figure 9–12 Favorite Channel Feeder stocks.

I watched it trade the first few minutes and noticed that despite the strong volume, it could not push to new highs. As usual, whenever a stock gaps up strongly, I expect a bit of a sell-off. Actually, my expectation is that the stock will "fill the gap." Although this does not happen 100 percent of the time, it is a great probability, so I trade accordingly.

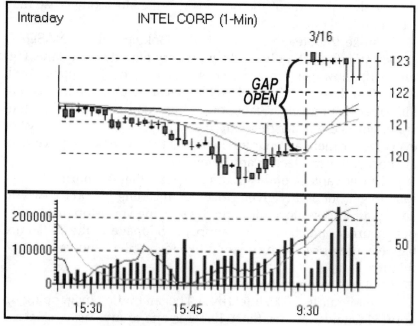

Figure 9–13 Intel—gap open.

See Figure 9–14 for the market-maker screens just minutes into the open. As you can see, just 4 minutes after the open, INTC is ¾ point off its high and is running into some good overhead resistance at 122⁹⁄₁₆.

Apparently thinking that INTC was heading lower, an ISLAND trader goes best ask, undercutting BTRD (Figure 9–15). Notice the lone Chippie (ARCHIP) bidding just above Goldman Sachs (GSCO) and crossing the market. Here it looks like there is some support at 122½ because both GSCO and Instinet (INCA) are bidding. But look at the depth of the ask. Additionally, INCA is selling 50,100 shares at 122⁹⁄₁₆.

GSCO now steps off the bid at ½ (Figure 9–16). A real tug-of-war is ensuing at this tier level between the buyers and sellers. Notice, too, that only 5 minutes into the session over 1.2 million shares have changed hands.

A minute later the sellers have dried up, so two Chippies and three Islanders are bidding (Figure 9–17). But notice that the first

Intel Corporation							
INTC	122 3/4		↑ +2 9/16	900	Ot		9:34
Bid ↓	122 1/2	**Ask**	122 9/16	**Vol**		1119000	
# Bid	4	**# Ask**	5		**Spread**		1/16
High	123 1/4	**Low**	122 5/8		**Close**	120 3/16	

Name	Bid	Size	#Best	Name	Ask	Size	#Best
NITE	122 1/2	400	6	SLKC	122 9/16	900	7
GSCO	122 1/2	1000	2	BTRD	122 9/16	300	6
INCA	122 1/2	2000	51	REDI	122 9/16	4500	8
ISLD	122 1/2	4800	23	INCA	122 9/16	54100	6
ISLAND	122 1/2	2000	0	ARCA	122 9/16	4500	3
DKNY	122 3/8	1000	0	ARCHIP	122 9/16	4500	0
FBCO	122 1/4	100	0	MONT	122 5/8	1000	0
NFSC	122 1/4	100	3	JPMS	122 5/8	100	0
MLCO	122 1/4	1000	1	ISLAND	122 5/8	100	0
JPMS	122 1/8	100	0	ISLD	122 5/8	100	14

Figure 9–14 Intel overhead resistance.

Intel Corporation

INTC	123 1/16 ↑	+2 7/8	100	0t	9:34
Bid ↓ 122 1/2	**Ask** 122 9/16	**Vol**			1145700
#Bid 2	**#Ask** 5	**Spread**			1/16
High 123 1/4	**Low** 122 1/2	**Close**			120 3/16

Name	Bid	Size	#Best	Name	Ask	Size	#Best
ARCHIP	122 9/16	200	0	ISLAND	122 143/256	1000	0
GSCO	122 1/2	1000	2	BTRD	122 9/16	300	6
INCA	122 1/2	2500	51	ARCA	122 9/16	4500	3
DKNY	122 3/8	1000	0	ISLAND	122 9/16	1000	0
FBCO	122 1/4	100	0	INCA	122 9/16	50100	6
NFSC	122 1/4	100	3	ISLD	122 9/16	2000	15
MLCO	122 1/4	1000	1	SLKC	122 9/16	100	7
JPMS	122 1/8	100	0	ARCHIP	122 9/16	4500	0
BRUT	122 1/16	300	0	MONT	122 5/8	1000	0

Figure 9–15 Intel—the ask is deep.

Intel Corporation

INTC	122 9/16 ↓	+2 3/8	100	0t	9:35
Bid ↓ 122 1/2	**Ask** 122 9/16	**Vol**	②		1226100
#Bid 2	**#Ask** 4	**Spread**			1/16
High 123 1/4	**Low** 121	**Close**			120 3/16

Name	Bid	Size	#Best	Name	Ask	Size	#Best
MSCO	122 1/2	1000	1	SLKC	122 9/16	100	7
HRZG	122 1/2	100	1	SBSH	122 9/16	1000	1
ISLAND	122 7/16	100	0	INCA	122 9/16	23300	6
ISLD	122 7/16	100	25	ISLAND	122 9/16	2000	0
ISLAND	122 25/64	700	0	ISLD	122 9/16	2000	17
INCA	122 3/8	100	52	MONT	122 5/8	1000	0
ISLAND	122 3/8	1200	0	JPMS	122 5/8	100	0
FBCO	122 1/4	100	0	REDI	122 5/8	2000	8
NFSC	122 1/4	100	0	RSSF	122 11/16	100	0

Figure 9–16 Intel—heavy volume on open.

Intel Corporation							

INTC	123 1/32 ↑	+2 27/32	100	0t	9:36		
Bid ↓	122 1/2	**Ask**	122 9/16	**Vol**	1355400		
#Bid	5	**#Ask**	2	**Spread**	1/16		
High	123 1/4	**Low**	121	**Close**	120 3/16		

Name	Bid	Size	#Best	Name	Ask	Size	#Best
ARCHIP	122 5/8	1000	0	SBSH	122 9/16	100	1
ARCHIP	122 9/16	500	0	SLKC	122 9/16	100	7
ISLAND	122 17/32	300	0	MONT	122 5/8	1000	0
ISLAND	122 33/64	4300	8	DKNY	122 5/8	100	1
ISLAND	122 127/256	1000	0	INCA	122 5/8	1000	6
MSCO	122 1/2	1000	3	ISLD	122 5/8	700	17
HRZG	122 1/2	100	1	ISLAND	122 5/8	400	0
DKNY	122 1/2	100	12	RSSF	122 11/16	100	0
INCA	122 1/2	17700		ISLAND	122 11/16	1000	0

Figure 9–17 Morgan Stanley is the first market maker bidding.

market maker to be found on the bid side, Morgan Stanley (MSCO), is only bidding ½.

Now, as shown in Figure 9–18, several ECN players are bidding, but again the sellers are the market makers. Also note that the buyers and sellers here are "head to head," meaning two buyers and two sellers with a spread of ¹⁄₁₆. The pace is slowing, and a pause ensues.

Believing that we're very near the top (Figure 9–19), I attempt a short on ISLD at 122¹³⁄₁₆, where a jubilant Islander takes my sell. I'm filled at ¹³⁄₁₆.

Note that I entered this trade on the expectation that the gap would be filled. At this early stage in the day, I didn't really expect that a channel would form. But that's exactly what happened.

Another key to this entry was that as the S&P futures were pushing higher (Figure 9–20), INTC was not able to do the same. This is significant because normally INTC will trade higher (or lower) in lockstep with the futures.

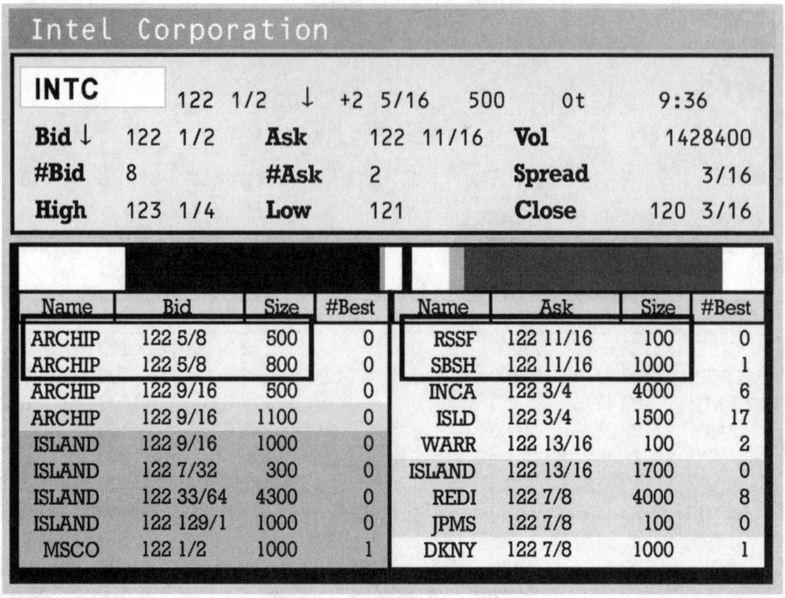

Intel Corporation

INTC	122 1/2	↓	+2 5/16	500	0t	9:36
Bid ↓	122 1/2	**Ask**	122 11/16	**Vol**		1428400
#Bid	8	**#Ask**	2	**Spread**		3/16
High	123 1/4	**Low**	121	**Close**		120 3/16

Name	Bid	Size	#Best	Name	Ask	Size	#Best
ARCHIP	122 5/8	500	0	RSSF	122 11/16	100	0
ARCHIP	122 5/8	800	0	SBSH	122 11/16	1000	1
ARCHIP	122 9/16	500	0	INCA	122 3/4	4000	6
ARCHIP	122 9/16	1100	0	ISLD	122 3/4	1500	17
ISLAND	122 9/16	1000	0	WARR	122 13/16	100	2
ISLAND	122 7/32	300	0	ISLAND	122 13/16	1700	0
ISLAND	122 33/64	4300	0	REDI	122 7/8	4000	8
ISLAND	122 129/1	1000	0	JPMS	122 7/8	100	0
MSCO	122 1/2	1000	1	DKNY	122 7/8	1000	1

Figure 9–18 Intel—head to head.

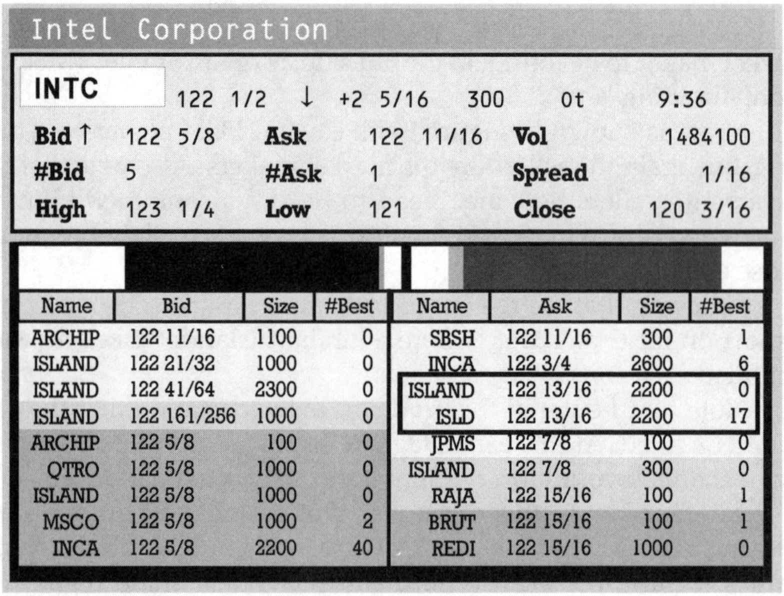

Intel Corporation

INTC	122 1/2	↓	+2 5/16	300	0t	9:36
Bid ↑	122 5/8	**Ask**	122 11/16	**Vol**		1484100
#Bid	5	**#Ask**	1	**Spread**		1/16
High	123 1/4	**Low**	121	**Close**		120 3/16

Name	Bid	Size	#Best	Name	Ask	Size	#Best
ARCHIP	122 11/16	1100	0	SBSH	122 11/16	300	1
ISLAND	122 21/32	1000	0	INCA	122 3/4	2600	6
ISLAND	122 41/64	2300	0	ISLAND	122 13/16	2200	0
ISLAND	122 161/256	1000	0	ISLD	122 13/16	2200	17
ARCHIP	122 5/8	100	0	JPMS	122 7/8	100	0
QTRO	122 5/8	1000	0	ISLAND	122 7/8	300	0
ISLAND	122 5/8	1000	0	RAJA	122 15/16	100	1
MSCO	122 5/8	1000	2	BRUT	122 15/16	100	1
INCA	122 5/8	2200	40	REDI	122 15/16	1000	0

Figure 9–19 Shorting Intel at 122¹³⁄₁₆.

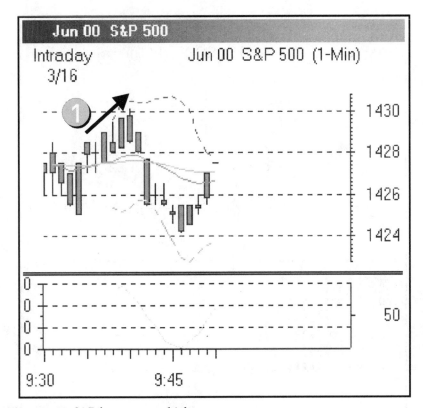

Figure 9–20 S&P futures move higher.

INTC can't take out $123, even as the futures move up at 9:36 (Figure 9–21). At 9:44 I cover at 121⅛, picking up 1¹¹⁄₁₆ in 8 minutes. For 1,000 shares traded, this equals $1,687.50. For 2,000 shares, it's $3,375 minus about $30 in commissions.

Figure 9–22 shows the chart at 10:08. As you can see, INTC totally closed the gap and then some. Also note that I didn't get out at the bottom, but I wasn't trying to. This goes along with one of my rules: "Sell or cover when you can, *not* when you have to!"

Actually, what is really important here is that INTC is setting up for the Channel Feeder play. The above trade, as I said, was based upon the expectation that INTC would fill the gap. I call this "shorting the open."

Now at 9:45 both the S&P futures (Figure 9–23) and INTC (Figure 9–24) have made their first high and low of the morning. I call

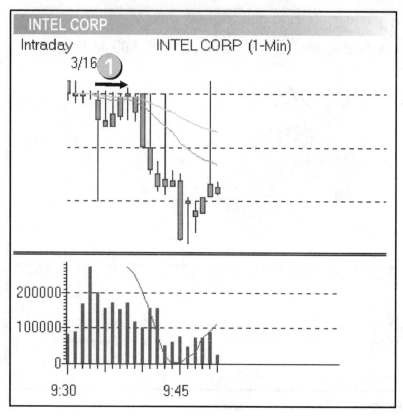

Figure 9–21 Intel moves sideways.

each high and low cycle an "oscillation," because it looks like a sine wave on a graph.

Now, based upon past experience and the knowledge I have gained from looking at literally thousand of charts, I change my expectation for INTC. Barring any news releases during the day that would affect INTC, the chip sector, or the market in general, I now expect that each successive price oscillation pattern will become smaller. Each successive high will be lower, and each successive low will be higher. This is the basic setup for the Channel Feeder strategy.

Now my trading is simple: Buy when the stock nears the bottom of the channel, and sell as it approaches the top. An even better technique is to "reverse" your position on the tops and bottoms. For example, if the channel is approximately 1 point wide, buy 100

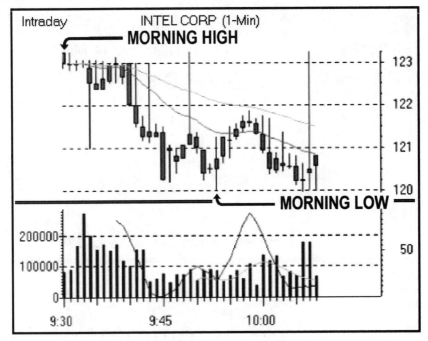

Figure 9–22 Intel has closed the gap.

shares at 120¼, and as the stock approaches 121¼, sell 200 shares. You are now net short 100 shares, which you cover as the stock approaches 120¼ once more.

Figure 9–25 shows how the INTC Channel Feeder actually looked during the morning of March 16, 2000. Notice the nice series of oscillations forming a channel.

I suggest that you trade small lot sizes when you're adapting to (or adopting) a new technique. In particular, the reversal techniques should only be attempted after you've attained plenty of experience with this play.

This pattern is very dependable. You may want to add it to your arsenal. Figure 9–26 presents a summary.

KNOWLEDGE KEYS

✓ Market-maker strategies are best suited for quiet market conditions (typically mid-day).

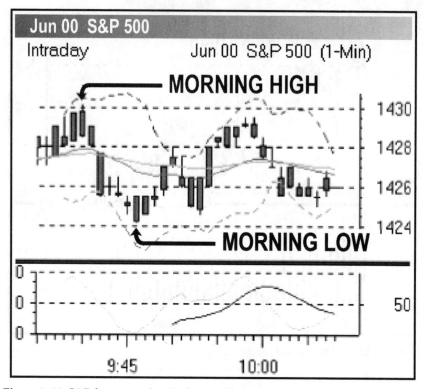

Figure 9–23 S&P futures makes its first oscillation.

✓ Market-maker strategies target smaller profits than do momentum strategies (typically a 1- or 2-R multiple).

✓ Useful market-making beliefs are the foundation for successfully trading these strategies.

✓ NYSE specialists control order flow and get to trade their own accounts. Because of this, they must let customer orders trade in front of theirs.

✓ Because you get to trade in front of the specialist, you can trade strategies such as the Stealth Specialist.

✓ NASDAQ market flow passes through multiple market makers in any given stock (and even around them via the ECNs).

✓ Market makers have three separate roles: They execute orders for institutional customers, they execute retail trades, and they trade their own accounts.

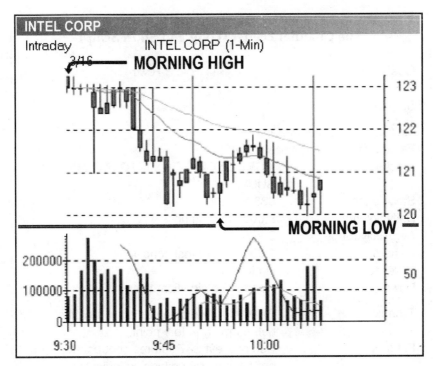

Figure 9–24 Intel makes its first oscillation.

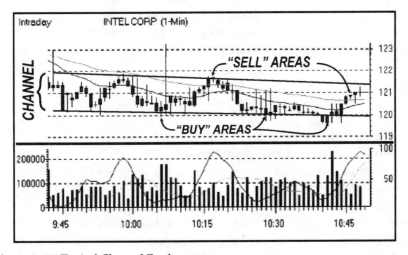

Figure 9–25 Typical Channel Feeder pattern.

The Channel Feeder (Long and Short Scalp)

Goal   ¼ to ¾   (1-R to 3-R win)

Stop loss   ¼   (1-R loss)

Factors to enter the trade:
Exchange   NASDAQ
Stocks   MSFT, CSCO, DELL, INTC, WCOM,
                      SUNW
Stock price $35 to $200
Daily volume   8,000,000 and up
Avg. daily range   2 to 5
shares   1,000 under most conditions
Order type   Limit only
News   None or no significant news

Technicals   Chart must indicate trading in a tight chan-
                      nel, normally ¼ to 1 point.
Futures   Use nearest S&P futures contract (top step
                      or first forward) as leading indicator. Lack-
                      ing news on the stock, correlation is 70
                      percent or better.
Time of day   This play is usually the best after the first
                      60 to 90 minutes of the trading day. Can be
                      especially good during mid-afternoon "dol-
                      drums" period.

Figure 9–26

✓ The ax is the market maker who exerts the most control over a
   NASDAQ stock at any given time.
✓ Identifying the ax and interpreting his trading activity can be a
   significant edge.
✓ During quiet markets, stocks that have no significant news
   impacting them tend to trade in defined channels.
✓ This tendency can be exploited in market-making strategies such
   as the Channel Feeder.

CALLS TO ACTION

✓ Develop your own set of market-making strategy beliefs. You can use the set of beliefs listed in this chapter as a starting point.

✓ Review your mission, self-assessment, and trading goals to determine if market-making strategies should be part of your overall trading plan.

✓ Learn the rules of order flow in the markets you are trading. Understand that they are significantly different in the NYSE and the NASDAQ.

✓ Practice (*live,* not paper trade) execution of the market-making techniques in this chapter with very small positions, say 10 to 100 shares, until you become proficient. Only then increase your share size.

NOTES

1. See Nasdaqtrader.com.
2. The NASDAQ says that for a market maker to stay actively qualified within a stock, she must make her market within a boundary of prices. See Nasdaqtrader.com.

## CHAPTER 10

Momentum Strategies

> We live in a moment of history where change is so speeded
> up that we begin to see the present only when it is already
> disappearing.
>
> *R. D. Laing*

Market-making strategies work very well in nontrending markets. However, what do you do when wild volatility is the norm?
Clearly another set of strategies is needed. Momentum trading
answers the call.

> **mo·men·tum,** noun: strength or force gained by motion or through
> the development of events

This definition from Merriam-Webster succinctly describes
momentum. Momentum trading is characterized by events and
rumors of events. For simplicity, I'll call all of this "news." In general, the better the news, the more the upside momentum. Conversely, the worse the news, the more the stock is driven by
momentum to the downside.

MOMENTUM PHILOSOPHY

If you spend much time at all getting to know top traders or if
you've done much reading about them, you'll know that most pro-

fessional traders agree that the best trading systems are often the simplest.

Momentum trading fits the "simple" description very well. Done correctly, it is simple. Yet it can be incredibly powerful and a very profitable trading style. As the name implies, this style of trading involves trading the larger-than-normal intraday movements of a stock. On any given market day, certain stocks will have the greatest momentum or movement due to trading activity. This momentum can be triggered by a number of factors, but news is often the prime factor driving momentum stocks.

One of the most important factors to consider when you are momentum trading is simply this: The stock is going up because people are buying it. The more that people or institutions buy, the higher the stock goes. The higher the stock goes, the more people that want it! Often this mentality leads to a self-perpetuating frenzy. And just as often, that frenzy leads to a final wild buying orgy, and the stock quickly reverses and heads in the opposite direction, sometimes more quickly than the speed it exhibited during its climb!

With a few differences, the converse is also true. As terror sets into the hearts of traders, they sell in a wild panic, often to have the stock "hard-reverse" and head up! What's needed is some method to systematize all this madness—a way to profitably trade, despite the wacky and sometimes irrational gyrations of "momentum" stocks.

Fortunately, several good methods do exist. An example for swing and position traders is William O'Neil's CANSLIM. It is a momentum system that combines both fundamental and technical data. However, if you used the CANSLIM system strictly for day trading, you'd be very disappointed, if not broke. This is because CANSLIM often buys "new highs." If you do this when day trading, you'll usually find yourself buying the high of the day. CANSLIM is a good system, but its time frame makes it, as a general rule, inappropriate for the strict day trader.

Momentum causes a stock to begin moving in patterns of oscillations that are often highly predictable (and therefore can be traded with a high probability). The price differential between the highs and lows (the stock's range for a given time period) is influenced by the underlying cause of the momentum. Some stocks move because of press releases; others move in sympathy with similar stocks in their sector that have news or are under momentum. Stocks move due to rumors, market-maker manipulation, institutional activity, and inside information.

The extent of each stock movement is affected by several factors: the dynamics of the market (market conditions), the reason (e.g., news) for its momentum, and the strength or weakness of the company and its sector. These movements can be recorded to calculate the probability of a pattern repeating, but the market is so dynamic that you should only use these patterns as general guidelines. Stocks can and do exhibit unexpected behavior due to market conditions, seasonal or day-of-the-week influences, market-maker manipulation, and trader activity or sentiment. Since this is the case, start with a general expectation but react appropriately to the behavior of the stock. Just as we did in Chapter 9, let's start off our discussion of specific momentum strategies by first looking at some foundational momentum beliefs, presented in Figure 10–1.

MOMENTUM PATTERNS

Two basic patterns that I use in momentum trading are ones that I have named "boomers" and "busters." (If these terms sound familiar, that's because you've already read a bit about them earlier in the book.) This is more than just some fun labeling. Each of these patterns has a specific trading expectation. That's important because it gives me a basis for both entering and exiting a trade. The specific behaviors exhibited by these stocks are a factor of (1) the company, (2) the news, (3) market conditions, and (4) current trader sentiment. That said, I've found the following patterns to be very reliable and tradable.

Boomers

Boomers are stocks that have gained approximately 20 percent or more of their value since the close of the last session's regular trading hours (the 4:00 p.m. Eastern Time close). These stocks are usually up on "good" news (e.g., beating projected earnings by a few cents), and the market usually overreacts.

Boomers are best bought from the first uptick at the open, or shorted when they reach their highs (see Figure 10–2). If the news is

Momentum Beliefs

1. Momentum strategies are best traded early or late in the day (the first 1 to 2 hours and the last 1 to 1½ hours of the trading day).

2. News is essential to drive momentum.

3. The public reaction to news is most often wrong and is especially prone to overreaction in the first 5 to 10 minutes after the news is released.

4. A good strategy is to fade the initial reaction to the news.

5. Bid-ask spreads must be ¼ or less—⅛ to ¹⁄₁₆ is best.

6. The previous day's high or low determines the initial resistance or support level for the current trading day. This assumes that the stock does not gap beyond the previous day's high or low.

7. Recent price action is the most important. For example, the support or resistance level of the last 15 minutes is more important than that of the last 30 minutes, which is more important than that of the last hour, etc.

8. Trade in the direction of the relative strength trend.

9. Gap opening plays are tradable.

10. Most boomers should be faded.

Figure 10–1

strong, the stock may make exceptional oscillations and be tradable from both the long and short side for much of the trading day. It is generally not wise to be in a hurry to short a boomer since it is under positive momentum. It is best to let the stock reach a point where profit taking sets in before going short. We'll look at this in more detail along with examples later in the chapter. (For a comprehensive explanation of news interpretation, see Chapter 8.)

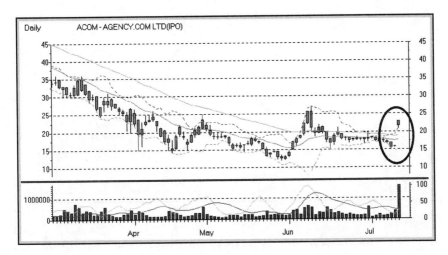

Figure 10–2 Boomer chart pattern.

Busters

Busters are stocks that have lost approximately 20 percent or more of their value since the close of the last session's regular trading hours (the 4:00 p.m. Eastern Time close). These stocks are usually down on "bad" news (e.g., missed projected earnings by a few cents, a merger that fell through), and the market again overreacts. These stocks will generally sell down from the open and then bounce back up (see Figure 10–3). A textbook buster, for example, will be a stock that closed at 20, opens at 16, sells down to 12, and then bounces back to 14 (regains 50 percent of what it sold down from at the open).

Boomers and busters also have some useful subcategories. I call them double (or triple) boomers and double (or triple) busters. A double boomer is a stock up greater that 20 percent on two consecutive trading days. A double buster is the converse. Triples are three in a row and are very rare. Again the reason for this labeling is to form a trading expectation from exhibited behavior.

Double Boomers

Double boomers are fun (and profitable) to trade because their patterns are very reliable (see Figure 10–4). The keys to double

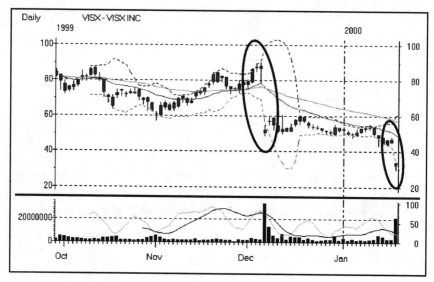

Figure 10–3 Buster chart pattern.

boomers are the strength of the news and the strength of the volume driving the momentum.

Here's what you can expect:

Double Boomers Gapping with Volume   Stocks exhibiting this behavior usually take one of two paths. They rarely go sideways for the remainder of the day.

1. They continue to climb at the open and at some point in the day (usually mid-to-late morning) fall back. These are good opening longs and then good shorts on the pullback.
2. They fall from the open with profit taking. These are good opening shorts.

Double Boomers No Gapping but with Volume   Stocks exhibiting this behavior usually sell down from the open, making good opening shorts.

Double Boomers Gapping Down   Stocks exhibiting this behavior usually sell down from the open, making good opening shorts.

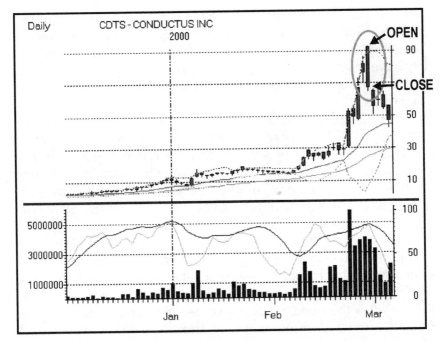

Figure 10–4 Double boomer chart pattern.

(*Note:* These stocks can oftentimes be shorted premarket, thus capturing a few more points. This, however, is only recommended for advanced traders and then only for those trading within their position-sizing algorithm. Premarket trading offers higher reward with higher risk.)

MARKET MAKERS DURING THE OPEN

To truly understand these momentum patterns, it's important to know how a market maker influences the early part of the trading day. A great way to read the mind of a market maker is to watch what she does during the market open. Most of the daily trading activity takes place in the first 2 hours and last hour of the trading day. So seeing how a market maker opens her stock can be quite informative.

As a review (see Chapter 8 for more detail), remember that the NASDAQ exchange is unlike the listed stock exchanges (NYSE,

AME), which are centralized and have a specialist through whom all orders flow. The NASDAQ, instead, has many market makers filling buy and sell orders for different customers or themselves. If they have any influence at all, they are vying to influence the opening. They are like poker players trying to figure out who's holding what cards.

They begin influencing the opening around 1 hour before the market open. They can gap a stock up or down several points without a single print (buy or sell). When there is news on a stock they are making a market in, they test the waters by bidding or offering stock on Level II to see what other market makers and traders are willing to buy or sell stock for. *This is totally without risk, since prior to the open they don't have to honor their quotes!*

The first 15 to 30 minutes after the open tends to be a "shaking-out" period when, quite often, market orders placed the night before or in the morning (people guessing what a stock is going to open at) are firing off well above or below the current bid and ask. Within ½ hour after the open, stocks have usually defined their trading range (their low/bottom/support and high/ceiling/resistance). This is not to say, however, that you have to wait 15 to 30 minutes before trading. There is tremendous potential during the first few minutes after the open for the astute trader who can determine the direction of a stock. And it is much easier to get a read if you've been following a stock and its ax for several days or more before actually trading it. This knowledge is even more helpful during the highly volatile opening period.

Often, some of the greatest profits can be made during the opening (and closing). However, the novice trader should probably avoid trading openings, because without the kind of knowledge I'm disclosing here, and without some real experience under more relaxed conditions, the novice will lose money very, very quickly during the opening half hour due to the increased volatility and fast market conditions.

You can gain a real edge by determining who the ax is in a particular stock and whether she is a net buyer or a net seller. If you can key on the ax during the premarket hours and the first half hour of the regular trading session (9:30–10:00 Eastern Time), you'll usually have a very good indication of the stock's direction for the rest of the day. Stocks in a trend tend to stay in that trend.

MARKET-MAKER MANIPULATION

Market makers (MMs) have substantial resources (deep pockets, expensive proprietary information systems, inside information); yet they still do everything they can to grab every dime of your trading capital.

You should also know that until recently, NASDAQ market makers were only required to quote a bid or ask price. They were not required to display the amount of shares they were willing to buy or sell. Now they must display the minimum number of shares they will buy or sell at each price level. Using Level II software, you can see the price and the quantity of shares that a market maker is bidding or offering (buying or selling). Market makers will change the quantity of shares they are bidding or offering to confuse other market makers and traders. They often jump back and forth from the inside bid to the inside ask for sometimes seemingly irrational reasons. They also hide behind Instinet (INCA) so they can conceal their identity. However, these tactics aside, when a stock is under momentum, the quantity of shares displayed by a market maker will normally represent the true number of shares she wants to buy or the number she has to sell. This information can be extremely informative to the perceptive trader. In short, the market maker can adjust her prices at any time, for any reason.

The following are some examples of the tactics market makers use in an attempt to take your money. An astute trader will learn their games and either wisely avoid trading stocks that are being heavily manipulated or turn adversity into opportunity.

Head-Fakes

Head-fakes are actions that MMs take to create the illusion of a short-term trend to induce panic buying or selling, and usually result in a short-term trend reversal. Panic buyers or sellers are "faked" out of their shares. An example of this would be when a group of MMs, or the ax controlling a stock, suddenly drop the bid by a significant amount. For example, stock ABCD is trading at 17¼ × 17⁵⁄₁₆. Suddenly the inside market (best bid or ask) drops to 16¾ × 16⅞. The stock has just dropped ½ point without any selling.

What happens? Panic. Sellers show up and immediately dump their shares, thinking there is a reason for the downtrend (possibly bad news or a downgrade). MMs accumulate cheap shares on the way down and sell for a profit on the way up. The ax will often do this hiding behind Instinet (INCA), an ECN often used by a MMs. Another example of this would be when a MM steps up to the best bid or ask with a large (e.g., 50,000) quote size hiding behind INCA. This is an obvious head-fake. Remember that MMs are like poker players. They do their best not to show their cards. They do not want other MMs or traders to know if they are buyers or sellers in a stock. It would undermine their efforts to collect cheap shares at lower and lower prices (if buying) or to dump expensive shares at higher and higher prices (if selling). Therefore, when MMs step up to the best bid or ask with a huge quote size, you will notice it is just as a trend is developing or has gained momentum. They step up with their phony quote, scare less experienced traders out of their shares, and then quickly disappear from the best bid or ask.

Fading the Trend

Fading the trend is when MMs, or the ax controlling a stock, use their resources of abundant shares and deep pockets to fight the trend and are successful in reversing it. An excellent example of this is INFO (see Figures 10–7 through 10–14). In the premarket, INFO gapped up from 6 to 7. At the market open, there was heavy selling or shorting between 7⅛ and 7⅜. Soon traders realized that in spite of the selling or shorting, the MMs were pushing the price up. The MMs managed to push the price all the way to 8 before letting it drop back down to 7½. It was evident that many traders either were profit taking (they had purchased the stock premarket or owned it previously) or were shorting the stock. Most traders probably thought that a 1-point gain on a $6 stock was significant enough for profit taking, and that the stock would fall. Traders' expectations were reasonable, but they were run over by the MMs' actions.

Short Squeeze

A short squeeze is most often a run-up in the price of an over-bought stock. This happens when a stock is outrageously overvalued, is in a sector that is in a state of "irrational exuberance" (e.g., many Internet, high-tech, and biotech stocks during 1998–2000), and has a high short interest. The stock typically climbs strongly on good news and is near its intraday top.

Without explanation, MMs begin to "step off the ask," and whole price tiers disappear without any significant prints. Short sellers panic in a rush to cover and start piling on the bids, driving the price even higher. The MMs sell into the panic, and all too frequently, the stock reverses and is then driven down to continually lower prices. The weak shorts are now bewildered and poorer. (It is usually weak-handed, undercapitalized traders who fall victim to a short squeeze.)

DETECTING MARKET-MAKER MANIPULATION

Fortunately, once you've learned how to use Level II, these manipulations become easier to detect. Here are two obvious situations to watch for:

1. You see a significant volume of sales go off at the bid, and yet MMs are lifting the ask, trying to coax the price higher.
2. A stock has not had news for days, the volume has dried up, and there is little pace (few prints), but yet the stock begins to move higher with little or no buying.

When a stock is being manipulated, it is being moved in a direction opposite the trend for reasons unknown to you. Often, the stock can no longer be traded with a high-percentage expectation. Therefore, trading the stock is gambling, which is not a good way to preserve your trading capital and survive as a stock trader. Thus when you see a stock behaving strangely, you have two choices: (1) If you're a new or otherwise an inexperienced trader, stay out of the stock. If already in, immediately exit. (2) Once you've become a seasoned trader, you can trade with or "shadow" the ax.

POSSIBLE INTERPRETATIONS OF THE MM'S ACTIVITIES

Given all these tactics (and more), how do you trade using this information? One way is to learn in interpret the MM's moves using Level II quote screens. Although these interpretations are not exact, they are tradable.

The Market Maker Is Buying Stock

Situation 1   The MM buys on the bid and doesn't change his quote. The inside market is 24⅞ × 25. The MM pays 24⅞ for some stock and then refreshes his quote.

Possible Interpretation: The MM is a buyer who believes that there are other MMs who are also interested buyers. In this situation, the MM is unlikely to change his quote.

Situation 2   The MM buys on the bid and lowers his bid one level. The inside market is 24⅞ × 25. The MM pays 24⅞ for some stock and then lowers his bid to 24¾.

Possible Interpretation: The MM is a buyer but is hoping to buy more stock at a lower price. He is testing the waters to see what will happen if he does not attract sellers. It is likely that he is buying stock for his own account, but he may be attempting to get a better price for an institutional order.

Situation 3   The MM pays 24⅞ for some stock and jumps from the bid to the ask. Remember that the inside market is at 24⅞ × 25. The MM pays 24⅞ and then offers to sell at 25.

Possible Interpretation: The MM is capturing the spread, or the MM bought stock and now he doesn't want it. The MM is not a buyer or would like you to think that he is not a buyer.

Situation 4   The MM pays 24⅞ for some stock and moves one level above the ask. Again, the inside market is 24⅞ × 25. The MM pays 24⅞ and then offers to sell at 25⅛.

Possible Interpretation: The MM is not a real buyer or seller at the present time. He is participating in the market, but only to fulfill his MM responsibility. In this situation, he bought stock on the bid and is holding it to sell a couple of levels higher on the ask. He is not the ax in the stock, but is not only capturing the spread, but also making money on the momentum of the stock.

The Market Maker Is Selling Stock

Now let's consider what might be happening when the MM sells stock. A MM is on the ask and makes a sale. How may he now behave?

Situation 1   The MM remains on the ask. The inside market is still 24⅞ × 25. The MM offers to sell stock at 25 and then refreshes his quote.
    Possible Interpretation: He has sold some stock and is willing to sell some more. The MM is a seller and evidently not a buyer at this level.

Situation 2   The MM sells stock and jumps one level above the ask. The inside market is 24⅞ × 25. The MM sells stock at 25 and then offers to sell more at 25⅛.
    Possible Interpretation: He is a seller and is trying to get a better price. He is testing the waters to see what will happen if he does not prevent the stock from climbing in price. He is likely to believe that there are no motivated sellers and that he can get a better price.

Situation 3   The MM jumps from the ask to the bid. The inside market is 24⅞ × 25. The MM sells stock at 25 and then offers to buy it back at 24⅞.
    Possible Interpretation: The MM is capturing the spread.

Situation 4   The MM sells stock at the ask and jumps one level beneath the best bid. The inside market is 24⅞ × 25. The MM sells stock at 25 and moves to the bid to buy at 24¾.
    Possible Interpretation: The MM is not a serious buyer or seller. He is participating in the market to fulfill his MM responsibility, to profit from capturing the spread, and to potentially capture more than the spread if the stock has momentum.

Interpreting the actions of market makers to determine their true intentions is speculation. However, we are not trying to be "right" about what the MM is doing. We're simply trying to form reasonable, tradable expectations. Remember, MMs do not need a single trade to go off, nor do they need to fill one order, before raising or lowering their bid or ask. They take on the risk of making a market on both sides of the trade and therefore will naturally adjust their prices to the level they feel offers the greatest profitability.

Before we move on to specific momentum tactics, let's take a quick look at an example of a MM's manipulation, in this case "fading the trend."

ILLUSTRATION OF FADING THE TREND

Finding the news items shown in Figures 10–5 and 10–6 in Briefing.com (one of my news sources) and noting the price was under $10, I had a good feeling that novice day traders would grab this stock and run with it.

Infonautics Inc. (INFO) 6-1/8: provider of Internet information services to schools, libraries, consumers and businesses **signs a definitive agreement with Bell & Howell;** INFO will receive 27% of the new company and BHW will own the balance of the new entity; see *press release.* . . .

Figure 10–5 Stories.

• **08:57 ET** *Infonautics (INFO)* 6: Company signs deal with Bell & Howell (BHW) to create a company focusing purely on the K-12 Internet market. Bell & Howell will be majority owner of the newly created company. INFO shares indicated 10% higher on the news.

Figure 10–6 In-Play.

I put the stock in a market minder window and brought up a T&S window to see the premarket prints (buys and sales) on INFO (see Figure 10–7). As I watched the stock climb significantly in price with good premarket volume (see Figure 10–8), I could have purchased the stock before the open. Of course, the premarket play is higher risk and potentially higher reward.

As the time got closer to the open, the stock maintained its gain and climbed higher (see Figure 10–9). This gave me an indication that the stock was likely to climb from the open.

Sure enough, at the open, the stock climbed rapidly (see Figure 10–10). My premarket expectation was confirmed.

When the market opened, INFO was at the top of my minder window (sorted by descending total volume). The fact that over 50,000 shares had traded premarket was a good sign. It showed the strength of the buying and selling interest in the stock. INFO had good momentum and pace. Figure 10–11 clearly shows the 1+ point gap since the close.

Lastly I noticed that in spite of the heavy selling (prices going off at the bid of 7⅛), market makers (lined up at the top three levels of the ask) were allowing the stock to rise. This is an example of fading the trend. The market makers were clearly selling into the strength (see Figure 10–11).

Note specifically in Figure 10–12 the heavy volume ("Tot. Vol.") and tight spread on INFO at the open. The last price was the bid price of 7⅛. The stock was selling, yet the price climbed. One easy way to spot a market maker fading a stock is to notice when most of the prints are at the bid price or below, while the MM has let the ask price rise.

The volume on INFO climbed. The last price was now 7⁵⁄₁₆. The stock was still selling at the bid, the volume began to accelerate, and the price climbed still higher (see Figure 10–13).

Traders were now following the trend that the market makers created. The stock had very good volume (over 500,000) shortly after the open (see Figure 10–14).

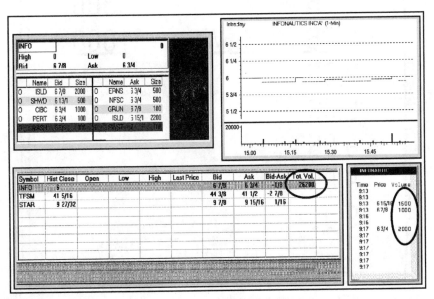

Figure 10–7 INFO trade setup.

INFONAUTIC...

‖——INFONAUTICS

Time	Price	Volume
9:04		
9:04		
9:04	6 5/8	1300
9:04	6 5/8	700
9:05		
9:05		
9:05	7	300
9:05	6 5/8	1000
9:05		
9:05		
9:05		
9:05		
9:05		

Figure 10–8 INFO is gapping premarket.

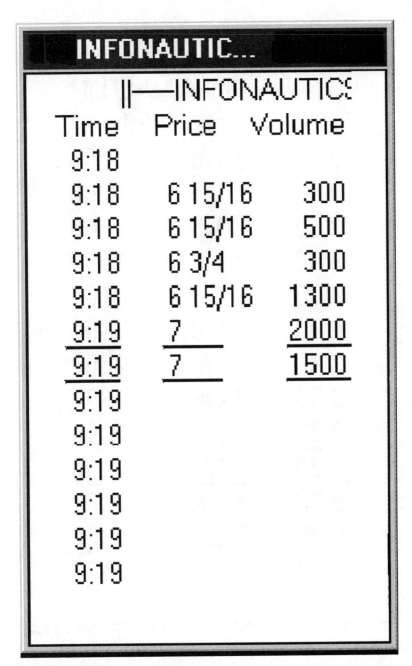

Figure 10–9 INFO continues higher.

INFONAUTIC

‖———INFONAUTICS		
Time	Price	Volume
9:30	7 1/8	200
9:30	7 1/8	1000
9:30	7 1/8	500
9:30	7 1/8	1000
9:30	7 1/8	100
9:30	7 1/8	100
9:30	7 1/8	2000
9:30	7 1/8	500
9:30	7 1/8	2000
9:30	7 1/4	400
9:30	7 1/8	1000
9:30	7 1/8	300
9:30	7 1/4	500

Figure 10–10 INFO opens at the high end of its premarket trading range.

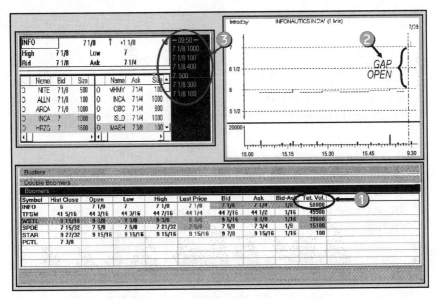

Figure 10–11 Market makers sell into the strength.

Symbol	Hist Close	Open	Low	High	Last Price	Bid	Ask	Bid-Ask	Tot. Vol.
INFO	6	7 1/8	7	7 1/8	7 1/8	7 3/16	7 1/4	1/16	58500
TFSM	41 5/16	44 3/16	44 3/16	44 1/2	44 3/16	44 7/16	44 1/2	1/16	52600
WSTL	8 15/16	9 3/8	9 3/8	9 3/8	9 3/8	9 5/16	9 3/8	1/16	39800
SPDE	7 15/32	7 5/8	7 5/8	7 21/32	7 21/32	7 5/8	7 3/4	1/8	18900
STAR	9 27/32	9 15/16	9 7/8	9 15/16	9 7/8	9 7/8	9 15/16	1/16	200
PCIL	7 3/8								

Figure 10–12 INFO selling at or below the bid, yet price rises.

Symbol	Hist Close	Open	Low	High	Last Price	Bid	Ask	Bid-Ask	Tot. Vol.
INFO	6	7 1/8	7	7 1/2	7 5/16	7 1/16	7 1/2	7/16	235000
WSTL	8 15/16	9 3/8	9 1/4	9 3/8	9 3/8	9	9 1/8	1/8	139800
TFSM	41 5/16	44 3/16	44 3/16	44 15/16	44 15/16	45 5/16	45 3/8	1/16	114500
SPDF	7 15/32	7 5/8	7 9/16	7 3/4	7 5/8	7 9/16	7 11/16	1/8	54000
SIAH	9 27/32	9 15/16	9 7/8	9 15/16	9 7/8	9 7/8	9 29/32	1/32	9200
PCTL	7 3/8								

Figure 10–13 Traders begin to "pay up" for INFO.

Symbol	Hist Close	Open	Low	High	Last Price	Bid	Ask	Bid-Ask	Tot. Vol.
INFO	6	6 5/8	6 1/2	7 31/32	7 3/4	7 5/8	7 11/16	1/16	541000
TFSM	41 5/16	44 3/16	44 3/16	48 3/8	46	46	46		433500
WSTL	8 15/16	9 3/8	8 15/16	9 3/8	9 1/4	9 1/4	9 5/16	1/16	388900
SPDF	7 15/32	7 5/8	7 15/32	7 3/4	7 1/2	7 7/16	7 9/16	1/8	164200
STAR	9 27/32	9 15/16	9 3/4	9 15/16	9 3/4	9 3/4	9 15/16	3/16	15900
PCTL	7 3/8	7 3/8	7 3/8	7 7/16	7 7/16	7 5/16	7 7/16	1/8	1000

Figure 10–14 Market makers have created a temporary "rally" and sell into it.

KEY MOMENTUM CONCEPTS

When trading momentum strategies, I keep three major concepts in mind. I use these as my reliable beliefs to help me set expectations.

1. Volume Determines Trends

I'm a big believer in volume. It's a very effective tool—and it's one of the easiest to understand. Day traders often find themselves overwhelmed with complex technical indicators, moving averages, and complex algorithms. However, sometimes it helps to step back and get down to basics. One of those basic indicators is volume (the number of shares bought and sold in any given day). Not long ago, a 100 million-share day on the New York Stock Exchange would have left brokers breathless. Volume has increased dramatically over the past few years, the simple result of having more money in play, driven by sharp increases in mutual fund and hedge fund assets. Now, in the wake of record-shattering days for the Dow, volume has spiked and has recently topped 1 billion shares per day. NASDAQ volume has regularly surpassed 2 billion shares per day.

As long as there has been trading, investors have used volume to get a read on where stocks are headed. And unlike most of the tools that technical analysts use, this one is easily found on almost any financial Web site or in any daily newspaper that has stock tables (usually expressed in thousands of shares), and of course in your EDAT software.

A trader can't live or die by any one indicator. But understanding volume can provide insight into a stock's behavior to help you determine its overall health. The most important guideline is this: *Volume precedes price.* Typically, before a stock price moves, volume comes into play. The beauty of this indicator is its flexibility. Changes in volume can be used intraday to determine short-term price movement, or they can be used over several days to determine a stock's 2- to 3-day trend.

Before learning how to interpret volume, you have to know what a stock's average daily volume is. Active traders were once relegated to writing down the volumes each day for their favorite stocks and then calculating the averages themselves. Now, of course, the Internet has made such information available to any investor online. (One of the best sites I've seen is Yahoo Finance at http://quote.yahoo.com. It will give you the average volume on any stock you choose.)

In general, a price change on relatively low volume for a particular stock suggests an aberration, whereas a price change on high volume portends a genuine trend. An active trader looks at volume to help determine a price trend. When momentum trading, the obvious goal is to trade in the direction of the major price trend. One of the best times to buy is when a stock is going down on low volume (with no news) after it has had recent increases on higher volume. This suggests that the selling is lighter and that the holders of the stock that are going to sell have finished selling and the rest are holding. Buyers of the stocks then may come back into the market when they see the price stabilize. *It's also not a bad idea to sell on high volume on the way up (if the volume appears to be tapering off), as this usually creates abnormally high prices that cannot be maintained very long.*

The basic theory is this: If price and volume are moving in the same direction, the trend of the stock price will continue. If they are running counter to each other, the trend will reverse.

Volume should never be used exclusively to time entries or exits, but it is an invaluable tool to gain insight into the markets and determine the current price trend. In other words, it helps the trader form tradable expectations.

2. Trade Relative Strength

Another phenomenal edge is to understand trading relative strength. Here I don't mean relative strength versus the S&Ps, as you might find in a newspaper. Neither do I mean a technical relative strength indicator. To a day trader, relative strength should be quite simple.

Strong Relative Strength

On days when the overall market is weak (the NASDAQ composite, the Dow, and/or the S&P futures), which stocks are up strongly? These are strong stocks relative to the market. They have strong relative strength that day or during the time of day you're screening for them.

The trading plan for stocks with strong relative strength in this situation is to determine the support and resistance. Once you find these levels, you buy the support levels. Once your trading skills have advanced, you may want to add to your position (called "scaling" or "pyramiding") each time the stock reaches support. Scaling in and out of positions is a very powerful position-sizing tool; it is, however, beyond the scope of this book.

Weak Relative Strength

On days when the overall market is strong (again, the NASDAQ composite, the Dow, and/or the S&P futures), which stocks are down sharply? These are weak relative to the market. They have weak relative strength that day or during the time of day you're screening for them.

The trading plan for stocks with weak relative strength in this situation is to determine the support and resistance. Once you find these levels, you sell (or short) the resistance levels. Again, for the accomplished trader, pyramiding or scaling is a great tool to increase profits.

3. Know Support and Resistance Levels

Usually within an hour after the open a stock has established its trading range. This will be the low (support) and high (resistance) that a stock trades within during that trading day. While breakouts (a stock making a new daily high or low) on news, market conditions, or insider or institutional activity do occur, they are not the norm.

Stocks usually establish support and resistance at whole numbers as a result of longer-term investor activity. An investor or position trader (who cannot or does not wish to play intraday stock movements) ordinarily will place a buy or sell order with her broker at a whole-dollar amount. Rarely does one call her broker and say "Buy ORCL at 31¾₆" or "Sell ORCL at 36¹¹⁄₁₆." Hence, once stocks hit a high or a low due to trading action, buy and sell orders are triggered, thus providing floors (support) and ceilings (resistance) for a stock. Seeing these trading ranges on a 1-minute chart is an extremely powerful tool for you, as it allows you to generate expectations.

When a stock is trading down to its support, a trader should be prepared to buy when the selling slows and he sees a reversal of the trend in the Level II window. When a stock has traded up to its resistance level, a trader should be prepared to sell (or short) when the buying slows and he sees a reversal of the trend in the Level II window.

MOMENTUM STRATEGIES—THE SONIC BOOM DIVE

Let's tie these concepts together by taking a look at another trade. The Sonic Boom Dive is truly one of my very favorite trading techniques. It's almost impossible to say how many thousands of times this pattern is repeated. A stock runs up wildly on "weak" news, euphoria reigns, and then suddenly, the boomer becomes a buster in one or two trading sessions. We'll take as an example the stock in Figure 10–15.

- 13:05 ET Tech Movers:NOPT+11 (receives favorable write-up in newsletter)...

Figure 10–15

Per my usual premarket preparation, I moved my previous day's boomers into my double-boomer minder window. I then pulled up a daily (200 day) and intraday (5 day) chart on NOPT.

I noted from the daily chart, shown in Figure 10–16, that Northeast Optical Network had very little movement (buying or selling interest) in the past few months. However, it had closed 12 points up the previous day (from $18 to $30, approximately 70 percent) on what can't even be considered news (a newsletter had put it on a buy list). My expectation was very high that this stock would make a good short at or near the open.

Next, I looked at the trading action from the previous day on an intraday chart. Almost the entire 12-point climb came during 20 minutes near the open. This is important. After the initial climb, the stock moved sideways the rest of the day—no follow-through. When a stock climbs this fast on such weak news, I expect it to drop down quickly, just as Figure 10–17 shows.

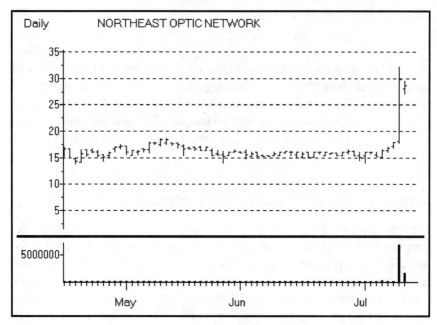

Figure 10–16 Northeast Optical 2 months prior to breakout.

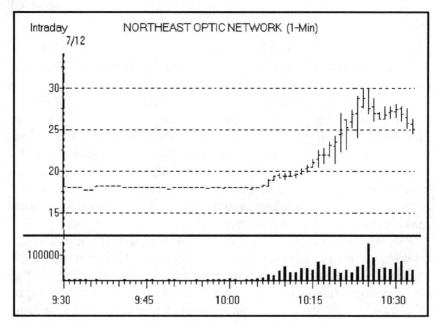

Figure 10–17 Fast breakouts often lead to quick reversals.

NOPT lost nearly 50 percent of its gain in 8 minutes. The old adage "What goes up must come down" plays out every day in the stock market. Usually the faster a stock climbs, the faster it falls. So if you missed the ride up, do not chase it higher. Rather, if you can borrow the stock for a short, catch the ride down.

As you can see from Figures 10–18 to 10–22, NOPT ran up quickly, retraced about 50 percent of its gain, and went absolutely nowhere the rest of the day.

While NOPT did not end the trading day at its high, it ended very near the high on good volume, which led me to believe that this stock would be in play the next day (see Figure 10–23). As it turned out, my expectations were right on the money (see Figure 10–24). A more detailed view demonstrating my expectations played out, as NOPT was shortable above $30 premarket and was between $28 and $29 at the market open (see Figure 10–25).

I took a quick look at NOPT's using my minder window (Figure 10–26). I then watched NOPT's activity in my Level II (market maker) window. I was ready to short this stock early. As no news was

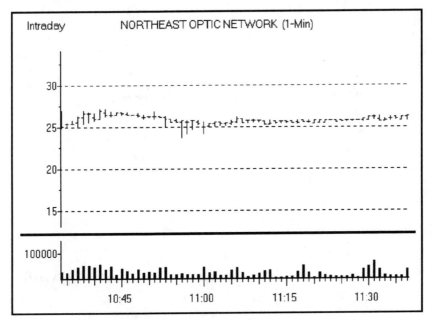

Figure 10–18 Northeast Optical—intraday pane 1.

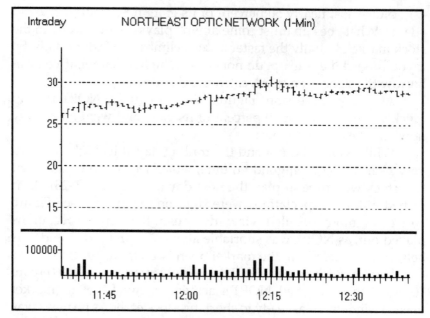

Figure 10–19 Northeast Optical—intraday pane 2.

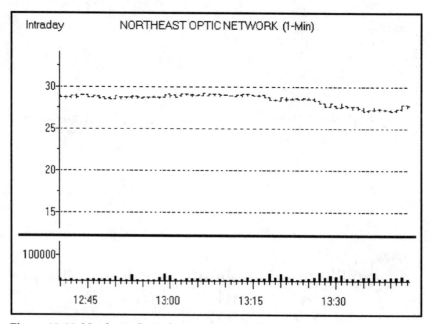

Figure 10–20 Northeast Optical—intraday pane 3.

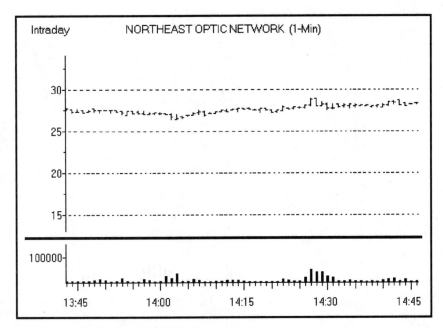

Figure 10–21 Northeast Optical—intraday pane 4.

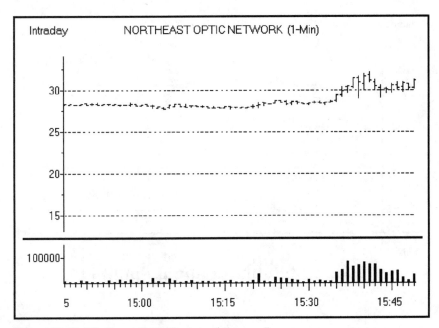

Figure 10–22 Northeast Optical—intraday pane 5.

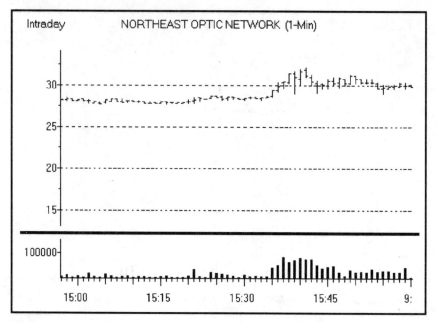

Figure 10–23 Northeast Optical closes near its daily high.

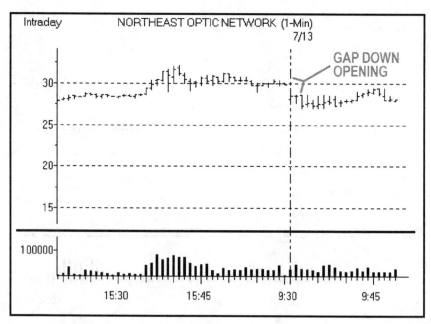

Figure 10–24 Northeast Optical gaps down the next morning.

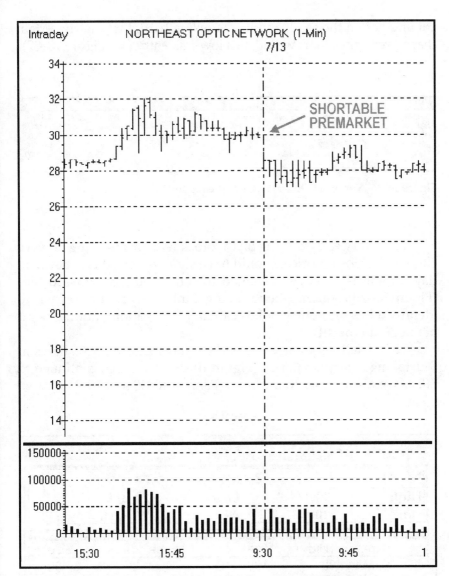

Figure 10–25 Northeast Optical was an excellent premarket short.

coming out on the stock and it was selling hard, I was fairly certain
that a premarket short would be a low-risk entry (see Figure 10–27).

Double Boomers									
Symbol	Hist Close	Open	Low	High	Last Price	Bid	Ask	Bid-Ask	Tot. Vol.
NOPT	17 15/16	18 1/8	17 3/4	32 1/8	29 7/8	30	29 1/4	-3/4	6986100
HERZ	6 5/16	6 7/8	7 7/32	10 13/16	8 1/32	7 15/16	8	1/16	3383400
ESPS	9 1/4	9 1/2	9 5/8	13 1/8	12 1/4	12 3/16	12 3/8	3/16	3222900
ELCO	5	5	4 7/8	5 5/16	5	5	5 1/16	1/16	364600

Figure 10–26 Northeast Optical (NOPT) premarket.

Note very early trading on the stock with prints going off very
close to the closing price. I could have shorted here, but patience in
day trading is an edge! I wanted to confirm the downward bias
(Figure 10–28). Again, when stalking a trade, my first priority is to
identify a low-risk entry point (capital preservation), not the point
of maximum profit!

NOPT fell very early premarket, and I shorted 300 shares at
$29, taking a very small risk (Figure 10–29). The stock continued to
fall as we drew closer to the open (Figures 10–30 and 10–31).

NORTHEAST OPTICS NETWORK

NOPT			30 1/4		+12 5/16		0
High		30 1/4		Low		27 3/4	
Bid ↓		30		Ask		28 3/16	

	Name	Bid	Size		Name	Ask	Size ▲
O	SHWD	30	100	O	ISLD	28 3/16	400
O	MASH	29 7/8	200	O	REDI	28 9/16	500
O	SLKC	29 1/2	100	O	INCA	28 5/8	1000
O	NITE	29 1/8	200	O	GSCO	29 1/4	1000
L	FBCO	28 5/8	100	O	ARCA	29 9/16	700 ▼

Figure 10–27 Northeast Optical market-maker screen—premarket.

NORTHEAST ...

‖—NORTHEAST		
Time	Price	Volume
8:16		
8:16		
8:17		
8:17		
8:21	30 1/4	900
8:21	30 1/4	900
8:22	30 1/4	900
8:26		
8:26		
8:28		
8:28		
8:30		
8:30		

Figure 10–28 Premarket—Northeast Optical is trading near prior day's close.

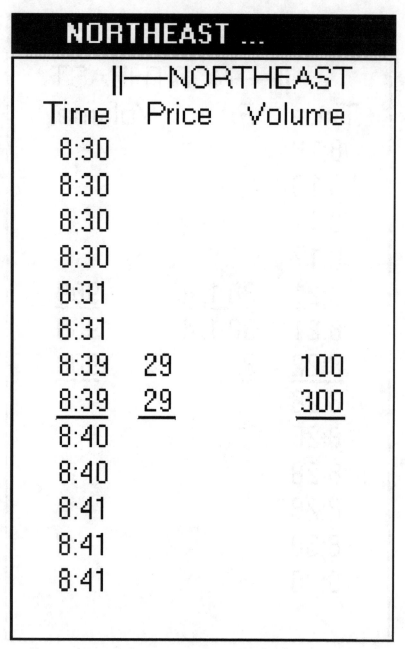

Time	Price	Volume
8:30		
8:30		
8:30		
8:30		
8:31		
8:31		
8:39	29	100
8:39	29	300
8:40		
8:40		
8:41		
8:41		
8:41		

Figure 10–29 Shorting a small lot premarket.

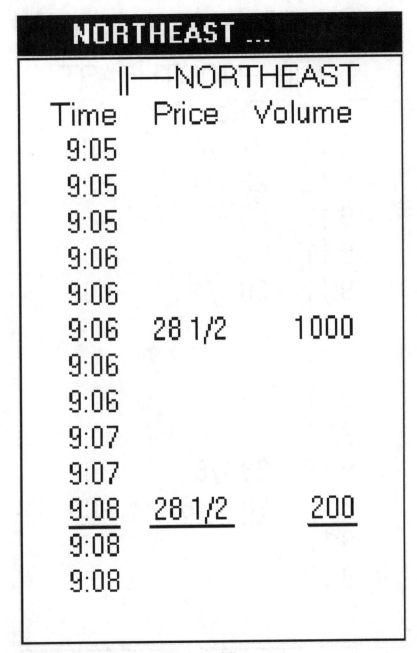

Figure 10–30 Northeast Optical begins to fall.

NORTHEAST ...

‖—NORTHEAST		
Time	Price	Volume
9:11	27 3/4	100
9:11	28 1/4	900
9:11		
9:11		
9:11	28 1/4	100
9:11		
9:11		
9:11		
9:11		
9:12	28 1/8	300
9:12	28 3/16	400
9:12		
9:12		

Figure 10–31 Northeast Optical continues to fall.

║—NORTHEAST		
Time	Price	Volume
9:24	28 3/4	600
9:25		
9:25		
9:25	28 13/16	400
9:25	28 13/16	600
9:25		
9:25		
9:26		
9:26		
9:26		
9:26		
9:26	28 1/2	} 300
9:26	28 13/16	} 100

Figure 10–32 Northeast Optical trades a bit higher.

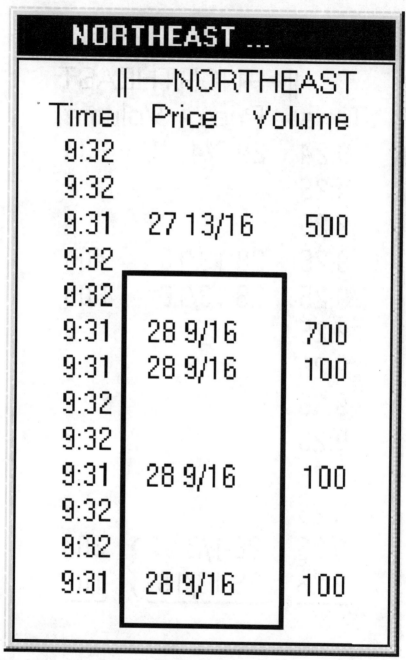

Figure 10–33 Northeast Optical's overall trend is lower.

NORTHEAST ...

||—NORTHEAST

Time	Price	Volume
9:34		
9:34		
9:32	27 11/16	300
9:32	27 11/16	200
9:32	27 11/16	300
9:32	27 11/16	100
9:32	28 9/16	200
9:32	27 1/4	1000
9:32	28 9/16	600
9:32	27 11/16	100
9:32	27 3/8	200
9:32	27 9/32	100
9:32	27 1/16	200

Figure 10–34 Covering Northeast Optical just after the open.

As we got even nearer to the open, NOPT started to climb, but the larger trend was down, so I felt comfortable staying with my short position (Figures 10–32 and 10–33). A couple of minutes into the open, with some prints going off well above the ask, I saw a near-term bottom and covered near 27⅜ for a 1⅝ gain (Figure 10–34). Figure 10–35 shows the playbook.

Goal	1 to 5	(1-R to 5-R win)
Stop loss	1	(1-R loss)

Factors to enter the trade:

Exchange	NASDAQ or NYSE
Stocks	Small caps that are out of favor and a boomer in one of the last 2 days
Stock price	$5 to $40, with a 50 percent or more opening gap on boomer day
Daily volume	10,000 to 200,000
Avg. daily range	1.5 or less prior to boomer day
# shares	1,000 minimum during trading day, 200–500 premarket
Order type	Limit only
News	None or no significant news on day of trade, weak news on boomer day
Technicals	Chart should indicate either a narrow channel or a downtrend prior to boomer day.
Volume	50 percent greater than average on boomer day, falling by 20 percent or more on day of trade
Time of day	This play is usually the best either just prior to the open or immediately after, during the first half hour of trading.

Figure 10–35 The Sonic Boom Dive (short momentum trade).

KNOWLEDGE KEYS

✓ Momentum strategies are best suited for the market open and for end-of-day trading when there is usually more volatility in the market.

✓ Momentum trades are typically driven by news or a mechanical setup based upon technical analysis.

✓ Momentum strategies target larger profits than market-making strategies—typically a 1.5- to 5-R multiple.

✓ Useful momentum beliefs are the foundation for successfully trading these strategies.

✓ On the NASDAQ, market makers will often display premarket quotes to test the strength or weakness of a stock. This is legal. It is also safe since they do not have to honor premarket quotes.

✓ Typical market-maker tactics include head-fakes, fading the trend, and short squeezes.

CALLS TO ACTION

✓ Develop your own set of momentum strategy beliefs. You can use the set of beliefs listed in this chapter as a starting point.

✓ Review your mission, self-assessment, and trading goals to determine if momentum strategies should be part of your overall trading plan.

✓ Learn to spot market makers' tactical maneuvers since they are more likely to be used when a stock is under momentum.

✓ Practice (*live*, not paper trade) execution of the momentum techniques in this chapter with very small positions, say 10 to 100 shares, until you become proficient. Only then should you increase your share size.

## PART FOUR

Feedback and Maintenance

Is Your Trading Rocket on Course?

Congratulations! You've come a very long way—especially if you've been doing the "Call to Action" items on your journey. Although this section is the last one, it is vitally important. As a driver, you know that to arrive at your final destination safely, you must make hundreds of very small course corrections along the way. It's called steering. Once in a while you have to make wholesale changes to your route (for instance, when there's a detour or a traffic jam). Making serious cash in the markets requires the same kinds of corrections.

Because all traders make errors, the very best have quick and simple methods of correcting them. Of course, too often the temptation is to ignore these issues by labeling them as unimportant details. It's just easier to keep on doing your same old routine. But we suspect that you really want to reach the pinnacle of your trading potential. To do that, let's take the last steps to the summit!

In this part, we'll review common errors that most EDAT traders make. Then we'll show you how to get feedback and make course corrections, and finally, in the last chapter, we'll discuss the components of peak performance trading—those components that separate the borderline trader from the outstanding trader.

## CHAPTER 11

Common Mistakes Everyone Makes—
And How You Can Avoid Them

The mistakes are all there, waiting to be made.

Chess Grandmaster Tartakower

Many of the mistakes that day traders make can be classified as errors of omission. There are the numerous tasks that they *should* do (the subject of the first two sections of this book!) to prepare themselves but that they avoid—either because of a lack of knowledge or because of wanting to choose a simpler, easier path. There are also numerous biases that traders have that lead them away from profits, just because their focus is misdirected. And lastly, there are numerous errors that traders make because they have not psychologically prepared themselves for winning.

A recent Securities and Exchange Commission study found that of the 68 day traders in the study, all 68 lost money during the period studied. Furthermore, 70 percent of them lost everything. The reason this occurs is because they made huge mistakes.

Fittingly enough, by describing in this chapter, many of the mistakes made by electronic day traders, we are summarizing many of the key points of this book. Thus, we can provide you with both a pathway toward success and, at the same time, the boundaries to keep you on that pathway and from falling into vicious traps that lead to financial ruin.

Let's look at Lenny M's trading.[1] Lenny had just gotten out of his old business with a bonus of $100,000. He was convinced that big money could be made through electronic day trading. He read three books on the subject, went to a conference where all the latest software was displayed, and even attended a workshop on how to pick stocks using Level II software. He was sure he knew the secret to making money in the market, but nevertheless, he was careful— or at least he thought so. He opened his account with his $100,000 fortune, and he just paper-traded for a few days until he'd assured himself that he could make a living through electronic day trading. Then his adventure began—he started trading.

His first trade was in EBAY. He'd been watching it for a couple of hours, and it was making new highs on lots of volume. It was now $179.50 bid and $180 asked. Lenny put an order in through ARCA to buy 1,000 at $179.50. The market kept moving without filling Lenny, and within 20 minutes EBAY was at $181.37. Lenny knew he'd let nearly $2,000 get away and was upset. He entered another order to buy it at the market, only to be filled at $182.13—a slight jump above the current asking price. The stock quickly moved to 182.50 and then started to plunge.

Lenny wanted to take his 37 cents per share of profit—after all, it amounted to $370—but he was also expecting the stock to move up a lot more. As a result, he stood his ground. When the stock dropped past his entry price, he decided to let it go down a couple of points to give it some room. It needed that room. Soon it was at $179.25. At that point, Lenny, feeling quite fearful, got out at a loss of almost $3,000. Lenny was so upset at himself that he couldn't trade the rest of the day.

That night he kept repeating to himself, even in his sleep, "Never take a market order—*never.*" The next day he was watching QCOM move to new higher ground. He purchased 1,000 shares at $125.38, slightly below the asked price, and felt proud of himself. The stock moved to $125.50 and then started to retreat. When it hit his entry point, Lenny again acted out of fear and sold his stock at $125.25 for a $130 loss.

Next, Lenny bought 200 LU at $72.37. It moved ahead slightly, and Lenny got out with a 1/16 profit. Lenny made five more trades but never covered his $130 loss from the morning. Then, at 3:30 Lenny decided to enter the market with 1,000 shares again. He was up on the trade $250 when he decided he needed to go the bathroom. There was a copy of a business newspaper in the bathroom, and Lenny started reading it and got involved in an article about people becoming millionaires through Internet stocks. When Lenny came back at 3:40, he stared at his screen in shock—his stock was down 2 full points. He couldn't believe it, and he just stared at the screen while the stock kept moving down. Now it was down 2.5 points. Lenny suddenly realized it was near closing and he wasn't sure whether to keep the stock or not. He decided that it would be too much to have nearly $5,000 in losses in 2 days, so he kept the position. That was a big mistake. In the after-hours trading the stock kept falling. Finally, Lenny couldn't take the pressure of the loss any more, and he just sold it at nearly a $5,000 loss.

Lenny now had lost 7 percent of his account in 2 days. He realized that he'd made the same mistake twice in a row—selling at the market—although he was totally unaware that he'd made over a dozen other mistakes as well. He'd expected to make several thousand dollars that week. Instead, he'd already lost $7,000. "I need to make $10,000 quickly," he thought.

From that point on, Lenny acted a little crazy. On the surface, he was cool as a cucumber. You couldn't tell he'd lost any money. But below the surface, something had snapped. He increased his positions from 1,000 shares or less to 3,000 shares or more. He listened to the financial news on television and acted on every news tip he heard.

For example, on Thursday of that same week he bought 2,000 of PCS at $51.25 on a news report that their losses would be less. The stock dropped 1.75 points that day and Lenny forgot he was a day trader. He bought 1,000 more at $50 and 500 more at the close at $49.5. He was down $4,000 at the end of the day and took home 3,500 shares of a declining stock. Lenny's thoughts—"When the earnings come out, I'll make a small fortune!"

The stock dropped another 1.5 points in the after-hours trading, and when Lenny woke up, he had $9,250 in paper losses and was facing a potential margin call. Lenny thought that's not so bad; at least my broker gave me 3 days to cover. He postponed action, knowing that a news release about PCS was coming out in the late morning. He actually had an order ready to go to buy another 1,000 shares. When the announcement came out, the losses were more than expected, not less. Lenny decided to start scaling out of his position, still hoping against all hope that the stock might stop on a dime and start moving in his direction. He looked at his order entry screen, saw 1,000 shares already entered, and hit the mouse button. But he forgot to change his order from buy to sell. That's right, Lenny bought another 1,000 shares.

When he realized his mistake, the market was plunging down. Lenny quickly sold 4,500 shares at the market, losing $2,625 through his mistake. That one day of trading had cost him $11,875.

Lenny continued his erratic behavior over the next month. His losses totaled $51,317 in 1 month—over half of his account. The only wise thing Lenny did was to quit trading after 1 month. He still had almost half of his account left.

The same events described for Lenny in the story above happen to many, many electronic day traders every day. As mentioned earlier, one study suggests that 70 percent of them will lose everything. The hope is that by learning to avoid the mistakes described in this chapter, you won't be among them.

Consequently, we'd like to devote the rest of this chapter to showing you how to avoid the kinds of mistakes that Lenny and most other electronic day traders make constantly. It is likely that much of this material will seem familiar to you. If that's the case, then congratulate yourself for having absorbed the important material in the earlier chapters of this book! These principles are so important that we're presenting them again to you here. In the sections that follow, we'll define the mistakes, illustrate how they happen, and then show you how to avoid them.

Mistake 1: Failure to define who you are and what your mission is as an electronic day trader.

One of the keys to the success of any business is a plan leading toward success. And the key to that plan is a mission statement that defines what the business is and what its objectives are going to be. What role are you playing, and what are the dynamics and risk profiles of that role? The answers to these key questions are the basis of your framework for decision making. Unless you understand these dynamics and can explicitly state them, you are sowing the seeds of failure before you start.

But wait a minute, you might say. "I know I'm Lenny M, and I want to make a lot of money doing electronic day trading. What more do I need to say?" The answer to that question is, "A lot!" You need to determine much more about yourself. What's your risk tolerance? What's your level of commitment? What's your stress tolerance, and how will you know when you've met it? What are you trying to accomplish? Are you trying to go from part-time day trader to a full-time professional? Have you stopped your regular job, did you set aside $100,000, and do you want to make at least $100,000 per year day trading so you don't have to work at a regular job? How much money do you need to make each week? What happens if you don't make that amount? You need to consider these questions and many others before you begin the task of day trading.

Most people don't, and that's a major mistake because they have not laid a foundation for decision making. Lenny, in our example, didn't even think in terms of a business plan for trading, or a mission statement, or a personal definition of who he was as a trader. Yet without such a foundation, you'll make numerous spur-of-the-moment decisions that will lead to financial disaster. And that's exactly what Lenny did.

Mistake 2: Failure to set objectives based upon your missions and your definition of who you want to be.

Once you've established who you are and what you are trying to accomplish as an electronic day trader, then you can set objectives to meet the parameters that you've defined for your role and the risk profile you've set for yourself. For example, if you have an idea for a new system, then you must ask yourself what kind of performance you'd expect from that system. Does that performance fit your mission statement?

While deciding on your trading strategies, you must decide if you're going to trade the most active stocks of the day. Usually, these are Internet stocks or stocks involved in laying the foundation for the Internet, telecommunications, or biotechnology. Most of these stocks are priced well over $100. They could move 3 points in a few seconds. You could take huge hits in these stocks and have very volatile performance. At the same time, if you understand the material in the position-sizing chapter, you'll find that you can make huge profits trading them.

Does that sort of trading fit into your mission? Does this type of volatile performance fit within your mission statement and your definition of who you want to be? Can you take the heat? What kind of drawdowns are you willing to tolerate? How many losses can you tolerate? If the answers to these questions fit within your personal definition and mission, then fine—you can do that type of trading. If they don't, or even if you're not sure, then you probably should avoid that type of trading at all costs.

Lenny M didn't even have a mission statement or personal definition. So it was impossible for him to evaluate anything with respect to how it fit within the framework of his mission statement. His decision making was random and emotionally generated.

Mistake 3: Failure to develop a specific set of rules to guide your trading based upon your mission and objectives.

Let's say you've defined your mission as a trader and defined who you want to be. You've also laid out objectives for your trading and decided on a particular system. You must now detail specific rules that you must follow in order to trade well and follow that system. These rules are to guide your decision making so that your decisions become automatic. You don't want to make decisions under high-stress conditions without predefining rules to guide you in those decisions. The rules will prevent you from making disastrous moves that have nothing to do with what you intended.

Lenny M had no rules to guide his trading. Had he had them, he could have avoided many of his mistakes.

Mistake 4: Failure to test and simulate a specific set of rules so that you know what to expect from the market in advance and so that you know the probabilities.

Your system should consist of (1) a set of setup conditions to screen your stocks against, (2) entry rules to apply to the stocks you select from your screen, (3) a worst-case stop-loss exit to define a 1-R loss, (4) your profit-taking rules, and (5) a set of rules to guide you in selecting the size of your position. Your system may also include re-entry rules. If you have such a system, then you can test it in three ways. First, you can simply trade it with small size until you've accumulated about 200 trades. Calculate the R multiple of each trade using the technique presented in Chapter 5. Also calculate the overall expectancy of your system by summing the R multiples and dividing by the number of trades. Second, you also can paper-trade through several virtual trading organizations. This way you will get actual fills and can determine the same information for free that you probably paid money for in test 1 (i.e., through trade losses). Third, you can use some software to test your system.[2] If you can use software to at least determine the distribution of R multiples for your system, then you'll be in good shape.

When you have the distribution of the R multiples that your system produces, then you have enough information to simulate your system. The easiest way is to simply put marbles in the bag that have the same distribution as your R multiples.[3] You then pick a position-sizing method (like trading 1 percent risk) and draw marbles out of the bag with replacement. Every 100 marbles you draw will give you a representation of what you might expect from the market. You'll know what to expect and whether or not you can live with it. More importantly, you'll begin to think of your system in terms of probabilities.

At this point, you now have a mission, an objective that is congruent with your mission, a system that meets your objectives, rules to guide your decision making, and a set of probabilities for your trading system that will help you control your emotions. Do you think Lenny had any of these valuable tools to help him in his trading? No, he had none of those tools. Can you now understand why traders like Lenny continually lose money?

Mistake 5: Failure to follow a set daily routine of tasks that are mission-important, but not urgent. These tasks include analyzing yourself, mentally rehearsing your day and how to deal with any problems that might arise, keeping a log of your trading, and doing a daily debriefing based upon that log.

In my home study course for traders and investors, you'll find a set of tasks that model what the highest-quality traders do regularly. Four of these tasks are absolutely critical for long-term survival in the markets. Yet most traders make the mistake of totally ignoring them, through either ignorance or laziness.

The first task is a daily self-analysis, usually done at the beginning of the day. You are the most critical aspect of your trading performance. Most people spend a lot of time analyzing the market, and no time analyzing themselves. Do you think Lenny, for example, spent time asking himself, "How am I feeling? Have I stifled any emotions, or are my emotions controlling my trading? Am I following my rules? What am I telling myself?" People who do this find that they gain tremendous control over their trading. People who ignore this task find themselves in the midst of irrational behavior that they can only shake their head about when they think back on it. Thus, it is critical for you to do a daily self-analysis so that you, and not your emotions or some irrational part of you, are in charge of your trading.

The next task you need to do on a daily basis is to mentally rehearse your day. Not doing this is a major mistake, because during a crisis you are unprepared. However, if you plan for the crisis ahead of time and then mentally rehearse how you'll respond, you can avoid all sorts of problems. This is one of the secrets of how most athletes achieve superperformance, and it should be one of your secrets as well—that is, if you want to be a top performer.

The third task of the day is to keep a log of your trading. Why did you make the trade? What was your abort point? What was going on inside of you when you made the trade? When you do this, you have a basis for analyzing your behavior and improving. When you don't keep such a log, you have no way of remembering what happened with various trades. They will soon all become a blur, and you'll have no way to profit from mistakes you might have made. And that's also a major mistake.

Lastly, you need to do a daily debriefing of your trading day. What happened during the day? Did you make any mistakes? (Here making a mistake means not following your rules.) And if you don't have any rules (see above), then you've made a mistake. Have you made any of the 25 mistakes listed in this section? During the daily debriefing, if you haven't made any mistakes, then pat yourself on the back. However, if you have made mistakes, then you need to determine what could happen that might cause you to repeat the mistake. Once you've done that, then mentally rehearse more appropriate behaviors so you don't repeat the mistake.

Now that you know about these four important tasks, think about Lenny. Do you think Lenny did any of them? There were some signs that he might have thought about mistakes he made, but he was not aware of most of his mistakes because he didn't do a self-analysis, go through a morning mental rehearsal, or keep a daily log. Lenny might have had some chance for long-term survival if he had at least done these four tasks.

Mistake 6: Entering a trade without immediately knowing when you will get out to preserve your capital. And a related mistake is letting losses get away from you even when you've set such a bailout point.

NASDAQ Level II trading has only recently allowed you to place a stop in the market using EDAT software. However, whether you use the software's capability to place stops or not, we expect day traders to be sufficiently aware of what is going on in the market and to be able to set mental stops. Once again, your stop-loss point is that point at which you commit to exit from your position, *no matter what,* in order to preserve your capital. I cannot stress how important this rule is and how big a mistake it is to break it. This was one of Lenny's biggest mistakes.

In addition, you must make sure that you execute your stop. If you must go away from a trade, as Lenny did once in one of his first trades, then have a stop with your broker or exit the position before you leave. You never know when some disaster might strike while you are gone. You could easily have a large chunk of your equity disappear just by taking a break while you have open positions that are not protected.

Mistake 7: A major mistake for most day trading systems, although this does not apply to the market-maker systems described in this book, is taking profits too soon.

Half of the golden rule of trading is to let your profits run. As we've said many times before, you want your winners to be large R multiples of your losers. And the only way you can do that is to hold onto winning trades so they get bigger. Electronic day traders can easily get R multiples of 5 or more.

As an electronic day trader, you'll need some rules to guide you in how to exit trades. Those rules should generally allow you to increase profits when a stock is moving in your favor. They should only help you exit when the stock stops moving or starts to erode some of your profits.

A common saying is that amateurs go broke because they cannot take a loss—they hang onto losses. However, most professionals go broke because they take profits too soon.

Lenny didn't make this mistake, but many professional traders do. Work on letting your profits run.

Mistake 8: Failure to monitor your trading and allowing distractions to enter your life so that you miss critical points in the market. In other words, not being focused on trading when you are tired or exhausted.

Many years ago, before electronic day trading even existed, I had a client who was day-trading the S&P 500. He kept mental stops, the same way you have to with electronic day trading. He was in and out of the market quickly. Generally, he made money every day.

One day while trading with a big position on, he got an emergency phone call. His girlfriend had been in a car accident. She was seriously injured and was at the emergency room of the hospital. He got up quickly, grabbed his coat, and left for the hospital. Guess what happened to his positions in the market? Yes, he totally forgot about them. In one day, he lost much of what he'd made that year.

These types of things will happen—perhaps they are inevitable. That's why worst-case contingency plans and mental rehearsal of those plans are so important. When you do that, closing out positions in situations like this becomes automatic. If you are a good trader, you want to do everything possible to avoid a 1-day loss that can wipe out a year's worth of profits.

Another good trader I heard about came in to work tired one day. Perhaps he'd partied too much the night before, or perhaps he was just exhausted from the grind of trading day in and day out. Anyway, he got into a trade in which he'd normally be out on a ¼-point loss. But in this case, the stock just kept falling. He didn't get out. Instead, he just stared at the screen with a blank look. The stock moved a full 2 points against him. At that point, he appeared to shake himself out of his daze and exited the position. He also then turned off his computer, went home, and took off the next 3 days.

This kind of mistake is typical of what happens with burnout or with lack of sleep. It can be avoided simply by doing a daily self-analysis, as suggested earlier in this chapter.

Mistake 9: Paying attention to what everyone else is doing and following the crowd.

When you don't have a plan and a set of rules to guide you, there is much uncertainty and anxiety in the day. You are overwhelmed with information. There are thousands of stocks to pick from—how do you know what to do? What most people do in this case is ask others for information—especially those who seem to be in the know. And there are plenty of sources for this information. You can log onto chat rooms where people are bragging about what they did or are more than happy to tell you what you should do. You can find plenty of information here. You can also watch the financial information on television. Here news reporters are perfectly willing to feed you all the information you want about stocks the "experts" are picking. However, you already know how little stock picking has to do with success in trading.

The results of believing these sources of information are usually disastrous. First, the crowd is usually wrong in these situations. In fact, you could probably develop a good trading system in which your screening technique is going against what you learn from these sources.

Second, even if the information is correct, people who follow these sources usually don't have a plan. They don't enter with an exit point in mind, and so it is very possible for them to turn a perfectly good trade into a loser.

Third, people who make such trades are usually acting on emotion. As you have seen, emotional trading can be, and usually is, disastrous.

When Lenny M, in the example given at the beginning of this chapter, went into his final tailspin, he was paying attention to rumors and what the crowd was doing. The results, of course, were huge losses in a very short period of time.

Mistake 10: Getting caught up in the excitement of trading, chasing trades, and forgetting your trading rules.

When I first started studying traders, I saw a lot of potential for addiction to the excitement of trading. In the early years at the Chicago Board of Trade, when the trading floor closed, floor brokers and locals used to get on a bus that stopped outside the building to take them to the racetrack. The excitement was so addicting that when it was over on the floor, these traders had to go where there was more of the same. My understanding is that they now go even further to get their excitement—to floating casinos.

Shortly after I got my Ph.D. in psychology, I spent a year working with compulsive gambler sociopaths. My experience suggested that the excitement of trading offered everything to the compulsive gambler that the casinos did. As a result, I went to some meetings of Gamblers Anonymous. At one of those meetings, I met George, who agreed to do an interview with me about gambling and the markets. That interview was published in my book *How to Develop Discipline for Traders and Investors*.[4] Here's an excerpt from that interview:

> From there, I would go to the brokerage house, the bookie joint, I would call it. [I would] sit there, totally consumed. It was the same feeling I would have when I walked into the MGM Grand or Caesar's Palace. I walked in there and the world shut down.
>
> Margin calls would come at the end of the day. After the end of the day, I would have to run around to make sure I do something, sign my wife's signature on my joint account. Somewhere, get enough money so my margins are taken care of, so I can be in action tomorrow.
>
> At the beginning, I remember, when I had to go and sign my wife's check, you know, forge my wife's signature in the joint account we had opened for the kids that required two signatures to take the money out. And I went through a lot of debate. It was very hard for me to do that. I didn't want to do it—it was my kids' money. My conscience was bothering me. Then I said, "Immediately, as soon as I make this money—I just can't take the loss and get the margin call—as soon as I make money, I'll put it back." And I went through subconscious rationalizations.
>
> There were winning days. When I had winning days, I would never touch the money. I was going to make the big score. The stock market afforded me a casino right in my backyard. I didn't have to fly to it. I mean it was a legitimate casino. My wife used to complain about it. I would say, "Honey, what are you talking about, all the people who are anybody are in the stock market and they invest. It's an investment.

I met another man in 1984 who was over $2 million in debt to the IRS from gambling in the stock market. He'd gotten money from whatever source he could, just to feed his craving for action. Unfortunately, the IRS taxes any "income" you get. It doesn't recognize stock market losses beyond $3,000 per year (unless you take the precautions outlined earlier that involve trading through a corporate entity or using trader status with a marked-to-market election), although it recognizes all stock market gains. This man hadn't filed a tax return for 4 years. He was afraid to because he owed so much money that he just didn't have. However, at the meeting I attended, he was about to promise to go to the IRS to ask for a payment plan. He knew he'd have to live on a minimum standard of income for many years to pay off his debt to them.

In today's electronic society, this kind of gambling is much easier. In the above story, the gambler's broker actually tried to slow him down and get him into managed accounts despite the fact that he was making huge commissions. Today, commissions have shrunk dramatically and your computer and a phone line have replaced brokers. At many discount firms, it's sometimes impossible to talk with a human being without having to wait on the phone for what seems like an eternity. Yet you can be in and out of trades in seconds and make hundreds of trades each day. It's an absolute "heaven" for the person who thrives on the action and excitement. And there are no obstacles in place for the compulsive gambler.

The key you must understand is that excitement has nothing to do with making money in the market. Good trading can be very boring. While trading on excitement may cost the compulsive gambler millions of dollars, many traders have a little bit of an urge for excitement. And once again, when you trade for excitement, that's what you get—excitement. It has nothing to do with making money.

This is one reason why a daily self-analysis and a trading log are so important. You must determine why you made the trade. If you get caught up in the excitement of the market, then you need to find an alternative source for your excitement needs. Good trading requires a plan, rules, and the discipline to follow them.

Mistake 11: Not knowing or understanding that position sizing is the key to making profits. In other words, trading too big or too small.

We've already talked about the importance of position sizing in Chapter 6. It is the key factor in meeting your objectives—it's not being right or picking the right stocks. It's not expectancy, although expectancy is critical. It's position sizing. That's the key to how much money you'll win or lose, and that's where most of your attention should be given. In fact, almost every mistake we've discussed in this chapter involved either hanging onto losses or a having a position that was way to big for the account size. Remember when Lenny had 4,500 shares of one stock? That is a major position-sizing error, and he lost 10 percent of his original account in that one trade.

Let's look at an extreme example. Let's say that a genie gives you a system in which you get 10-R winning trades 99 percent of the time. That system could make you a billionaire in a year. Since you are right 99 percent of the time and only have a 1 percent chance of losing, you risk everything on your first trade. Unfortunately, the 1 percent chance of a loss happens immediately, and you lose all your money. You are now broke and cannot capitalize on that magic system. Position sizing is the most important factor in your bottom line, and the biggest mistake most traders make—the most costly—is trading too big.

The secret to making money is to realize that the worst that might happen could happen today. When your position sizing is appropriate for that, then you'll survive and prosper in the long term.

Mistake 12: Allowing your life to get out of balance to such an extreme that you sabotage your trading.

Let's look at Alex and his trading. Alex was a very committed trader. He did everything that we've talked about so far in this book. He spent a lot of time soul-searching and made a decision that he was committed to be a professional trader and to make slow, steady money through electronic day trading. He developed a mission statement and some conservative objectives. He developed a great trading system and found a position-sizing algorithm that met those objectives. He also tested the system to determine its probabilities. He simulated it to know he could live through the worst possible scenarios. He also performed all those daily tasks—self-analysis, mental rehearsal, keeping a log of his trading, and doing a daily debriefing. In short, he seemed like the model trader, except in one area.

The one area in which Alex was falling short was the rest of his life. He was spending 18 hours a day on trading. You might be able to do that for a while when you first get started. That might be part of your commitment to trading well. However, there are parts of you that will only stand to be neglected for so long.

Alex had a wife and three children. He hadn't spent any time with them for almost 2 years. They agreed that his commitment was important to begin with, and they gave him time to get his trading business going. But 3 months of 18-hour days turned into 6 months, and then a year, and then 2 years. Suddenly, his wife was gone with the children. Alex was facing lawyers and a divorce. Now Alex was spending 18 hours a day in emotional turmoil and grief, and in dealing with lawyers and trying to protect his trading account from an angry spouse. His trading performance fell apart.

You must set limits on your trading to avoid this kind of experience. If you neglect parts of yourself—the parts committed to family or to relationships or to even having fun—then eventually those parts will undermine your trading. Consequently, once your trading is set up and run like a business, make sure you keep your life balanced. Don't neglect the rest of yourself. When you do, it's a major mistake. And eventually, it will come back and sabotage everything you've built for yourself as a trader.

Mistake 13: Trading during major life-changing events.

There are certain life changes that are so dramatic that when they occur, you must suspend trading and devote effort to settling those changes. If you don't, in my experience, your trading will fall apart. In the example above with Alex, his trading fell apart when he went through a divorce.

Divorce isn't the only major change that can affect your trading. Moving is usually a major change. When you move your office or your home, you need to suspend trading until you are settled. If you don't, your trading will usually suffer.

Another example is a new addition to the family. When a baby comes along, for instance, life is disrupted. Sleep becomes a short commodity. Lifestyles are totally changed, and these changes may totally disrupt trading. We've had men in various stages of our trader programs add a child into their lives. All of them disappeared from trading for almost a year.

A lawsuit is another distracter. This often creates havoc with a person's time and focus during a divorce. However, a lawsuit having to do with anything can result in lost time and lost concentration.

Another major change that can disrupt your life is a significant illness. Obviously, becoming ill yourself will disrupt your trading.

But the same thing will happen when a close family member becomes ill.

In all these cases, the change becomes a major distraction from trading. You lose focus. Your mind wanders during the day. You neglect important tasks because of the distraction.

The most critical mistake you can make during these times is to attempt to trade while you are distracted. It usually results in significant losses.

The next most important mistake you can make is not to plan for such contingencies before they occur. Determine everything that might be a significant distraction in your trading. When you've done that, develop a plan for how to work through it with the least disruption possible, or better yet, how to avoid it. Mentally rehearse that plan many times, and you'll minimize the possible errors you could make.

Mistake 14: Becoming too confident and thinking you can control the market in some way.

Have you noticed that when you talk to other traders, they typically tell you about how much money they are making in the market? Several months ago, after completing one of our seminars, we took some clients to dinner at a nice restaurant in town. We mentioned to the waiter that we'd just finished doing a workshop, and he wanted to know what sort of workshop. When he learned that it had to do with trading, he promptly informed us that he was a superb trader. He'd made over 170 percent in the markets in the first 9 months of 1999. He spent the next half hour telling us how great his trading was, what his philosophy of trading was, and how much more he was going to make in the markets.

There is a fine line between believing in yourself and being overconfident. A great trader knows the probabilities of her system. She knows what she'll make on the average each month simply based on the probabilities. She knows what to expect in different sorts of markets. She knows what her worst-case situation might be, and she generally plays the probabilities.

The person who is unsure of himself, in contrast, will really bask in the glory of success. He'll extend his rates of returns way into the future and talk about where he'll be someday. This sort of talking gives him courage. Suddenly, he takes unnecessary trades, and his position size increases dramatically. When this happens, a major loss is usually just around the corner.

The cure for this mistake is to make sure that you understand the probabilities of your system and have thoroughly simulated it. Know the potential downside of your system and take trades that allow you to survive the worst possible situation in the short run so you can obtain your expectancy over the long run.[5]

Mistake 15: Allowing your emotions to get in the way of trading well and in the way of following your rules.

Your emotions can affect your trading immensely. Here are some examples:

- Jeff became fearful about taking trades. The fear grew and grew until he was no longer able to trade.
- Ellen became angry whenever she opened a position and it immediately went against her as if the market had her number. Often she became so angry that it distracted her from rational behavior. She'd miss good opportunities and also distract others from trading well.
- Peter became overwhelmed whenever he got too much information about a stock or a number of stocks. When he went into this overwhelmed state, it was as if his head were spinning. He couldn't think. He couldn't process what was going on, and he went into a state of paralysis. This was fine if he was no longer in the market—it kept him out of trouble. But when it happened while he was in the market, he didn't act on what was happening with his current trades, and this usually resulted in large losses.

If you are emotional about something that happened in your trading, you'll probably find that that kind of response is a pattern in your life. Whether the emotion is fear or anger or greed or whatever, you probably behave that way consistently. The fact that your reactions are more than one-time occurrences suggests that you have something to do with those emotions.

Most people believe that events happen and cause them to be emotional. This implies that the events are controlling your behavior. They are not—you are causing your own behavior. In fact, there are many ways to change your emotional state instantly. If you can change your emotions, then you are definitely in control of how you behave—you make things happen.

If your emotions get in the way of your trading, you can learn your patterns by keeping a trading diary, as suggested earlier in this chapter. When you discover your patterns, you can then use the wizard technique suggested in Chapter 13 to change your mental state. When you start to do this regularly, you will have done a lot to control your mental state. (In addition, the *Peak Performance Course for Investors and Traders* has an entire volume devoted to discipline and controlling one's mental state.)

Mistake 16: Staying with a stagnant trade or trading when the market is doing nothing and doesn't offer you an opportunity.

One of the big advantages you have as a trader is that you don't have to trade. You can select when you trade and only take good opportunities. This is a huge advantage if you use it. As an electronic day trader, you are able to seize opportunities that only exist for a second or so. They might be imbalances in the market. They might be a momentary overevaluation or underevaluation of a stock's price or a huge bid-ask spread. However, these are not advantages at all if you don't take them and you trade just to trade.

Some people think that they have to continually trade just to be in the market and be active—and this includes people who are not necessarily in it for the excitement. They just think they have to trade. They are so eager for opportunities that they use any excuse to trade.

Typically, if the market is doing nothing at all, then you don't need to trade. If you are in a trade and it's doing nothing, then you are tying up valuable resources and energy in a lost opportunity. Get out of the trade. It's probably not doing what you expected it to do, so get out now.

Mistake 17: Not knowing the ECN you are trading with or the software you are using.

Different ECNs, as described in the early chapters, have different characteristics. Having numerous choices means that you can select any one of them. However, if the ECN you select doesn't fit the type of trading you want to do, you could be making a big mistake. You might not get filled at your price and the stock might get away from you, which might happen if you use ARCA or SelectNet to trade a fast-moving stock. Similarly, if you use SOES to trade odd lots, you'll be giving up the bid-ask edge. And if you are a beginner and you trade on ISLD, you might get eaten by the sharks. Know the characteristics of each exchange before you trade on it. Study the material in this book and the brochures that explain the various ECNs. Prepare yourself first.

Mistake 18: Carrying a stock overnight, or worse yet, carrying a stock overnight and getting a margin call.

When you decide to become an electronic day trader, you are committing to a certain style of trading that involves taking a "house-type" edge and moving rapidly. Most of your trades should last a few seconds to, at most, a few hours. If this is your style of trading, and that's the style of trading this book is about, then you should not take positions home overnight. If and when you do, it probably will be one of your worst mistakes as an electronic day trader.

Lenny, in our initial example, took home 3,500 shares of a stock because he expected an earnings report that would positively influence the stock. It was one of his worst mistakes.

When you carry a stock overnight, you are subject to events that occur during off hours that might affect your stock or the market as a whole. What would you do if some disaster happened and the market opened down 300 points on the NASDAQ and 100 points on the S&P? You could lose much of your equity by this one mistake. Similarly, what would you do if some disaster happened to your stock? For example, what if the president of the corporation died in his sleep and the stock opened down 40 points? You are trading for small losses, but a 40-point move against you could amount to an 80-R loss. It doesn't take too many of those to ruin the expectancy of your system.

Lastly, when you trade the same stock several times during the day and then take it home with you, you could be subject to a margin call. All your trades may be winners, but the exchange (or your broker) will still want some money from you in the morning. And if you don't pay up, you might have your account suspended.

Again, be prepared. Read and understand the rules for using margin (all EDAT accounts are margin accounts) before you trade.

Mistake 19: Trading after hours—especially as a beginner. A related mistake for a beginner would be to trade the first 15 minutes or the period from 12:30 to 3 p.m.

There are certain time periods during the day when it is very dangerous—especially for a beginner—to trade. One such time period is the opening of the market, the first 15 minutes. During this period, the professionals are testing the market on most issues. Is it a buyer's market or a seller's market? What happens if the price goes up or down? Until you understand the ins and outs of early trading, we strongly suggest that you avoid this period.

Another key time period for the beginner *not* to trade is the period from 12:30 to 3 p.m. Here the market is typically much slower. As a result, market makers can move stock by large amounts in a short period of time. And once again, if you do not know what you are doing, you could get hurt badly.

Finally, there are after-hours markets when you can trade if you want to and have to. Here the market is very illiquid. You can trade during this time period, but it will cost you dearly. People have been known to pay 10-point premiums (or more) just to be able to trade these hours. There should be no need to do so.

Mistake 20: Exposing yourself to too much information and becoming overwhelmed.

The average human being has a capacity to process about seven chunks of information at one time, where a chunk is however much one can process as a single unit. For example, you might be able to process seven stocks at a time, or three stocks and their prices. This really is a big problem for most traders because there are thousands of stocks you can trade, with a massive amount of information available on each. There are news services for investors, information services, television coverage of the markets, and chat rooms to get other people's opinions. If you succumb to this information overload, trying to absorb it all, you'll soon become overwhelmed. And when you become overwhelmed, you probably won't be able to trade, or at least trade well.

One of our objectives in writing this book is to help you filter through information, finding out what is useful. You need to follow some of the suggestions in this book to develop a plan and objectives that fit you. You also need to focus on information that fits your plan. When you do that, you'll be able to cope with the huge amount of information currently available to traders.

Most people who come to the markets with no set plan, like Lenny, have a real problem with information overload. They don't know what to look at, so they look at everything. They especially gravitate to the opinions of others, because that feels emotionally comforting. However, such opinions are usually quite dangerous.

Mistake 21: Trading on gossip or rumors you hear in the chat rooms or on the financial stations.

As mentioned in mistake 9, traders with no plan tend to get "expert" advice from chat rooms or television programs. However, this information seldom is valuable—it's just emotionally satisfying. Typically, people in chat rooms will talk about a stock, bragging about their skills in picking it, right when it's at a high. Or news will come out about a stock, and it will get the attention of CNBC. When the information comes out, there might be a temporary run-up, but then the stock will tumble. Thus, the traders who gravitate toward this information to figure out what to do will typically have a major problem when the stock changes direction.

Again, the most important thing you can do is develop a plan, objectives that fit within the framework of the plan, and then a system that fits the plan's objectives. Once you have a system, you'll have rules to guide your behavior, and you won't be looking to others for advice on what to do. You'll have specific stock screening criteria that fit your style of trading, and when you enter a position, you'll know how to manage it through intelligent exits. These aspects of trading are critical to achieving success and to focusing on the important aspect of trading.

Mistake 22: Averaging down a loss.

This mistake is a continuation of mistake 6—knowing when you must get out of a stock to preserve your capital. If this type of rule is not in place, then most people continue the mistake by averaging down. The logic behind averaging down is, "If the stock was a good deal at $100, then at $98 it's a super deal and I should buy more." And when the price drops to $95, the logic becomes, "Now when the stock goes back to my original entry price, I'll be way ahead." Now let's look at the reality.

The reality behind averaging down is that you have no exit to preserve your capital. Instead, you've become enamored with some particular stock and have no means to preserve your capital if you are wrong. And you only have to be wrong once in averaging down a stock to suffer a huge R-multiple loss. The effect of a 30-R loss to an account can be devastating.

We've seen long-term traders lose everything by averaging down in a stock they like. When a short-term trader does it—especially an electronic day trader—it just means that it takes a lot less time to lose everything.

A friend who runs an electronic day trading firm recounted the following story:

> We had one guy who had done very well trading IPOs. He was up $120,000 in 3 months. One day he was trading, and he shorted Net-Bank. His first 1,000 shares went against him, and so he shorted more. He shorted still more just ahead of the CEO talking on CNBC. Within a 2-hour time frame, he was 35 points out of the money on 3,000 shares. The saddest part was when he was going to cover his shorts; he was trying to pick his exit points down to the ⅛ instead of just getting out. This exit strategy probably cost him another $5,000. For a few weeks after that, he was like a walking ghost. Losing $115,000 in a 2-hour period really can take its toll on a guy.

Mistake 23: Mixing two styles of trading in the same account, especially before you are competent in either of them.

Let's say you are a scalper, practicing the market-maker style of trading we recommend in Chapter 9. You make 15 trades each day and are right about 9 of them on the average. You make ¹⁄₁₆ when you are right and lose ¹⁄₁₆ when you are wrong, although you occasionally have a 2-R winner or 2-R loser.

Now let's say you are trading XYZ stock in this manner. Suddenly a story comes out, and you decide you really like XYZ. You buy some in your account as a core holding that you don't plan to sell—you decide that it's your retirement nest egg. You now have a preference for XYZ. When you switch styles and buy XYZ as a market maker, it becomes hard to sell it for a $\frac{1}{16}$ profit. So you switch over to a momentum trading style.

What you've done when you mix styles like this is break down the discipline of the rules you've worked so hard to develop. It's now easy to change your mind and ignore rules. And when you start to play this dangerous game, you'll find your discipline totally breaks down and you've entered the road to disaster.

Pick one style of trading and master it. Prove to yourself that you can make money consistently using the style that you've picked. When you've mastered it, then (and only then) can you add another style of trading for diversification.

If you elect to add another style of trading, trade the second style in a separate account. Have separate written rules for each account, and be sure you can follow both and be disciplined about it. If you find yourself breaking the rules, even when you have different accounts, then go back to one style of trading.

Mistake 24: Keyboard mistakes of various types.

When I was last in London, pit trading in the futures market was being replaced by electronic day trading. Most pit traders couldn't make it away from the floor, but a few were flourishing. However, many rumors were floating around about how dangerous electronic trading could be. The nastiest rumor was one that said a trader decided to sell 100 contracts of some futures. He entered the order and pressed the "Sell" button. However, the button stuck and, to his horror, sell order after sell order appeared on his screen and was executed.

While I have no idea whether this story was true or not, it does illustrate one of the potential mistakes that you can make with electronic day trading—major keyboard errors. It's easy to hit the wrong key, sending the wrong order out to the markets. In this day of very rapid markets, that order could be filled many times over before you could correct it.

For example, you might want to close out an order, but hit "Buy" instead of "Sell," thus doubling the size of your position. This type of error, and its converse, happens all the time.

Another error that electronic day traders make is an error in a stock symbol. As a result, they end up sending in an order for a stock they don't want. While this type of error is unlikely, it could happen.

Most electronic day traders make several keyboard errors each year. The hope is that they are minor and can be corrected quickly. However, you need to be aware that they do occur. They tend to disappear as you gain more experience with the markets, but they also tend to reappear when you are tired, emotional, or overwhelmed or when your life is out of balance. Thus, it becomes very important to monitor your condition and health.

Mistake 25: Not planning for what could go wrong.

The last critical mistake that traders make is the failure to take a step that could correct many of the first 24 mistakes—planning for them in advance. When you don't know about such errors and you don't plan for them, you'll probably act foolishly when they happen and just compound them. Instead, plan for such errors, because many of them will be a regular part of trading.

As part of your business or trading plan, include a section called "Worst-Case Contingency Planning." Let your brain run wild about what could go wrong, what could happen to disrupt your trading. Whenever you come up with something, and we've suggested many ideas in this chapter, write it down.

When you can no longer think of things that might go wrong, take your list and look at each item. Now imagine that thing happening. If it did happen, how could you react to minimize its consequences? Write down how you might respond to each situation to minimize the damage. Also consider what conditions might set up such problems and what you might do to prevent them from ever occurring. Write down everything you can think of.

Now look at your list of action items. What are the three best things you could do to minimize each event or its effects. Circle those items and then mentally rehearse doing them. If you mentally rehearse them now, they will become automatic to you when you need them in the heat of battle.

By simply avoiding the last mistake and doing what we've suggested, you can minimize the effects of most errors. And the more errors and mistakes you can eliminate or minimize, the more your account will grow.

KNOWLEDGE KEYS

✓ A trading mistake is defined as not following your rules.

✓ The first key to avoiding mistakes is understanding the most common ones that are made.

✓ The most significant mistake you can make is trading without a mission, objectives, and a trading plan in place.

✓ A trading log or journal will help you to identify mistakes you've made and make plans for how to avoid them in the future.

✓ Visualization or mental rehearsal is another key part of your daily routine that will help you to plan in advance to avoid and/or minimize trading mistakes and their impact on your trading equity.

✓ Adding a section on disaster contingency planning to your business and/or trading plan can save you thousands of dollars in trading losses.

CALLS TO ACTION

✓ Do not trade again until you have a written mission, written trading objectives, a written business plan, and a written trading plan.

✓ Make sure either your business plan or your trading plan has a section on disaster contingency planning.

✓ Establish and follow a written daily trading routine that includes doing a self-analysis ("Am I fit to trade today spiritually, mentally, emotionally, and physically?"), going through mental rehearsals, maintaining a trading log, and performing a daily debrief.

✓ If you are already an active trader, review the list of 25 common mistakes from this chapter and pick the top 3 that you need to work on most. Design a plan to minimize their impact on your trading.

NOTES

1. Lenny M is a fictional name, but his experience is based upon many real-life stories that I gathered interviewing various electronic day traders.

2. I know of no software that will do an adequate job of testing everything in your system. For some of the issues involved, see *Trade Your Way to Financial Freedom* by Van K. Tharp.

3. We also have a game that will allow you to plug in your actual R-multiple distribution and simulate your trading.

4. Dr. Tharp's *Peak Performance Course for Investors and Traders*. Available from IITM at 1-800-385-IITM or 919-852-3994.

5. Part of Van K. Tharp's *Peak Performance Course for Investors and Traders*.

6. This statement, by the way, is my definition for a low-risk idea.

## CHAPTER 12

Getting Feedback and Refining the Process

The unexamined life is not worth living.
Socrates

At the end of the trading day, your first impulse is probably to shut down all your equipment and get far away from trading. Trading is a strenuous activity, much like taking an exam. If you can remember the feeling of a very strenuous all-day test, like taking the SAT college entrance exams, the trading process is the same—it drains you. It drains you because you are using large amounts of your brain processing capacity while you trade.

But even though you may feel drained at the end of the day, you need to discipline yourself either to continue on with a daily debriefing process or to do it later on at a set time that evening. The daily debriefing is a critical part of your trading success. This process will have a critical impact on your bottom line—a positive one if you do it and a negative one if you skip it.

There are several steps to this debriefing process: (1) reviewing your trades, (2) determining whether or not you made mistakes during the day, (3) learning from your mistakes when you do make them, (4) doing periodic reviews, and (5) refining the process of trading.

REVIEW YOUR TRADES: LIVE AND LEARN

When you use today's direct-access trading software, you will have a record of every trade you make during the day. We strongly suggest that you take that raw information and put it into a database of some sort that will make it useful for you in the future, so that you can understand your trading patterns. The simplest suggestion would be to use an Excel spreadsheet, similar to the spreadsheet described in Chapter 5. That spreadsheet is divided into nine columns, with each row being an individual trade.

The most critical elements to include in your spreadsheet (as column headings) are the following:

1. Date and time
2. Symbol for what you traded
3. Your entry price
4. Your initial risk (i.e., your stop price)
5. How many shares you traded
6. Your total risk exposure in that trade (which we call R)[1]
7. Your total gain or loss, after commissions
8. Your R multiple

Your Level II software will write the price for the entry and exit and the number of shares traded to your hard drive, but you will have to copy this information to your spreadsheet and fill in the blank columns. In addition, we also suggest that you make notes at the end on why you entered and exited that particular trade (if you can remember) and any emotional reactions you had to the trade. Since important psychological information is both subjective and qualitative, the sooner you do your spreadsheet after you finish trading, the more likely you are to remember what happened.

Environmental Influences

When you're doing your journal, capture as much information as possible. Did environmental influences have any impact? Note the lighting, outside distractions such as children or spouses talking to you, other distractions such as the telephone ringing—anything having to do with the environment external to yourself. What will happen over time if you pay attention to these things is that you'll learn to set your environment up in a way to reduce or eliminate their impact on your trading. Earlier in the book we talked about the temperature of a room during trading. The reason we know about how hot a room can get is because Brian June kept a trading journal that talks about it. Minimize your negative environmental factors and enhance the positive ones. How does your chair feel? It took Brian almost a week to figure out that sitting at a card table chair was killing his back, but that might have taken longer without a trading journal. So you'll want to capture those personal thoughts.

Personal Thoughts

Your thoughts have a great effect on your trading. So when you are not under intense pressure from trading, keep a journal of your thoughts, with a time stamp for each thought. Notice how you are thinking during the day and how those thoughts are impacting your trading. For instance, when you lose money on a trade, what do you say to yourself? If you're using words like "stupid," "ignorant," or "loser" or statements like "I can never do anything right" or "I always do everything wrong," you're using very disempowering language. You're teaching your brain to actually attract the negative as opposed to attracting the positive.

If you catch yourself using negative self-talk, concentrate on positive issues. Reward yourself verbally and mentally when you keep your trading rules, meaning you made a good trade. Do not punish yourself when you do not keep your trading rules. Instead, use something more empowering. For instance, if you break one of your trading rules by failing to stop out when your rules dictate, don't say to yourself, "Dummy, you didn't stop out!" It's better to use language such as this: "I recognize that I broke my trading rule. I assume personal responsibility for that. Next time, in order to enhance my self-worth, I will adhere to my trading rule." These seemingly small things make a big difference. And you are not likely to recognize these changes unless you've taken the time to make a journal. Because once you've taken hundreds or thousands of trades, you simply won't remember anymore. That's when you can get yourself into trouble as a trader.

Market Influences

As much as you can during your journaling, notice the market influences for each trade. I go back to my five indexes that I keep all the time: the Tick, the TRIN, the S&P futures (first forward contract), the NASDAQ composite, and the Dow Jones. I actually have a format where I write down the trades and then the condition of these key indexes, so that I will know whether the market was positive, negative, uptrending, downtrending, or consolidating. You will also want to include in your spreadsheet the impact of news, positive or negative, and any sector news. For example, if you're trading biotech stocks, it's important to know how the other biotechs are trading at the time. If you're trading Internet stocks, then note what the Internet index is doing.

Equipment and Support

Although we hope we've prepared you to deal with equipment and support problems already, you should note problems in these areas in your journal. For example, note when your data feed, software, or ISP goes down and how you deal with it. What happens when you have computer problems? Again, we already discussed these issues, but if they are impacting your day, then make a note of that in your journal. As an extra benefit, with your connectivity and computing history captured in your journal, you'll be able to troubleshoot problems much more effectively.

DEBRIEFING THE TRADES: RULES ARE *NOT* MADE TO BE BROKEN

The key to debriefing your trades is to ask yourself one critical question: "Did I follow my trading rules?" If you can say yes with certainty, then pat yourself on the back—even if you lost money (*especially* if you lost money!). Pay close attention to this comment: Following your rules has nothing to do with making or losing money. When you follow your rules, no matter how good your strategic plan is, you'll still lose money on some days. It's particularly important to pat yourself on the back when this happens, because you need to congratulate yourself for following your rules.

You must understand this critical distinction right now. *If you followed your trading plan—particularly your exit rules and your position-*

sizing rules (discussed in Chapter 6)—*then you made a good trade, regardless of whether you made money or not.* You have to consider such trades to be good trades. When you do that, you will mentally and emotionally reinforce the longer-term aspects of good trading as opposed to the shorter-term aspects of making money. By defining a good trade as one in which you followed your rules, you will reinforce the discipline that you need on a long-term basis to stick with your plan and therefore remain profitable over the long term.

Similarly, bad trades, by our definition, are those trades in which you didn't follow your trading rules or your trading plan. And here's the key: If you didn't follow your trading rules and you still made money, you must classify that trade in your mind as a particularly bad one. You must do everything in your power to keep from reinforcing bad habits! As you progress as a trader through the program we are giving you, we hope that you'll find that you actually have very few bad trades.

In my own trading, I'm to the point where I don't often have bad trades. The reason I know this, of course, is because I've kept a trading journal. Again, I'm not saying that I only have a few losing trades! I'm saying I have just a few trades where I don't stick to my trading rules or my trading plan. And my goal is to get these down to zero. Actually, if you look at my written trading plan, one of my top goals is to have zero bad trades, meaning trades where I didn't follow my rules or my plan. I've found that over time that's been easier and easier to accomplish. It's also easier if you do the research in advance and you know your system well. The better you understand your system and the more precisely you write it down, the less likely you are to break your trading rules.

All errors are basically psychological. And while that is the case, we can still classify mistakes into four categories: (1) execution errors, (2) entry or setup errors, (3) exit errors, and (4) position-sizing errors. Chapter 11 presented a much more thorough discussion of psychological mistakes and how to correct them. That material is critical, and you should read it several times before you start doing your debriefings.

Execution Errors

This is where you fumble with the actual execution side. You see your setup, but you delay taking your trade, or you select the wrong route for your trade. In general, these are mechanical errors that are fairly easy to fix or improve once you've identified them. If you find that the error is really a psychological one, it really belongs in one of the categories below.

Setup and Entry Errors

There are really two types of setup and entry errors: (1) entering a trade without a predefined setup and (2) failing to enter a trade when a clear signal was given. Boredom can be a real problem for day traders, particularly day traders trading at home by themselves. You have no one to talk to, other than CNBC, and there are a lot of times during the mid-day doldrums when nothing is happening. At these times you might be tempted to manufacture setups out of your head. A certain friend of mine, whom I shall not name, has done that from time to time, doing damage to his account, I might add, by taking setups out of what I will call boredom. There's nothing really going on, and there's no setup there, but he takes the trade anyway and ends up losing money. I take care of this potential problem by using the trade playbook that I have developed. I take no trades that are outside the playbook.

Exit Errors

The next type of error occurs when you violate or ignore your exit rules. The exit rules also fall into two categories: stop-loss errors and profit-taking errors. Many momentum traders will get into trouble when a trade is going in their direction. They get too greedy, and as the stock turns and starts to move against them, they convince themselves that it's only temporary. And they let a lot of profits run into losses by doing this. The way to protect against this trading error is to thoroughly understand your profit-taking exit strategy before you get into the trade. This will set you up to act decisively when the trade moves against you, whether you're profitable or not.

Another example of an exit error is blowing your stops. Some of the most serious errors are stop-loss errors. Earlier in this book we defined R, your initial risk, and R multiples—defining your profits and losses in terms of R. From my experience, which includes my own trading and that of other traders that I know, I would say that running your stops is the most frequent problem for most traders. I have the personal belief that if you would subject yourself to very rigorous stop rules on stop losses, you could almost do a random market entry at any time. In other words, buy or sell short almost anywhere and stop out quickly if you're wrong. I'm not suggesting that you do this; I'm only suggesting that you could have a totally random entry system and still be profitable if you're willing to stop out when you're wrong. It's that important.

Position-Sizing Errors

By far the most serious errors a trader can make are position-sizing errors. While blowing a stop can be deadly, giving you huge R-multiple losses, you can still survive them if your position sizing is adequate. However, most traders don't even understand the impact of position sizing and have never been taught its significance. One position-sizing error can cause you to go broke or nearly put you out of the game. Several position-sizing errors will usually assure you of a total blowout of your account.

Although we've classified mistakes as falling into four types, all of them tend to be the result of lapses in your mental state. As a result, you will want to keep track of your mental state for each trade. What is going on for you emotionally? What is your state of mind? Are you bored? Excited? Ill? Tired? If you're overwhelmed by some feeling or some thought at the time you take the trade, make a note of it right then or you may forget it. Oftentimes, these will be clues about what's going on inside of you at the time you're taking your trades, and you know by now that what's going on inside of you is more important than what's happening in the market.

CORRECTING MISTAKES ON THE SPOT: DO IT NOW OR FORGET IT LATER

These are the key questions you need to answer when you make a mistake:

- What were the psychological underpinnings of the mistake?
- Under what conditions did you make that mistake?

- What conditions might arise that would cause you to repeat the mistake?
- What are some solutions that would give you a better alternative behavior under those conditions?

Answer these questions and come up with several alternative behaviors. Rehearse these alternatives until they are second nature to you.

TAKE THE 30,000-FOOT VIEW FOR LOFTIER PROFITS

You'll want to augment these daily debriefs by following them up with weekly, monthly, quarterly, and annual debriefs. I suggest that if you don't have a trader friend or you're not part of a trading group where you have others that you can rely on, you should go through these weekly, monthly, and quarterly debriefs with a coach. The reason you should do this is because it's very, very difficult to be objective about your own performance. This is the way I handle it. Reviewing my trading results with other traders helps me to be more objective and also helps to keep me accountable (i.e., not let these reviews "slip through the cracks").

You might wonder why it's necessary to do weekly, monthly, and quarterly debriefs, and even an annual debrief, especially if you're already doing a daily debrief. Think of it this way: As you drop back to each time frame, you're looking farther out and taking a more broad view of your trading and your trading effectiveness.

On a weekly debrief, you want to look back and try to find patterns of effective trading that you'd like to continue, or patterns of ineffective habits that might be forming that you'd like to stop. If you ran more stops than normal this week, could there have been a reason for that? Is there an outside influence in your life that caused you to do something different this week than you did last week? A weekly debrief probably should be done on Friday afternoon or over the weekend, looking back at what happened so that you can then incorporate your findings into next week's trading. It may only take 45 minutes, an hour, or an hour and a half to go back and look through your trading records and try to spot these types of patterns.

A monthly debrief doesn't necessarily have to take place on the 30th or 31st of the month, but may be on a weekend following a month's trading. You're looking for even larger pictures of patterns of things that you have done right and that you want to reinforce in yourself. Here, you really want to go back and check your trading results versus your trading goals. Did you reach your monthly goals in terms of your process goals and how you traded, and also in terms of your results-oriented goals? Did you reach the profit levels and avoid the drawdowns as you have spelled out in your trading goals? This monthly debrief probably doesn't take much more time than a weekly debrief (provided you've regularly done your daily and weekly debriefs)—maybe an hour or an hour and a half every month.

A quarterly debrief might be a little bit different. Once a quarter, you might want to break out and take a couple of hours, or maybe even half a day, to go back and look over everything and check the effectiveness of your trading. Here again, you're going to have enough information on your trading to drop back yet another level and look at the effectiveness of your trading strategy itself. Is the strategy performing up to the levels that your back testing showed it should? When you arrived at this trading strategy, you certainly had some expectation for the percentage of trades that would be profitable, for the ratio of average win to average loss, for average profit per trade, and for other metrics that you'll want to compare. Look to see if your trading strategies are measuring up to their expected performance. If not, this is the time to try to figure out why not. Again, during this quarterly debrief you'll want to take a bit more time than the shorter-period reviews.

Lastly, the annual debrief probably should be more of a mission and goal-oriented look at your systems and your trading style and strategies. Make sure they're still consistent with you as a person and that they're matching up with how you want to trade going forward into the new year. This should probably be some sort of retreat you will want to do. Go away for a whole day, or maybe even a whole weekend, and do this type of debrief.

The last point that we would make about this debriefing and feedback to yourself is to reemphasize that you want to be able to check yourself and compare the effectiveness of your performance, not only in a dollar sense, but also in a process-oriented or qualitatively oriented sense. You should quantify your performance where possible—percent wins, percent losses, dollars won and lost, etc. But in those areas that you can't easily quantify, you'll want to use some sort of qualitative variables. For example, at the end of the day, you might want to rate each day in terms of how well you traded from a process perspective on a scale of 1 to 10. Did you follow your rules? If you followed every rule scrupulously and traded just perfectly from a process perspective, whether or not you made money, give that day a 10. If there were some hiccups, you might give it an 8, etc.

That type of scale will allow you to go back and check over time how well you did. You might be able to tell the weeks, or months, where you traded well and you had things running pretty smoothly in your life, or a week where you traded poorly when you had a lot of outside stressors in your life. So it's a very useful exercise to go back and apply a qualitative scale to the types of process-oriented trading review that you want to do.

REFINING THE PROCESS: IF IT AIN'T BROKE, FIX IT (A LITTLE) ANYWAY

The final task to undertake when doing the debrief-and-refine process is, of course, to refine. Now that you've taken the time to journal and to go through the feedback process, what do you need to do to refine and to improve your trading results? In all cases, you should base these decisions on the actual insights that you've gleaned from your journaling and from your feedback processes. Do you need to refine your goals and your strategies? Earlier today, D. R. and I were talking about one of our trading strategies that we use for a gap and trap entry. D. R. traded that particular strategy today and commented that the strategy worked perfectly, just the way we had envisioned it; however, he didn't get to enjoy the profits of that trade because he stopped out. When we took a look at the stop rules, we decided that maybe we needed to refine our stop strategy for that particular trade and that particular stock. This is an example of using real feedback and the real journaling process to refine our trading.

Some words of caution here: When you're refining, be careful not to throw the baby out with the bath water. In particular, there are two broad mistakes you can make here. First, if you're trading very, very well and you're profitable (notice that those are two separate events), the mistake that you're likely to make is one of complacency—you're doing so well, you stop looking at the refining process altogether. But your growth as a trader will be curtailed if you do that, and it is likely you will be taken by surprise (shaken out of your complacency) if circumstances change. For instance, if you've been using a momentum-based strategy but the market goes into a real consolidation phase, what are you going to do? How are you going to trade when market conditions minimize (or eliminate) the effectiveness of your momentum strategies?

The second broad mistake you can make occurs if you're trading poorly and/or you're losing money. Then the tendency is to jump to the conclusion that your trading strategies are poor and that they're not working. So traders in this particular case tend to throw the whole system out. Here's where you see traders (particularly traders who don't do all the process-oriented work that we espouse) go through one system after another. They'll buy system after system after system, spending literally fortunes on the next "sure thing" trading system; and they discard each one of them once they get into a drawdown situation. There is a big difference between a strategy that is in a predictable drawdown period and a strategy that has failed. You rarely need a howitzer in the refining process!

So when you do your refining process, make sure that you only use the degree of adjustment that's necessary. There's a scientific term called "degrees of freedom." I don't really want to get deep into the definition of degrees of freedom here, but let me give you a very brief explanation. Let's go back to the example that we used earlier of the trade with D. R. and the gap and trap strategy. In our discussion, D. R. and I determined that perhaps we needed to adjust our time frame for our stop, or perhaps we needed to adjust the stop itself. In other words, maybe we needed to give the trade more time, or maybe we needed to make a larger stop. That would be two degrees of freedom.

The problem is, you can't test both at once, and that's what most people try to do. They would try to adjust both of them at the same time. But the more degrees of freedom you have, the less certain you are about the results that you've achieved. That's because you don't know which adjustment was responsible for the changed results. So when you're adjusting your strategies, change only one variable (one degree of freedom) at a time. Change one thing, and test only that one thing, in order either to eliminate it as a possible problem or to conclude that it's the variable that needed to be dealt with. The bottom line is that well-researched and well-thought-out trading strategies need only small refinements at a time. Think of taking baby steps instead of giant leaps.

The work that you do *after* the trading is done will be among the most valuable tasks that you will undertake. No trading strategy or system works perfectly in all markets at all times. Your posttrading reviews and the refinements that result will give you your best chance of maintaining an effective and profitable trading strategy in various market conditions. These same reviews will also allow you to assess and upgrade the key aspects of your trading psychology. Your post-trading activities will help ensure consistency and continuous improvement as you strive to attain the "promise" that is inside you.

KNOWLEDGE KEYS

✓ A daily review of your trading activity is an essential part of successful trading

✓ An organized spreadsheet or database containing key information on each trade that you make provides the foundation for your trading review.

✓ A trading journal is equally (or more) valuable as a tool for tracking and improving your trades.

✓ Your trading journal should contain key issues about your trading day and your individual trades, including your personal thoughts and feelings, environmental influences, market influences, and the impact of your equipment, connections, or other support issues.

✓ If you do nothing else, you should at least debrief every trade you make with one simple but critical question, "Did I follow my rules for this trade?"

✓ A good trade is one in which you follow your trading rules. Period.

✓ A bad trade is one in which you break a trading rule. Period.

✓ Trading errors fall into one of four main categories: (1) execution errors, (2) entry or setup errors, (3) exit errors, and (4) position-sizing errors.

✓ Weekly, monthly, quarterly, and annual debriefings (in addition to your daily debriefing) will help you improve your trading effectiveness by providing a broader perspective.

✓ When you refine your trading strategy, make changes in small steps.

CALLS TO ACTION

✓ Prepare a spreadsheet (or database) of your individual trades to use in your daily debriefs.
✓ Keep a trading journal that captures your personal thoughts and other important information about your trading day.
✓ Classify every trade you make based on whether or not you followed all your trading rules.
✓ Plan ahead to make weekly, monthly, quarterly, and annual trading reviews.

NOTES

1. R is the risk per share times the total number of shares. It represents what you hope will be your worst-case initial loss. See Chapter 5 for a more extensive discussion of R, R multiples, and expectancy.

## CHAPTER 13

Peak Performance Trading—The Keys to Gaining Control of Your Trading

Effort only fully releases its reward after a person refuses to quit.

Napoleon Hill

One of the great secrets of trading success is to make the assumption that you are responsible for what happens to you in the markets. Many great traders that I have worked with have always assumed that the market is a great university for teaching money secrets. If they are willing to learn, then they profit more and more. If they decide not to learn, then they will make the same mistakes over and over again. *The question you must ask yourself is: "Do I want to learn from the markets or not?"*

As mentioned previously, I like to teach position sizing by taking people through a trading simulation game. The game is quite simple. We draw marbles out of a bag to simulate a trading system in which 60 percent of the marbles are winners, while 40 percent are losers. Most of them have a 1 to 1 payoff, but there is a 10 to 1 winner and a 5 to 1 loser in the bag. In addition, the marbles are always replaced, so you never know what's going to happen on a given trade—just like you never know what's going to happen with a given trade in the market. This game actually has a better payoff than the way most people play the market. In addition, it is much better than any casino game. After 50 trades, everyone should make money if the sample distribution is anywhere near the population of the marbles in the bag.

Typically, only a third of the participants in the room will make money playing 50 draws in such a game. In fact, about a third of them usually go bankrupt. Why?

In a game such as this, you are going to have some long losing streaks—probably 5 to 7 losses in a row with perhaps a 5 to 1 loser in the group. To be successful in the game, you have to devise a position-sizing strategy, as discussed in Chapter 6, to survive that kind of losing streak. Most people don't have such a strategy. That's part of their lesson, but most people don't learn the lesson. Instead, they elect to blame someone else or something else for their failure.

I typically select some people in the audience to draw out the marbles. When a losing marble comes up, I will ask the person who picked it to keep drawing until he picks a winner. This means that should a long losing streak occur, it will be associated with a particular person. And when I ask participants, "How many of you think you lost money (or went bankrupt) because Jim (i.e., the person who pulled the losing streak) took us into a bear market?" many people will raise their hands. In other words, they believe their loss was Jim's fault for pulling losing marbles. With this belief, they are assuming their loss had nothing to do with how they *played* the game—with their position-sizing strategy.

If you are looking for a "Jim" to blame for your misfortunes in the markets, you can always find one. There is always someone to blame for what happens. You can blame the officers of the stock company. You can blame the insiders on Wall Street. You can blame your broker. You can blame the market makers for manipulating stock prices. And you can even blame the person who took the other side of your trade. If it makes you feel better, then you can always find someone to blame. But finding someone to blame will *never* help you correct your own mistakes.

Thus, the most useful attitude to have when trading is to assume that *you are responsible for whatever happens to you in the market*. The moment you decide that you are responsible for the results of your trading is the exact moment you also make the decision to be in control of your trading. This decision gives you an enormous responsibility that you also must assume. It requires that you do the following:

- Completely *commit yourself* to trading and to the inner search that is so important to trading well.
- Continuously engage yourself in soul-searching so that you know who you are deep inside. This means that you understand your psychological issues and your emotions.
- Understand the psychological biases that most people bring to the market—such as the need to try to control things and the need to want to be right so badly that it becomes more important than making money. Not only must you know about those biases, but also you must commit yourself to overcoming them.
- Be aware of how your emotions can rule your life, and be willing to take responsibility for controlling yourself.
- Develop some objectives for what you want to accomplish in the market. Defining your objectives can be as much as 50 percent of the task of developing a trading system.
- Design a system that will meet those trading objectives. Responsibility also assumes that you know how to design such a system and are willing to follow that system. And as you design your system, keep in mind that position sizing is the main part of your system that will help you meet your objectives.
- Develop rules to follow that will guide you through trading your system. Responsibility also means that you understand that your trading system might be wrong 60 percent of the time, because making money has nothing to do with being right about a particular trade. Losing trades are just part of playing the game.
- Define the parameters for a mistake. A mistake means not following your rules. Taking responsibility means that you commit yourself to not making such mistakes. And that's difficult to do if you haven't also committed yourself to all of the above conditions.

These eight points define what it means to be responsible for your trading results. They are essential for success, and we'll be covering all eight points in more detail in this chapter.

COMMITMENT TO YOURSELF AND TRADING

The most critical aspect of taking total responsibility for your trading, and perhaps the one you should do first, is to commit yourself totally to the trading process. Commitment means congruency. It means that all of your parts (all of you) are working together for a common purpose.

For example, imagine yourself in a situation where you just made a small paper profit in your tested system, but in doing so, you broke your rules. How would you feel? Probably, you'd feel conflicted and unsure of yourself.

Now imagine yourself in a situation in which you have a small paper profit and you've followed all your rules. What's the difference in the feeling? In the second case, you probably feel together and congruent. You feel committed to the situation.

When you are internally fragmented, you have conflict and there is always the temptation to withdraw or retreat. However, when you are working while internally balanced, when you are committed, retreat doesn't even come into the picture. Instead, there is no question that you are moving ahead.

When you are not committed, you'll always find distractions that get you off track. Some event will happen, and the next thing you know, your focus will be entirely on that new event. You'll become emotional about something and lose your focus on trading. You'll fail to carry through on important tasks—all because you've failed to commit totally to trading.

PSYCHOLOGICAL AWARENESS (SOUL-SEARCHING)

The next key to taking control of your trading is to become aware of how you influence your own performance. Trading performance is your performance. It reflects your training and conditioning just as much as if you were a trained athlete competing in the Olympics. Those who have trained well and have a good coach will do well. Those who have not prepared themselves and know little about themselves will not do well.

So what is psychological awareness? Psychological awareness means knowing your emotions and knowing the patterns in your behavior. It requires that you realize that there is a connection between your thoughts and emotions and your performance in the market.

Here's a simple exercise for you. On a separate sheet of paper, list your three biggest trading problems. Now these may not necessarily *be* your three biggest trading problems, but they are the ones you are most aware of at this particular time. Do that now before you read on.

Now that you've completed the exercise, examine the problems you have listed. They could take two forms. The first form is that of a problem that you do not own. Problems of this nature include the following: (1) "My system is not adequate." (2) "The market makers are always taking advantage of me." (3) "The market's too volatile for me." (4) "My spouse doesn't understand my trading." (5) "If I just had better equipment or faster access to the floor, my trading problems would be solved." And people can find many, many more.

Note that all those problems are outside of you and outside of your control, and they are outside of you by choice. And as long as the problems appear to be outside of you, you will continue to repeat them. You can only solve them by bringing them under your control.

What that means is that each of them could be placed inside you and thus be within your control—this is the second form that problems could take.

For example,

- Instead of saying "My system is not adequate," you might say, "I haven't defined who I am and what I'm trying to do in the markets, so I have not been able to find the system that's right for me."
- Instead of saying "The market makers are always taking advantage of me," you might say, "I'm too emotional, and I haven't learned my system, nor have I learned how to execute it properly. In addition, I haven't learned market-maker patterns."
- Similarly, instead of saying, "The market's too volatile for me," you might begin to think, "I get upset when the market gets away from me."
- You might substitute for the problem, "My spouse doesn't understand my trading," the idea that "When my spouse

complains about not understanding my trading, I get
angry and that affects my performance."

- And lastly, instead of looking for better equipment, you
  might notice the reaction you have to the equipment you
  currently own.

In each case, putting the problem inside of you starts to give
you some control. You can work on your emotions and your behavior, but you cannot fix what is outside of you.

I would strongly suggest that you keep a psychology journal of
your reactions to the market. Write down your thoughts when you
buy and sell stock, particularly noticing your emotions. In addition,
when you feel emotional, write down what's going on inside you. If
you write down something every day, then by the end of a week or
two, you'll probably start to notice some patterns. Noticing these patterns is the first major step to correcting them.

You need to also become aware of any internal conflict you
might have. Internal conflict exists when part of you wants to do
one thing and another part of you wants to do something else. For
example, part of you might know you need to work on yourself,
while another part of you says, "Just get on with the trading—self-
work is a waste of time." That's a typical example of internal conflict. Another example might be that part of you wants to follow
your trading rules, while another part of you just wants the action
and excitement of the trade. That second part of you always wants
to be in the market, even when it violates your rules.

As you keep your psychological journal, just notice any feelings of conflict that you might have. Periodically review your journal, and you will begin to see distinct patterns emerge. In addition,
you'll begin to understand what parts of you might exist. These
parts could include roles you play, emotions you have, or even representations of significant people in your life. Each part was created
to carry out some positive intention (e.g., protect you in some way).
However, the behaviors associated with the positive intentions of
your various parts may be in conflict. This is why it's so important
to know what is going on inside of you. And you can begin to solve
some of your conflict by simply acknowledging your parts. When
you find a part that conflicts with good trading habits, give it something more constructive to do while still maintaining its original

intention. For example, an excitement part will typically come out in trading when it has no other outlet. Give it another outlet.

OVERCOMING PSYCHOLOGICAL BIASES

Psychological researchers have expended a great deal of effort on the biases that affect human decision making. Basically, human beings must process a tremendous amount of information in order to make decisions. In fact, the amount of information we must deal with doubles each year. Yet our conscious mind can only deal with about seven chunks of information at one time. How do we cope?

We humans deal with all this information by developing judgmental heuristics or shortcuts. These shortcuts enable us to make decisions quickly when confronting a vast amount of information, but they also cause us to make some questionable decisions. In fact, the research as a whole shows that we human beings are very poor decision makers.

Economists are beginning to pick up on this research and have formed a unique school of economics called "behavioral finance." They are beginning to realize that markets are not efficient, as proposed by the random walk theory. Instead, they are inefficient because of the judgmental heuristics that psychologists are now uncovering. However, the economist's approach to solving the problem is to determine how the markets are inefficient and use that as a prediction tool. In my opinion, this will get them nowhere because market success is not about prediction. Instead, market success comes from knowing all about these biases[1] and overcoming them in your own approach to the market.

Although there are more than 50 such biases that could affect your performance as a trader, only 2 are appropriate for discussion here. These biases, which affect almost all day traders and keep them from making money in the market, are (1) the need to be right and (2) the lotto bias.

The Need to Be Right

The average adult who is playing the market has gone through 12 to 16 years of education in a system that teaches you that 70 percent or less is failure and that 94 percent or better is an A.[2] Now you are faced with trading the markets in which most good systems are seldom right even 50 percent of the time. And if you don't understand this concept, then reread Chapter 5 on expectancy. However, the need to be right is a lot more deadly than just looking for trading systems that are right 70 percent of the time or better. There is a big psychological cost.

Suppose you need to be right about a trade. You've purchased EBAY at 144. It's now at 147 and you have a 3-point profit. You are going to have a strong desire to take that profit, especially when the price starts dropping. It suddenly drops to 145.5 and you sell. You've made $1.50 per share, less commissions. But now the stock goes up again and closes out at 153. You've lost $7.50 per share (in opportunity cost) because of your need to be right. It was more important to sell before your profit turned into a loss (i.e., to be right) than it was to have a large profit later. A trader who is fully prepared would have a trading plan that establishes rules that tell how much open profit can be given back in a trade. With such rules on paper, you can help yourself avoid this need to be right.

Let's look at another example. If you got to make this choice once a day for a month, which would you prefer?

   a. A sure profit of $900
   b. A 95 percent chance of a profit of $1,000 and a 5 percent chance of no profit at all

Make your decision now.

Now that you've answered the question, calculate the expectancy of "b." If you multiply 1,000 times 0.95 and subtract 0 times 0.05, you have an expectancy of $950. That's better than the sure $900, so you should have picked b. However, most people would pick "a" because of the desire to be right and take the sure profit.

Both of these examples, the EBAY example and the tendency for people to pick the sure gain over the higher-expectancy gamble, violate the golden rule of trading, which is to *cut your losses short and let your profits run*.

Now let's look at the other side of the need to be right—hating to take losses. Let's suppose you have that problem—you hate to take losses. You've purchased EBAY at 145, and now it goes against you. You've decided to put a stop at 140, but the stock gaps down to 139. What do you do if you hate to take losses? What the average person does is to do nothing except to hope that it will come back.

Another 20 minutes pass, and EBAY drops again to 133. And if a 6-point loss was hard to take at 139, how do you feel about a 12-point loss at 133? That's horrible, so you don't take it. It'll come back—you just know it. However, it's suddenly a really bad day for EBAY and the bottom falls out. It drops to 118. Now you've got a 27-point paper loss in just a few hours. What do you do? If you hate losses, you certainly don't want to take it now, but if you're trading on margin, you might be forced to do so—and all because *you want to be right and hate to take losses.*

OK, now let's look at another exercise. Which of the following would you prefer?

   a. A sure loss of $900
   b. A 95 percent chance of a $1,000 loss and a 5 percent chance of recovering your losses and getting back to break even

Make your decision now.

If you are like most people, you picked "b." You'll do whatever it takes to not have the loss and get back to even. But let's look at the expectancy of "b." You need to multiply 0.95 times negative $1,000 and then add to it 0.05 times 0. The net result is an expectancy of a loss of $950, which is worse than a sure loss of $900. However, most people will take the unwise gamble (b) over the sure loss (a).

Once again, both of these examples go against the first part of the golden rule of trading—cut your losses short. In the EBAY example, you should have sold out at 139 for a 6-point loss. Instead, your hatred of losses may have forced a 27-point loss. And in the exercise to choose between two losses, if you took the unwise gamble, you also failed to cut your losses short.

You can see why the need to be right is such an insidious bias. Most people would rather be right than make money.

The Lotto Bias

Many states in the United States make a lot of money through state-run lotteries. In these lotteries, the chances of winning a million dollars is estimated to be about 13 million to 1. How do they get people to play with those kinds of odds? The lottery organizers get people to play by giving them an illusion of control—let them pick the numbers. All you have to do is match seven of them and you win a fortune. Seems easy enough, and after all, you get to pick the numbers. You can pick your birth date or your anniversary. You can open a fortune cookie and pick those "lucky" numbers. You can buy numbers from so-called experts who claim they have an edge. You can consult your local astrologer about the numbers. You can buy software that will analyze the past numbers picked and give you an idea of which numbers were more likely in the past. You can even buy random number generators that will pick the numbers for you, just like the lottery machine. In fact, a whole industry has sprung up to help people pick the numbers—much like a whole industry exists to help you pick the right stocks. It's the same bias, because you appear to be in control.

However, in the lottery the numbers that the lotto machine picks make the money. They have nothing to do with the numbers you pick. Similarly, making money in the markets has little to do with the stocks you pick, but because of the "lotto bias," most people believe "stock picking" is everything. Instead, in the markets, you make money by your exits—cutting losses short and letting profits run. I know this is still a stunning revelation for many of you, but making money in the markets has very little to do with picking the right stocks. (Reread Chapter 5 on expectancy if you need to reinforce this concept.) However, it's very difficult to convince most people that stock picking has little to do with long-term success because of the lotto bias.

There are countless other biases that also affect your trading—the gambler's fallacy, the availability bias, the randomness bias, the law of small numbers, the need-to-understand bias, the representation bias, the reliability bias, the conservatism bias, the not-giving-yourself-enough-protection bias, the postdictive error bias, and the degrees-of-freedom bias, just to name a few.[3] You owe it to yourself to learn about these biases and how they may apply to you. When you understand them, then you can fix them so they no longer apply.

EMOTIONS AND TRADING

The next area that you must understand is how your emotions affect you. Most people think that events happen and then we get emotional about them. For example, if the market goes against you, you get angry. However, the father of American psychology, William James, said, "The emotions come first." And I believe he was right.

Here's how it might work. First, as we grow older, we learn to judge our emotions. Some emotions are good, while others are bad. Fear and anger, for example, are usually considered bad. If you were fearful, your parents might have said, "Be brave. Have a little courage." Or if you were angry, your parents certainly didn't understand your temper, and they took steps to suppress it.

Emotions are not good or bad—they just are. In fact, many people love fear. That's why they ride on roller coasters and go to horror movies. And they love to watch news stories that evoke negative emotions, believing the emotions are outside of them. Emotions are neutral. However, once you judge an emotion as being bad, you typically are not willing to feel it to its conclusion. Instead, you suppress bad emotions. The result is that your stored emotions come up over and over.

Imagine as a child that you made friends with a new child. However, that child took your favorite toy to play with and you hit him. As a result, your mother punished you. And when you got angry about being punished, the punishment became even more severe. So you learned to suppress your anger.

What happens? When you see your old friend, the anger comes to the surface. But he really didn't do anything. Even when he took your toy, he was just playing and didn't mean to hurt you. But you now have stored anger. You have an inner voice that says, "He'll take things away from me," and you get angry. You might even generalize that to other people who have similar mannerisms to his or who look like him—their presence makes you feel angry because a little voice pops up and says, "They'll take things away from you."

Now if you have that sort of anger, imagine what might happen in the market. You get into a position with a stop. The market immediately goes against you and moves down to your stop. It's the low price of the day, and you are taken out. Immediately, that stored anger comes up as a little voice says, "They took it away from you." As the price retraces to your entry point, you can just see what happened and you get furious. However, that doesn't stop the stock from rising, and soon it's past your original entry point. Within an hour of being stopped out, you notice that you would have had a 20-point profit. You are even more furious. And at the end of the day you would have had a 30-point profit. Not only that, you suddenly realize that you missed another entry point when the stock hit a new high for the day—one that would have still given you a nice profit. As a result, you go home angry, yell at your spouse, and kick your dog. Yet does your response have anything to do with being stopped out? No, it had to do with having stored anger and finding something to justify its expression.

The first step toward solving these kinds of emotional problems is to become aware of them. At first, you are going to think, "It's not me. It's all out there." The market makers keep getting you. However, as you analyze what is happening and start to say to yourself, "How am I creating this?" you'll suddenly become aware of repetitive patterns. And that awareness is a major step toward ridding yourself of these sorts of emotional curses.

KNOWING AND STATING WHAT FITS YOU

As I stated in *Trade Your Way to Financial Freedom*, the holy grail is when you know yourself and what you want and then design a method that fits your personality. It's an important step that you must take, but most people gloss over it without giving it much thought. Here's what one of my clients recently said about this key ingredient.

> Take, for instance, the question of defining your objectives. For a long time I'd thought that success in trading depended on developing a set of low-risk trading methodologies, mixing them with wise money management algorithms, and formulating a business plan. [And even that thinking is way above average.]
>
> Then, gradually, the fallacy of that thinking dawned on me. What are you trying to accomplish? What are your objectives? How can you formulate a business plan if you do not know what your objectives are? I'd thought of my objectives on and off for a while and then shelved them. It's one thing to mouth what you need to do; actually doing it is quite another. How often have you said to yourself, "Cut your losses short and let your profits run?" It's the same with, "Define your objectives."
>
> Where do you begin? How do you know what your objectives are without knowing what it is that you really want? How do you know what you want without knowing yourself? What does knowing yourself really mean? How many of us have actually taken a week of our lives and spent the entire time considering what it is that

we value the most? One of the questions that Dr. Tharp's Basic Trader Program forces you to consider is that problem. Actually, it's one of the exercises in Dr. Tharp's home study course, which I had casually detoured around and skipped over (without even knowing it) until I came face-to-face with it again. And if you wish to understand your own belief system and arrive at a set of objectives for your endeavor, you'll have to spend the time and seriously consider the question until at least you can feel it in your bones if not actually come up with an answer. . . .

[As I continued this process], I began seeing some aspects of me I had never considered before—both strengths and weaknesses—particularly weaknesses. Example: One of my trading methodologies consisted of selling naked Treasury Bond options at short-term turning points. Fixed, limited rewards of premium collected offset by high system reliability of 75% or more. These were comfortable trades most of the time. But once in a while the Bond market makes an absolutely terrifying adverse explosion of implied volatility which threatens to kill you unless you make a decisive life-saving move out of the market. Remember Victor Niederhoffer? That well-known trader and author of *The Education of a Speculator*,[4] in the fall of 1997 went short a whole bunch of S&P puts when the market exploded against him. He refused to cut his losses and get out, eventually blowing himself and all of his investors out of the water. If Niederhoffer can fall into a loss trap, what about me? It only takes a quirk of psyche lulled into complacency or driven into terror to create this malignant trap which no amount of historical backtesting can predict. I'd been there. I am prone to such psychological weakness. But to avoid such a situation, I can't count on a disciplined response. I scratched this system from the library of my trading methods.[5]

As you continue to explore yourself (we hope you took the time to start that journey at the end of Chapter 2), you can begin to realize what your patterns are. If you cannot immediately design something to fit the person that you really are, then you can at least avoid doing things that don't fit you. Preserving capital by avoiding foolish actions is one of the secrets of great traders. However, as you come to know yourself better and better, you can begin to formulate goals and desires. And as you formulate those desires, then you can develop reasonable objectives and design a trading system that meets them perfectly. But without self-knowledge, this all-important task is impossible.

At a recent electronic day trading seminar we did, a fairly new trader remarked, "I know exactly what my objectives are. I want to shoot for the moon, and I'm willing to risk whatever comes along. I want to get the biggest possible returns, and I don't care what happens in the interim." I love statements like that because it gives me a chance to prod. And prod is what I did.

> VAN: Would you be willing to risk a 50 percent drawdown to get the maximum return?
>
> TRADER: Well, I wouldn't like it, but yes I would.
>
> VAN: Well, what if the probability of a 50 percent drawdown were about 75 percent? Would you be willing to risk that?
>
> TRADER: No, that's too much.
>
> VAN: What probability would you be willing to tolerate?
>
> TRADER: Well, zero probability of a 50 percent drawdown is probably the best outcome, but I'd be willing to go with a 10 percent chance of a 50 percent drawdown, I think.
>
> VAN: Would you be willing to risk a 10 percent chance of a 50 percent drawdown and a 90 percent chance of a 25 percent drawdown?
>
> TRADER: When you put it that way, probably not. Maybe a 25 percent chance of a 25 percent drawdown.

The prodding certainly clarified things a bit. We went from "I want to shoot for the moon, and I'm willing to risk whatever comes along" to "I'd be willing to go with a 10 percent chance of a 50 percent drawdown, I think" and "Maybe a 25 percent chance of a 25 percent drawdown." That's quite a shift as we get more specific. And the response is still theoretical. What happens when real money is at stake and the trader is living through a real drawdown? Knowing yourself and how your trading objectives tie in to your mission allows you to calmly weather those inevitable drawdowns, as we'll explore in the next section.

KNOWING YOUR OBJECTIVES AND USING POSITION SIZING TO MEET THOSE OBJECTIVES

Once you know who you are, you can begin to develop objectives for yourself.

In my book *Trade Your Way to Financial Freedom*, I provide readers with a questionnaire to help them in developing objectives. In that questionnaire, I ask questions such as:

- How much time do you have to devote to trading?
- How much money do you need to live on each year and how much of that must come out of trading profits?
- How many distractions can you expect during the day?

Interestingly enough, some people have asked me, "What do questions like those have to do with setting objectives?" To answer what the relationship is, let's take a closer look at some of the questions.

How much time do you have to devote to trading? If you don't have the entire market day (or at least a significant portion of most market days) to devote to trading, then you probably shouldn't become an electronic day trader. Day trading is time-intensive. You must spend time watching the market. If you only have a half hour each day to devote to trading, then you are better off position-trading with stocks, or adopting a buy and hold strategy with wide stops, or even doing mutual fund switching. Electronic day trading is not for you. As a result, this question is very important in helping you determine your time frame for trading.

How much money do you need to live on each year and how much of that must come out of trading profits? The relevance of this question to objectives seems fairly obvious, and it is vitally important. If you need $100,000 per year to live on and all of it must come from trading profits, then you have a minimum objective. If this amounts to earning a return of 50 percent or more per year on your trading equity, then you need to assess whether this goal is realistic for you. You also need to determine whether you can tolerate the pressure of having to perform at a very high level just to get by and make the money you need. It's a key question. I've seen many traders who could trade well when they didn't need money, but when they had to make it, they failed miserably.[6]

How many distractions can you expect during the day? Day trading, especially intuitive (or discretionary) day trading, requires intense focus. Distractions could easily disrupt the flow of your system and cause you to lose money. If you have a lot of disruptions, then electronic day trading may not be for you, or at minimum you need something that is very mechanical to assist you in your trading (or you need to find a way to minimize the distractions).

These are just a few of the many questions you must ask yourself in order to develop a system you can live with—one that's right for you. And when you have such a system, then you have a reasonable chance to attain your objectives. Without asking these sorts of questions and determining the implications of your responses for your objectives, you can never expect to develop reasonable objectives.

Once you've developed objectives for yourself, then you can begin the process of developing a trading system that fits you. In my opinion, that's the key to your success in the markets. And much of this book is about doing just that—understanding who you are and building a trading plan and routine around your unique personality. Add this to examples of some strategy that really works and an understanding of the importance of position sizing, and you have the foundation for long-term trading success.

Many people who think they don't have time to develop or adapt strategies for themselves buy "canned" trading systems. Brian summarized quite well our thoughts on canned trading systems in Chapter 2. The practice almost always fails because of a mismatch in the beliefs used to design the system (which are almost never adequately disclosed) and the beliefs of the person who bought the system. We've provided you with some good strategies in Chapters 9 and 10. They work, but can you make money with them? Probably not without "tweaking" them in a major way so that they fit you. And certainly not unless you fully adopt the beliefs on which they were built. However, they are still useful because they provide you with some background for developing your own systems.

In addition, by understanding the importance of position sizing, you can customize most of the systems we've talked about to meet your objectives. This topic is discussed extensively in Chapter 6.

RULES AND KNOWING WHAT TO EXPECT FROM YOUR SYSTEM

If you design a system based on expectancy and high-R multiples from historical data, then you will have some idea what it did in the past. Your system will also give you a set of rules to guide your behavior and make your trading less subject to your emotional whims. However, there still are two important aspects of the system you don't know. How well does your historical sample of data represent your system's performance in the actual market today, and what is it like to trade the system day in and day out? That is why simulation of your system is important.

How would a simulation work? You would take the distribution of R multiples that you have from your system and, assuming these are a good representation of what your system would actually be like in the market, randomly sample from it. That's when you begin to learn what it is like to live with your system. Once you've lived through it, you won't be constantly changing it.

For example, if your system produced the sample of trades shown in Table 5–1, you would want to look at the distribution of R multiples in those trades. You could then take that distribution of trades and represent it by a bag of marbles, with one marble representing the R multiple for each trade.

Let's say you make 100 trades each month. Each time you draw out 100 marbles from the bag of marbles, replacing each marble after it is drawn, you would have a new example of what a month of trading might be like for you. You could look at your losing streaks and see what it is like to live through each of them. You could practice different position-sizing strategies and notice the drawdowns you get and your psychological reactions to them. What happens when you have an exceptionally good streak? Do you get out of control?

Every month of trading that you simulate and live through will make it that much easier to trade your system. And I'd recommend that you simulate a minimum of several years' worth of trading.[7] Go back and review the discussion of system simulation in Chapter 6 until you thoroughly understand what is involved. You might also try IITM's trading game. This will allow you to simulate many trades with any R-multiple distribution you select.

HOW TO CORRECT MISTAKES

Though we covered this material in some detail in Chapter 12, I'm presenting it again here with a slightly different slant. I'm doing this so that you can further absorb its importance and so you can gain a deeper understanding of the psychological basis for these important steps. In order to correct your trading mistakes, you need to do three things on a regular basis: (1) Keep a log of your trading; (2) based upon those logs, do a daily debriefing at the end of each day; and (3) do a daily mental rehearsal before you trade. These tasks are essential as you progress from a beginner or unsuccessful trader to a very profitable electronic day trader.

The Trading Log

Your trading log is essential in order to gain awareness about your trading. What are your patterns? What mistakes are you making?

At minimum, you should include the following information in your log. First, you must include the details of the trade—this is essential if you are to correct mistakes. Second, you must include your rationale for the trade. Why did you open the position? And why did you close it out? Lastly, it is critical to both notice and include any emotional responses you had to the trade. Were you attached to the stock and afraid of missing out on something? Did you move a stop because of emotional responses? What went on inside of you while you held the position?

The Daily Debriefing

At the end of the day, you need to review all your trading logs with the following question in mind. "Did I follow my trading rules?" If you followed your rules, even if you lost money, then I recommend that you simply tell yourself, "Good job," and pat yourself on the back. On the other hand, if you didn't follow your rules, then you made a mistake. And if you have no trading rules, as recommended earlier, then you also made a mistake by trading without rules.

When you make a mistake, the procedure for correcting it is to determine what circumstances occurred that caused you to make that mistake. How might you react to those circumstances in the future to improve? Once you've done that, then you need to begin a mental rehearsal process.

The Mental Rehearsal Process

When you fail to follow your rules, it is usually due to some emotional response. There are a number of techniques to help you overcome such emotional responses, including changing what you are doing with your body and changing your breathing.[8] In fact, in my chapter in Jack Schwager's book, *Market Wizards,* I recommended a particularly effective technique, which I will repeat here.

> *The Market Wizards Technique:* When you notice yourself getting emotional, move away from your current position. If possible, move at least ten feet away and then turn around and imagine yourself in your old position doing what you were doing. What did you look like? What was your breathing like? Notice any tension in your body. Notice your breathing. Just notice what you were like while doing that behavior. Next, imagine a great trader in the same situation. What would that trader look like? How would he respond to the situation? Notice all the details of his posture and breathing. Lastly, return to your old trading position and jump into the body of your model trader. At this point you will find that your behavior is quite different.

Try it. It only requires a little imagination.

CHECKLIST FOR PEAK PERFORMANCE TRADING

As a way of helping you assess whether electronic day trading is right for you, we've designed the following checklist of items that you should consider. We recommend that you be able to check at least 12 of the items below before you commit substantial funds to day trading.

_____ 1. Am I totally committed to trading? Can I totally commit to doing whatever it takes to be successful, including going at it full time and doing the necessary work?

_____ 2. Am I willing to devote time to self-analysis and soul-searching, knowing that I'm the most important factor in my trading?

_____ 3. Am I willing to spend as much time on self-analysis as I spend on market analysis?

_____ 4. Am I willing to lose (small amounts) on 50 percent or more of my trades, knowing that making money in the market comes from expectancy, not from being right?

_____ 5. Am I willing to give up trying to control the markets and focus instead on controlling my exits?

_____ 6. Am I willing to notice my emotions, realizing that they are coming from me and not from the market or some other external situation?

_____ 7. Am I willing to find my emotional patterns and work on solving them?

_____ 8. Am I willing to spend time figuring out who I am and what I want before I start working on my trading system?

_____ 9. Am I willing to design an EDAT system that totally fits my personality and who I am?

_____ 10. Am I willing to set objectives that fit me before I start trading?

_____ 11. Am I willing to work on developing a position-sizing algorithm to meet those objectives?

_____ 12. Am I willing to simulate my system to determine how I can expect it to perform under numerous market conditions?

_____ 13. Am I willing to develop rules to guide my behavior?

_____ 14. Am I willing to keep a daily log of my trades?

_____ 15. Am I willing to do a daily debriefing of my trading in order to determine what mistakes I've made?

_____ 16. Am I willing to do mental rehearsals on a regular basis to overcome problems, correct mistakes, and improve what I'm already doing well?

KNOWLEDGE KEYS

✓ Understand the psychological biases that most people bring to the market—such as the need to try to control things and the need to want to be right so badly that it becomes more important than making money.

✓ Be aware of how your emotions can rule your life, and be responsible for controlling yourself.

✓ Assume that you, and no one else, are responsible for whatever happens to you in the market.

✓ Completely commit yourself to trading and do the inner search that is so important to trading well.

✓ Develop some objectives for what you want to accomplish in the market.

✓ Design a system that will meet those objectives.

✓ Develop rules to follow to guide you through trading your system.
✓ Complete the checklist for Peak Performance Trading. Be sure that you are able to check at least 12 of the items on it before you commit substantial funds to day trading.

N O T E S

1. One of the best sources of information about judgmental heuristics as they apply to investors and traders is a book called *Mindtraps* by Roland Barach. Van K. Tharp also discusses judgmental shortcuts extensively in his *Peak Performance Course for Investors and Traders* and in *Trade Your Way to Financial Freedom*. All three sources are available from IITM, Inc., by calling 919-852-3994, or they can be ordered online through www.iitm.com.

2. In the case of schooling, being right only means giving back what the teacher wants.

3. Some excellent books on this topic include *Mindtraps* by Roland Barach and *Beyond Fear and Greed* by H. Shefrin.

4. Niederhoffer, Victor. *The Education of a Speculator*. New York: John Wiley & Sons, 1997.

5. Reprinted from *Market Mastery*, 1999, Volume 4, Number 12, with permission.

6. The converse is also true for others—some can only make money when the have to do so.

7. You must also remember that you are assuming that your sample of trades actually represents a month's worth of your trading.

8. At least 15 such techniques are contained in volume 4 of my home study course for traders and investors. See the Bibliography for ordering information.

Glossary

Algorithm   Rules for computing, i.e., procedures for calculating mathematical functions.

Antimartingale strategy   A position-sizing strategy in which position size is increased when one wins. Any position-sizing strategy based upon one's equity will be an antimartingale strategy.

ARCA   The four-letter market participant designation for the Archipelago ECN.

Ax   The market participant who, at any given time, is controlling most of the trading in a given security.

Bearish   The opinion that the market will be going down in the future.

Best-case example   Many books show you illustrations of their key points about the market (or indicator) which appear to perfectly predict the market. However, most real-world examples of these points are not nearly as good as the one that is selected, which is known as a best-case example.

Bias   The tendency to move in a particular direction. This could be a market bias, but most of the biases discussed in this book are psychological biases.

Bid arrow   An arrow that displays the direction of the last bid. If the last bid is equal to or higher than the previous one, this arrow will point up and is displayed in green on many software platforms. If the last bid is lower than or equal to the immediately previous bid, the arrow will point down and will usually be red.

Bid book   The left side of the Level II montage that shows all the market participants currently bidding to buy stock.

Broadband   The common-use term that describes high-bandwidth-speed Internet connections.

Bulletin-board stocks   Stocks that have different order handling rules and different exchange status than the typical stock traded via EDAT. They are, therefore, not eligible for EDAT. These stocks can be identified in a Level II window by the symbol "Kk" displayed in the top portion of the window.

Bullish   The opinion that the market will be going up in the future.

Candlesticks   A type of bar chart, developed by the Japanese, in which the price range between the open and the close is either a white rectangle (if the close is higher) or a black rectangle (if the close is lower). These charts have the advantage of making the price movement more obvious visually.

CME   The acronym for the Chicago Mercantile Exchange. "The Merc," as it is also known, trades futures and options on futures for many financial instruments and agricultural commodities. It is notable to the EDAT trader as the exchange where the S&P futures are traded.

Connectivity   The term used to describe a computer's overall connection to the Internet. This includes your computer, modem, interface to your ISP (cable, phone line, satellite, etc.), ISP servers, servers you communicate with, and the route back to your computer.

Consolidation   A pause in the market during which prices move in a limited range and do not seem to trend.

Crossed market   The unusual condition where the ask price of one market maker for a security is lower than the bid price of another market maker.

Deep price tiers   Price levels on the Level II montage that are at least two or three price tiers removed from the inside bid or ask price level.

Direct-access trading   (see *Electronic direct-access trading*)

Disaster stop   A stop-loss order to set your worst-case loss in a position.

Discretionary trading   Trading that depends upon the instincts of the trader, as opposed to a systematic approach. The best discretionary traders are those who develop a systematic approach and then use discretion in their exits and position sizing to improve their performance.

Divergence   A term used to describe two or more indicators failing to show confirming signals.

Drawdown   A decrease in the value of your account because of losing trades or because of "paper losses" that may occur simply because of a decline in the value of open positions.

Dynamic real-time data   A data feed that updates itself automatically (i.e., does not require screen refreshes) and that has no delay relative to the data that are being delivered from the exchanges.

ECN   The acronym for electronic communication network. An ECN is formally defined as an electronic system that takes orders that are entered by market participants, widely disseminates those orders to third parties, and permits the orders to be executed against in whole or in part. The most common ECNs for EDAT are Island, Archipelago, Redibook, and Attain, although there are others.

Electronic direct-access trading (EDAT)   The type of trading characterized by a direct connection to the stock exchange servers (through your broker's servers, of course). The key here is that this connection involves no outside human interaction—your keystrokes or mouse clicks are routed directly to the market. The software system for EDAT is built on "client-server" technology.

Electronic order book Lists all buy and sell orders for a particular stock that come in through an individual routing system.

Equity The value of your account.

Equity curve The value of your account over time, illustrated in a graph.

Expectancy How much you can expect to make on the average over many trades. Expectancy is best stated in terms of how much you can make per dollar you risk. Formulas are given in Chapter 6 that show you how to calculate expectancy.

Fill The price at which your order was executed; includes the number of shares that you bought or sold. Hence, you can receive a partial fill (less than the number of shares that you bid or offered).

Form T Refers to the fact that the trade occurred in the after-market, between 4:02 p.m. and 4:39 p.m.

Fundamental analysis Analysis of the market to determine the supply and demand characteristics. In equities markets, fundamental analysis determines the value, the earnings, the management, and the relative data of a particular stock.

Gambler's fallacy The belief that a loss is due after a string of winners and/or that a gain is due after a string of losers.

Globex The CME's electronic trading system. Its common usage refers to after-hours sessions (e.g., overnight) for the CME's futures contracts—notably the S&P futures contract.

Hidden (reserve) orders Orders that allow you to enter a larger order than you wish to have displayed in the system. The user defines the display quantity, and the balance of the user-specified reserve quantity remains hidden from other market participants. The display quantity is automatically refreshed from the reserve.

Hit rate The percentage of winners you have from trading or investing. Also known as the reliability of your system.

Holy grail system A mythical trading system that perfectly follows the market and is always right, producing large gains and zero drawdowns. No such system exists, but the real meaning of the holy grail is right on track. It suggests that the "secret" is inside you.

INCA The four-letter market participant designation for the Instinet ECN.

Indicator A way of summarizing data in a "meaningful" way to help traders and investors make decisions.

Inside market Shows the "best" bid and the "best" offer. The best bid is the most a buyer is willing to pay for a stock. The best ask or offer is the least amount a seller will accept for his or her stock. When you get a quote from your broker, you're quoted the inside market.

Investing A term that refers to a buy and hold strategy that most people follow. If you are in and out of trades frequently or you are willing to go both long and short, then you are trading.

Irregular trade A trade than has been reported "out of sequence," or a trade that occurred prior to or after regular trading hours.

ISLD The four-letter market participant designation for the Island ECN.

ISP The acronym for Internet service provider. An ISP is the company that provides electronic access to the Internet for its customers.

Level II screen Known formally as the NASDAQ Level II Quotes Montage. It shows the up-to-date bids and offers of all market participants of a given stock.

Leverage The relationship between the amount of money one needs to put up to own something and its underlying value determines the amount of leverage one has. High leverage increases the potential size of profits and losses.

Liquidity The ease and availability of trading in an underlying stock or futures contract. When the volume of trading is high, there is usually a lot of liquidity.

Long Owning a tradable item in anticipation of a future price increase. Also see *Short*.

Low-risk idea An idea that has a positive expectancy and that is traded at a risk level that allows for the worst possible situation in the short term so that one can realize the long-term expectancy.

Market maker A company that maintains a firm bid and offer price in a given security by standing ready to buy or sell at publicly quoted prices.

Martingale strategy A position-sizing strategy in which the position size increases after you lose money. The classic martingale strategy is where you double your bet size after each loss.

Maximum adverse excursion (MAE) The maximum loss attributable to price movement against the position during the life of a particular trade.

Mental rehearsal The psychological process of preplanning an event or strategy in one's mind before actually doing it.

Minder window A simple, customizable window in EDAT software that presents real-time dynamic data on individual stocks and indexes in a tabular format.

Modeling The process of determining how some form of peak performance is accomplished and then passing on that training to others.

Momentum A term that refers to an indicator that represents the change in price now from some fixed time period in the past. Momentum is one of the few leading indicators. Momentum as a market indicator is quite different from momentum as a term in physics.

Money management A term that was frequently used to describe position sizing, but has so many other connotations that people fail to understand its full meaning or importance. For example, it also refers to managing other people's money, controlling risk, managing one's personal finances, and achieving maximum gain, in addition to many other concepts.

Moving average A method of representing a number of price bars by a single average of all the price bars. When a new bar occurs, that new bar is added, the last bar is removed, and a new average is then calculated.

NASDAQ The acronym for the National Association of Securities Dealers Automated Quotation system.

Negative expectancy system   A system in which you will never make money over the long term. For example, all casino games are designed to be negative expectancy games. Negative expectancy systems also include some highly reliable systems (i.e., with a high hit rate) which tend to have occasional large losses.

NeuroLinguistic Programming (NLP)   A form of psychological training developed by systems analyst Richard Bandler and linguist John Grinder. It forms the foundation for the science of modeling excellence in human behavior. However, what is usually taught in NLP seminars are the techniques that are developed from the modeling process. For example, we have modeled top trading, system development, and money management at IITM. What we teach in our seminars is the process of doing those things, not the modeling process per se.

Number best   The number of times that a market participant has been the *only* participant left at any give price level.

Offer book   The right side of the Level II montage that shows all the market participants currently offering to sell stock.

Oscillator   A term that refers to an indicator that de-trends price. Most oscillators tend to go from 0 to 100. Analysts typically assume that when the indicator is near zero, the price is "oversold," and that when the price is near 100, it is "overbought." However, in a trending market, prices can be overbought or oversold for a long time.

Parabolic   A term that refers to an indicator that has a U-shaped function, based upon the function ($y = ax^2 + bx + c$). Because it rises steeply, it is sometimes used as a trailing stop that tends to keep one from giving back profits.

Peak-to-trough drawdown   A term used to describe one's maximum drawdown from the highest equity peak to the lowest equity trough prior to reaching a new equity high.

Pink sheets   Daily printed listings that have quotations for many thousands of over-the-counter stocks not listed on any of the major stock markets. Dealers who are acting as market makers in the individual securities enter these quotations. The National Quotation Bureau prints the pink sheets.

Position sizing   The most important of the six key elements of successful trading. This element determines how large a position you will put on throughout the course of a trade. In most cases, algorithms for determining position size are based upon one's current equity.

Position trader   One who holds trades longer than 1 to 2 weeks with the expectation of taking advantage of longer-term trends.

Positive expectancy   A term used to describe a system (or game) that will make money over the long term if played at a low enough risk level.

Postdictive error   A term that refers to an error that is made when you take into account future data that you should not know. For example, if you buy on the open each day if the closing price is up, you will have the potential for a great system, but only because you are making a postdictive error, because you don't know today's closing price.

Prediction   A process of determining what will likely happen that many people depend on in hopes of making money. For example, analysts are employed to predict prices. However, great traders make money by "cutting losses short and letting profits run," which has nothing to do with prediction.

Price divergence   The price improvement that is sometimes available on an ECN such as Island or Archipelago because your limit order is the best match for a new or preexisting order on that ECN that offers a fill at a better price.

Price tiers   On a Level II screen, the individual price levels that group the individual participants and their share volume at a given price. Price tiers are displayed in descending groups on the bid side of the Level II screen and in ascending order on the ask side.

R multiple   All profits can be expressed as a multiple of the initial risk (R). For example, a 10-R multiple is a profit that is 10 times the initial risk. Thus, if your initial risk is $10, then a $100 profit would be a 10-R-multiple profit.

R value   The initial risk taken in a given position, as defined by one's initial stop loss.

Random number   A number determined by chance. A number that cannot be predicted.

REDI   The four-letter market participant designation for the Redibook ECN.

Reliability   A term that refers to how accurate something is or how often it wins. Thus, a 60 percent reliability means that something wins 60 percent of the time.

Retracement   A price movement in the opposite direction of the previous trend. A retracement is usually a price correction.

Reward-to-risk ratio   The average return on an account (on a yearly basis) divided by the maximum peak-to-trough drawdown. Any reward-to-risk ratio over 3 that is determined by this method is excellent. It also can refer to the size of the average winning trade divided by the size of the average losing trade.

Scalping   A term that refers to the actions of traders, usually floor traders, who buy and sell quickly to get the bid and ask price or to make a quick profit.

Setup   A term that refers to a part of one's trading system in which certain criteria must be present before you look for an entry into the market.

Short   Selling an item in order to be able to buy it later at a lower price. When you sell before you have bought the item, you are said to be "shorting" the market.

"Sit on the ask"   A trading term used to describe a market participant (usually a market maker) who is selling shares from the inside ask position and continues to refresh his or her bid and sell more at the same price level. This usually prevents the price of the stock from moving up as long as the market participant "sits on the ask."

Slippage   The difference in price between what you expect to pay when you enter or exit the market and what you actually pay. For example, if you attempted to buy at 15 and you end up buying at 15.5, then you have a half point of slippage.

SOESable   A term that means that a market participant is subject to the mandatory filling of orders placed through the Small Order Execution System (SOES).

Specialist   A member of a stock exchange (typically the NYSE or ASE; there are no specialists for NASDAQ listed stocks) through which all trades in a given security pass.

Stairmaster A momentum-based trading strategy that is founded on the expectation that a stock experiencing fundamentally sound positive news will trend upward in a stair-stepping pattern. Trades are entered (or added to) during the repeating basing periods that precede up moves.

Stalking A term that refers to the process of getting ready to get into a position. This is one of the ten tasks of trading from Dr. Tharp's model.

Stochastic An overbought-oversold indicator, popularized by George Lane, that is based upon the observation that prices close near the high of the day in an uptrend and near the low of the day in a downtrend.

Swing trader One who holds trades from 2 to 5 days with the expectation of taking advantage of a short- to intermediate-term price movement.

System A set of rules for trading. A complete system will typically have (1) some setup conditions, (2) an entry signal, (3) a worst-case disaster stop to preserve capital, (4) a profit-taking exit, and (5) a position-sizing algorithm. However, many commercially available systems do not have all these criteria.

Tick The minimum fluctuation in price of a tradable item.

TICK (indicator) Measures the number of advancing versus the number of declining stocks on the New York Stock Exchange (not the NASDAQ) at any given moment.

Tick arrow An arrow that shows the direction of the last actual trade. It will point up if the last price is unchanged from or higher than the previous trade. This is an up tick. Often the arrow will be green on an uptick. If, however, the last sale was lower than or equal to the immediately previous trade, the arrow will point down and usually will be red. This is a downtick.

Time & sales window A record of every transaction executed as well as a time-stamped record of all the bid and offer changes of the market participants.

Trade distribution A term that refers to the manner in which winning and losing trades are achieved over time. It will show the winning streaks and the losing streaks.

Trade opportunity One of the six keys to profitable trading. It refers to how often a system will open a position in the market.

Trading Opening a position in the market, either long or short, with the expectation of either closing it out at a substantial profit or cutting losses short if the trade does not work out.

Trailing stop A stop-loss order that moves with the prevailing trend of the market. This is typically used as a way of exiting profitable trades.

Trend following The systematic process of capturing extreme moves in the market with the idea staying in the market as long as the market continues its move.

Trending day A day that generally continues in one direction, either up or down, from the open to the close.

TRIN (indicator), or Arms Index Named after its inventor, Richard Arms, the formula involves both the volume and price of advancing and declining issues.

Validity   A term that indicates how "real" something is. Does the thing measure what it is supposed to measure? How accurate is it?

Volatility   A term that refers to the range of prices in a given time period. A highly volatile market has a large range in daily prices, whereas a low-volatility market has a small range of daily prices. This is one of the most useful concepts in trading.

Web-based trading   Typified by a browser-based order entry system. The orders you enter on your computer are routed to a computerized trading desk. As such, your orders are basically glorified e-mails to a broker, which you use instead of a phone call.

Bibliography

Barach, Roland. *Mindtraps.* Raleigh, NC: International Institute of Trading Mastery, 1996, 2d ed. Good book about the psychological biases we face in all aspects of trading and investing.

Chande, Tushar. *Beyond Technical Analysis: How to Develop and Implement a Winning Trading System.* New York: John Wiley & Sons, 1997. One of the first books to really go beyond just emphasizing entry.

Colby, Robert W., and Thomas A. Meyers. *Encyclopedia of Technical Market Indicators.* Homewood, IL: Dow-Jones Irwin, 1988. Excellent just for its scope.

Connors, Laurence, and Linda Bradford Raschke. *Street Smarts.* Malibu, CA: M. Gordon Publishing Group, 1995. A book with lots of good short-term setups and entries.

Covey, Stephen R., A. Roger Merrill, and Rebecca R. Merrill. *First Things First.* New York: Simon & Schuster, 1994. An instant classic on time and life management.

LeFevre, Edwin. *Reminiscence of a Stock Operator.* New York: John Wiley & Sons, 1993. New edition of an old classic.

Nasser, David S. *How to Get Started in Electronic Day Trading.* New York: McGraw-Hill, 1998. A good place to start if you have little or no exposure to electronic direct-access trading.

Niederhoffer, Victor. *The Education of a Speculator.* New York: John Wiley & Sons, 1997.

Robbins, Anthony, and Frederick L. CoVan. *Awaken the Giant Within.* New York: Fireside, 1993. A great text on the science of success.

Schwager, Jack. *Market Wizards.* New York: New York Institute of Finance, 1988. A must-read for any trader or investor.

Schwager, Jack. *The New Market Wizards*. New York: HarperCollins, 1992. Continues the tradition, and again it is a must-read. William Eckhardt's chapter alone is worth the price of the book.

Shefrin, H. *Beyond Fear and Greed*. Boston: Harvard Business School Press, 2000.

Song, Chull. The Basic Trader Test. *Market Mastery*, 1999, vol 4, No 12.

Tharp, Van K. *Trade Your Way to Financial Freedom*. New York: McGraw-Hill, 1999. "If you intend to trade, you'd better know what's in this book"—Ed Seykota from the dust jacket.

Tharp, Van K. *The Peak Performance Course for Investors and Traders*. Raleigh, NC: International Institute of Trading Mastery, 1988–1994. This is Van's model of the trading process, presented in such a way so as to help you install the model in yourself. Call 919–852–3994 to order.

Tharp, Van K. *How to Develop a Winning Trading System That Fits You: A 3–Day Seminar on Tape*. Raleigh, NC: International Institute of Trading Mastery, 1997. IITM's original systems seminar, which has great information for all traders and investors. Call 919–852–3994 to order.

Index

About the Authors

Van K. Tharp, Ph.D., is president of the International Institute of Trading Mastery (IITM) and has been a consultant to traders and investors for over 15 years. Internationally recognized as today's number one coach and trainer for traders, Dr. Tharp is the author of *Trade Your Way to Financial Freedom* as well as a five-volume home study course, a monthly newsletter on systems and psychology, and a number of articles in industry publications. His trading models and techniques were featured in the book *Market Wizards: Interviews with Great Traders.*

Brian June moved directly from a successful corporate career into a sizable income as an electronic day trader. A popular speaker at day trading seminars and expositions, Mr. June has written numerous articles for *Market Mastery*, the IITM newsletter, and is an expert at applying sound business principles to achieve trading success. He also developed a popular workshop on electronic day trading tactics and strategies.

A Personal Invitation from Van K. Tharp and Brian June

GET YOUR NEXT TRADING STRATEGY FOR FREE

If you want to get the most out of your trading, then you must have comprehensive strategies to fit all market conditions. We presented several in this book to get you started. However, there are many more! If you'd like another strategy to add to your arsenal, fill out a request form at our Web site, and we'll send you the complete system totally free and without obligation. The strategy includes the setup, entry rules, profit-taking exits, position-sizing strategy, and examples. Don't miss out on this great opportunity! Make your request online at www.oneminutetrader.com/freestrategy.

GET A FREE NEWSLETTER

We publish a monthly newsletter, *Market Mastery*, that includes tips on how to develop a system and how to improve your performance by changing your thinking. One of the topics not covered extensively in this book is the subject of trading data—both what can go wrong and how to find good data. As a way of saying "thank you" for your interest, we're offering you a free copy of our newsletter that addresses this important topic. It also includes a book review and valuable information on how to protect yourself in today's market. You can have it for free by making your request online at www.oneminutetrader.com/marketmastery.

PLAY A FREE MARKET SIMULATION GAME ON OUR WEB SITE

We believe that one of the best ways to learn to trade or invest well is through simulation games—especially if those games teach the most important factors first. We've designed a game on our Web site that teaches you how to do position sizing and how to protect your profits—the keys to success. The game costs nothing to play and provides a tremendous education. Find out more about it on our Web site at *http://www.oneminutetrader.com/*. It's free, so try it now.

If you don't have access to the Web at this time, then you may request a CD, which gives you access to the first level of the game, by writing to the following address:

One Minute Trader Corporation
21 Woodshaw Road
Newark, DE 19711
866-852-4993 (toll free—U.S. only)
919-852-4993
919-852-3942 fax
info@theoneminutetrader.com e-mail

Please include $5.00 shipping costs for the CD with your request.